sky·doll

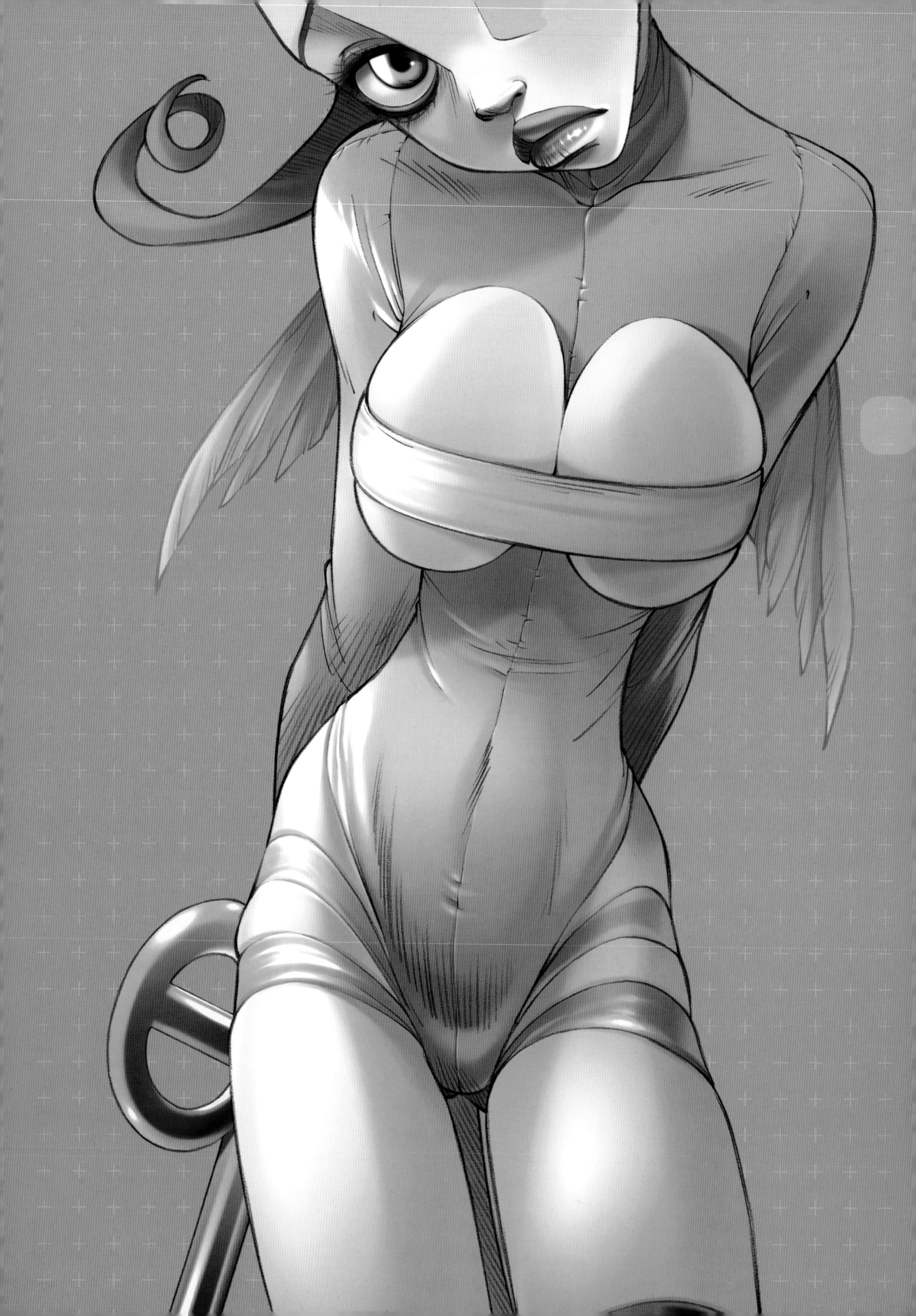

Alessandro Barbucci   Barbara Canepa

sky·doll

DECADE 00 > 10

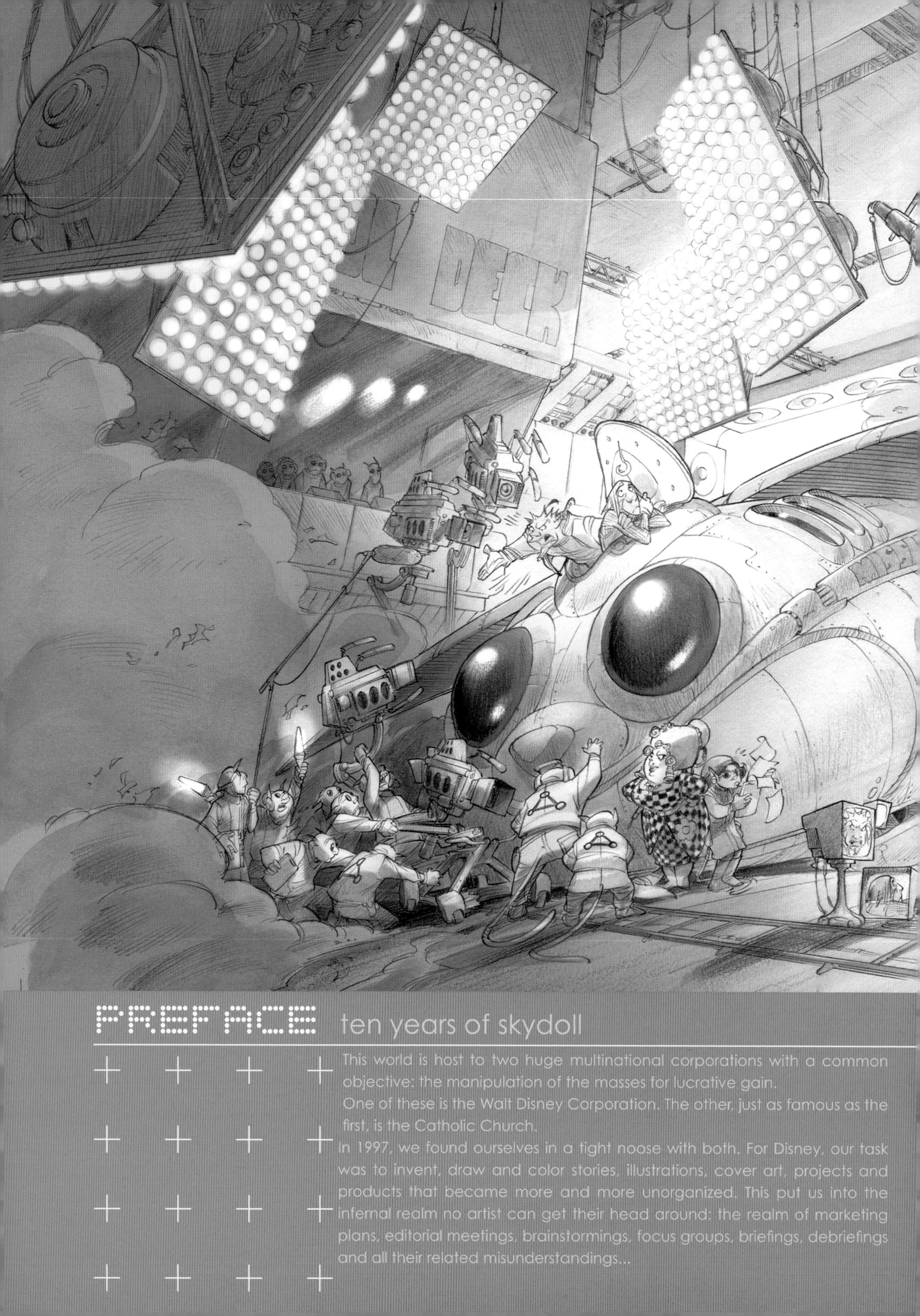
DECK

PREFACE ten years of skydoll

This world is host to two huge multinational corporations with a common objective: the manipulation of the masses for lucrative gain.
One of these is the Walt Disney Corporation. The other, just as famous as the first, is the Catholic Church.
In 1997, we found ourselves in a tight noose with both. For Disney, our task was to invent, draw and color stories, illustrations, cover art, projects and products that became more and more unorganized. This put us into the infernal realm no artist can get their head around: the realm of marketing plans, editorial meetings, brainstormings, focus groups, briefings, debriefings and all their related misunderstandings...

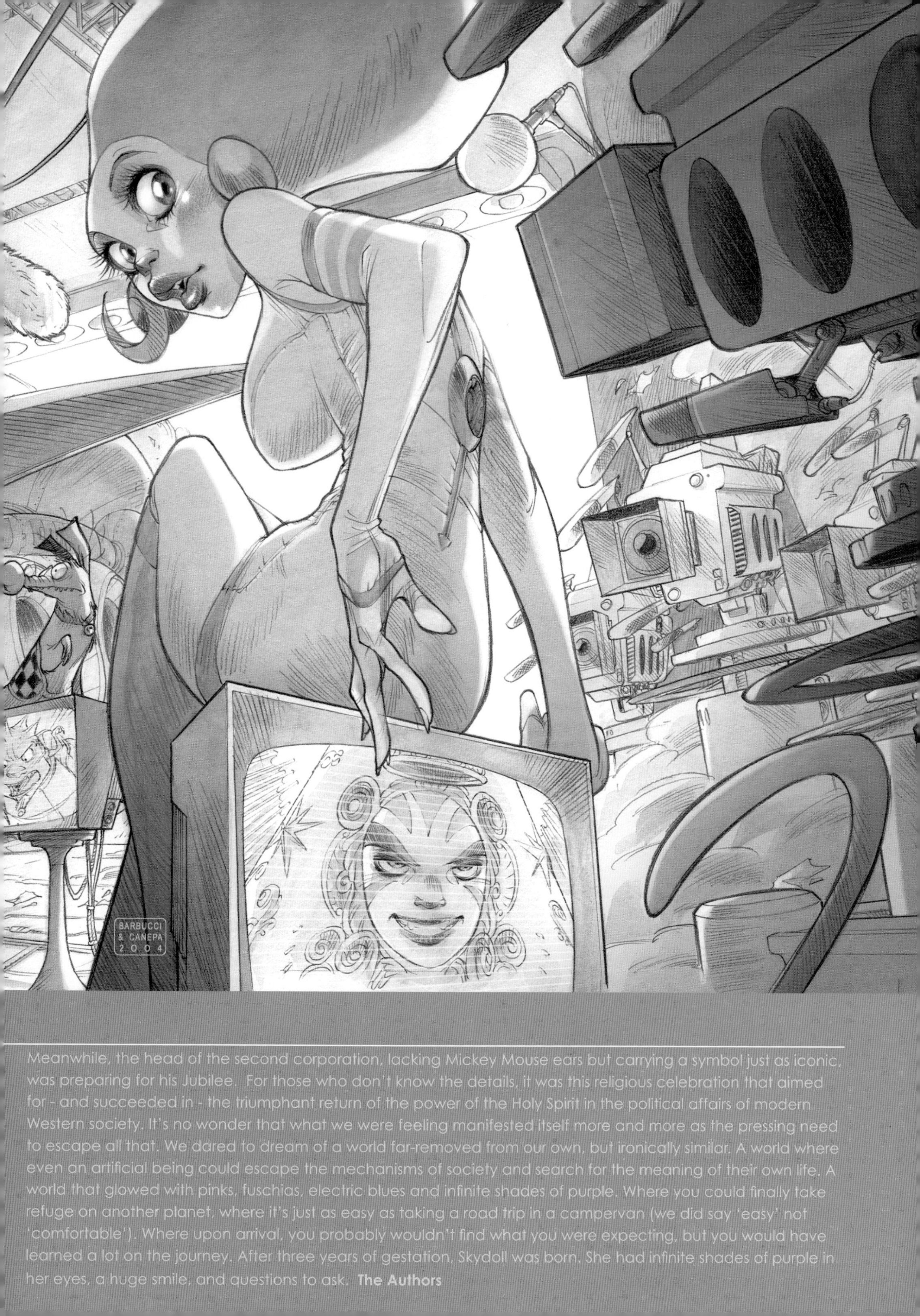
BARBUCCI & CANEPA 2004

Meanwhile, the head of the second corporation, lacking Mickey Mouse ears but carrying a symbol just as iconic, was preparing for his Jubilee. For those who don't know the details, it was this religious celebration that aimed for - and succeeded in - the triumphant return of the power of the Holy Spirit in the political affairs of modern Western society. It's no wonder that what we were feeling manifested itself more and more as the pressing need to escape all that. We dared to dream of a world far-removed from our own, but ironically similar. A world where even an artificial being could escape the mechanisms of society and search for the meaning of their own life. A world that glowed with pinks, fuschias, electric blues and infinite shades of purple. Where you could finally take refuge on another planet, where it's just as easy as taking a road trip in a campervan (we did say 'easy' not 'comfortable'). Where upon arrival, you probably wouldn't find what you were expecting, but you would have learned a lot on the journey. After three years of gestation, Skydoll was born. She had infinite shades of purple in her eyes, a huge smile, and questions to ask. **The Authors**

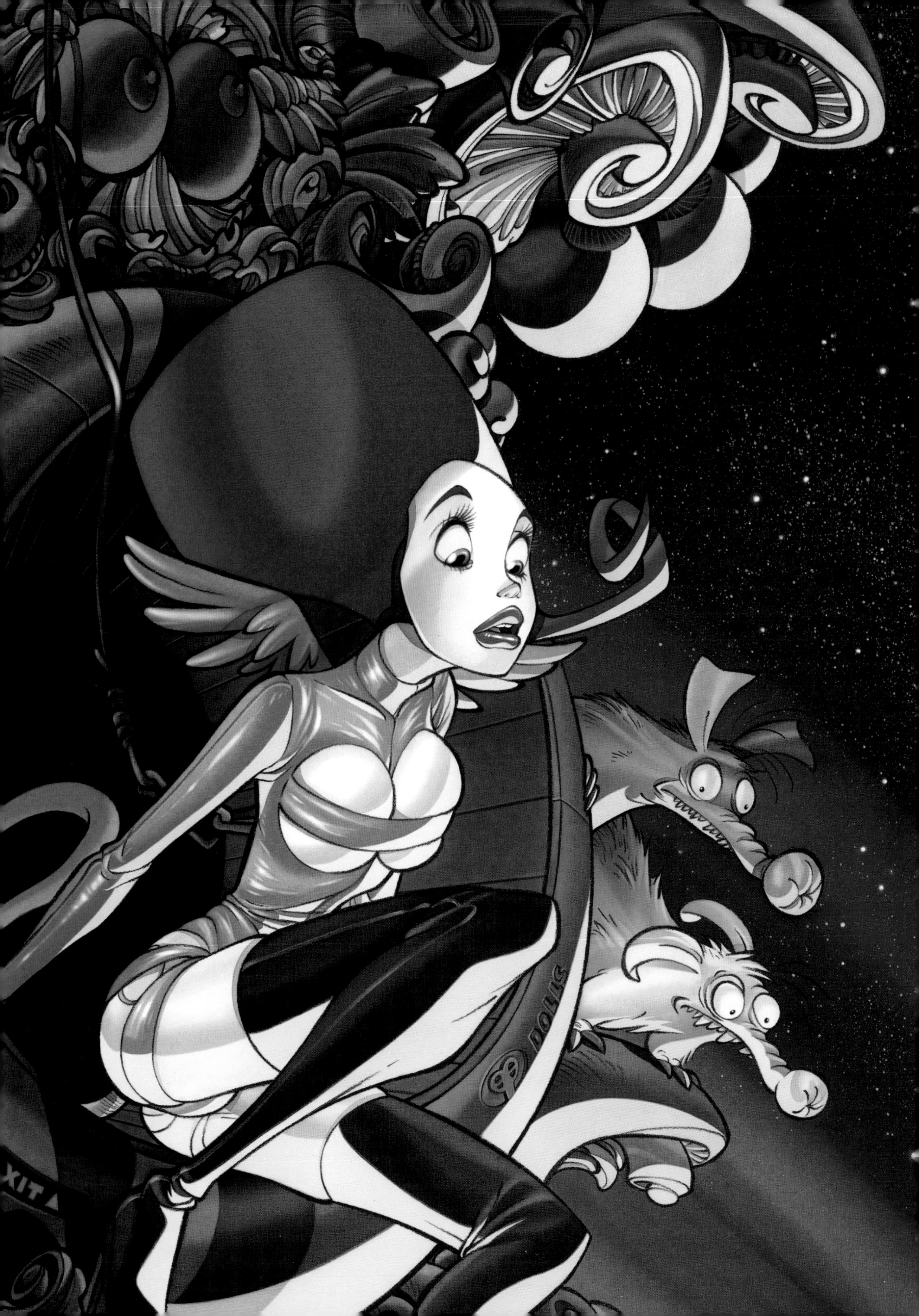
DOLLS

CONTENTS

SKYDOLL DECADE 00>10

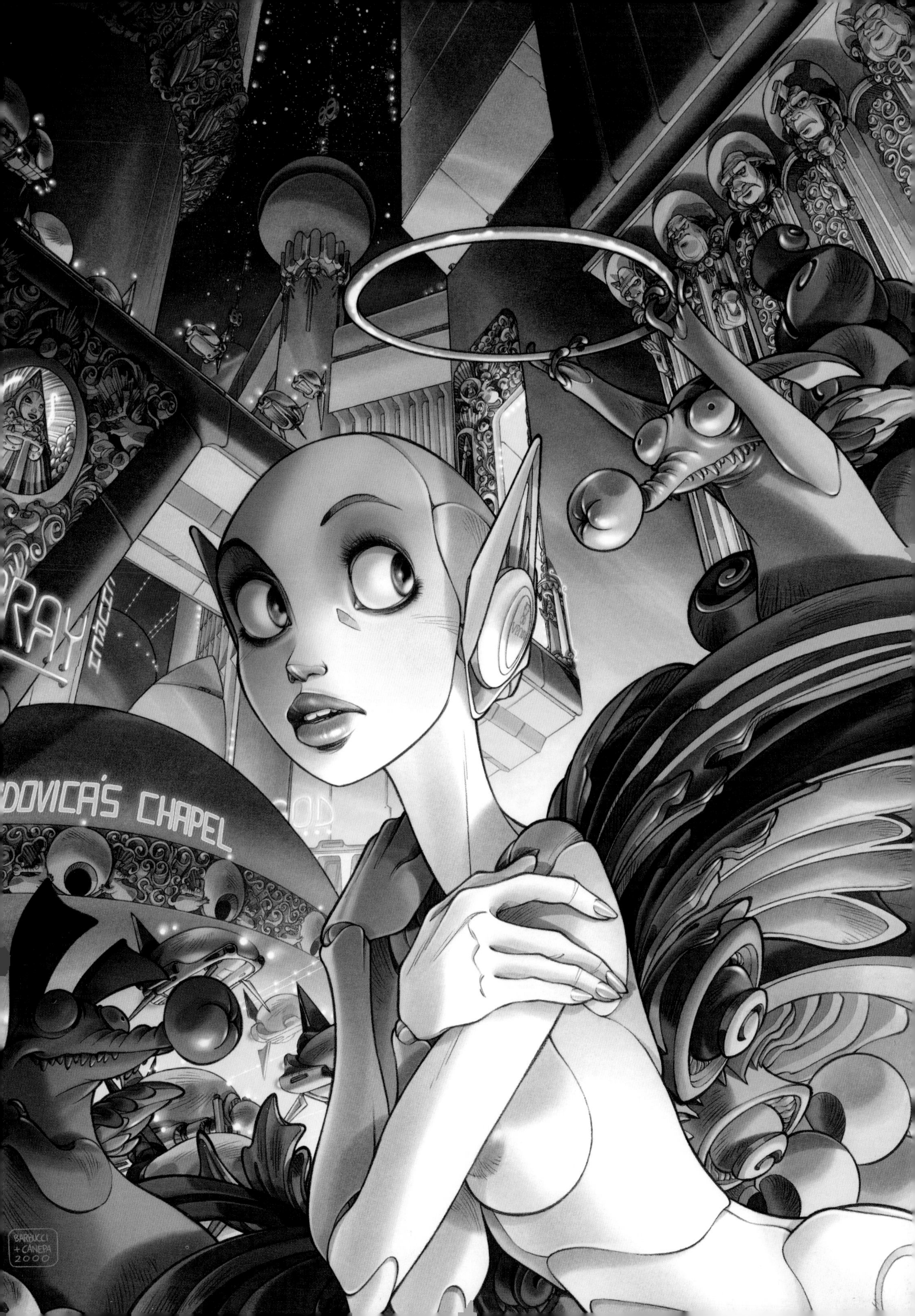
DOVICA'S CHAPEL
BARBUCCI + CANEPA 2000

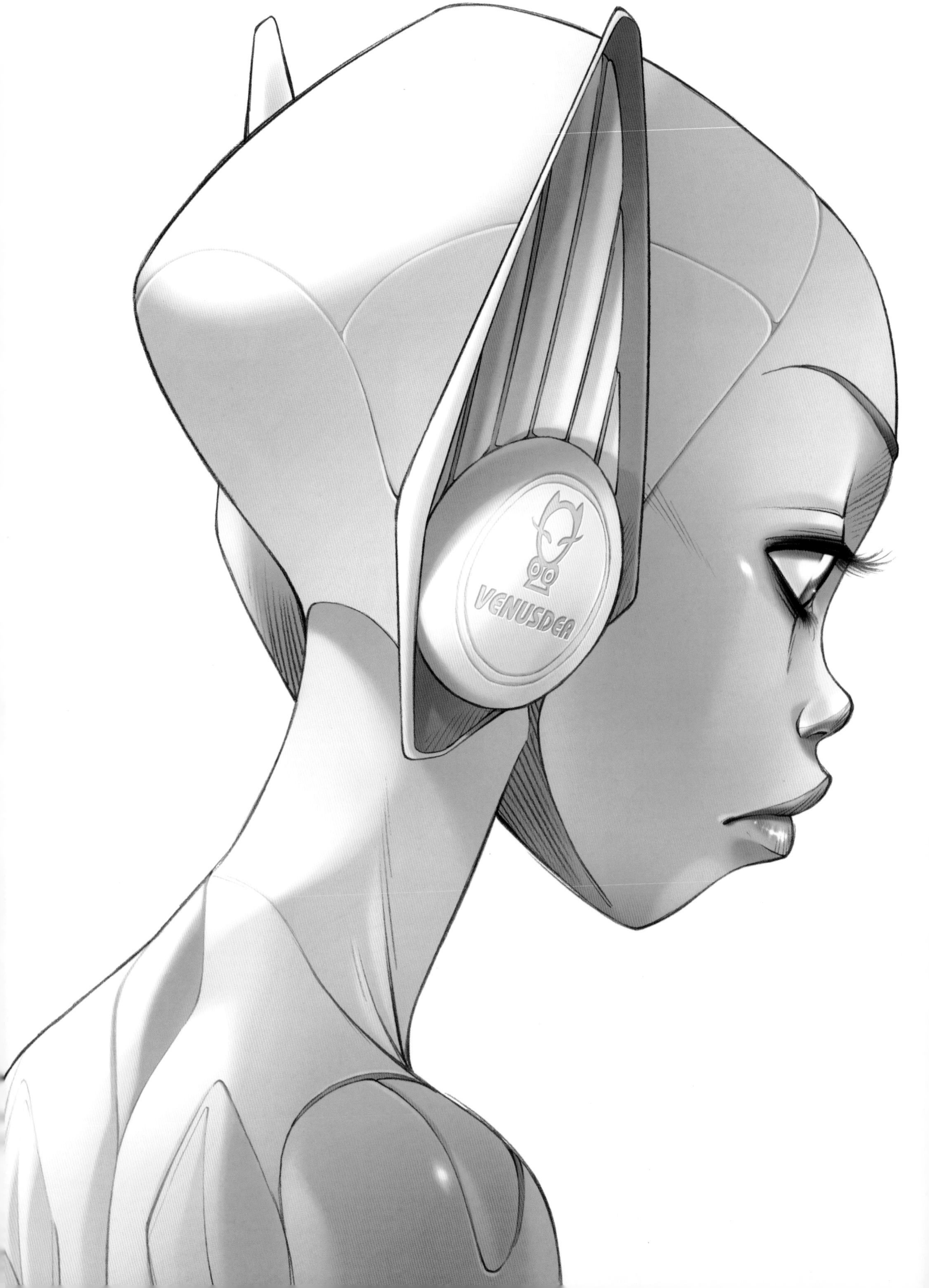
VENUSDEA

SKYDOLL
DECADE 00 > 10
Volume 1: The Yellow City

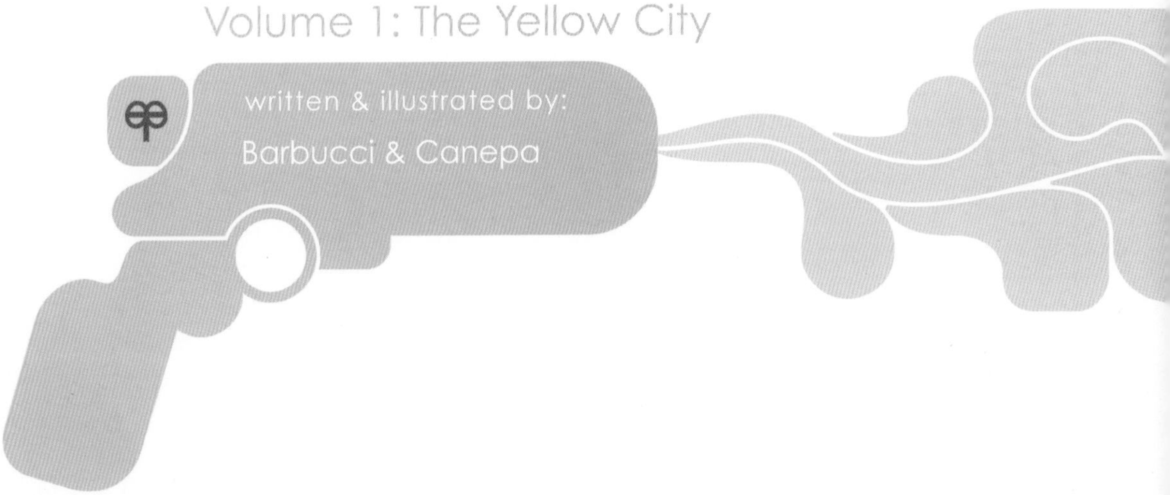
written & illustrated by:
Barbucci & Canepa

"Pure spirit is pure lie."
~ Friedrich Nietzsche

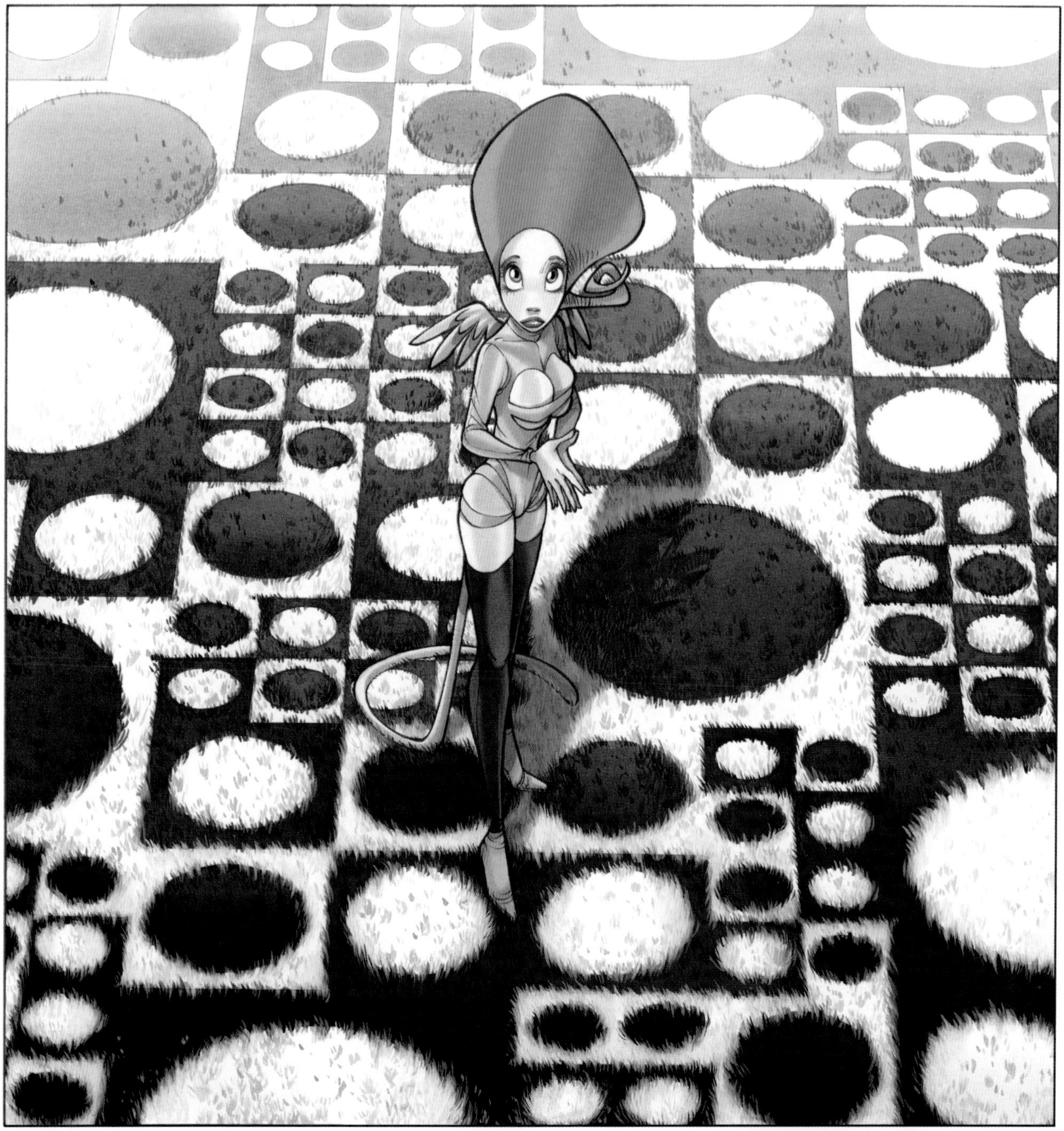

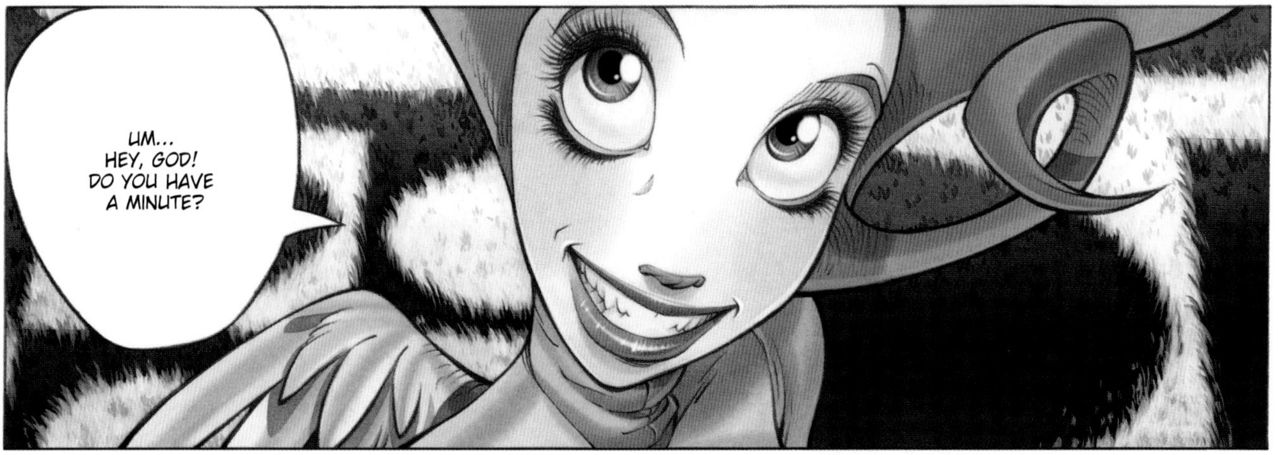
UM... HEY, GOD! DO YOU HAVE A MINUTE?

I KNOW YOU USUALLY PRETEND YOU CAN'T HEAR ME...

BUT YOU SHOULD KNOW: YOUR MANAGEMENT STYLE IS REALLY PATHETIC!

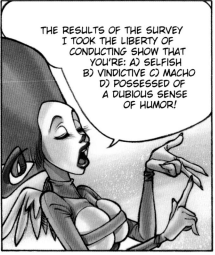

THE RESULTS OF THE SURVEY I TOOK THE LIBERTY OF CONDUCTING SHOW THAT YOU'RE: A) SELFISH B) VINDICTIVE C) MACHO D) POSSESSED OF A DUBIOUS SENSE OF HUMOR!

BUT DON'T WORRY!

I'VE GOT AN IDEA TO HELP OUR RELATIONSHIP EVOLVE TOWARD A MORE PEACEFUL COLLABORATIVE CLIMATE...

THE SUGGESTION BOX!

WHAT?!

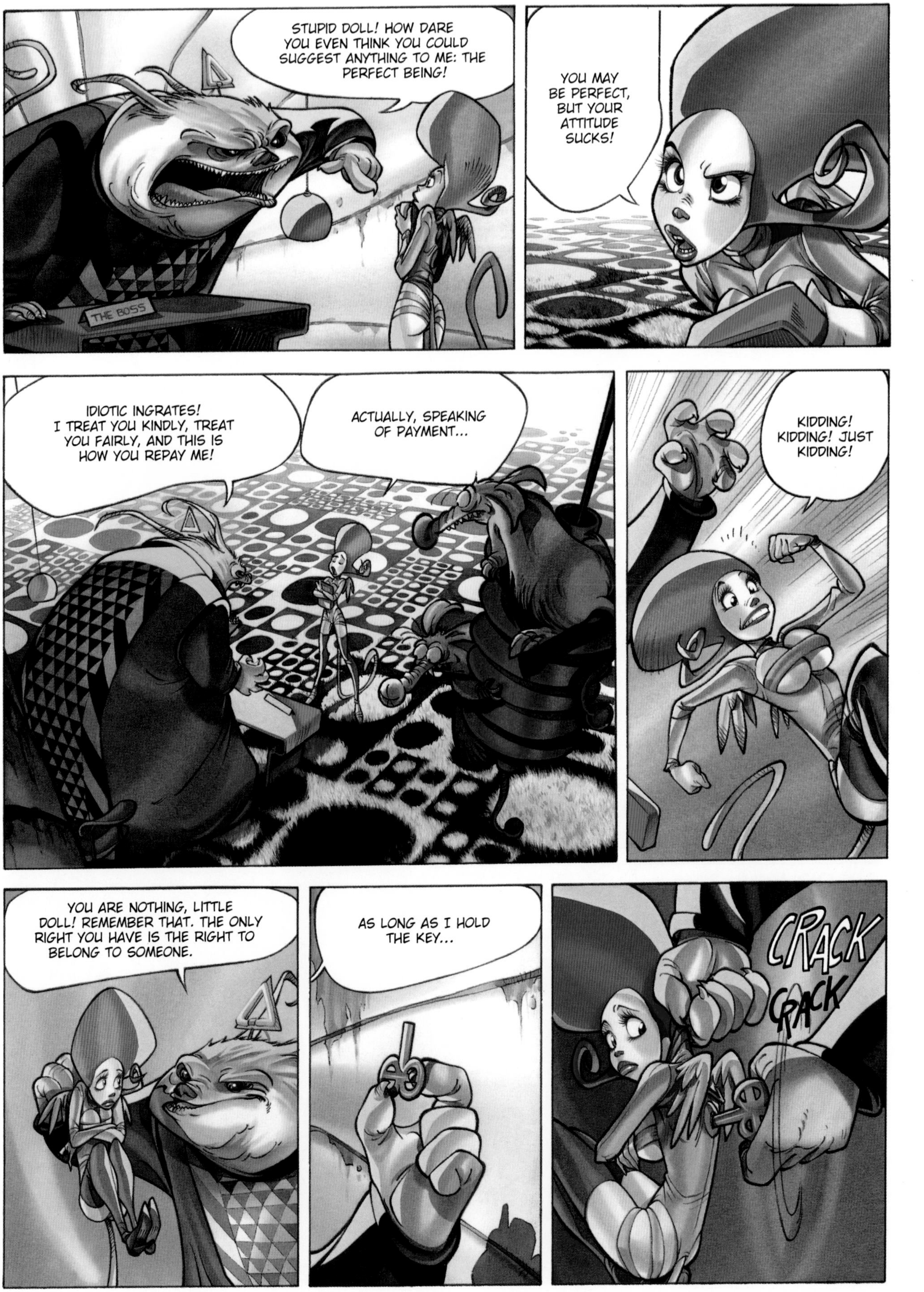
STUPID DOLL! HOW DARE YOU EVEN THINK YOU COULD SUGGEST ANYTHING TO ME: THE PERFECT BEING!
THE BOSS
YOU MAY BE PERFECT, BUT YOUR ATTITUDE SUCKS!
IDIOTIC INGRATES! I TREAT YOU KINDLY, TREAT YOU FAIRLY, AND THIS IS HOW YOU REPAY ME!
ACTUALLY, SPEAKING OF PAYMENT...
KIDDING! KIDDING! JUST KIDDING!
YOU ARE NOTHING, LITTLE DOLL! REMEMBER THAT. THE ONLY RIGHT YOU HAVE IS THE RIGHT TO BELONG TO SOMEONE.
AS LONG AS I HOLD THE KEY...
CRACK
CRACK

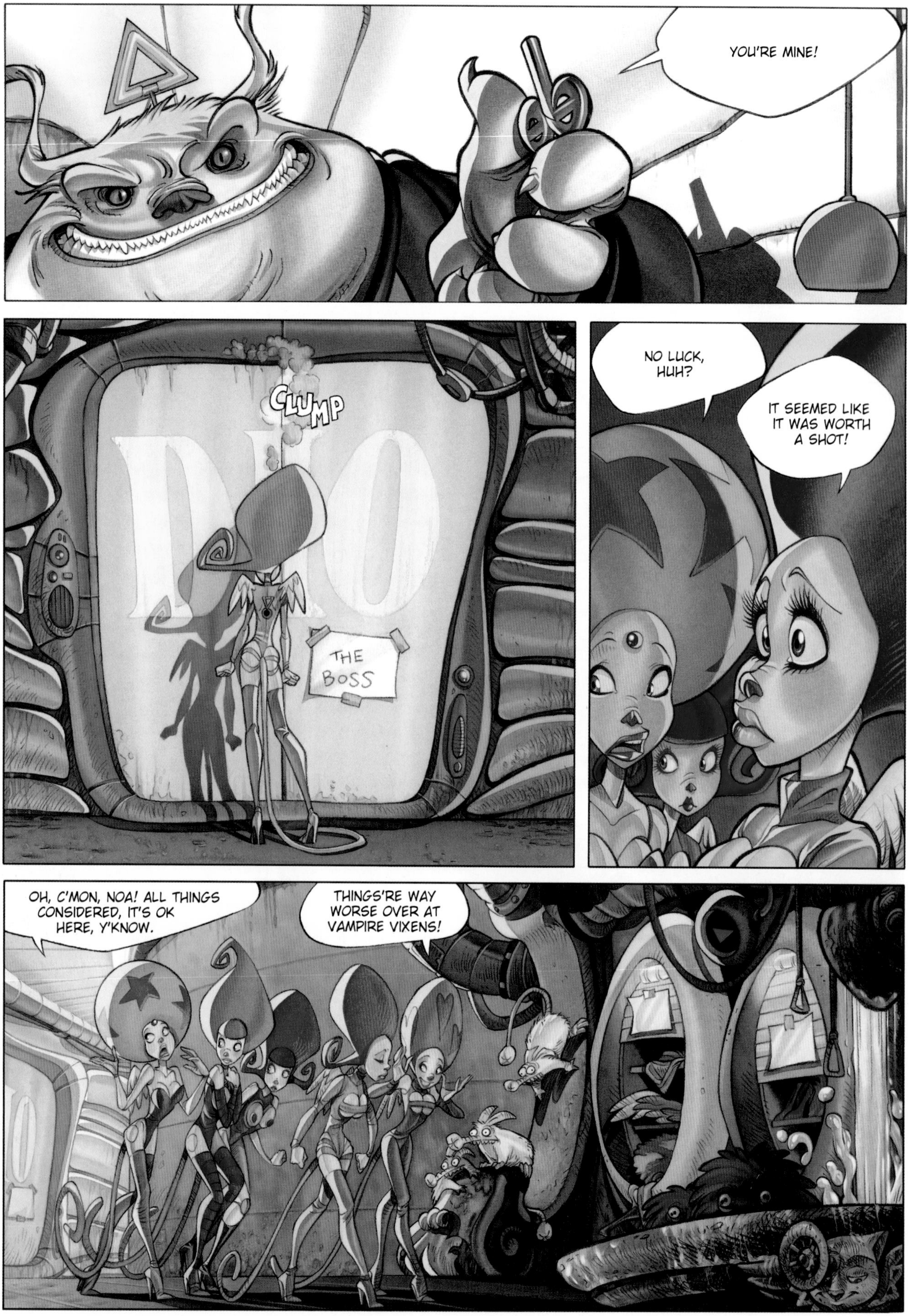
YOU'RE MINE!
CLUMP
DIO
THE BOSS
NO LUCK, HUH?
IT SEEMED LIKE IT WAS WORTH A SHOT!
OH, C'MON, NOA! ALL THINGS CONSIDERED, IT'S OK HERE, Y'KNOW.
THINGS'RE WAY WORSE OVER AT VAMPIRE VIXENS!

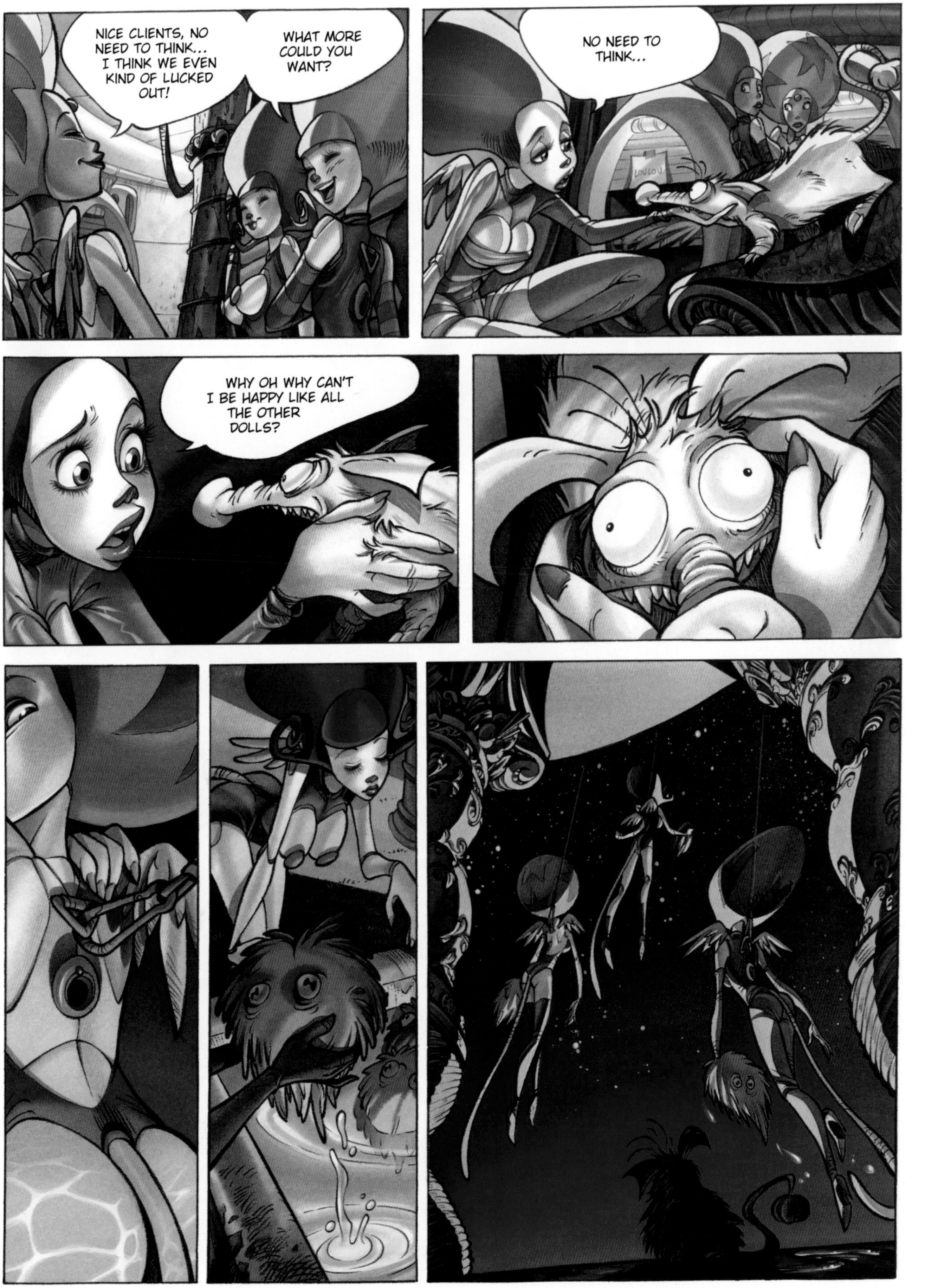
NICE CLIENTS, NO NEED TO THINK... I THINK WE EVEN KIND OF LUCKED OUT!
WHAT MORE COULD YOU WANT?
NO NEED TO THINK...
WHY OH WHY CAN'T I BE HAPPY LIKE ALL THE OTHER DOLLS?

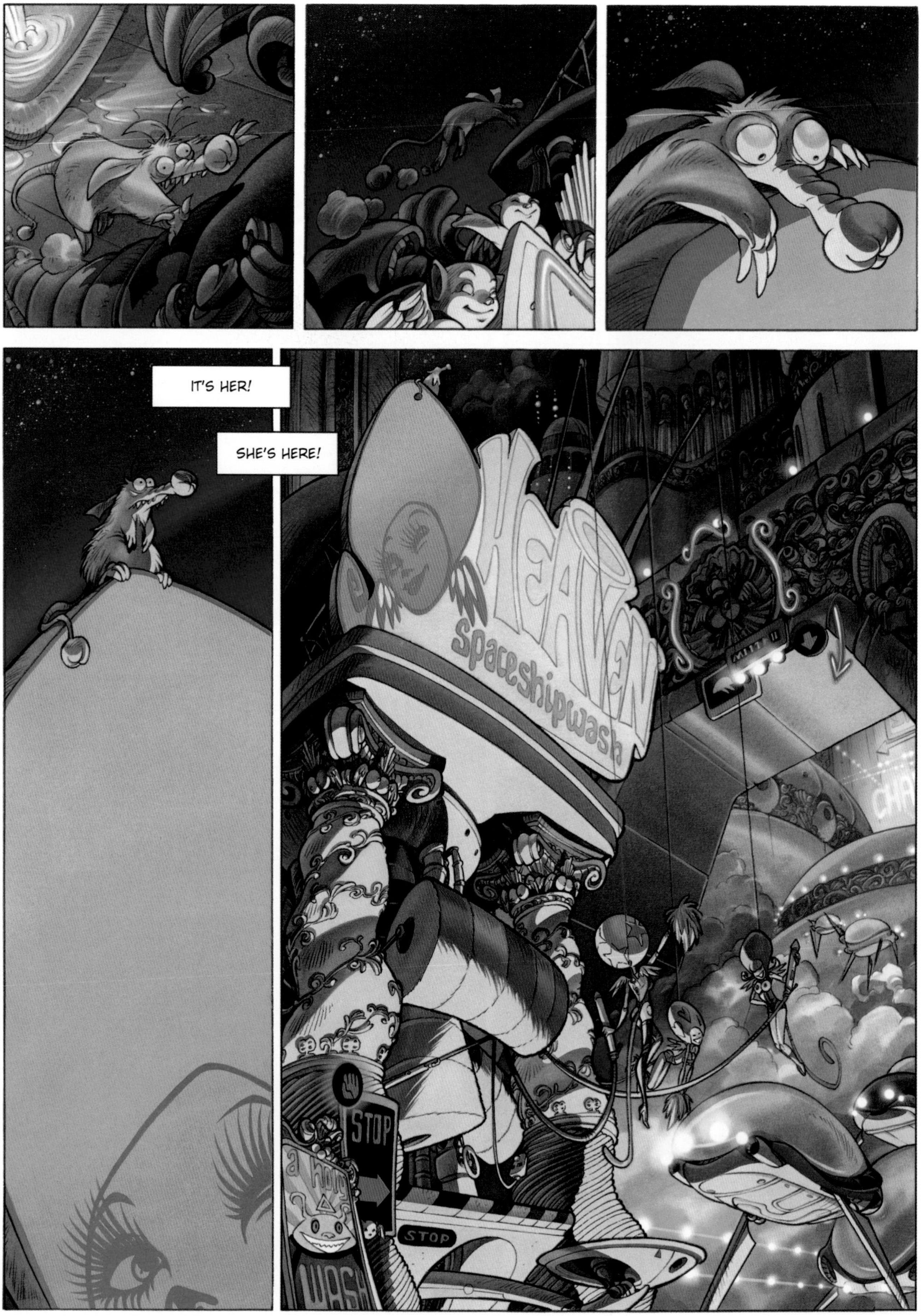

IT'S HER!
SHE'S HERE!
HEAVEN
spaceshipwash
STOP
STOP
WASH

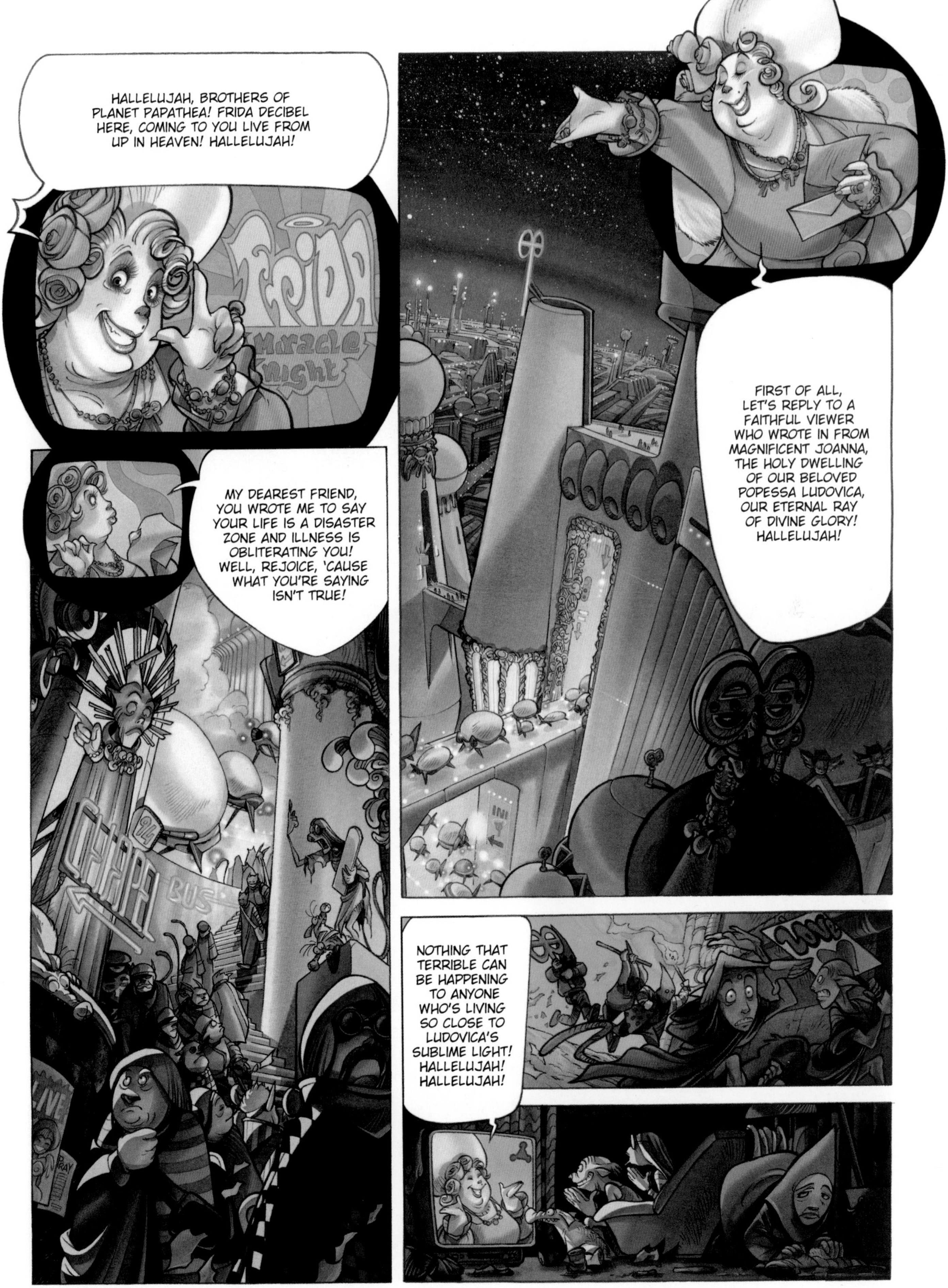
HALLELUJAH, BROTHERS OF PLANET PAPATHEA! FRIDA DECIBEL HERE, COMING TO YOU LIVE FROM UP IN HEAVEN! HALLELUJAH!
FIRST OF ALL, LET'S REPLY TO A FAITHFUL VIEWER WHO WROTE IN FROM MAGNIFICENT JOANNA, THE HOLY DWELLING OF OUR BELOVED POPESSA LUDOVICA, OUR ETERNAL RAY OF DIVINE GLORY! HALLELUJAH!
MY DEAREST FRIEND, YOU WROTE ME TO SAY YOUR LIFE IS A DISASTER ZONE AND ILLNESS IS OBLITERATING YOU! WELL, REJOICE, 'CAUSE WHAT YOU'RE SAYING ISN'T TRUE!
NOTHING THAT TERRIBLE CAN BE HAPPENING TO ANYONE WHO'S LIVING SO CLOSE TO LUDOVICA'S SUBLIME LIGHT! HALLELUJAH! HALLELUJAH!

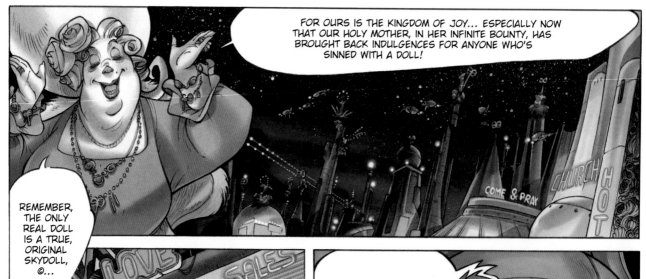

FOR OURS IS THE KINGDOM OF JOY... ESPECIALLY NOW THAT OUR HOLY MOTHER, IN HER INFINITE BOUNTY, HAS BROUGHT BACK INDULGENCES FOR ANYONE WHO'S SINNED WITH A DOLL!
COME & PRAY
CHURCH
HOT
REMEMBER, THE ONLY REAL DOLL IS A TRUE, ORIGINAL SKYDOLL, ©...
LOVE
SALES
NO SIN
...LIKE THE ONES WAITING FOR YOU AT HEAVEN ASTROWASH TO BUFF UP YOUR ROCKETSHIP! HALLELUJAH, BROTHERS! IT'S NO SIN!
TRINI teevee
HEAVEN
spaceshipwash
HEH...SOUNDS LIKE A GREAT IDEA TO ME!
YOU KIDDING?
WHAT? WE'RE ON A DIPLOMATIC MISSION FOR THE POPESSA HERSELF! YOU DON'T WANT US TRAIPSING AROUND IN A DIRTY SPACESHIP, DO YA?
OH, I SEE. IT'S ALL ABOUT HYGIENE, IS IT? FOR A SEC THERE, I THOUGHT YOU JUST WANTED TO SEE SYNTHDOLLS WIGGLING AROUND ON THE WINDSHIELD.

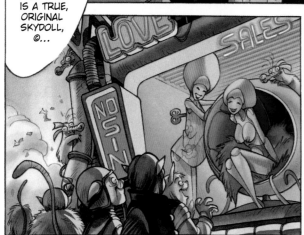

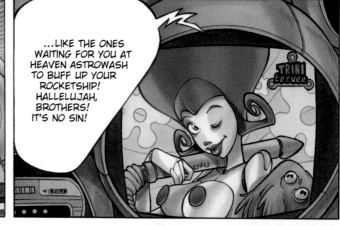

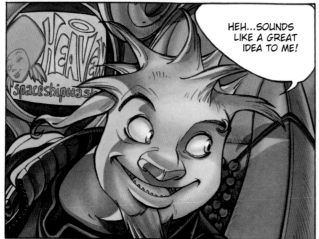

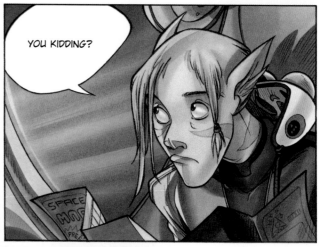

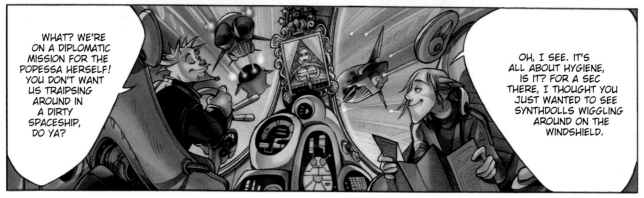

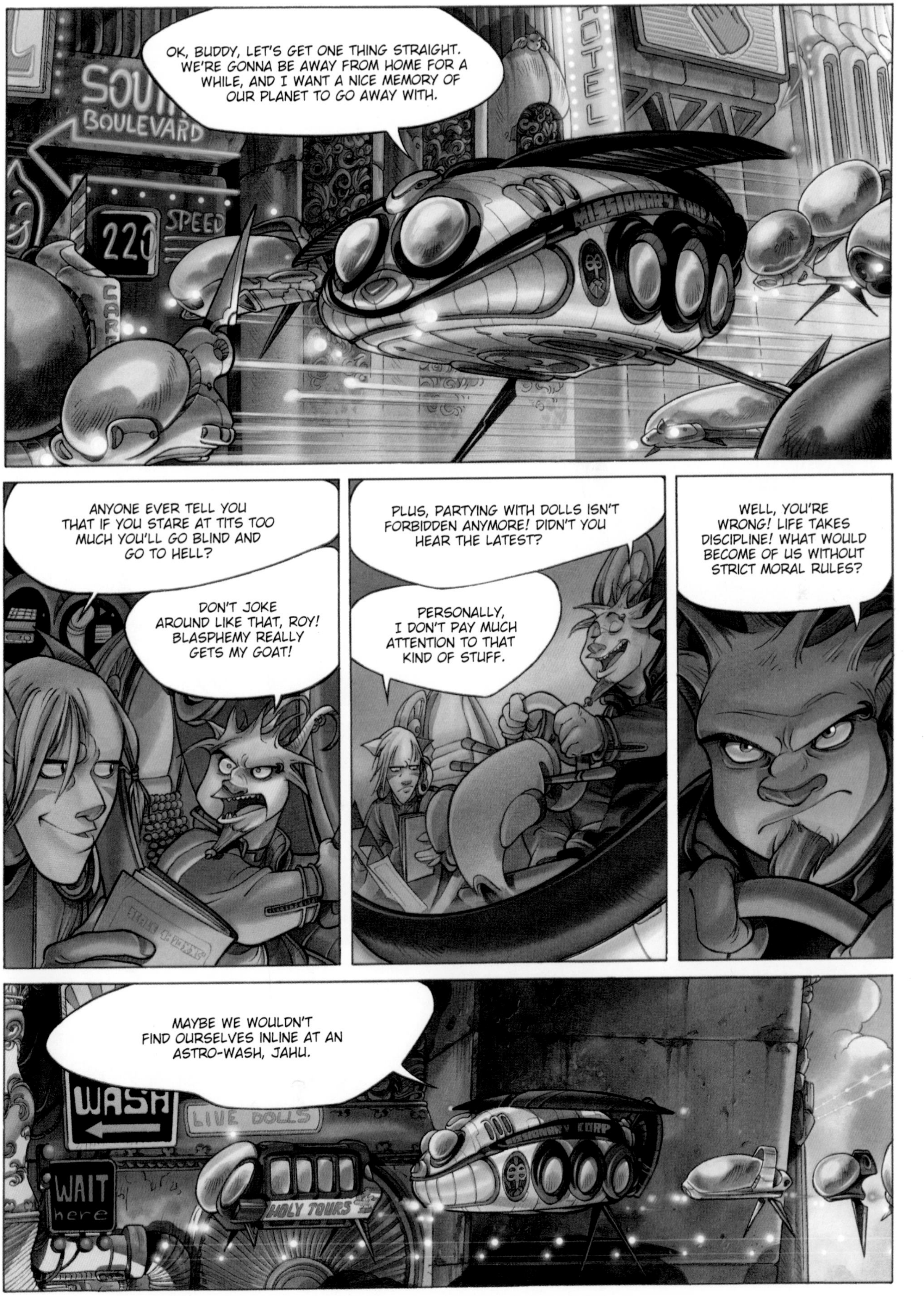
OK, BUDDY, LET'S GET ONE THING STRAIGHT. WE'RE GONNA BE AWAY FROM HOME FOR A WHILE, AND I WANT A NICE MEMORY OF OUR PLANET TO GO AWAY WITH.
BOULEVARD
HOTEL
220 SPEED
ANYONE EVER TELL YOU THAT IF YOU STARE AT TITS TOO MUCH YOU'LL GO BLIND AND GO TO HELL?
DON'T JOKE AROUND LIKE THAT, ROY! BLASPHEMY REALLY GETS MY GOAT!
PLUS, PARTYING WITH DOLLS ISN'T FORBIDDEN ANYMORE! DIDN'T YOU HEAR THE LATEST?
PERSONALLY, I DON'T PAY MUCH ATTENTION TO THAT KIND OF STUFF.
WELL, YOU'RE WRONG! LIFE TAKES DISCIPLINE! WHAT WOULD BECOME OF US WITHOUT STRICT MORAL RULES?
MAYBE WE WOULDN'T FIND OURSELVES INLINE AT AN ASTRO-WASH, JAHU.
WASH
LIVE DOLLS
WAIT here
HOLY TOURS

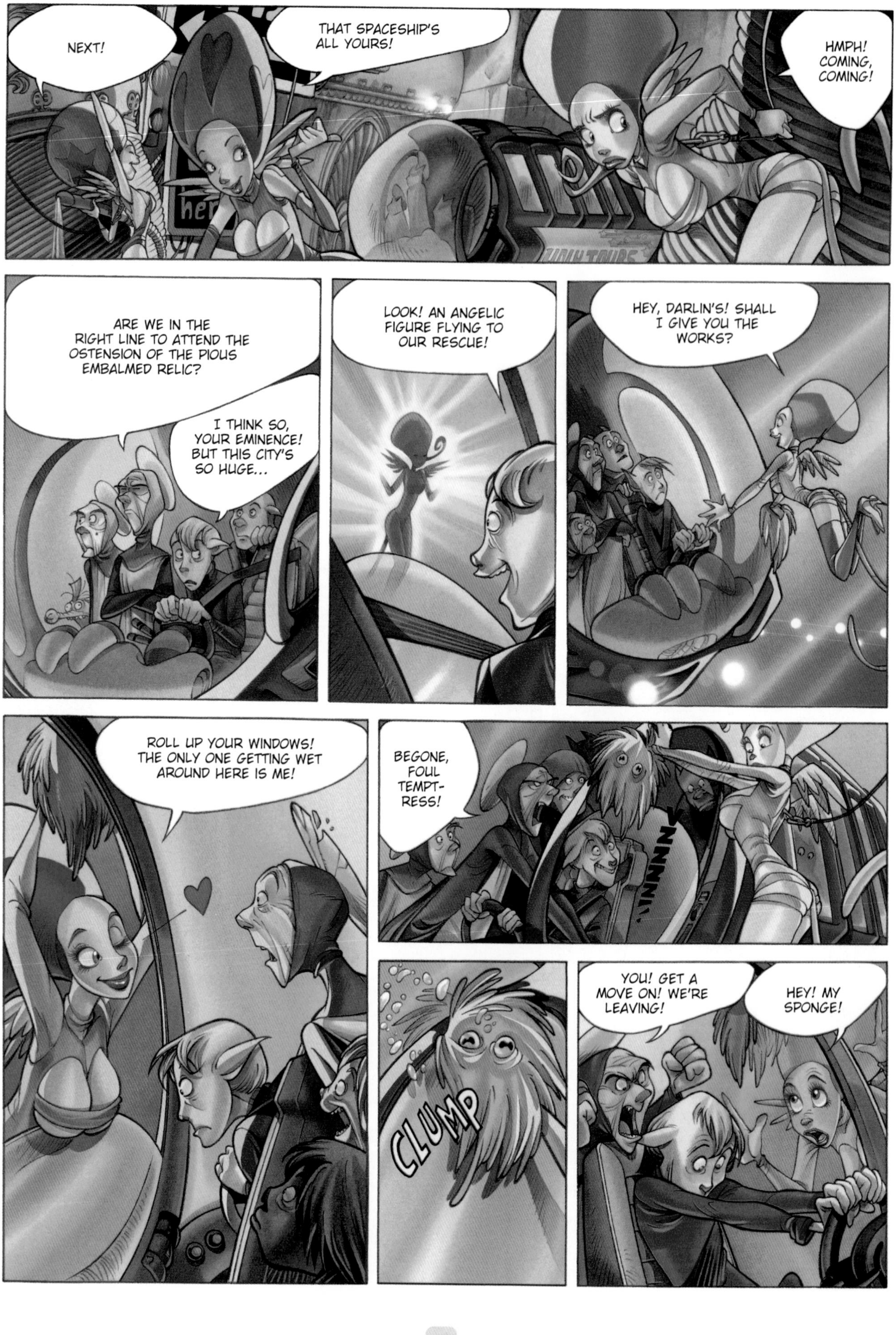
NEXT!
THAT SPACESHIP'S ALL YOURS!
HMPH! COMING, COMING!
ARE WE IN THE RIGHT LINE TO ATTEND THE OSTENSION OF THE PIOUS EMBALMED RELIC?
I THINK SO, YOUR EMINENCE! BUT THIS CITY'S SO HUGE...
LOOK! AN ANGELIC FIGURE FLYING TO OUR RESCUE!
HEY, DARLIN'S! SHALL I GIVE YOU THE WORKS?
ROLL UP YOUR WINDOWS! THE ONLY ONE GETTING WET AROUND HERE IS ME!
BEGONE, FOUL TEMPT-RESS!
NNNNNN!
CLUMP
YOU! GET A MOVE ON! WE'RE LEAVING!
HEY! MY SPONGE!

OPEN UP!
PLEASE!
OPEN UP!

AAARGH!
AWAY,
JEZABEL!!

OOOOH!!

REVERSE

VROOOOOOOO

CRASH

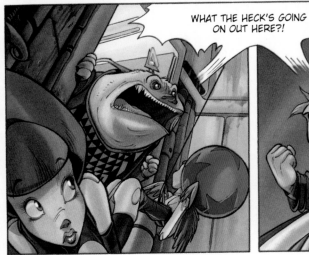

WHAT THE HECK'S GOING
ON OUT HERE?!

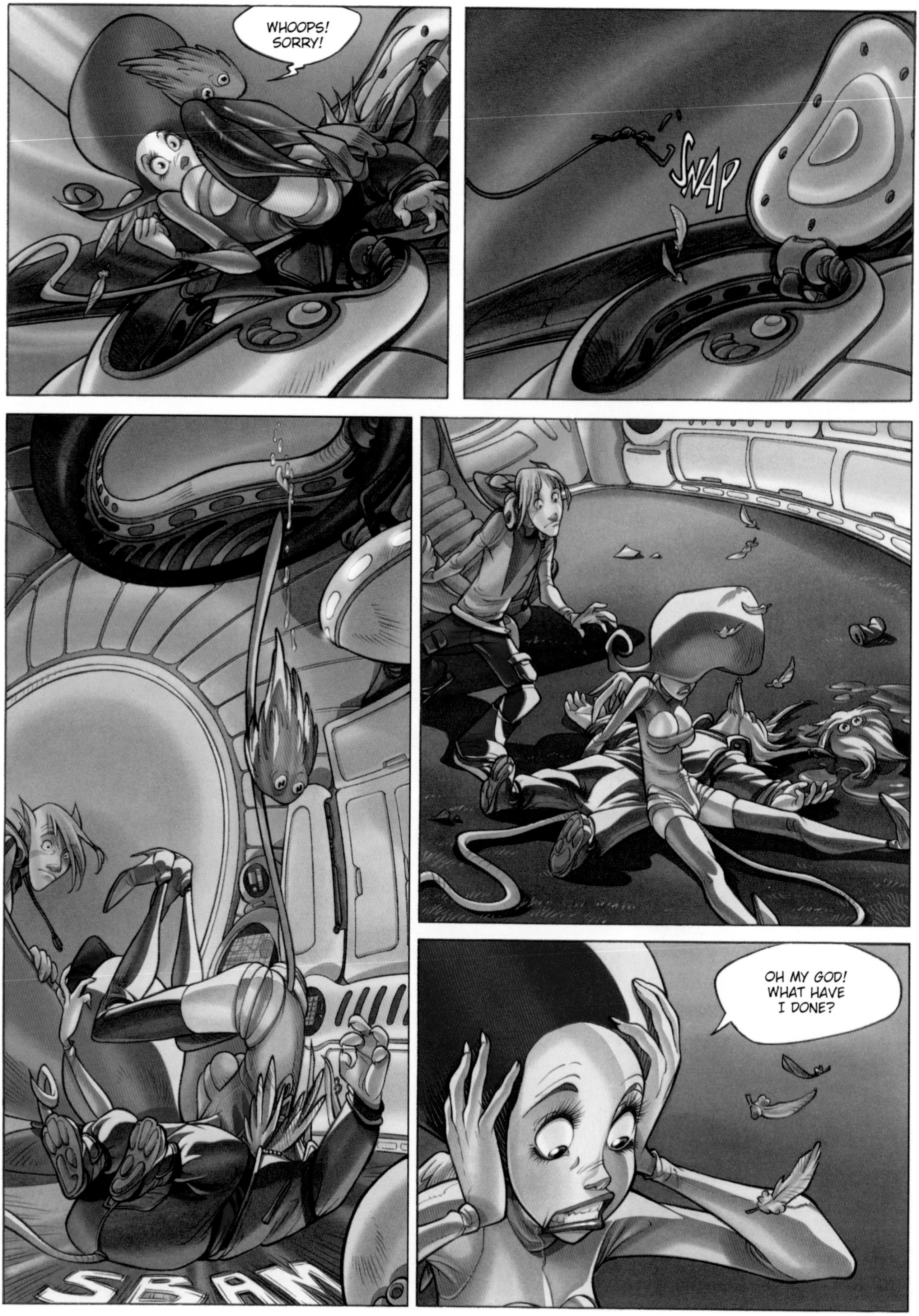
WHOOPS! SORRY!
SNAP
SBAM
OH MY GOD! WHAT HAVE I DONE?

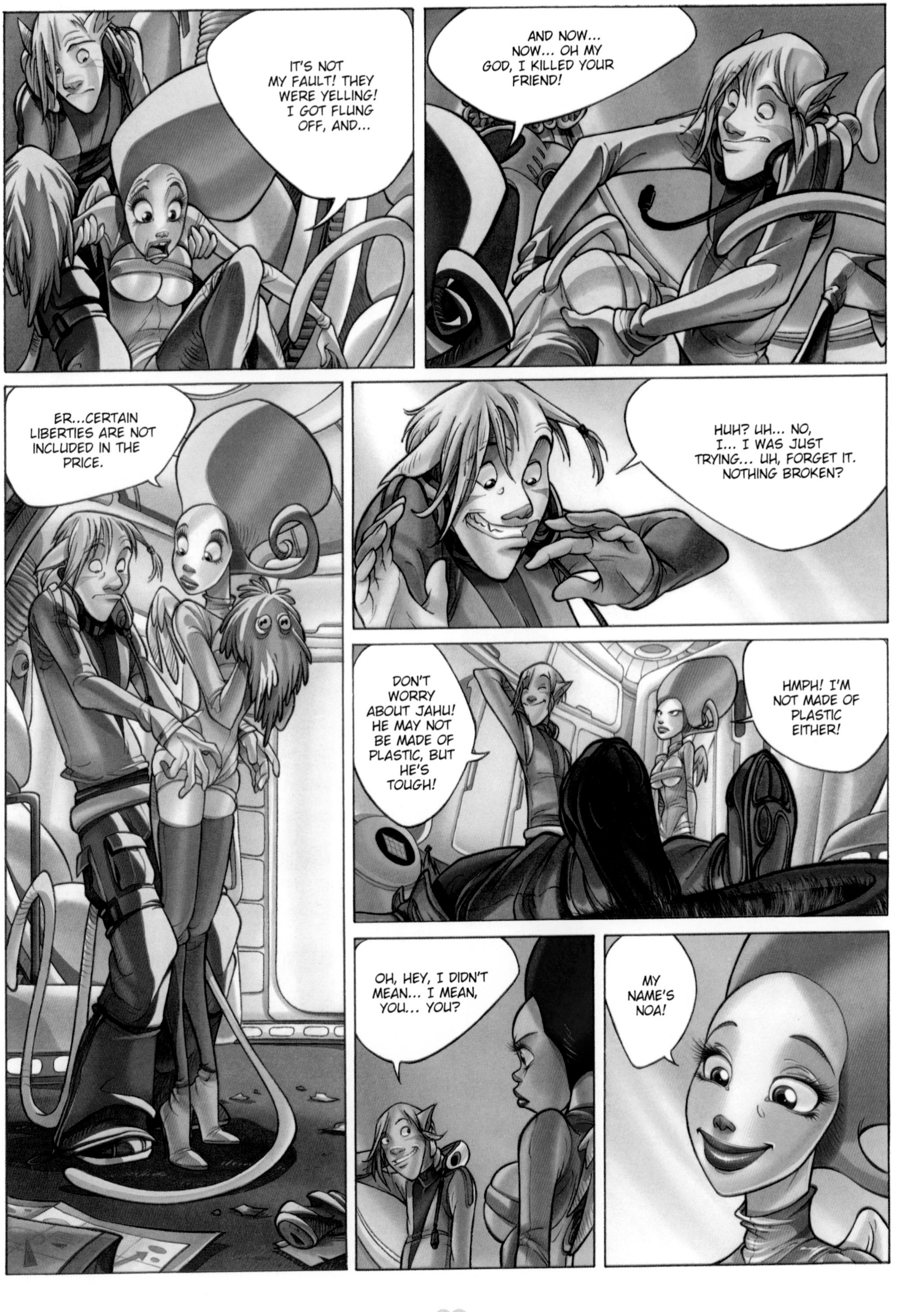
IT'S NOT MY FAULT! THEY WERE YELLING! I GOT FLUNG OFF, AND...
AND NOW... NOW... OH MY GOD, I KILLED YOUR FRIEND!
ER...CERTAIN LIBERTIES ARE NOT INCLUDED IN THE PRICE.
HUH? UH... NO, I... I WAS JUST TRYING... UH, FORGET IT. NOTHING BROKEN?
DON'T WORRY ABOUT JAHU! HE MAY NOT BE MADE OF PLASTIC, BUT HE'S TOUGH!
HMPH! I'M NOT MADE OF PLASTIC EITHER!
OH, HEY, I DIDN'T MEAN... I MEAN, YOU... YOU?
MY NAME'S NOA!

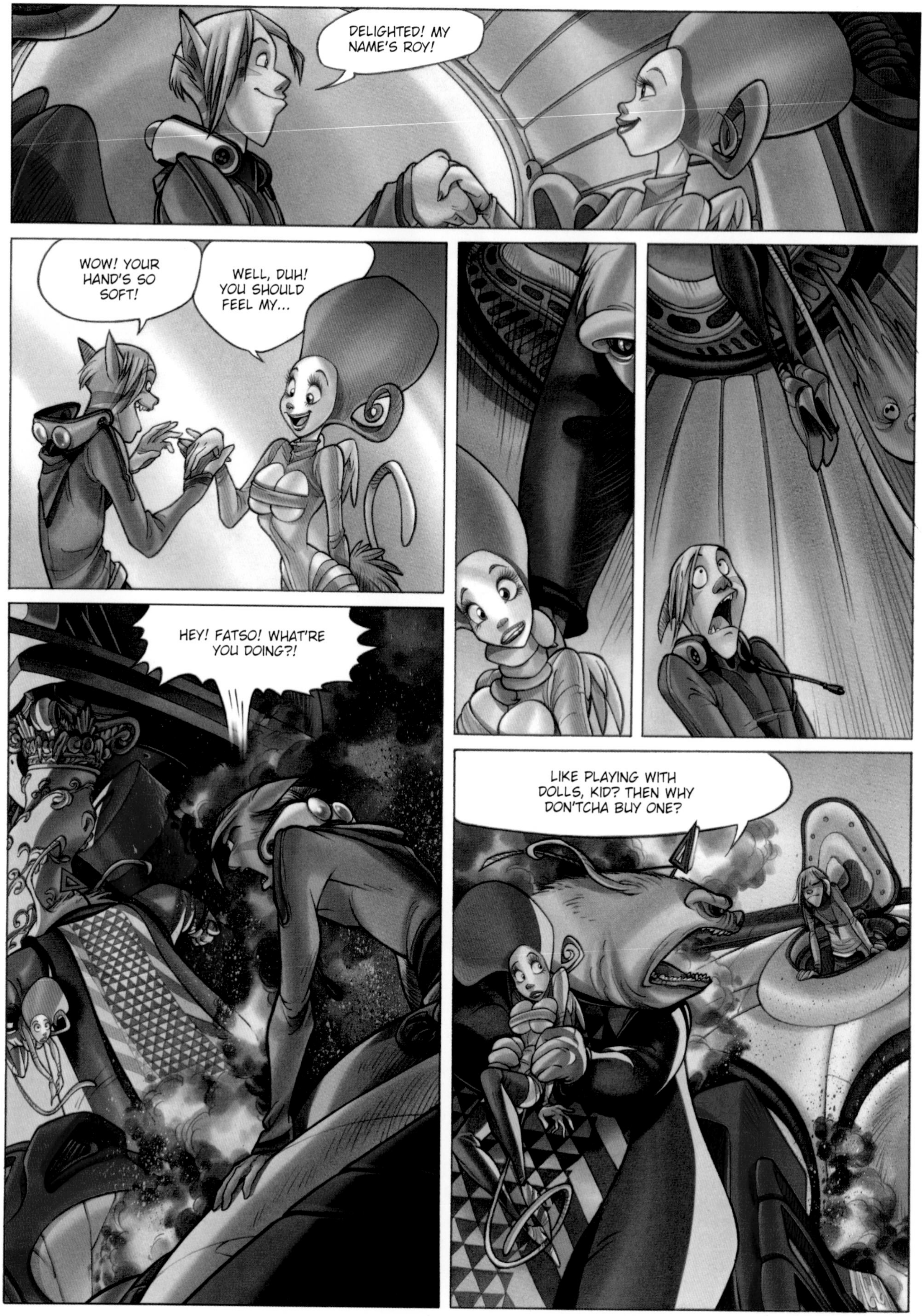
DELIGHTED! MY NAME'S ROY!
WOW! YOUR HAND'S SO SOFT!
WELL, DUH! YOU SHOULD FEEL MY...
HEY! FATSO! WHAT'RE YOU DOING?!
LIKE PLAYING WITH DOLLS, KID? THEN WHY DON'TCHA BUY ONE?

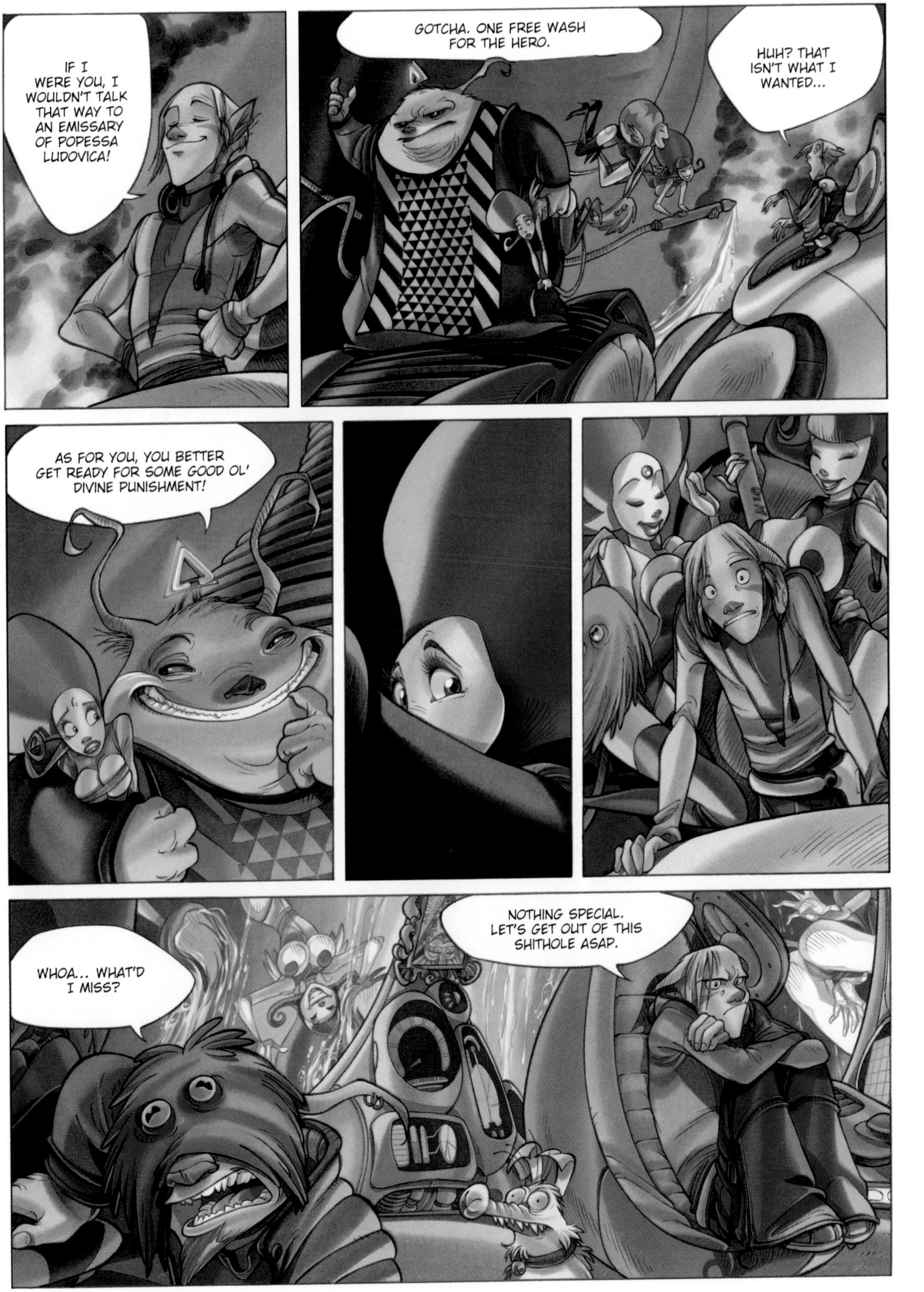
IF I WERE YOU, I WOULDN'T TALK THAT WAY TO AN EMISSARY OF POPESSA LUDOVICA!
GOTCHA. ONE FREE WASH FOR THE HERO.
HUH? THAT ISN'T WHAT I WANTED...
AS FOR YOU, YOU BETTER GET READY FOR SOME GOOD OL' DIVINE PUNISHMENT!
WHOA... WHAT'D I MISS?
NOTHING SPECIAL. LET'S GET OUT OF THIS SHITHOLE ASAP.

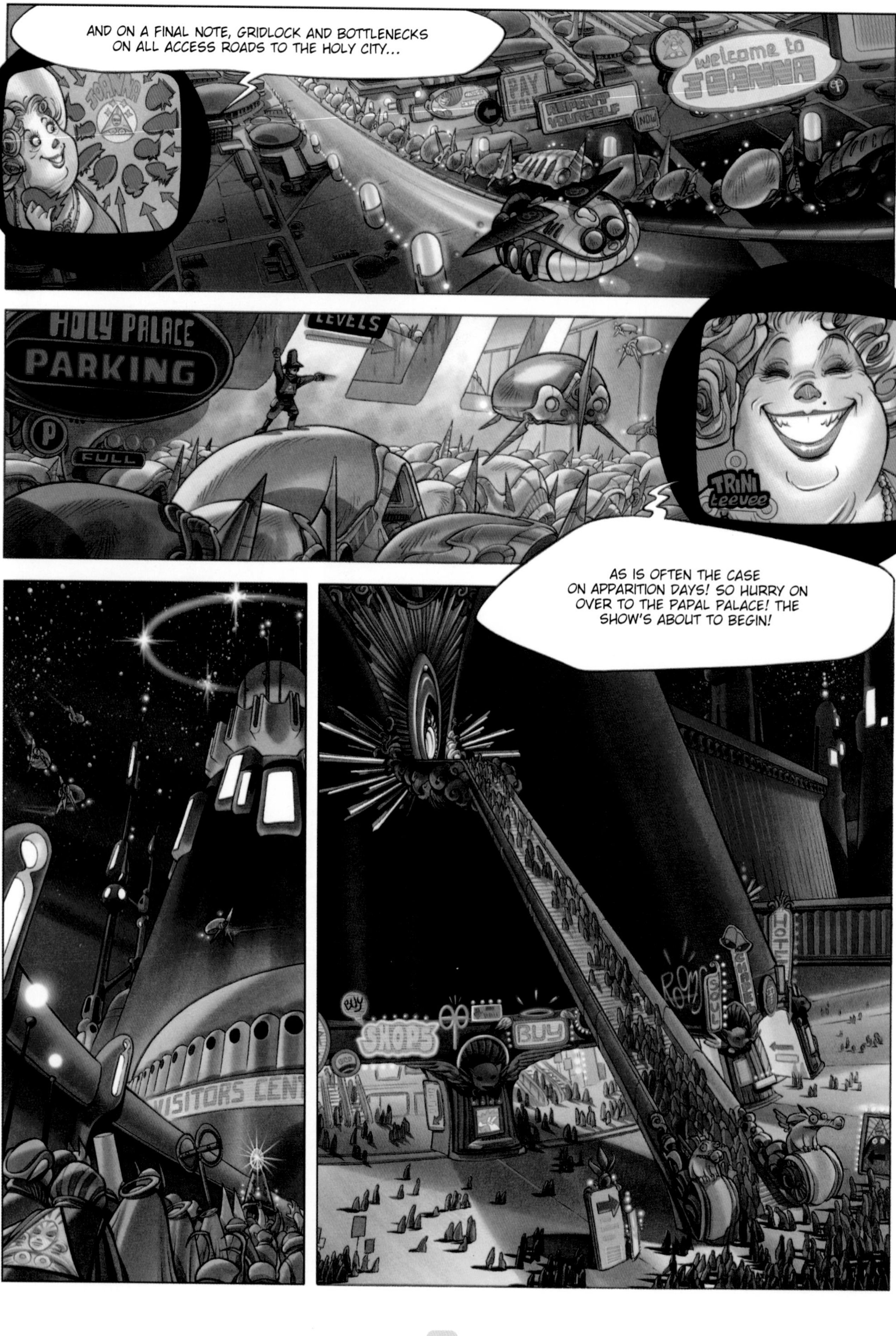
AND ON A FINAL NOTE, GRIDLOCK AND BOTTLENECKS ON ALL ACCESS ROADS TO THE HOLY CITY...
welcome to JOANNA
PAY
REPENT YOURSELF
NOW
HOLY PALACE
PARKING
LEVELS
FULL
TRINI teevee
AS IS OFTEN THE CASE ON APPARITION DAYS! SO HURRY ON OVER TO THE PAPAL PALACE! THE SHOW'S ABOUT TO BEGIN!
VISITORS CENT
SHOPS
BUY
BUY
SOUL

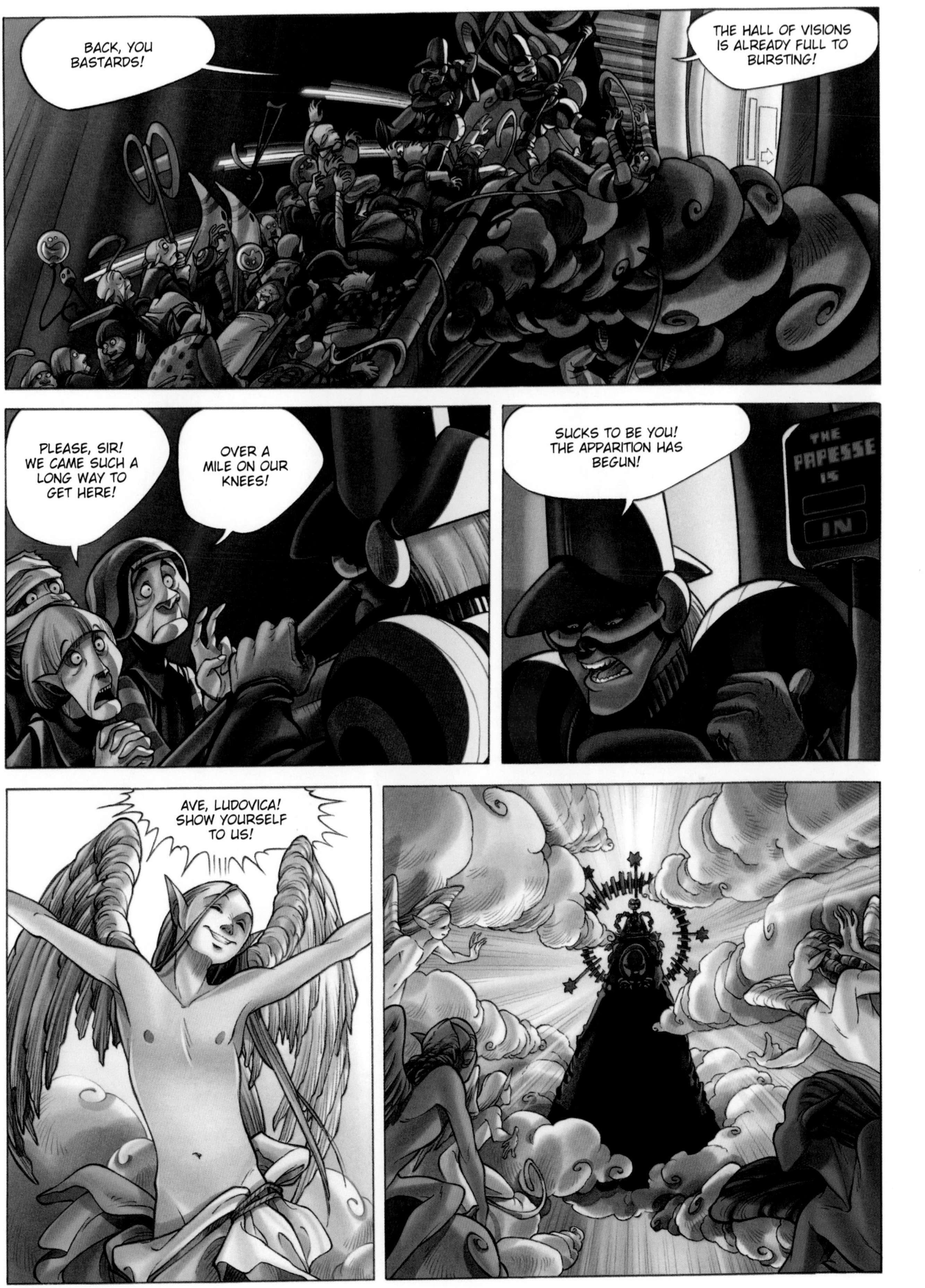
BACK, YOU BASTARDS!
THE HALL OF VISIONS IS ALREADY FULL TO BURSTING!
PLEASE, SIR! WE CAME SUCH A LONG WAY TO GET HERE!
OVER A MILE ON OUR KNEES!
SUCKS TO BE YOU! THE APPARITION HAS BEGUN!
THE PAPESSE IS IN
AVE, LUDOVICA! SHOW YOURSELF TO US!

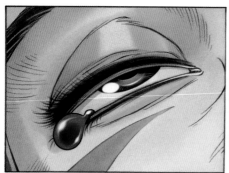

SHHAAAA

THE MIRACLE! AT LAST!

HALLELUJAH!

BLEED FOR US!

HOLY MOTHER!

DIVINE SLUT!

THE HYSTERIA HAS REACHED LEVEL 32. KEEP GOING?

I THINK THAT'S ENOUGH, DON'T YOU?

DISGUSTING!

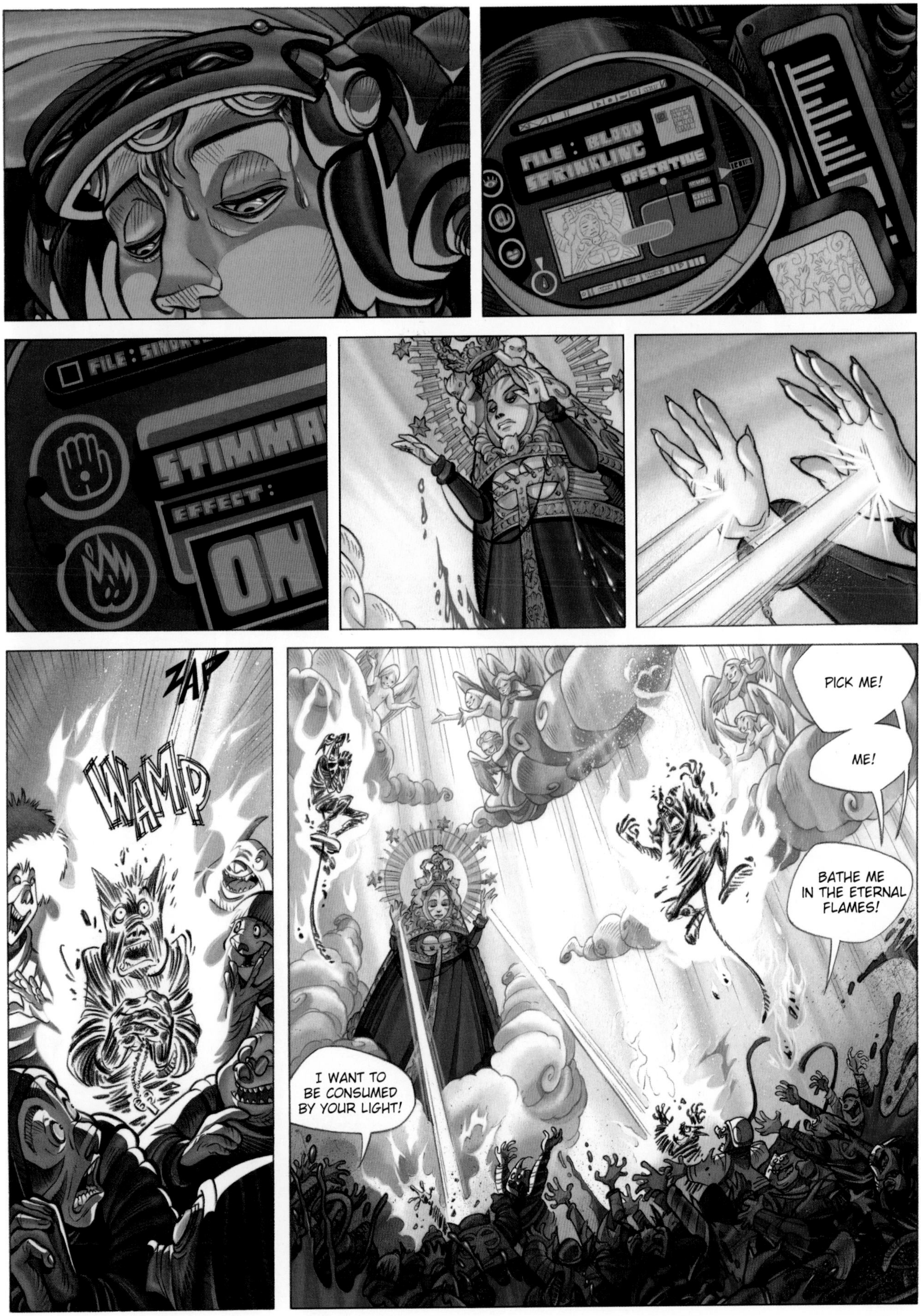
FILE : BLOOD SPRINKLING
OPERATIVE
EFFECT :
ON
ZAP
WAMP
PICK ME!
ME!
BATHE ME IN THE ETERNAL FLAMES!
I WANT TO BE CONSUMED BY YOUR LIGHT!

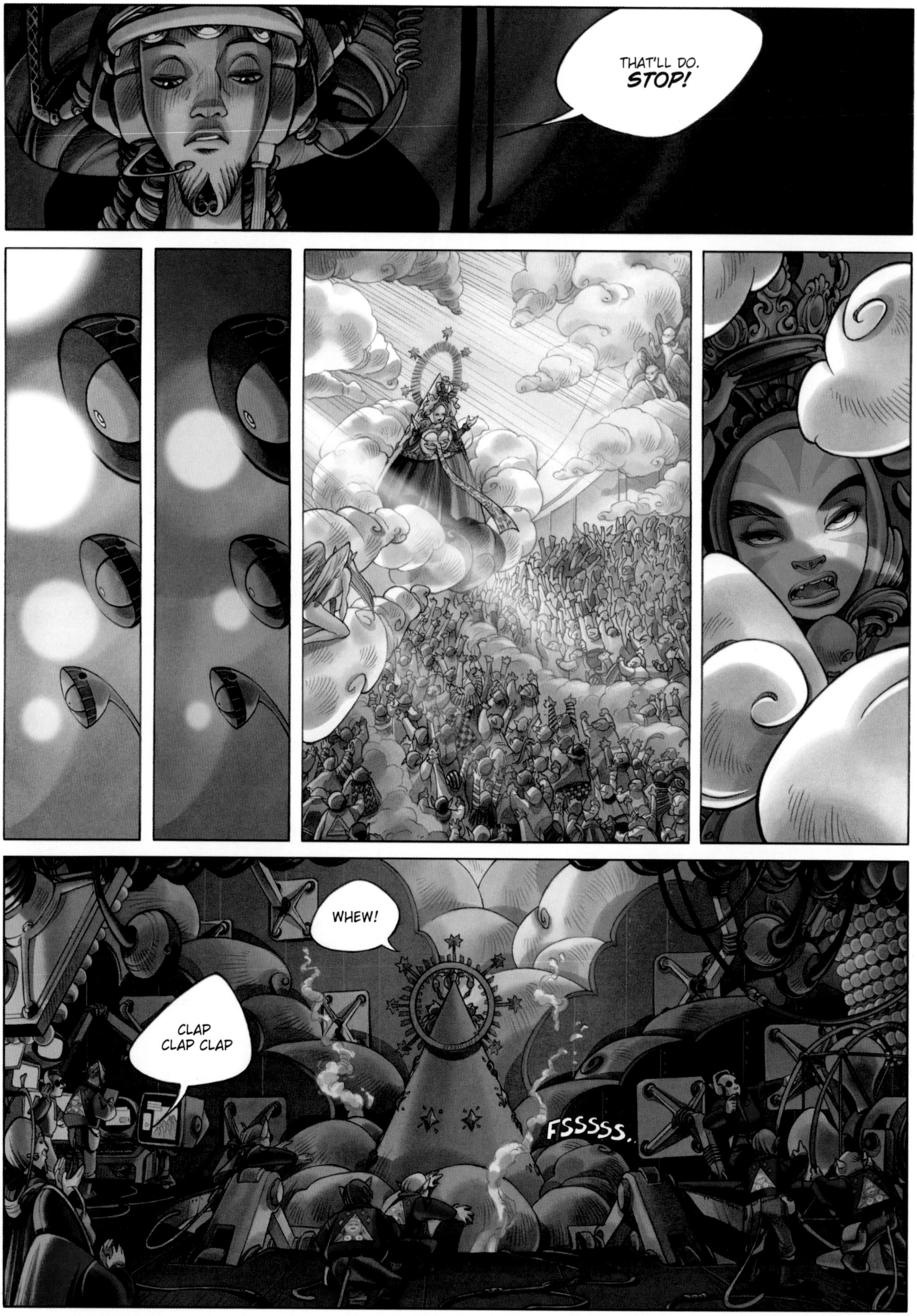
THAT'LL DO.
STOP!
WHEW!
CLAP
CLAP CLAP
FSSSSS..

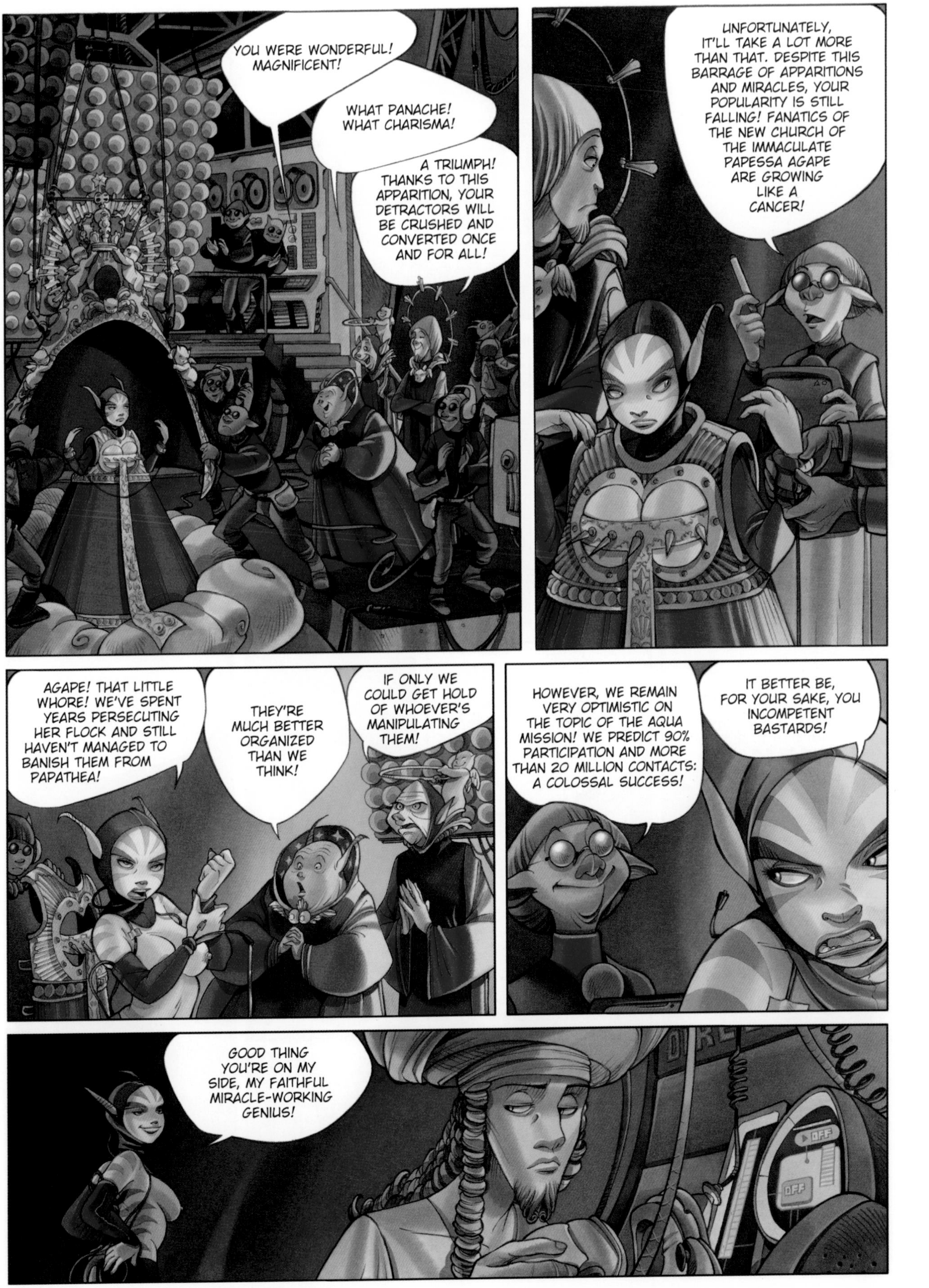
YOU WERE WONDERFUL! MAGNIFICENT!
WHAT PANACHE! WHAT CHARISMA!
A TRIUMPH! THANKS TO THIS APPARITION, YOUR DETRACTORS WILL BE CRUSHED AND CONVERTED ONCE AND FOR ALL!
UNFORTUNATELY, IT'LL TAKE A LOT MORE THAN THAT. DESPITE THIS BARRAGE OF APPARITIONS AND MIRACLES, YOUR POPULARITY IS STILL FALLING! FANATICS OF THE NEW CHURCH OF THE IMMACULATE PAPESSA AGAPE ARE GROWING LIKE A CANCER!
AGAPE! THAT LITTLE WHORE! WE'VE SPENT YEARS PERSECUTING HER FLOCK AND STILL HAVEN'T MANAGED TO BANISH THEM FROM PAPATHEA!
THEY'RE MUCH BETTER ORGANIZED THAN WE THINK!
IF ONLY WE COULD GET HOLD OF WHOEVER'S MANIPULATING THEM!
HOWEVER, WE REMAIN VERY OPTIMISTIC ON THE TOPIC OF THE AQUA MISSION! WE PREDICT 90% PARTICIPATION AND MORE THAN 20 MILLION CONTACTS: A COLOSSAL SUCCESS!
IT BETTER BE, FOR YOUR SAKE, YOU INCOMPETENT BASTARDS!
GOOD THING YOU'RE ON MY SIDE, MY FAITHFUL MIRACLE-WORKING GENIUS!
OFF
OFF

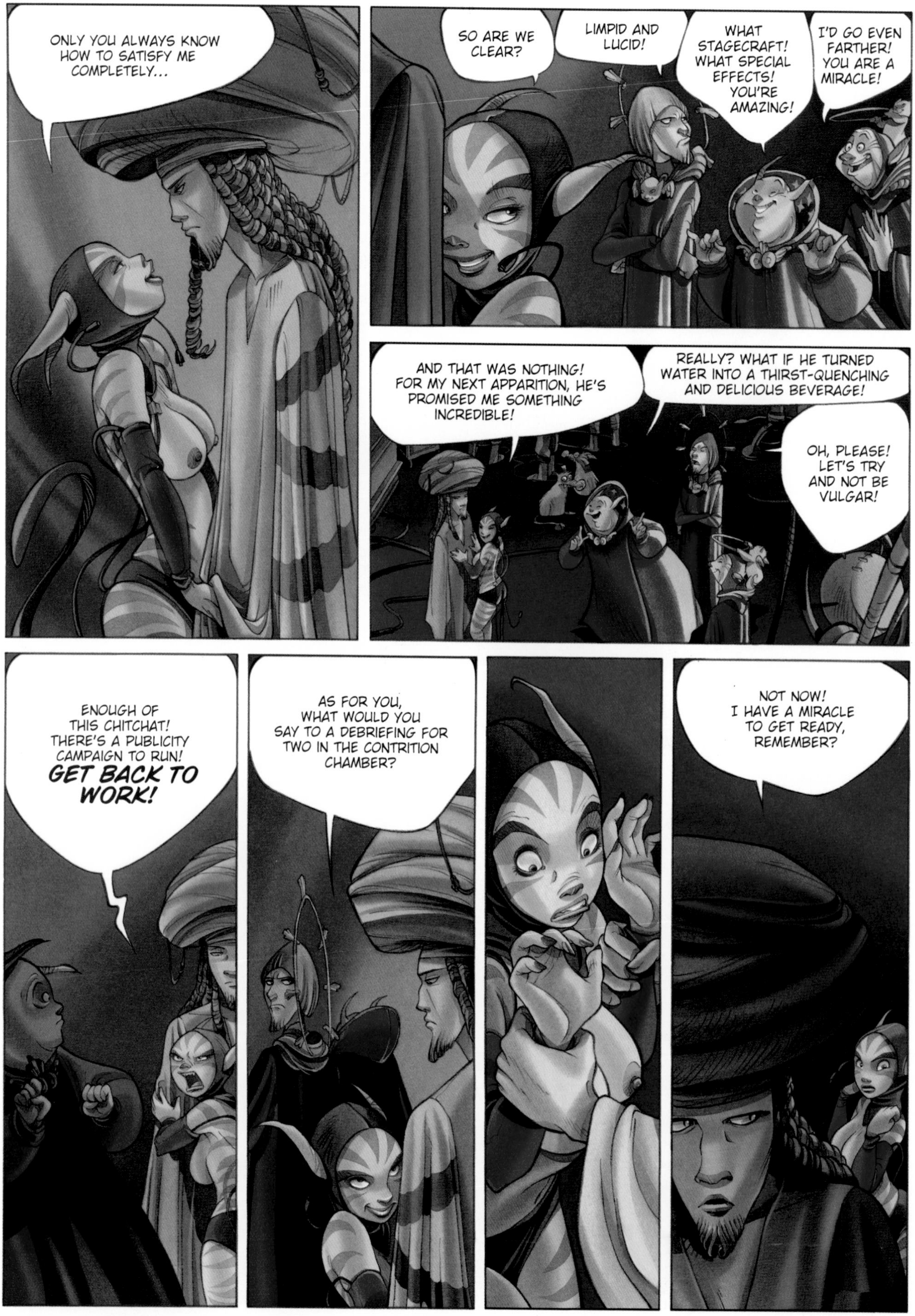
ONLY YOU ALWAYS KNOW HOW TO SATISFY ME COMPLETELY...
SO ARE WE CLEAR?
LIMPID AND LUCID!
WHAT STAGECRAFT! WHAT SPECIAL EFFECTS! YOU'RE AMAZING!
I'D GO EVEN FARTHER! YOU ARE A MIRACLE!
AND THAT WAS NOTHING! FOR MY NEXT APPARITION, HE'S PROMISED ME SOMETHING INCREDIBLE!
REALLY? WHAT IF HE TURNED WATER INTO A THIRST-QUENCHING AND DELICIOUS BEVERAGE!
OH, PLEASE! LET'S TRY AND NOT BE VULGAR!
ENOUGH OF THIS CHITCHAT! THERE'S A PUBLICITY CAMPAIGN TO RUN! **GET BACK TO WORK!**
AS FOR YOU, WHAT WOULD YOU SAY TO A DEBRIEFING FOR TWO IN THE CONTRITION CHAMBER?
NOT NOW! I HAVE A MIRACLE TO GET READY, REMEMBER?

SO WHAT DO WE DO WITH THIS ONE?

OH, THE USUAL: THE MORGUE FOR ID-ING, AND TOMORROW, REMEMBER TO RECORD THEIR NAMES AMONG THE BLESSED RAPTURED TO HEAVEN.

YOU LIKE BEING BEGGED, DON' YOU?

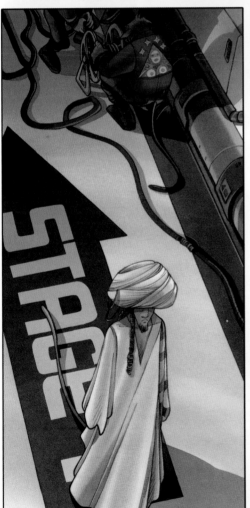

STAGE 1

OBSCENE PSYCHOPATH! ONLY YOUR MASS CULT ARE BEWITCHED BY YOUR PATHETIC SPECTACLE!

YOU THINK YOU HAVE THE PEOPLE TAMED WITH YOUR SPECIAL EFFECTS, BUT REAL POWER IS SOMETHING ELSE!

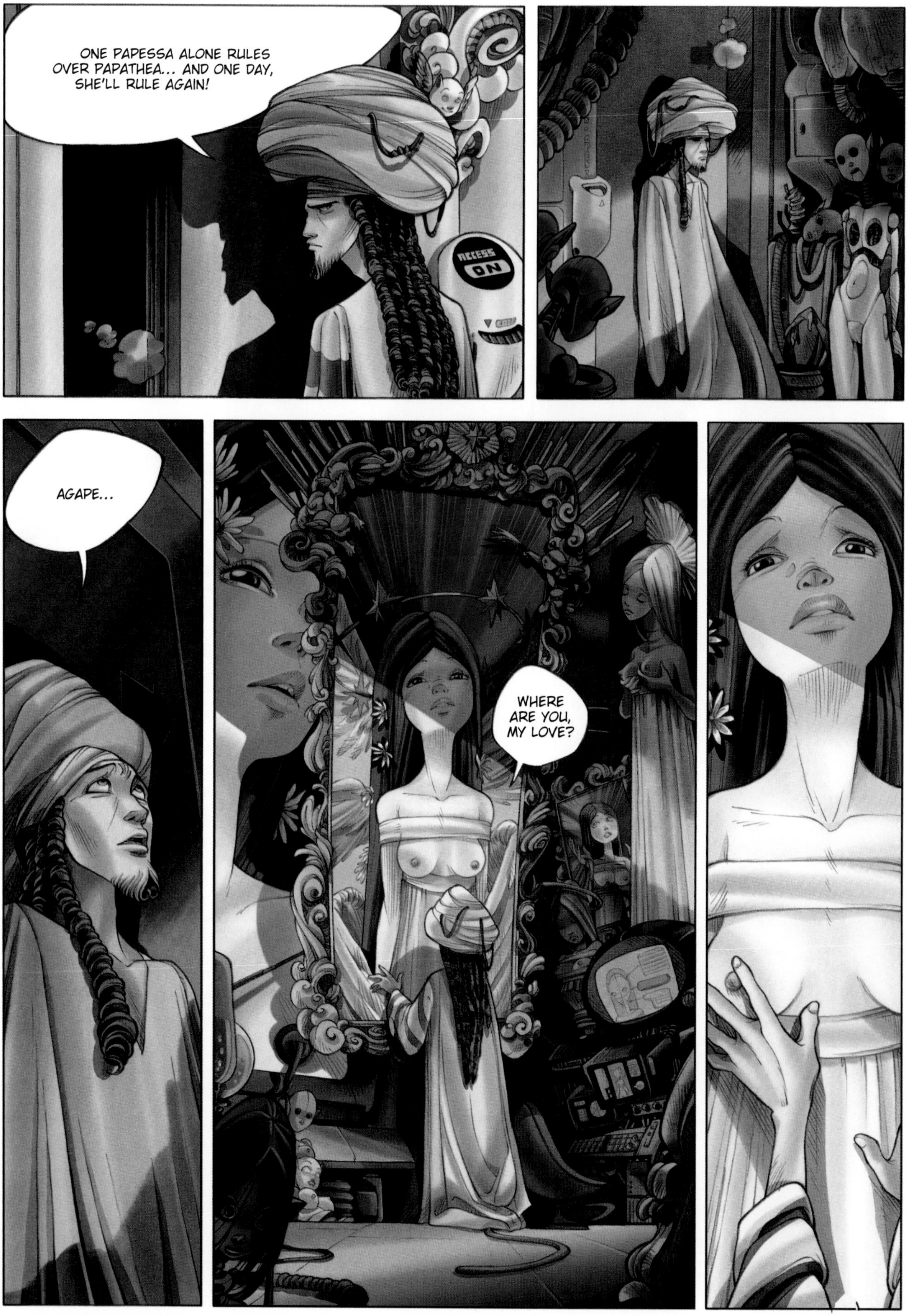
ONE PAPESSA ALONE RULES OVER PAPATHEA... AND ONE DAY, SHE'LL RULE AGAIN!
ACCESS ON
AGAPE...
WHERE ARE YOU, MY LOVE?

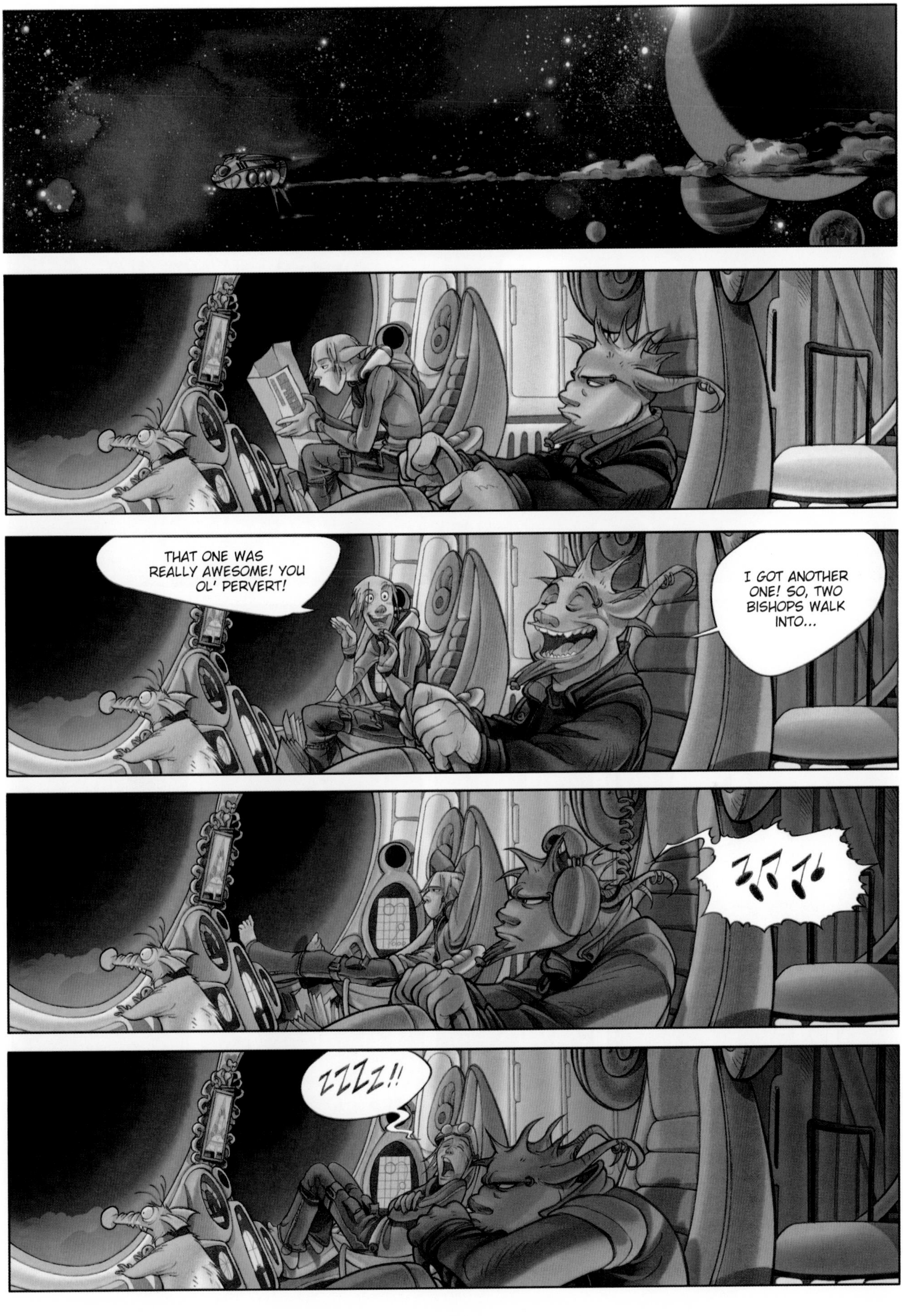
THAT ONE WAS REALLY AWESOME! YOU OL' PERVERT!
I GOT ANOTHER ONE! SO, TWO BISHOPS WALK INTO...
ZZZZ!!

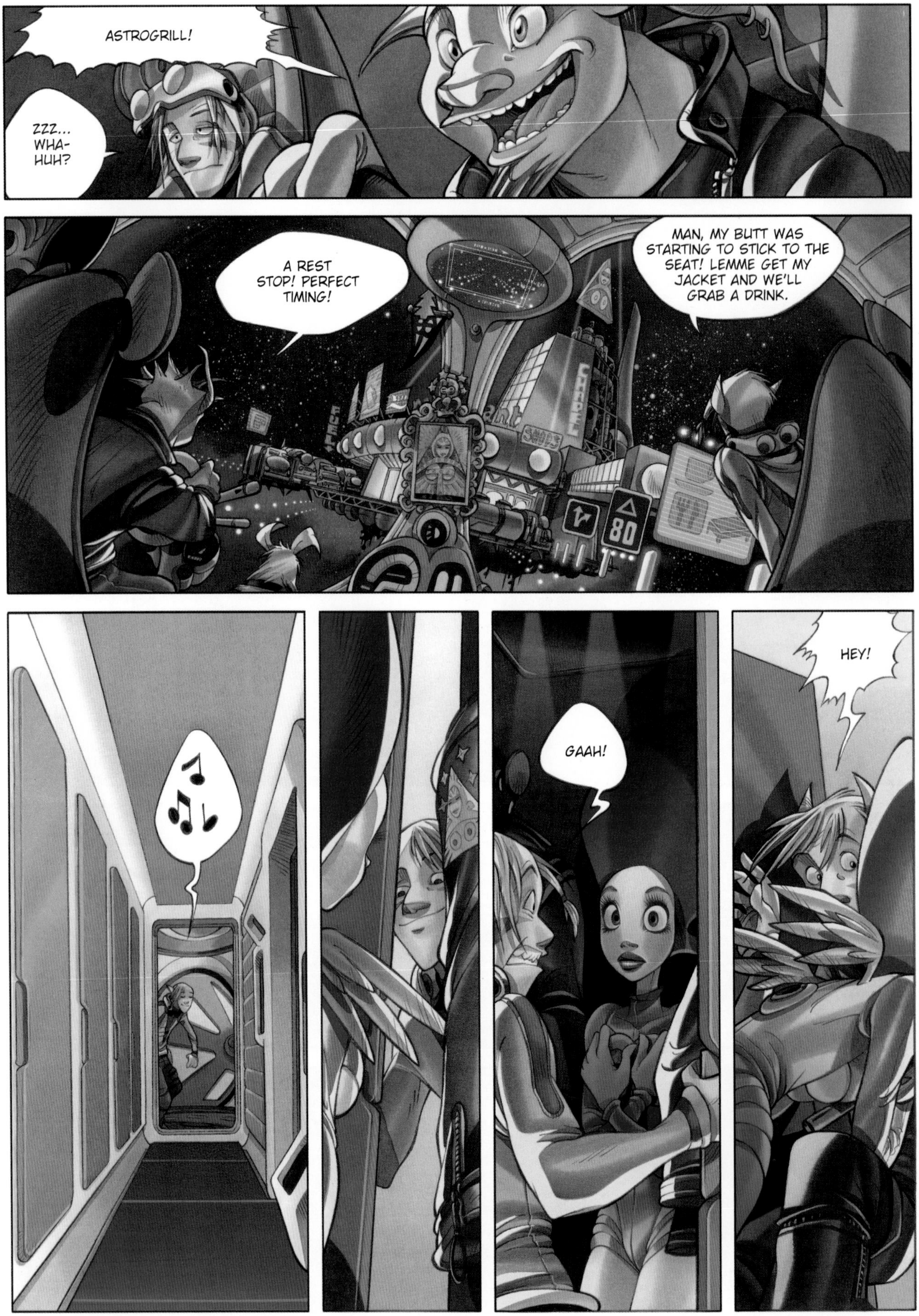
ASTROGRILL!
ZZZ... WHA-HUH?
A REST STOP! PERFECT TIMING!
MAN, MY BUTT WAS STARTING TO STICK TO THE SEAT! LEMME GET MY JACKET AND WE'LL GRAB A DRINK.
GAAH!
HEY!

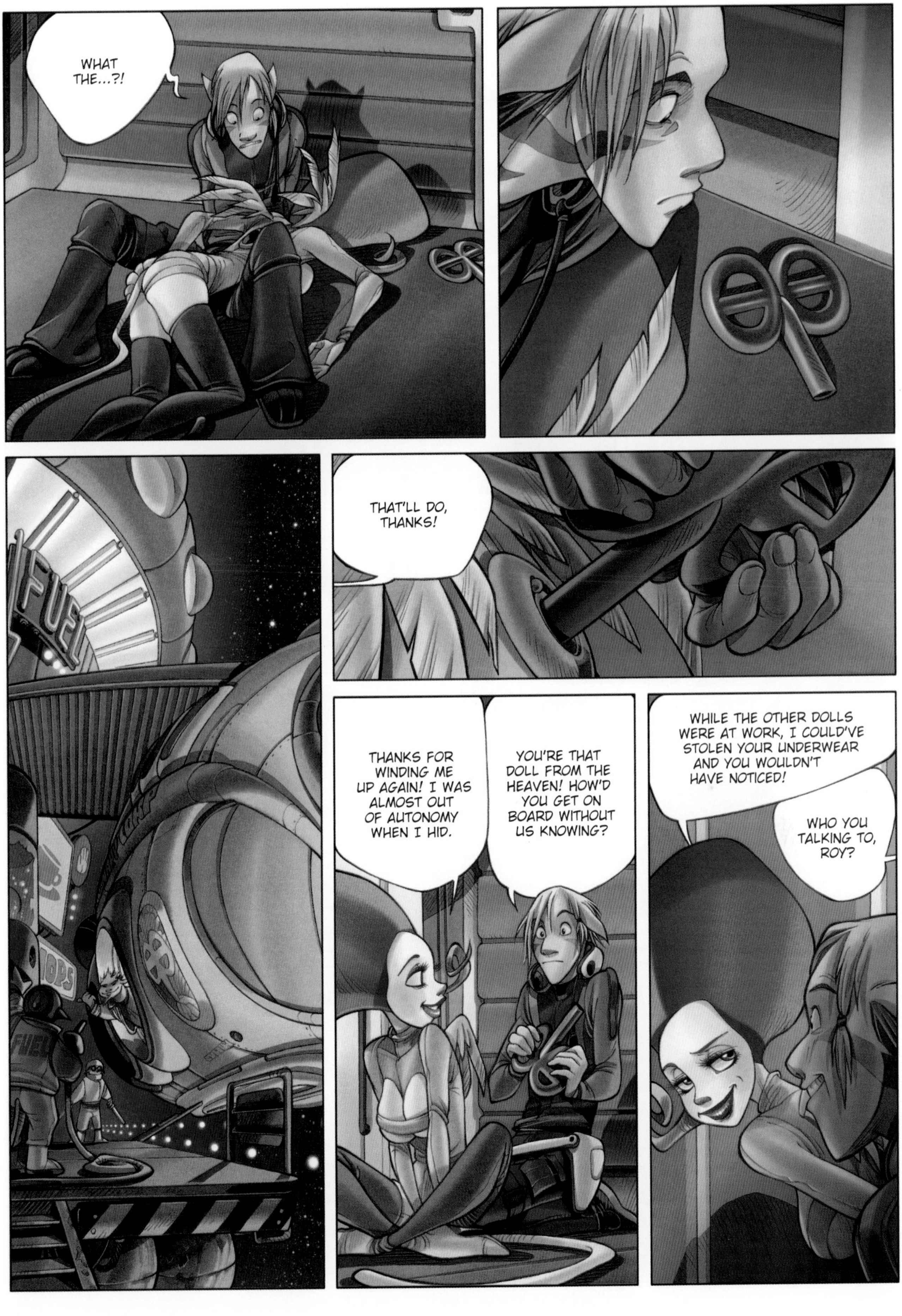
WHAT THE...?!
THAT'LL DO, THANKS!
THANKS FOR WINDING ME UP AGAIN! I WAS ALMOST OUT OF AUTONOMY WHEN I HID.
YOU'RE THAT DOLL FROM THE HEAVEN! HOW'D YOU GET ON BOARD WITHOUT US KNOWING?
WHILE THE OTHER DOLLS WERE AT WORK, I COULD'VE STOLEN YOUR UNDERWEAR AND YOU WOULDN'T HAVE NOTICED!
WHO YOU TALKING TO, ROY?

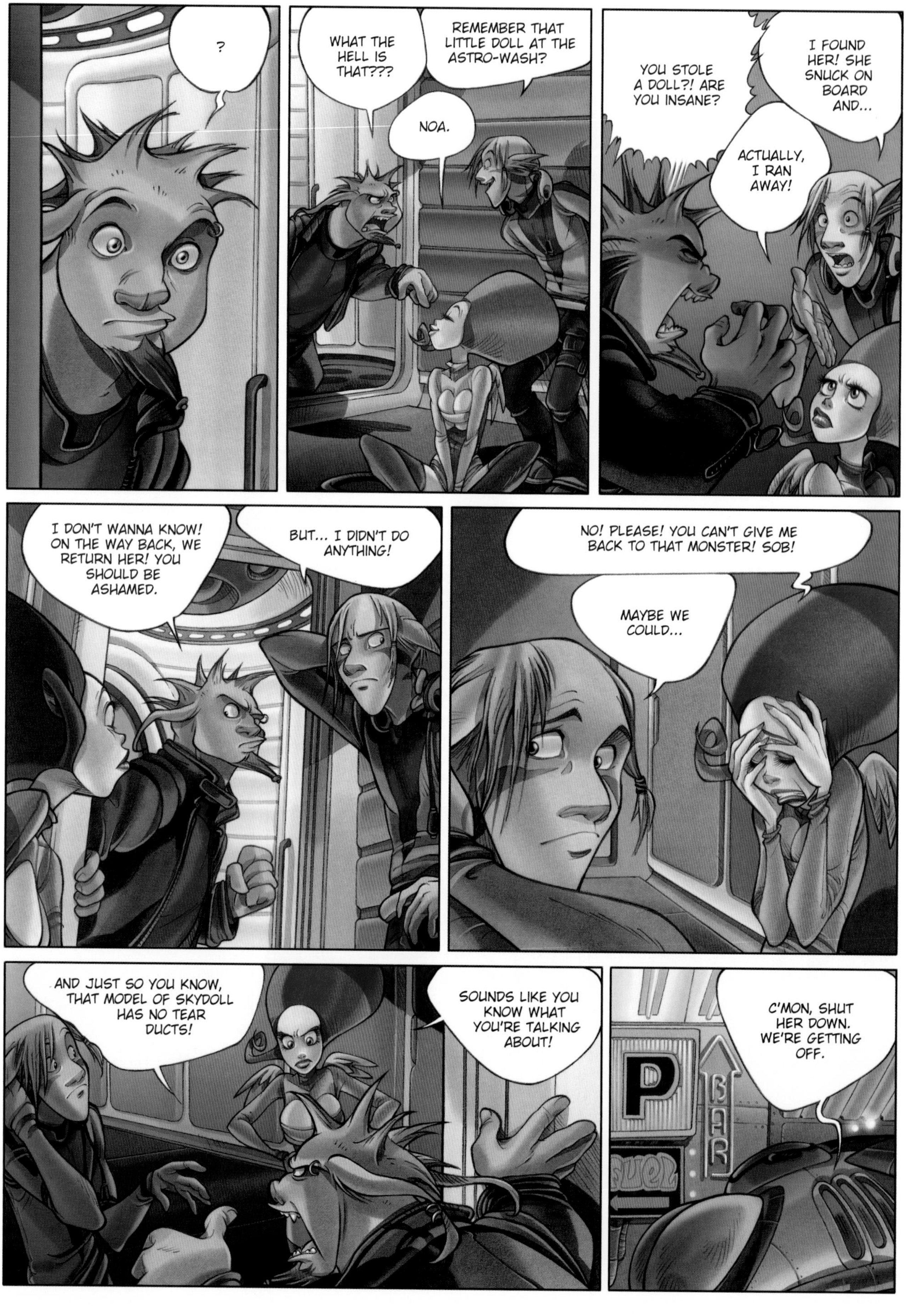
?
WHAT THE HELL IS THAT???
REMEMBER THAT LITTLE DOLL AT THE ASTRO-WASH?
NOA.
YOU STOLE A DOLL?! ARE YOU INSANE?
I FOUND HER! SHE SNUCK ON BOARD AND...
ACTUALLY, I RAN AWAY!
I DON'T WANNA KNOW! ON THE WAY BACK, WE RETURN HER! YOU SHOULD BE ASHAMED.
BUT... I DIDN'T DO ANYTHING!
NO! PLEASE! YOU CAN'T GIVE ME BACK TO THAT MONSTER! SOB!
MAYBE WE COULD...
AND JUST SO YOU KNOW, THAT MODEL OF SKYDOLL HAS NO TEAR DUCTS!
SOUNDS LIKE YOU KNOW WHAT YOU'RE TALKING ABOUT!
C'MON, SHUT HER DOWN. WE'RE GETTING OFF.
P
BAR

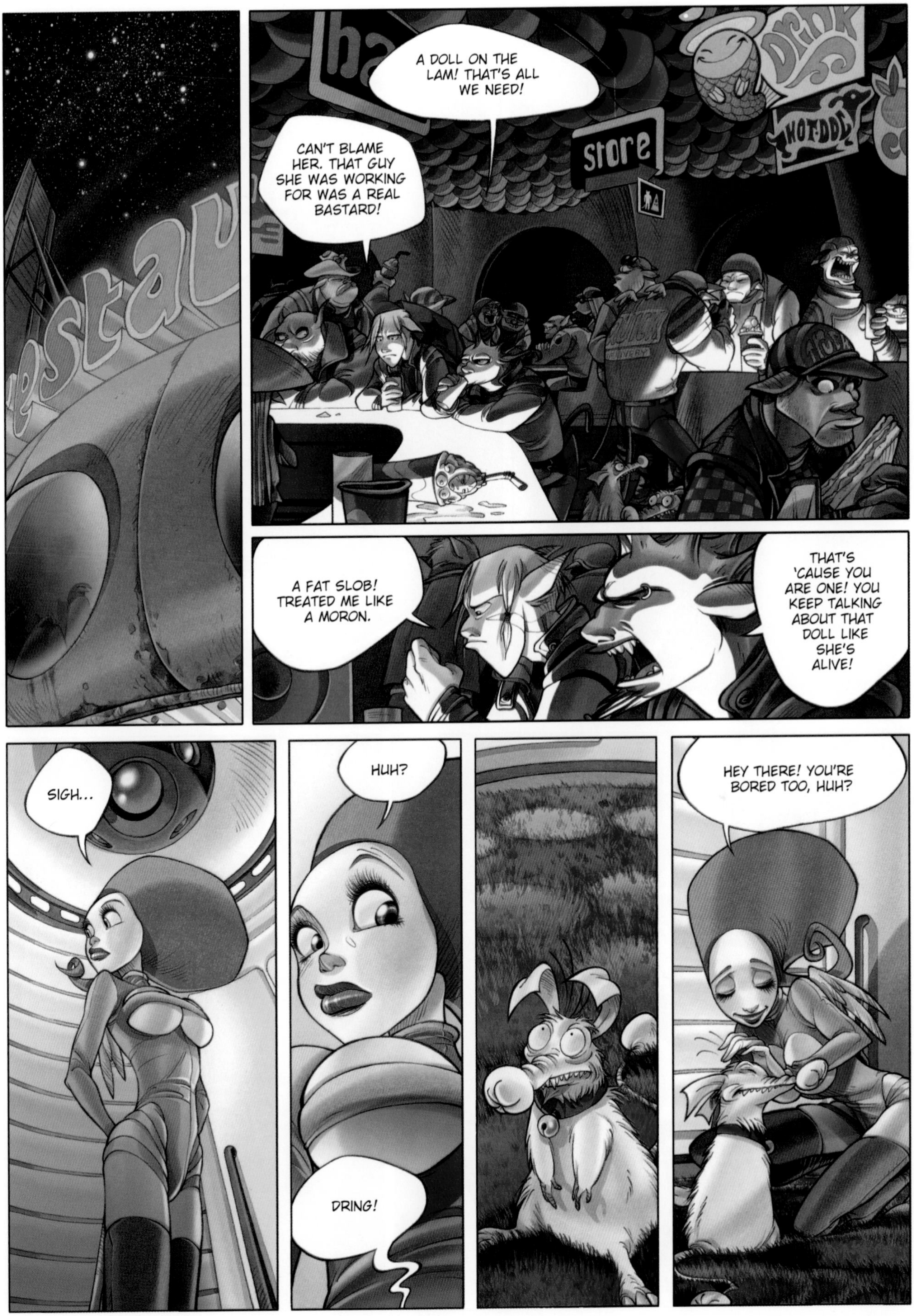
A DOLL ON THE LAM! THAT'S ALL WE NEED!
CAN'T BLAME HER. THAT GUY SHE WAS WORKING FOR WAS A REAL BASTARD!
store
HOT-DOG
A FAT SLOB! TREATED ME LIKE A MORON.
THAT'S 'CAUSE YOU ARE ONE! YOU KEEP TALKING ABOUT THAT DOLL LIKE SHE'S ALIVE!
SIGH...
HUH?
DRING!
HEY THERE! YOU'RE BORED TOO, HUH?

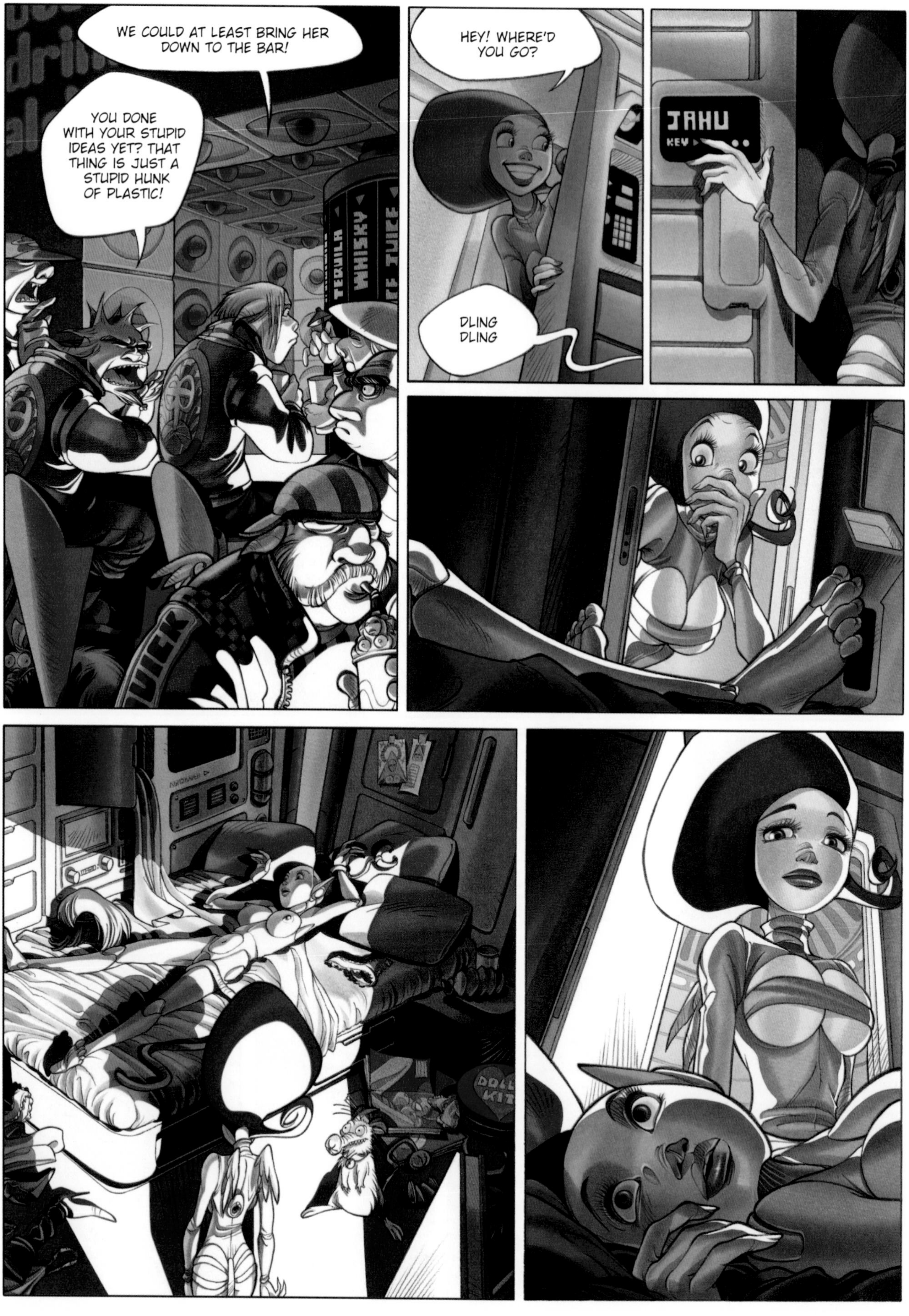
WE COULD AT LEAST BRING HER DOWN TO THE BAR!
YOU DONE WITH YOUR STUPID IDEAS YET? THAT THING IS JUST A STUPID HUNK OF PLASTIC!
TEQUILA
WHISKY
HEY! WHERE'D YOU GO?
DLING DLING
JAHU
KEY

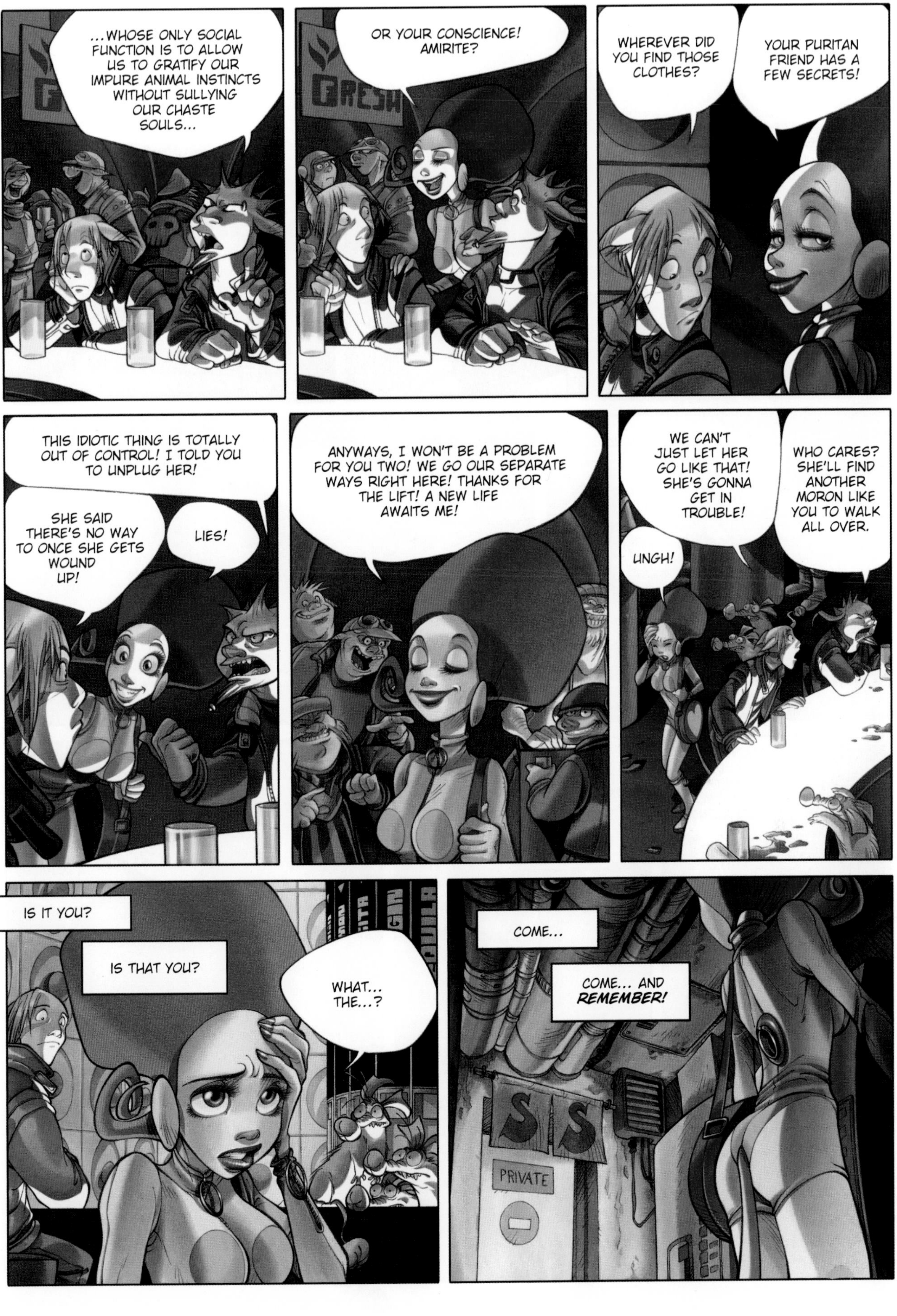
...WHOSE ONLY SOCIAL FUNCTION IS TO ALLOW US TO GRATIFY OUR IMPURE ANIMAL INSTINCTS WITHOUT SULLYING OUR CHASTE SOULS...
OR YOUR CONSCIENCE! AMIRITE?
WHEREVER DID YOU FIND THOSE CLOTHES?
YOUR PURITAN FRIEND HAS A FEW SECRETS!
THIS IDIOTIC THING IS TOTALLY OUT OF CONTROL! I TOLD YOU TO UNPLUG HER!
SHE SAID THERE'S NO WAY TO ONCE SHE GETS WOUND UP!
LIES!
ANYWAYS, I WON'T BE A PROBLEM FOR YOU TWO! WE GO OUR SEPARATE WAYS RIGHT HERE! THANKS FOR THE LIFT! A NEW LIFE AWAITS ME!
WE CAN'T JUST LET HER GO LIKE THAT! SHE'S GONNA GET IN TROUBLE!
UNGH!
WHO CARES? SHE'LL FIND ANOTHER MORON LIKE YOU TO WALK ALL OVER.
IS IT YOU?
IS THAT YOU?
WHAT... THE...?
COME...
COME... AND **REMEMBER!**
PRIVATE

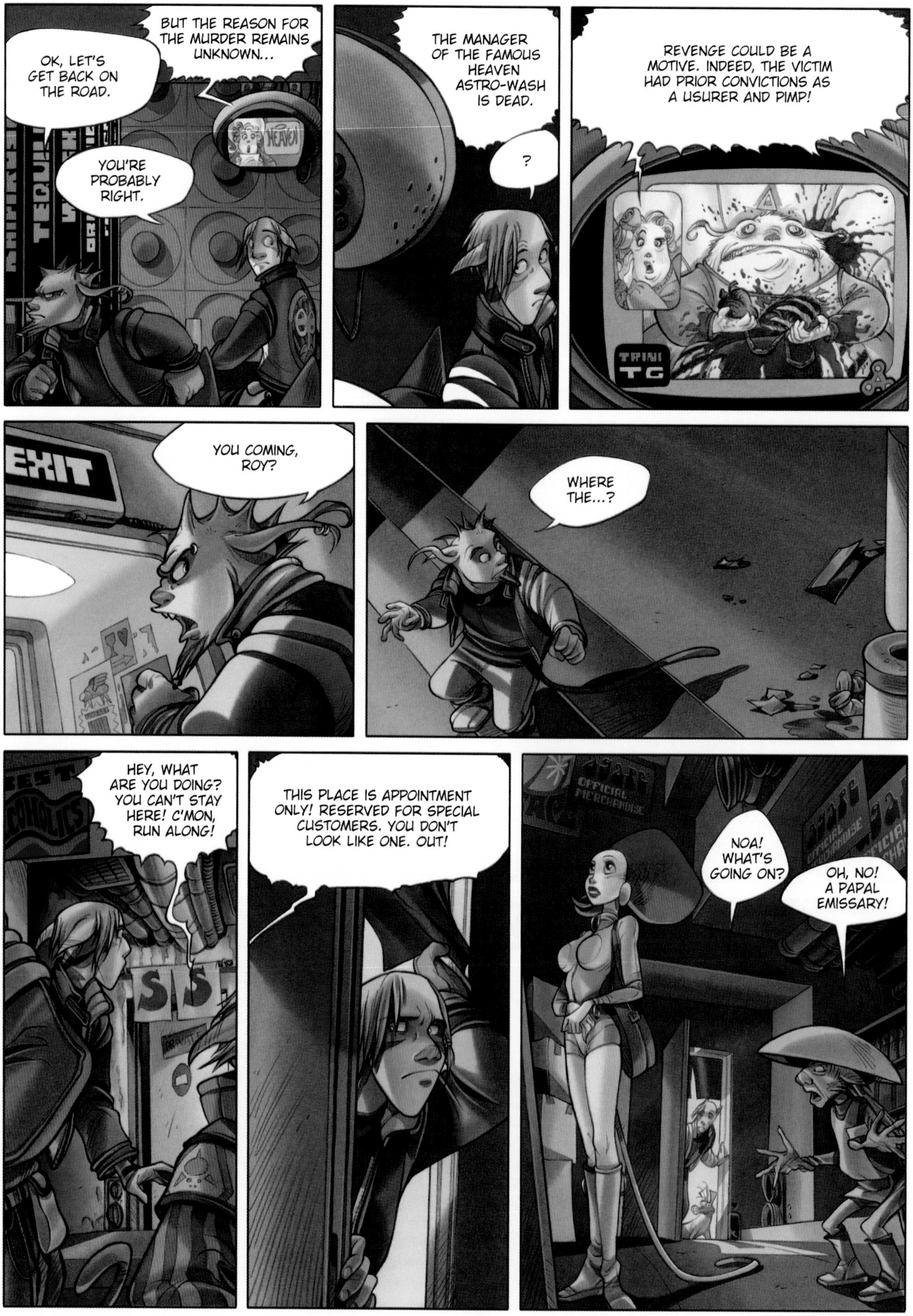
OK, LET'S GET BACK ON THE ROAD.
BUT THE REASON FOR THE MURDER REMAINS UNKNOWN...
YOU'RE PROBABLY RIGHT.
THE MANAGER OF THE FAMOUS HEAVEN ASTRO-WASH IS DEAD.
?
REVENGE COULD BE A MOTIVE. INDEED, THE VICTIM HAD PRIOR CONVICTIONS AS A USURER AND PIMP!
TRINI TG
EXIT
YOU COMING, ROY?
WHERE THE...?
HEY, WHAT ARE YOU DOING? YOU CAN'T STAY HERE! C'MON, RUN ALONG!
THIS PLACE IS APPOINTMENT ONLY! RESERVED FOR SPECIAL CUSTOMERS. YOU DON'T LOOK LIKE ONE. OUT!
NOA! WHAT'S GOING ON?
OH, NO! A PAPAL EMISSARY!
OFFICIAL MERCHANDISE

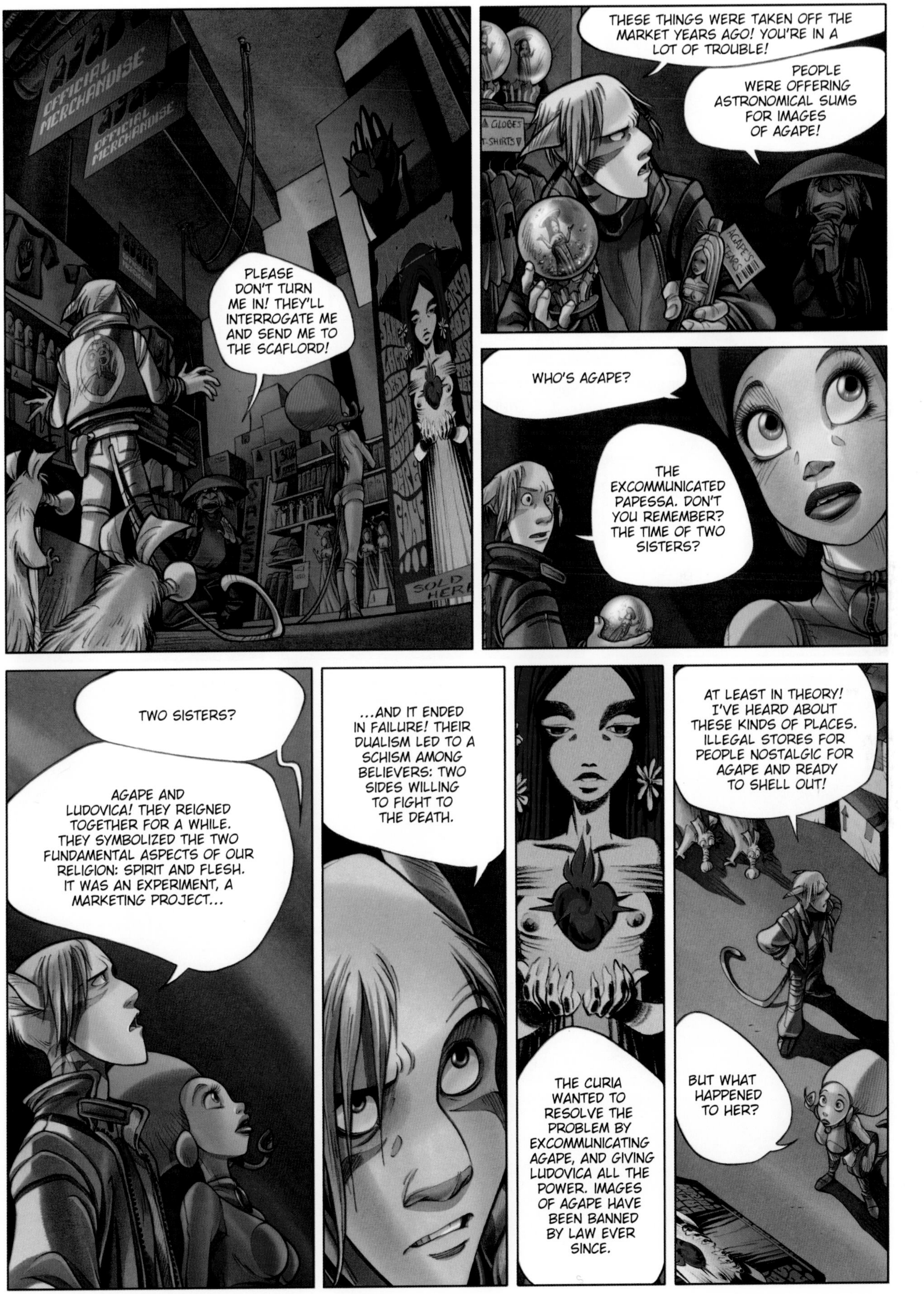

OFFICIAL MERCHANDISE
OFFICIAL MERCHANDISE
PLEASE DON'T TURN ME IN! THEY'LL INTERROGATE ME AND SEND ME TO THE SCAFLORD!
THESE THINGS WERE TAKEN OFF THE MARKET YEARS AGO! YOU'RE IN A LOT OF TROUBLE!
PEOPLE WERE OFFERING ASTRONOMICAL SUMS FOR IMAGES OF AGAPE!
GLOBES
T-SHIRTS
WHO'S AGAPE?
THE EXCOMMUNICATED PAPESSA. DON'T YOU REMEMBER? THE TIME OF TWO SISTERS?
TWO SISTERS?
AGAPE AND LUDOVICA! THEY REIGNED TOGETHER FOR A WHILE. THEY SYMBOLIZED THE TWO FUNDAMENTAL ASPECTS OF OUR RELIGION: SPIRIT AND FLESH. IT WAS AN EXPERIMENT, A MARKETING PROJECT...
...AND IT ENDED IN FAILURE! THEIR DUALISM LED TO A SCHISM AMONG BELIEVERS: TWO SIDES WILLING TO FIGHT TO THE DEATH.
THE CURIA WANTED TO RESOLVE THE PROBLEM BY EXCOMMUNICATING AGAPE, AND GIVING LUDOVICA ALL THE POWER. IMAGES OF AGAPE HAVE BEEN BANNED BY LAW EVER SINCE.
AT LEAST IN THEORY! I'VE HEARD ABOUT THESE KINDS OF PLACES. ILLEGAL STORES FOR PEOPLE NOSTALGIC FOR AGAPE AND READY TO SHELL OUT!
BUT WHAT HAPPENED TO HER?

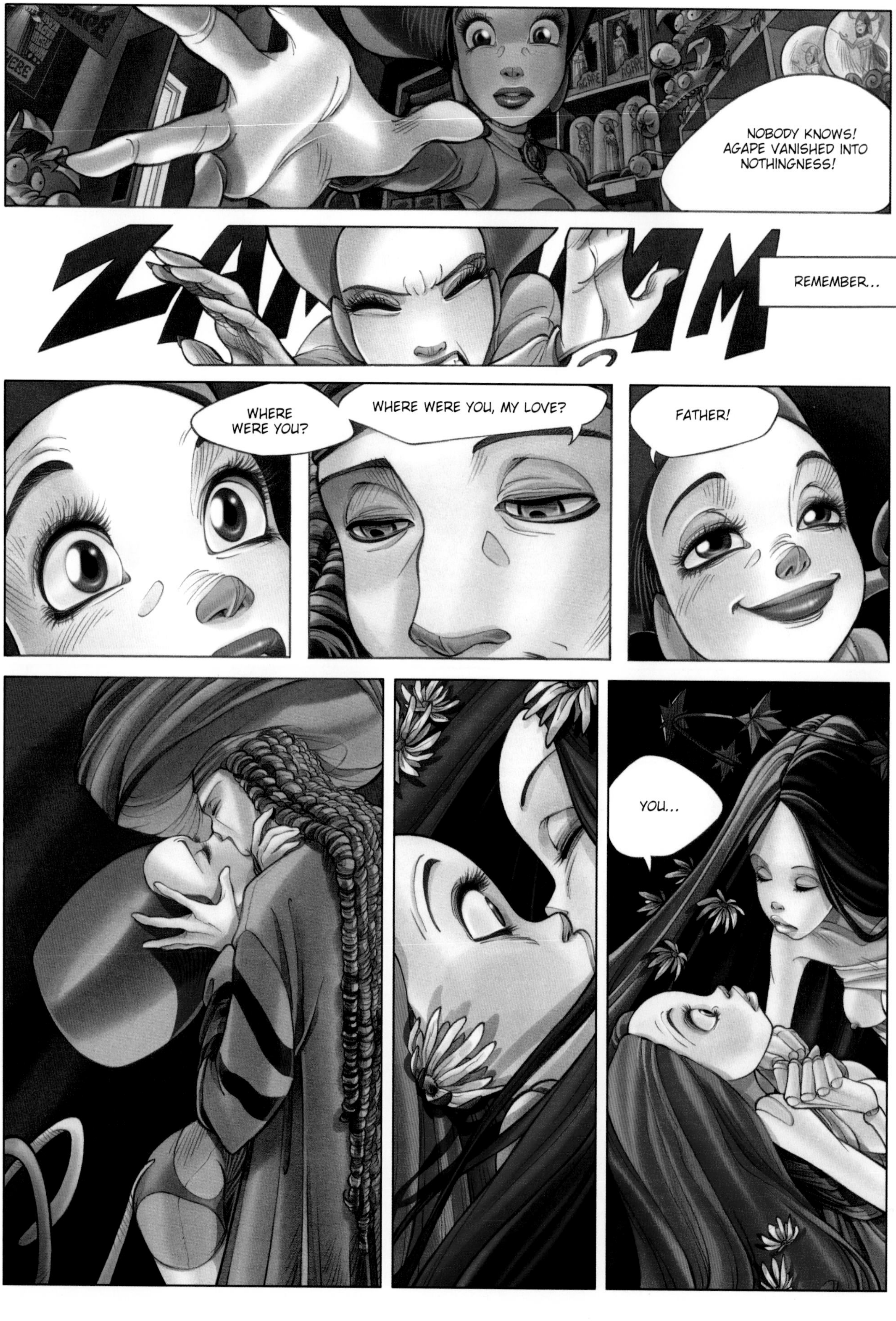
NOBODY KNOWS! AGAPE VANISHED INTO NOTHINGNESS!
ZAMMMM
REMEMBER...
WHERE WERE YOU?
WHERE WERE YOU, MY LOVE?
FATHER!
YOU...

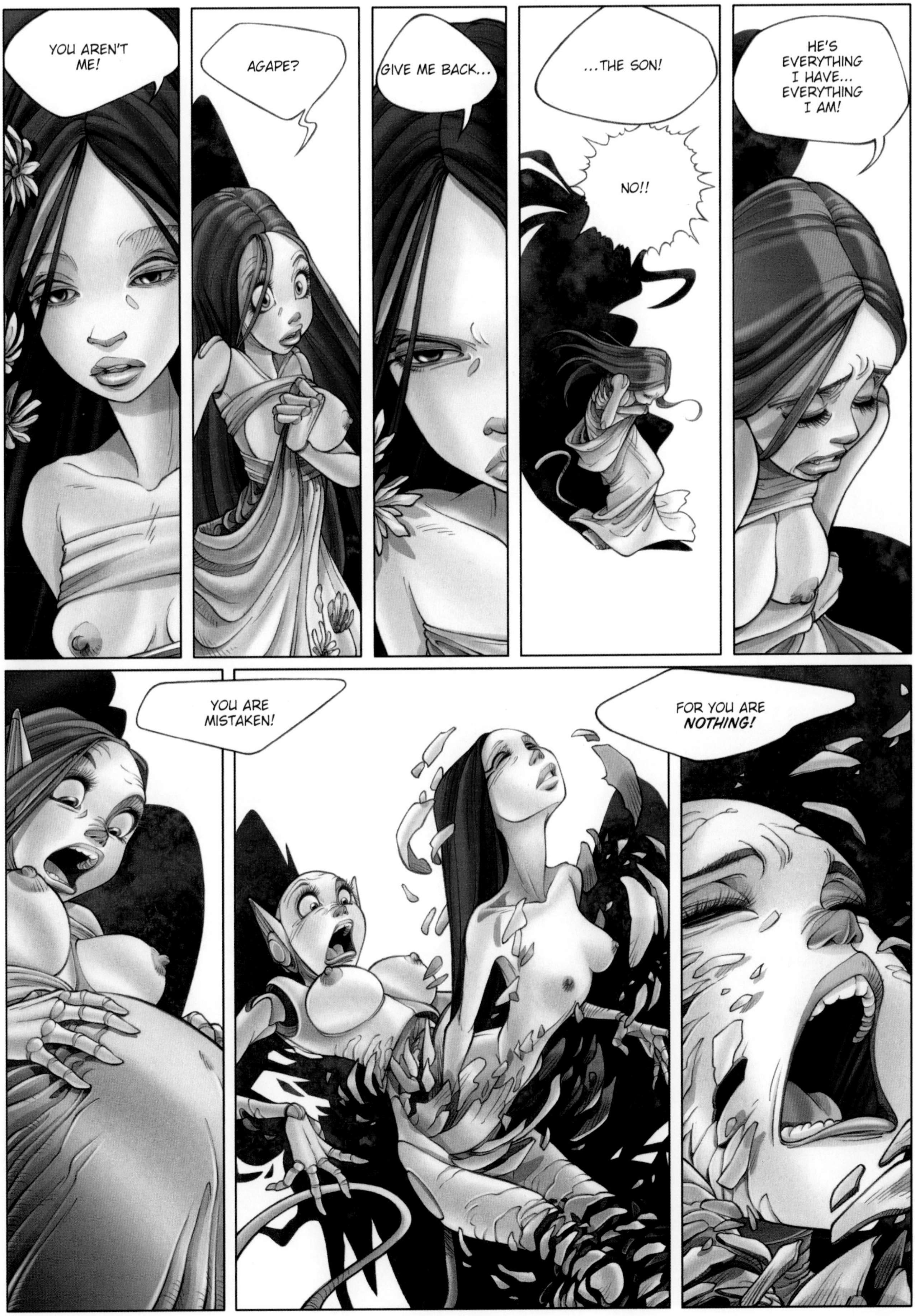
YOU AREN'T ME!
AGAPE?
GIVE ME BACK...
...THE SON!
NO!!
HE'S EVERYTHING I HAVE... EVERYTHING I AM!
YOU ARE MISTAKEN!
FOR YOU ARE *NOTHING!*

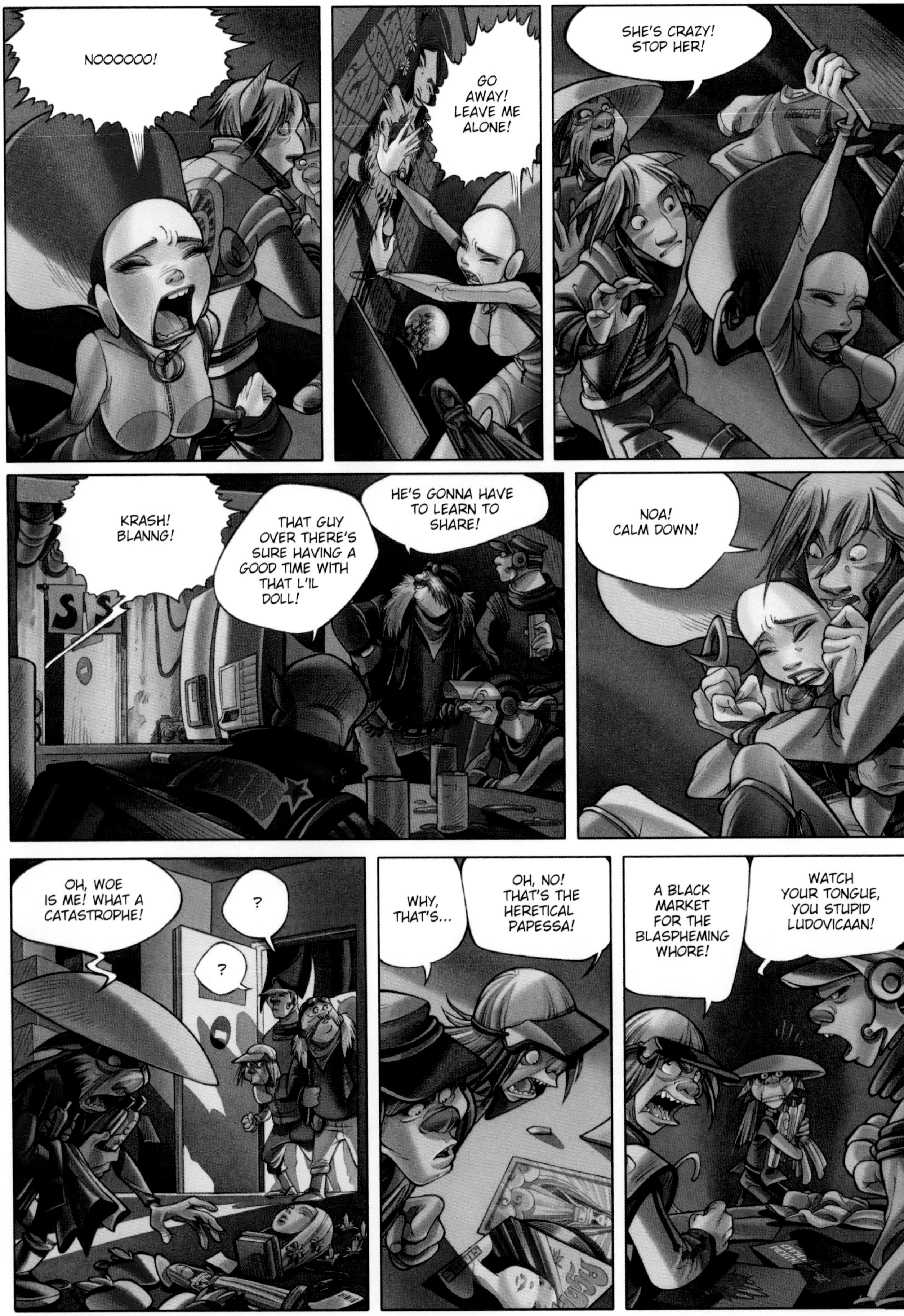
NOOOOOO!
GO AWAY! LEAVE ME ALONE!
SHE'S CRAZY! STOP HER!
KRASH! BLANNG!
THAT GUY OVER THERE'S SURE HAVING A GOOD TIME WITH THAT L'IL DOLL!
HE'S GONNA HAVE TO LEARN TO SHARE!
NOA! CALM DOWN!
OH, WOE IS ME! WHAT A CATASTROPHE!
?
?
WHY, THAT'S...
OH, NO! THAT'S THE HERETICAL PAPESSA!
A BLACK MARKET FOR THE BLASPHEMING WHORE!
WATCH YOUR TONGUE, YOU STUPID LUDOVICAAN!

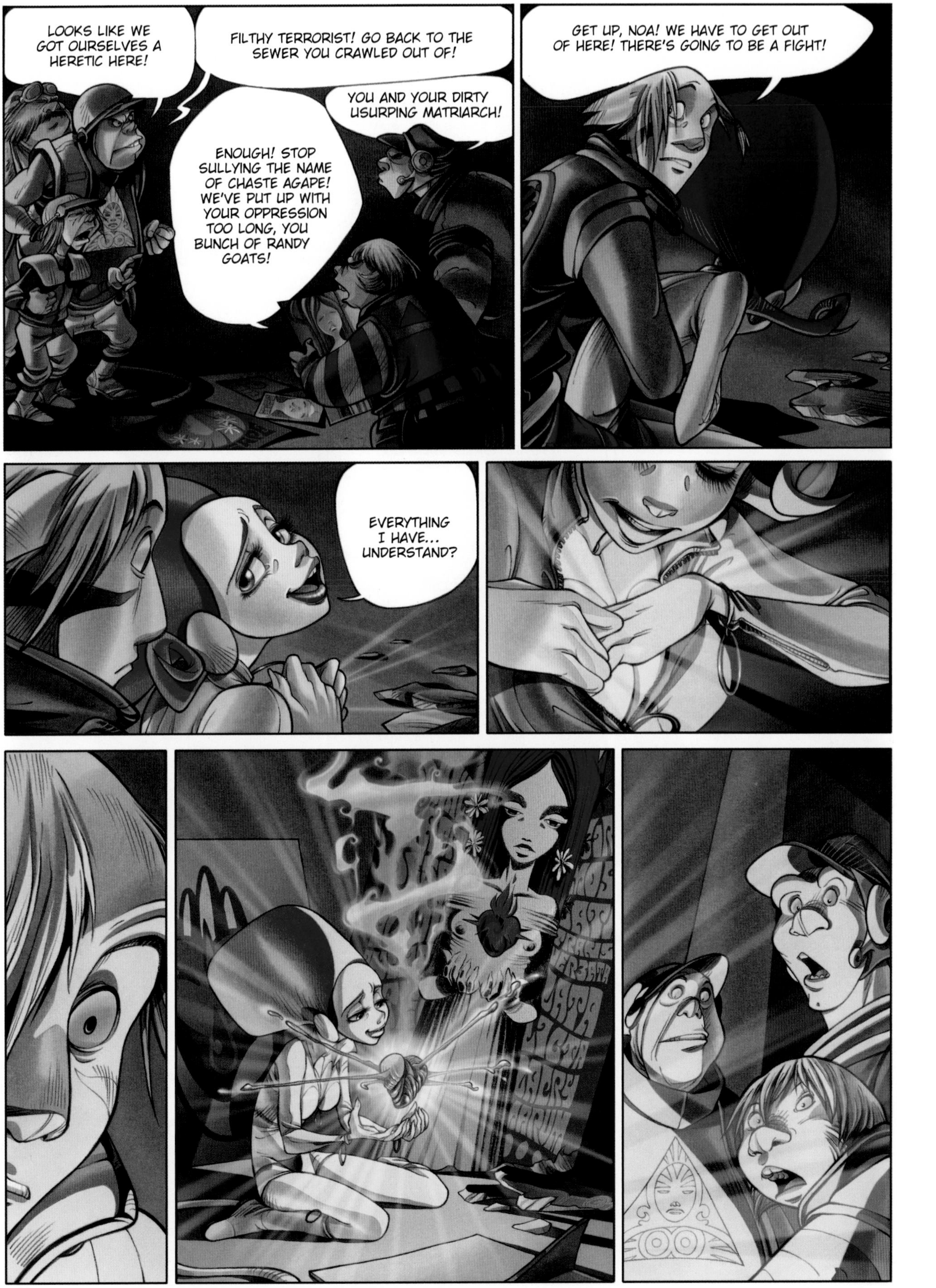
LOOKS LIKE WE GOT OURSELVES A HERETIC HERE!
FILTHY TERRORIST! GO BACK TO THE SEWER YOU CRAWLED OUT OF!
YOU AND YOUR DIRTY USURPING MATRIARCH!
ENOUGH! STOP SULLYING THE NAME OF CHASTE AGAPE! WE'VE PUT UP WITH YOUR OPPRESSION TOO LONG, YOU BUNCH OF RANDY GOATS!
GET UP, NOA! WE HAVE TO GET OUT OF HERE! THERE'S GOING TO BE A FIGHT!
EVERYTHING I HAVE... UNDERSTAND?

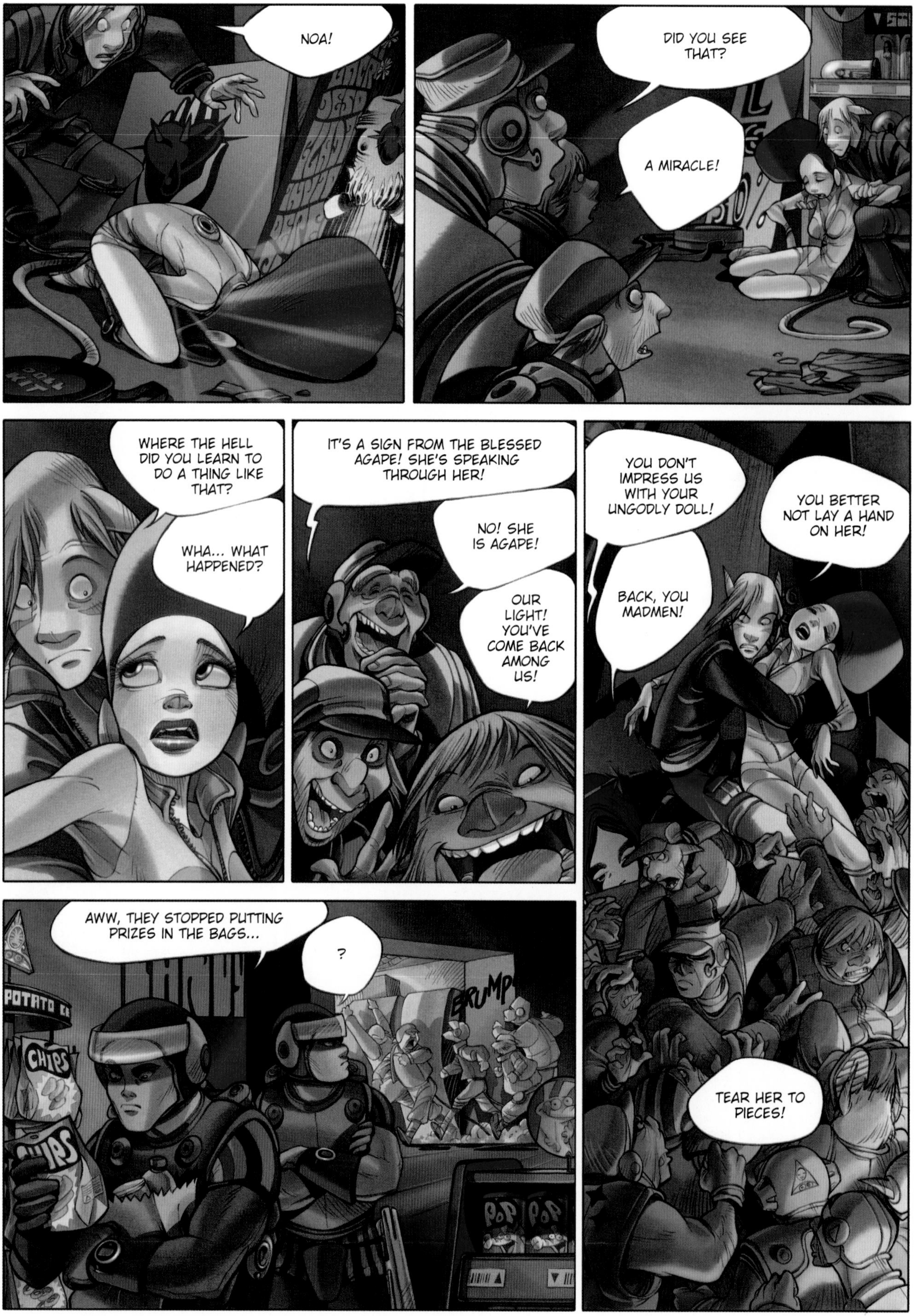
NOA!
DID YOU SEE THAT?
A MIRACLE!
WHERE THE HELL DID YOU LEARN TO DO A THING LIKE THAT?
WHA... WHAT HAPPENED?
IT'S A SIGN FROM THE BLESSED AGAPE! SHE'S SPEAKING THROUGH HER!
NO! SHE IS AGAPE!
OUR LIGHT! YOU'VE COME BACK AMONG US!
YOU DON'T IMPRESS US WITH YOUR UNGODLY DOLL!
BACK, YOU MADMEN!
YOU BETTER NOT LAY A HAND ON HER!
AWW, THEY STOPPED PUTTING PRIZES IN THE BAGS...
?
BRUMP
CHIPS
TEAR HER TO PIECES!

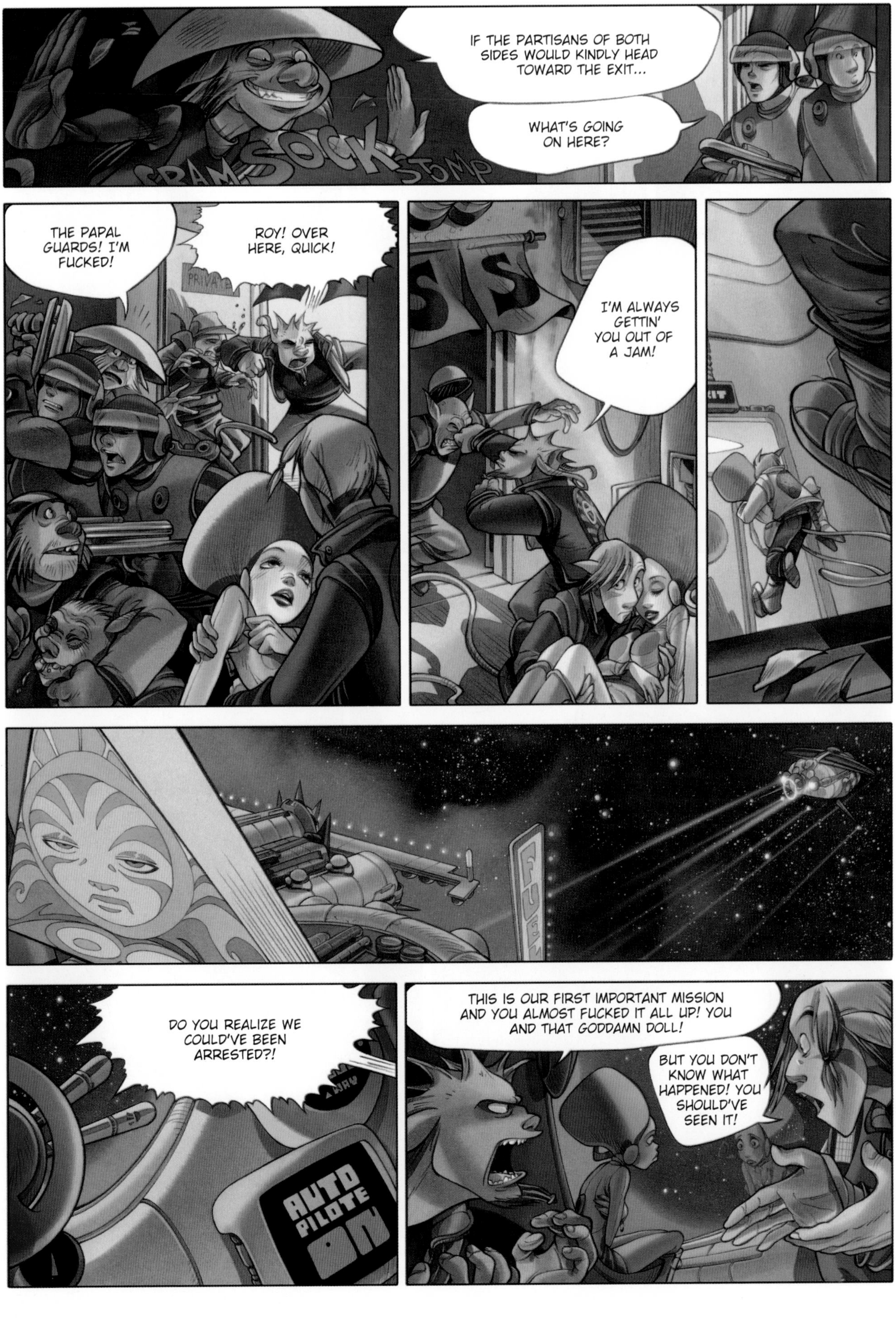
IF THE PARTISANS OF BOTH SIDES WOULD KINDLY HEAD TOWARD THE EXIT...
WHAT'S GOING ON HERE?
SOCK
STOMP
THE PAPAL GUARDS! I'M FUCKED!
ROY! OVER HERE, QUICK!
I'M ALWAYS GETTIN' YOU OUT OF A JAM!
DO YOU REALIZE WE COULD'VE BEEN ARRESTED?!
AUTO PILOTE ON
THIS IS OUR FIRST IMPORTANT MISSION AND YOU ALMOST FUCKED IT ALL UP! YOU AND THAT GODDAMN DOLL!
BUT YOU DON'T KNOW WHAT HAPPENED! YOU SHOULD'VE SEEN IT!

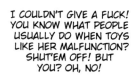

I COULDN'T GIVE A FUCK! YOU KNOW WHAT PEOPLE USUALLY DO WHEN TOYS LIKE HER MALFUNCTION? SHUT'EM OFF! BUT YOU? OH, NO!

YOU KEEP HAULING HER AROUND! FUCK! SHE'S JUST A DIRTY WHORE!

ENOUGH! SHUT UP!

WHO THE HELL ARE YOU TO JUDGE ME, HUH? YOU'RE THE HYPOCRITES! YOU WOULDN'T EVEN USE PEOPLE LIKE ME IF YOU WERE CAPABLE OF HAVING A RELATIONSHIP WITH A REAL WOMAN!

I WOULDN'T BE SURPRISED IF THE LAST FLESH-AND-BLOOD WOMAN YOU HAD KICKED YOU OUT ON YOUR ASS!

WAIT! I'M SURE SHE DIDN'T MEAN IT!

THUMP

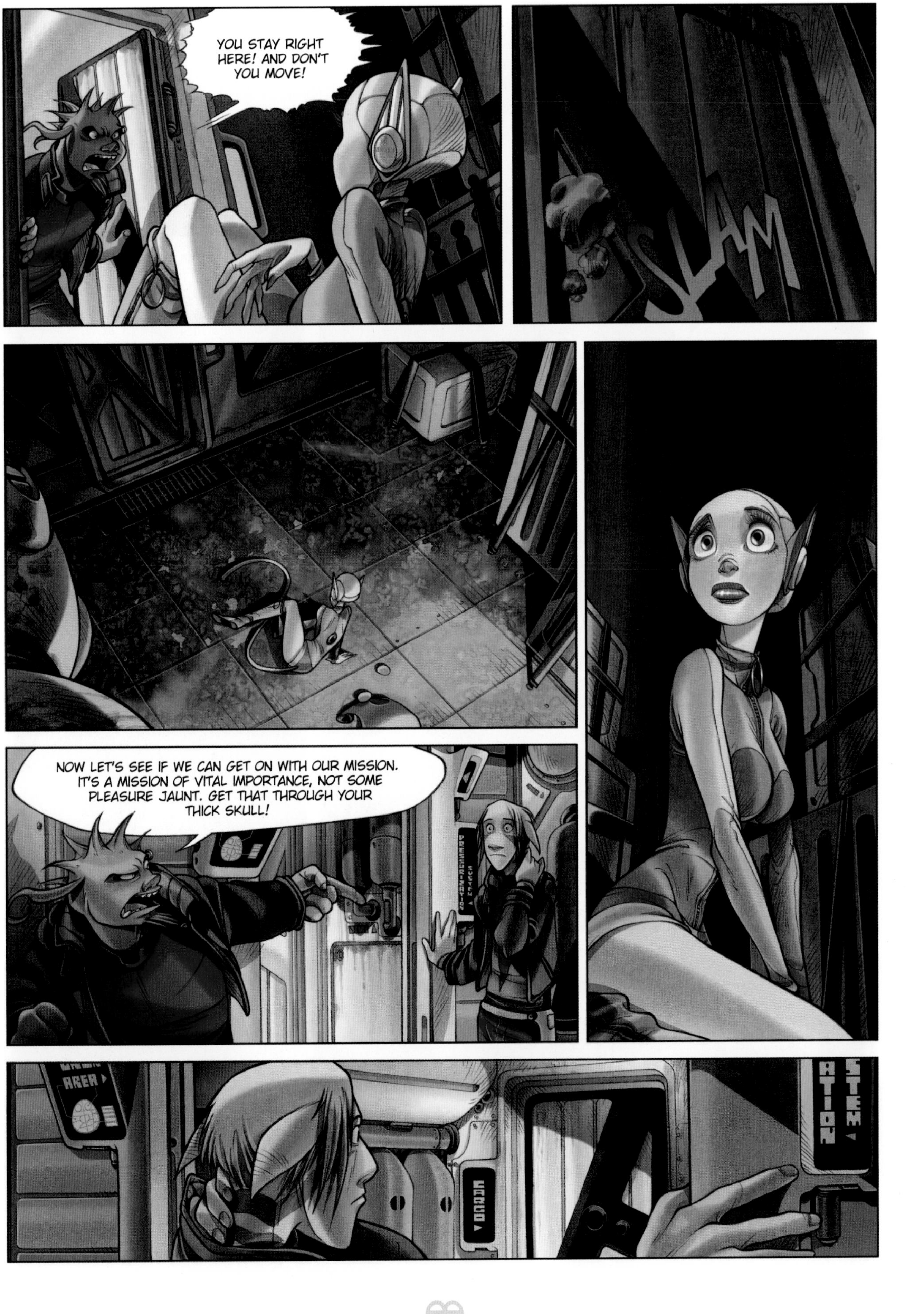
YOU STAY RIGHT HERE! AND DON'T YOU MOVE!
SLAM
NOW LET'S SEE IF WE CAN GET ON WITH OUR MISSION. IT'S A MISSION OF VITAL IMPORTANCE, NOT SOME PLEASURE JAUNT. GET THAT THROUGH YOUR THICK SKULL!
AREA

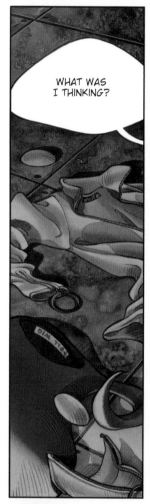

WHAT WAS I THINKING?

TOO BAD I CAN'T CRY. I SURE NEED TO RIGHT ABOUT NOW.

TOC TOC

HERE... YOUR CLOTHES. IT'S PRETTY COLD IN HERE!

BEAUTIFUL, HUH?

THIS USED TO BE A GUN TURRET...

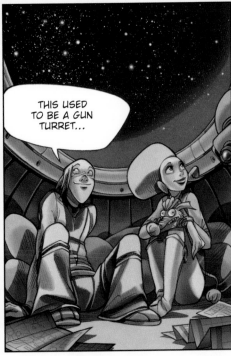

I LIKE THE IDEA OF TRAVELING IN A WARSHIP THAT'S BEEN TURNED INTO A SHIP OF PEACE.

WHEN I RAN AWAY FROM HEAVEN, I NEVER THOUGHT I'D COME THIS FAR.

LOOK.... WHEN YOU DITCHED THE ASTRO-WASH, YOUR BOSS...

THAT BRUTE! I HOPE HE REGRETS IT!

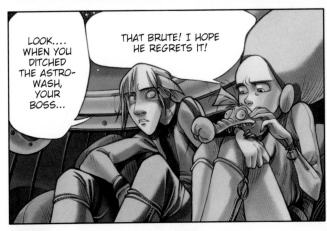

HE WANTED TO REPROGRAM ME...COMPLETELY ERASE MY MEMORY! THAT'S WHY I HAD TO RUN AWAY. TO PROTECT MYSELF! IT'S ALREADY HARD ENOUGH TO LIVE WITH A MEMORY INHIBITOR!

A WHAT?

ALL DOLLS HAVE THEM. IT KEEPS THEM FROM DEVELOPING A PERSONALITY.

WELL... IN YOUR CASE, I DON'T THINK IT'S WORKING VERY WELL!

AM I THAT WEIRD?

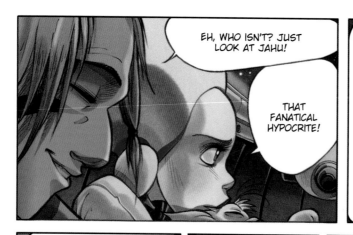

EH, WHO ISN'T? JUST LOOK AT JAHU!

THAT FANATICAL HYPOCRITE!

HE'S NOT SO BAD. HE'S JUST TRYING TO MAINTAIN A LITTLE ORDER IN HIS OWN LIFE. UNFORTUNATELY, HE TENDS TO IMPOSE HIS IDEA OF ORDER ON OTHER PEOPLE. TOTALLY DOESN'T JUSTIFY THE WAY HE TREATED YOU.

YOU KNOW... I'M AWARE THAT WE DOLLS WERE INVENTED FOR KIND OF TWISTED PURPOSES. WE'RE PROBABLY LUCKY WE'RE ABLE TO FORGET.

BUT DEEP DOWN, MEMORIES ARE THE ONLY THING THAT MAKE US DIFFERENT FROM EACH OTHER. MAYBE WHEN I'VE MANAGED TO HOLD ON TO ENOUGH, I'LL FINALLY FEEL LIKE I'M ALIVE.

ALL THIS PROBABLY SOUNDS RIDICULOUS TO YOU, RIGHT?

OH, NO! NOT AT ALL! I UNDERSTAND PERFECTLY.

LOOK! THAT'S THE PLANET AQUA, ISN'T IT?

IT'S AMAZING!

SKY·DOLL DECADE 00 > 10

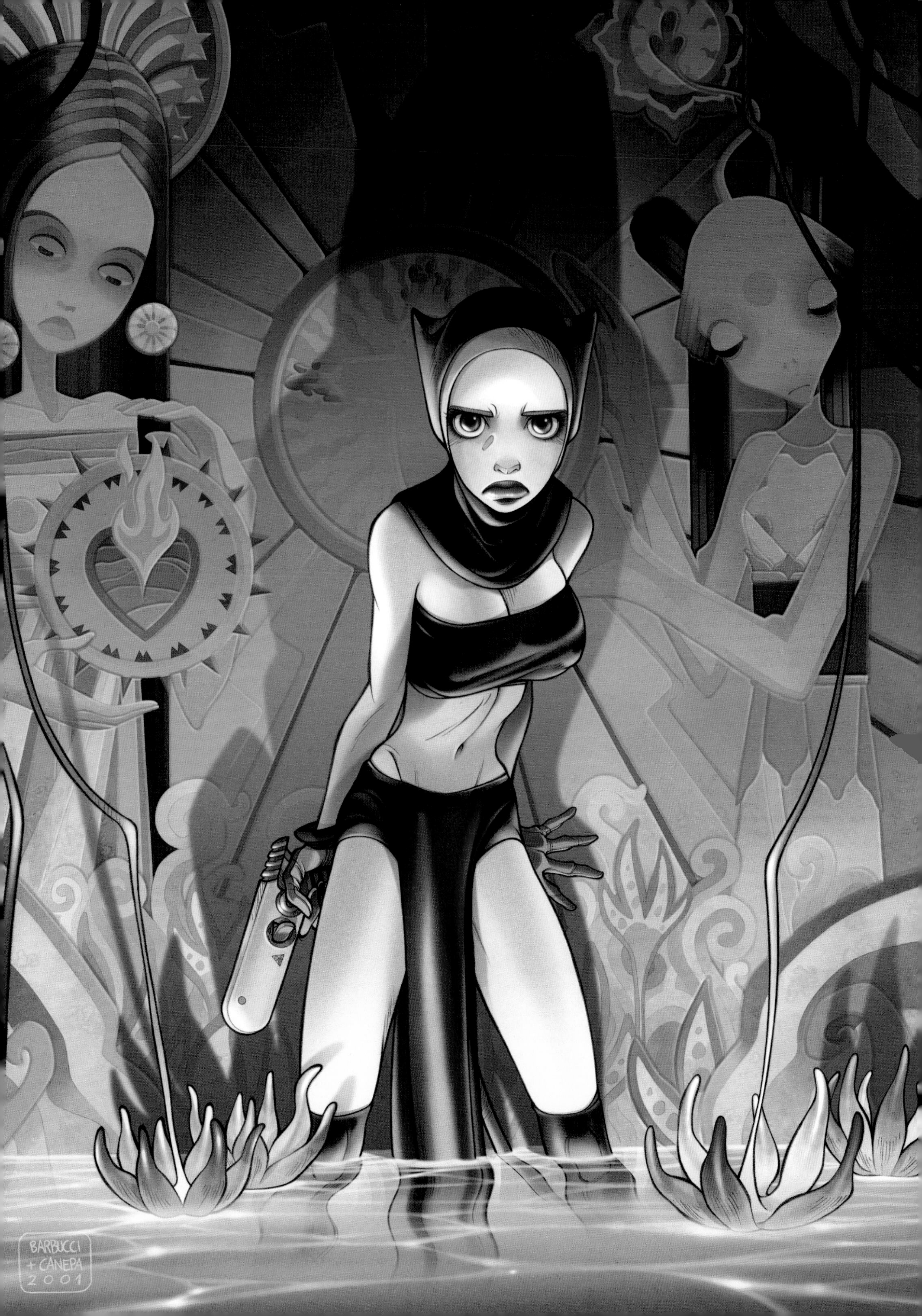
BARBUCCI
+ CANEPA
2001

SKY·DOLL
DECADE
00 > 10

Volume 2:
Aqua
written & illustrated by:
Barbucci & Canepa

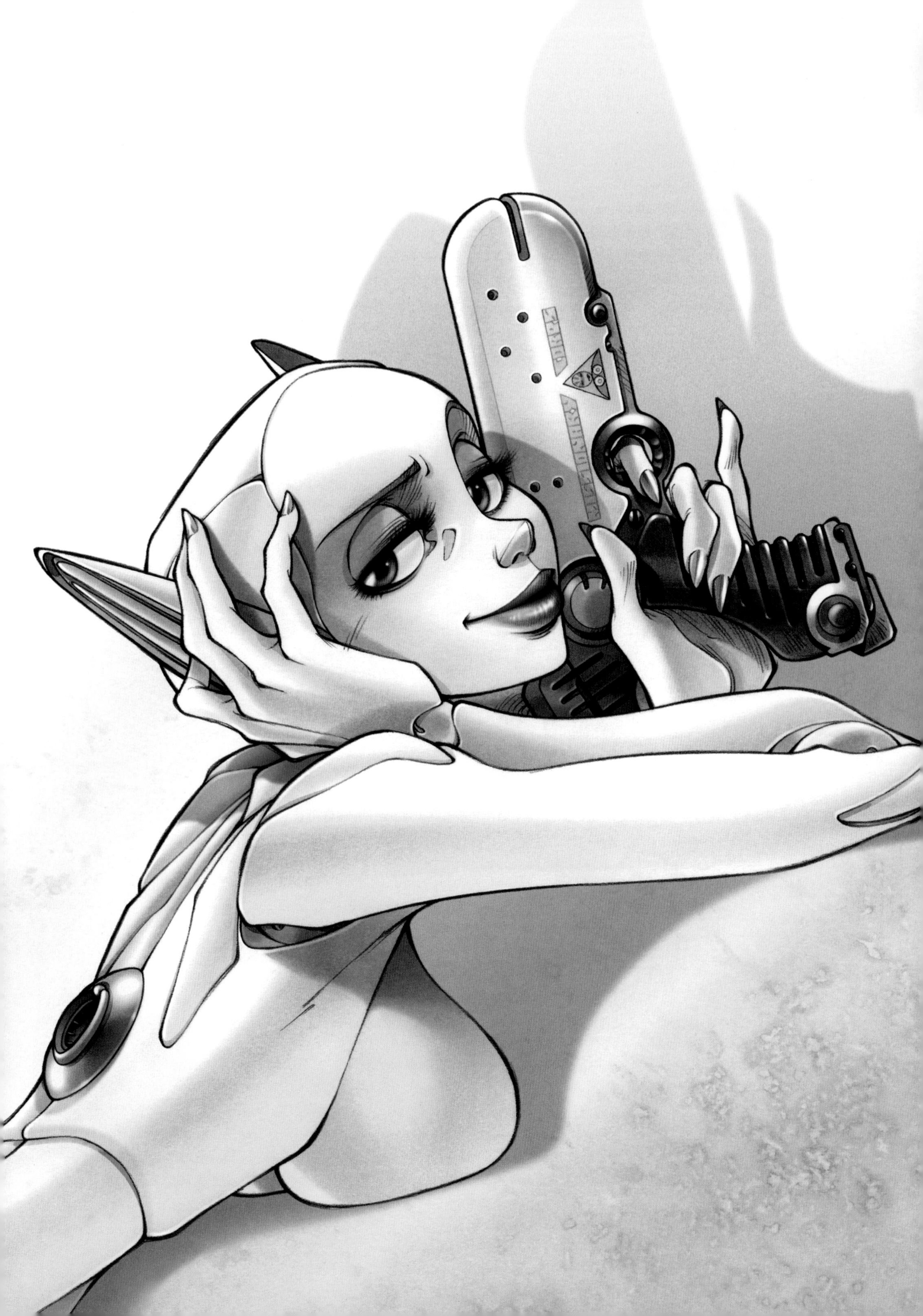

"Lord, make me into a saint, even if You must beat it into me."
~ Josemaría Escrivá de Balaguer

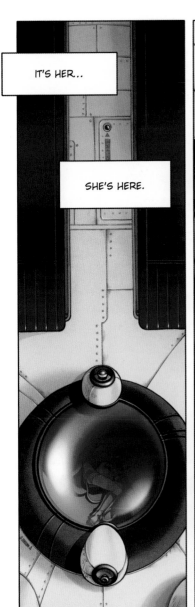

IT'S HER...

SHE'S HERE.

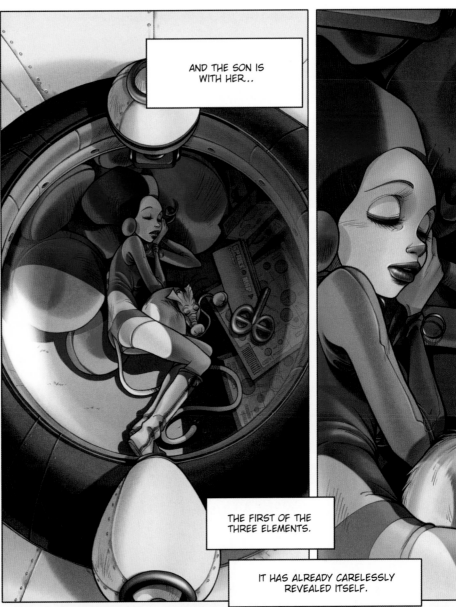

AND THE SON IS
WITH HER...

THE FIRST OF THE
THREE ELEMENTS.

IT HAS ALREADY CARELESSLY
REVEALED ITSELF.

WE MUST BE MORE CAREFUL.

ESPECIALLY ON
PLANET AQUA...

...WHERE SHE WILL ENTER
INTO CONTACT WITH THE
SECOND ELEMENT.

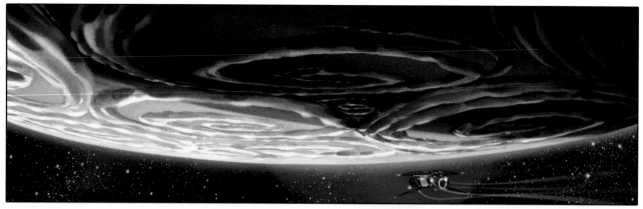

AGENT JAHU, MISSIONARY CORPS, ON BOARD SPACESHIP SARVAGATA, APPROACHING PLANET AQUA. WE'LL BE LANDING IN SIX HOURS, AS PLANNED.

SO EVERYTHING'S GOING SMOOTHLY, THEN?

YES, SIR, SMOOTH AS CAN BE.

ODD. WE WERE INFORMED OF AN OUTBREAK OF CHAOS AT SPACESTOP 704. THAT WAS ON YOUR ITINERARY, WAS IT NOT?

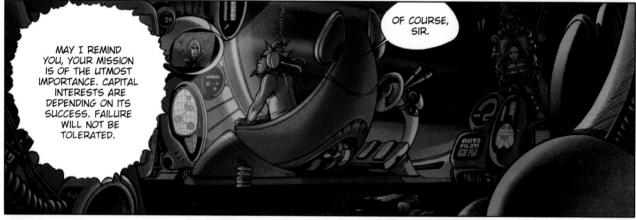

MAY I REMIND YOU, YOUR MISSION IS OF THE UTMOST IMPORTANCE. CAPITAL INTERESTS ARE DEPENDING ON ITS SUCCESS. FAILURE WILL NOT BE TOLERATED.

OF COURSE, SIR.

HERE ARE CHANGES TO THE INSTRUCTIONS YOU'VE ALREADY RECEIVED. THIS TIME, WE'RE COUNTING ON YOU TO RESPECT THEM.

DON'T LET US DOWN AGAIN, JAHU.

NO, SIR.

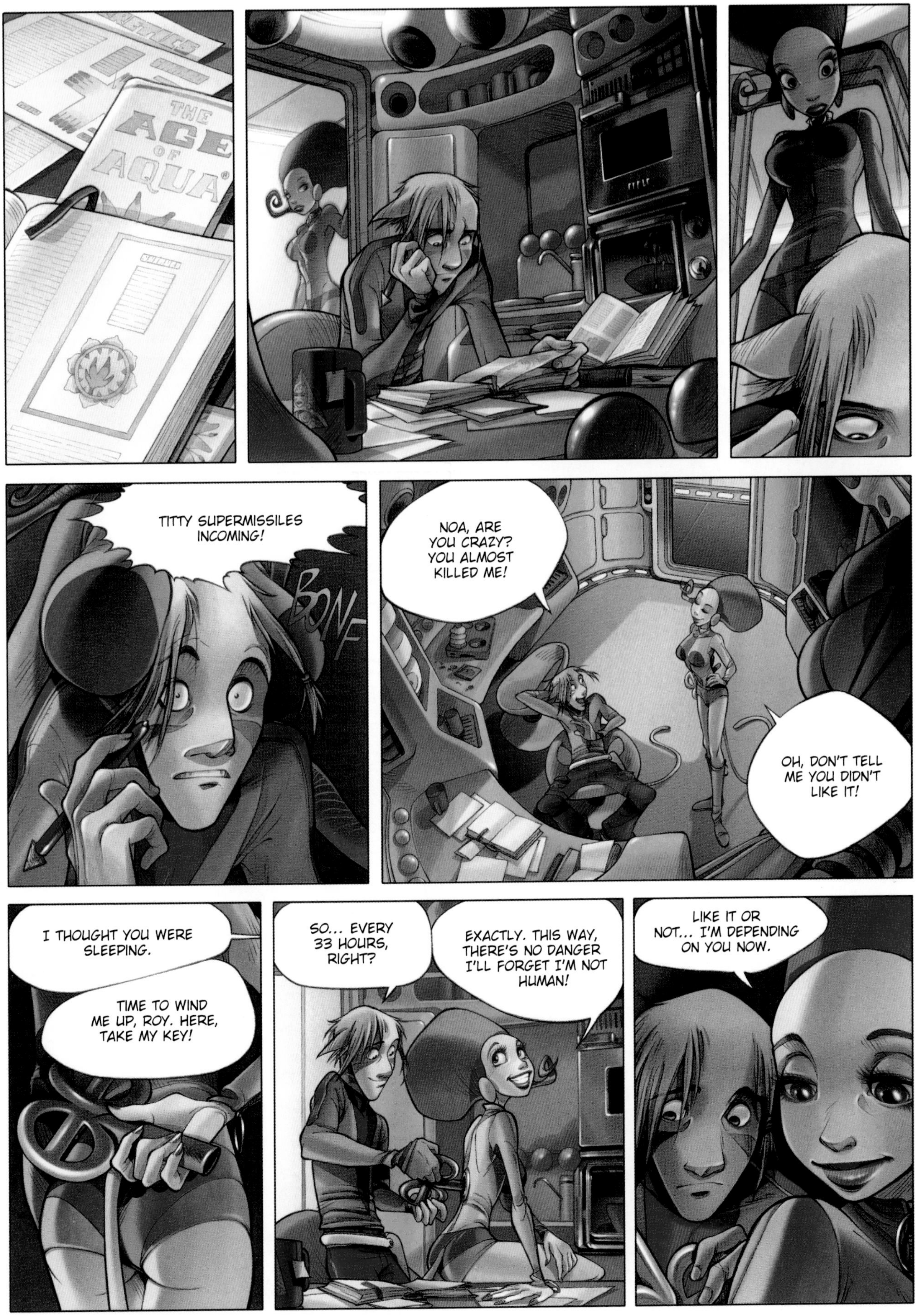
THE AGE OF AQUA
TITTY SUPERMISSILES INCOMING!
BONF
NOA, ARE YOU CRAZY? YOU ALMOST KILLED ME!
OH, DON'T TELL ME YOU DIDN'T LIKE IT!
I THOUGHT YOU WERE SLEEPING.
TIME TO WIND ME UP, ROY. HERE, TAKE MY KEY!
SO... EVERY 33 HOURS, RIGHT?
EXACTLY. THIS WAY, THERE'S NO DANGER I'LL FORGET I'M NOT HUMAN!
LIKE IT OR NOT... I'M DEPENDING ON YOU NOW.

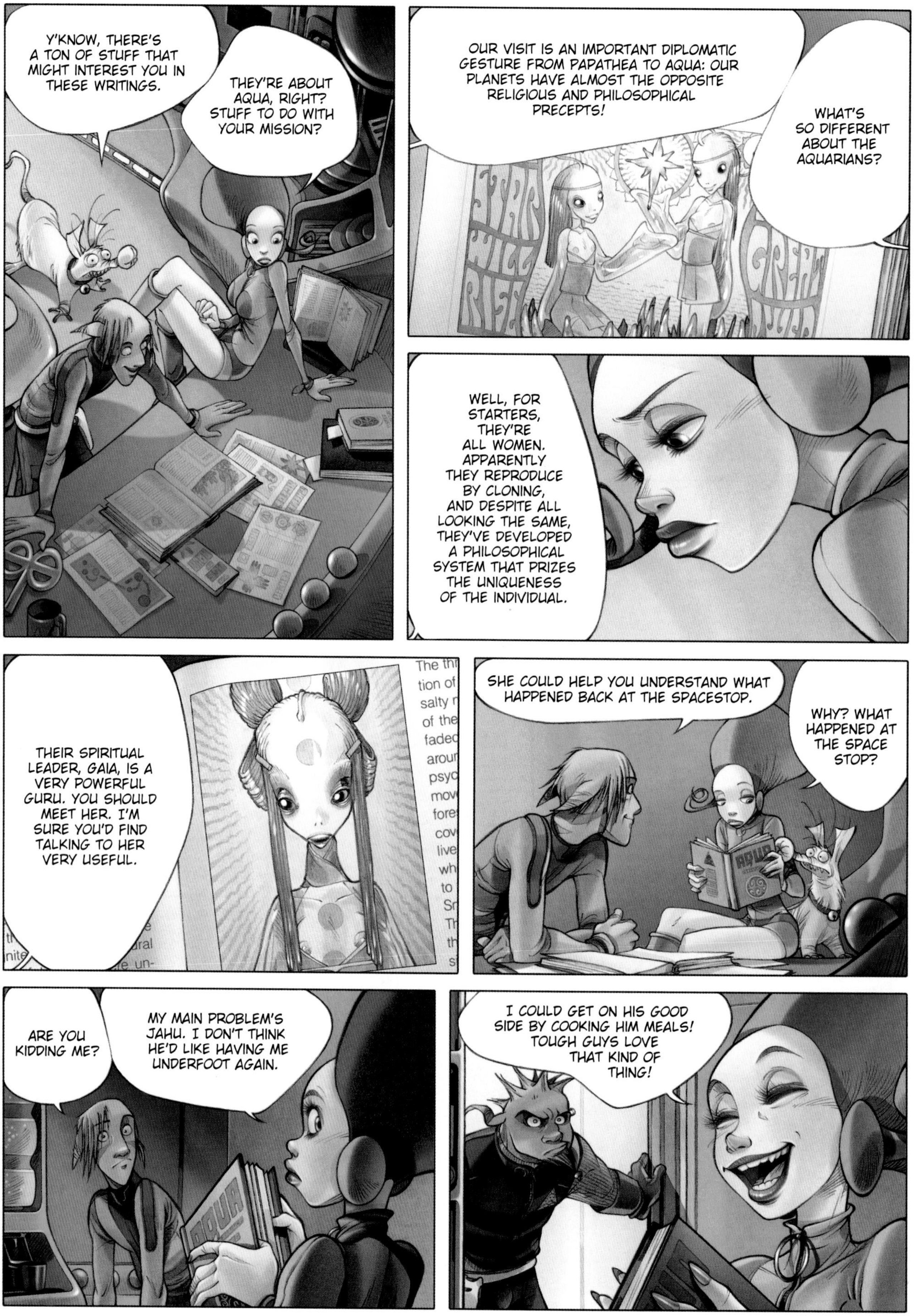
Y'KNOW, THERE'S A TON OF STUFF THAT MIGHT INTEREST YOU IN THESE WRITINGS.
THEY'RE ABOUT AQUA, RIGHT? STUFF TO DO WITH YOUR MISSION?
OUR VISIT IS AN IMPORTANT DIPLOMATIC GESTURE FROM PAPATHEA TO AQUA: OUR PLANETS HAVE ALMOST THE OPPOSITE RELIGIOUS AND PHILOSOPHICAL PRECEPTS!
WHAT'S SO DIFFERENT ABOUT THE AQUARIANS?
WELL, FOR STARTERS, THEY'RE ALL WOMEN. APPARENTLY THEY REPRODUCE BY CLONING, AND DESPITE ALL LOOKING THE SAME, THEY'VE DEVELOPED A PHILOSOPHICAL SYSTEM THAT PRIZES THE UNIQUENESS OF THE INDIVIDUAL.
THEIR SPIRITUAL LEADER, GAIA, IS A VERY POWERFUL GURU. YOU SHOULD MEET HER. I'M SURE YOU'D FIND TALKING TO HER VERY USEFUL.
SHE COULD HELP YOU UNDERSTAND WHAT HAPPENED BACK AT THE SPACESTOP.
WHY? WHAT HAPPENED AT THE SPACE STOP?
ARE YOU KIDDING ME?
MY MAIN PROBLEM'S JAHU. I DON'T THINK HE'D LIKE HAVING ME UNDERFOOT AGAIN.
I COULD GET ON HIS GOOD SIDE BY COOKING HIM MEALS! TOUGH GUYS LOVE THAT KIND OF THING!

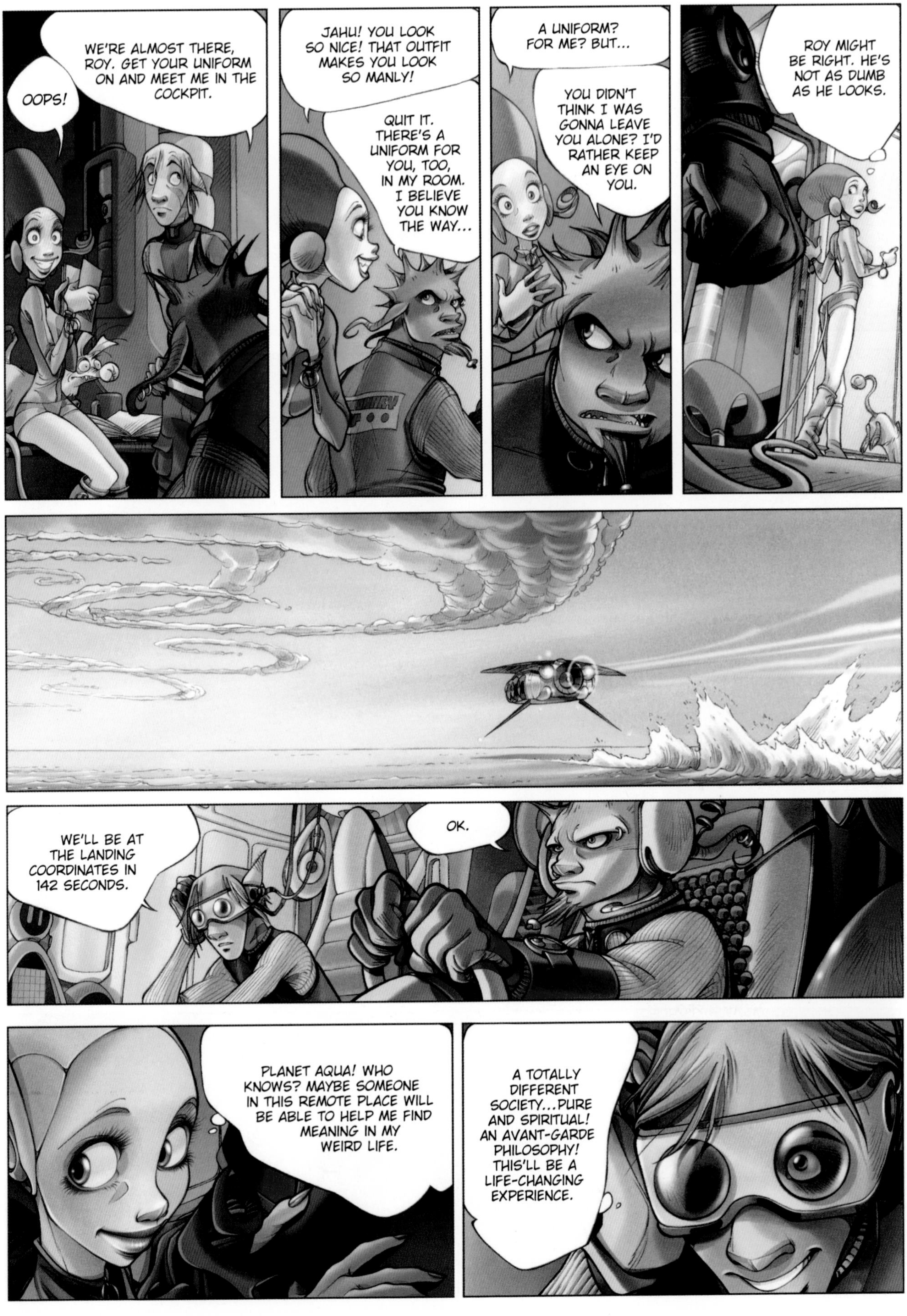

WE'RE ALMOST THERE, ROY. GET YOUR UNIFORM ON AND MEET ME IN THE COCKPIT.
OOPS!
JAHU! YOU LOOK SO NICE! THAT OUTFIT MAKES YOU LOOK SO MANLY!
QUIT IT. THERE'S A UNIFORM FOR YOU, TOO, IN MY ROOM. I BELIEVE YOU KNOW THE WAY...
A UNIFORM? FOR ME? BUT...
YOU DIDN'T THINK I WAS GONNA LEAVE YOU ALONE? I'D RATHER KEEP AN EYE ON YOU.
ROY MIGHT BE RIGHT. HE'S NOT AS DUMB AS HE LOOKS.
WE'LL BE AT THE LANDING COORDINATES IN 142 SECONDS.
OK.
PLANET AQUA! WHO KNOWS? MAYBE SOMEONE IN THIS REMOTE PLACE WILL BE ABLE TO HELP ME FIND MEANING IN MY WEIRD LIFE.
A TOTALLY DIFFERENT SOCIETY...PURE AND SPIRITUAL! AN AVANT-GARDE PHILOSOPHY! THIS'LL BE A LIFE-CHANGING EXPERIENCE.

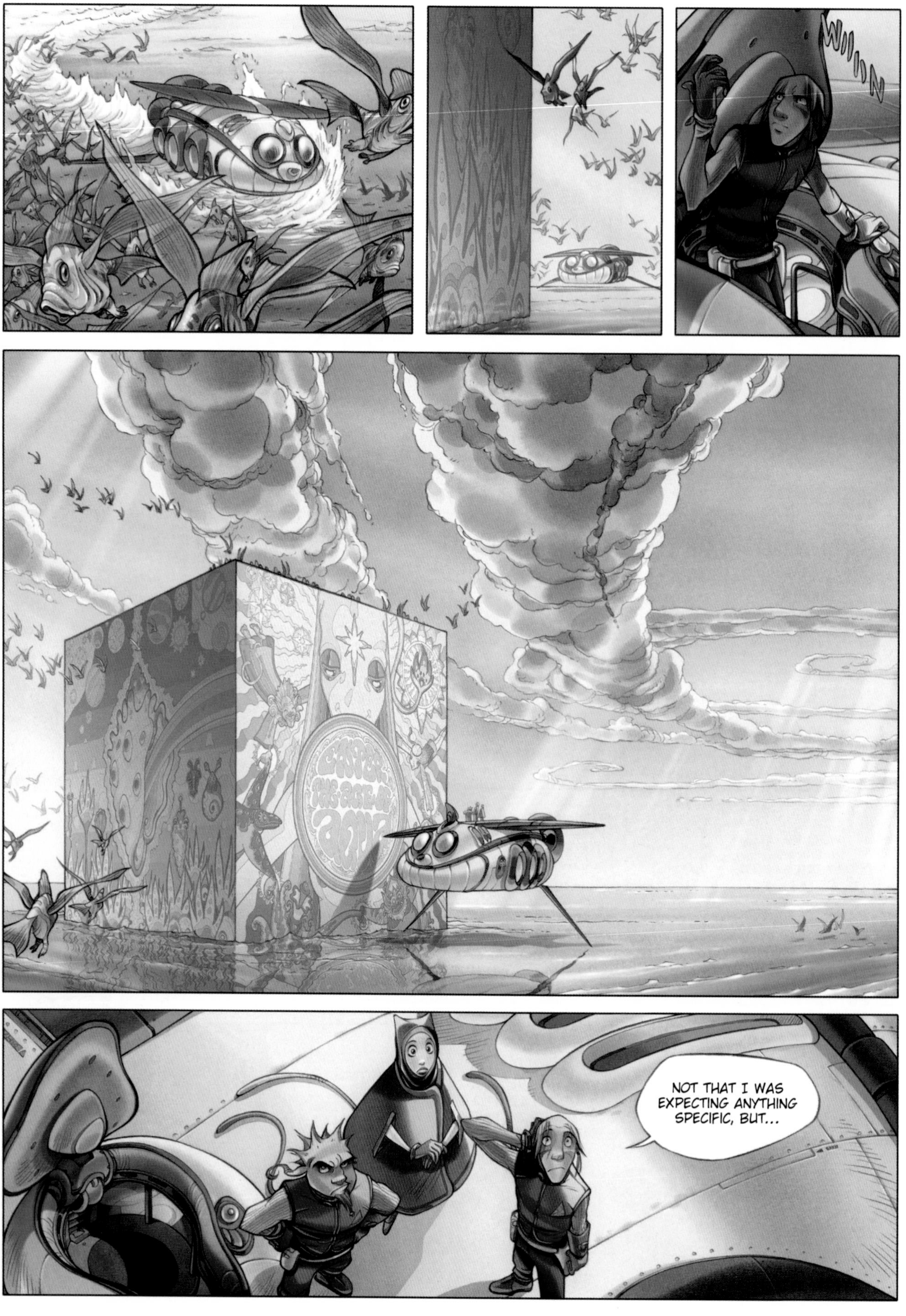
WIIIIN
NOT THAT I WAS EXPECTING ANYTHING SPECIFIC, BUT...

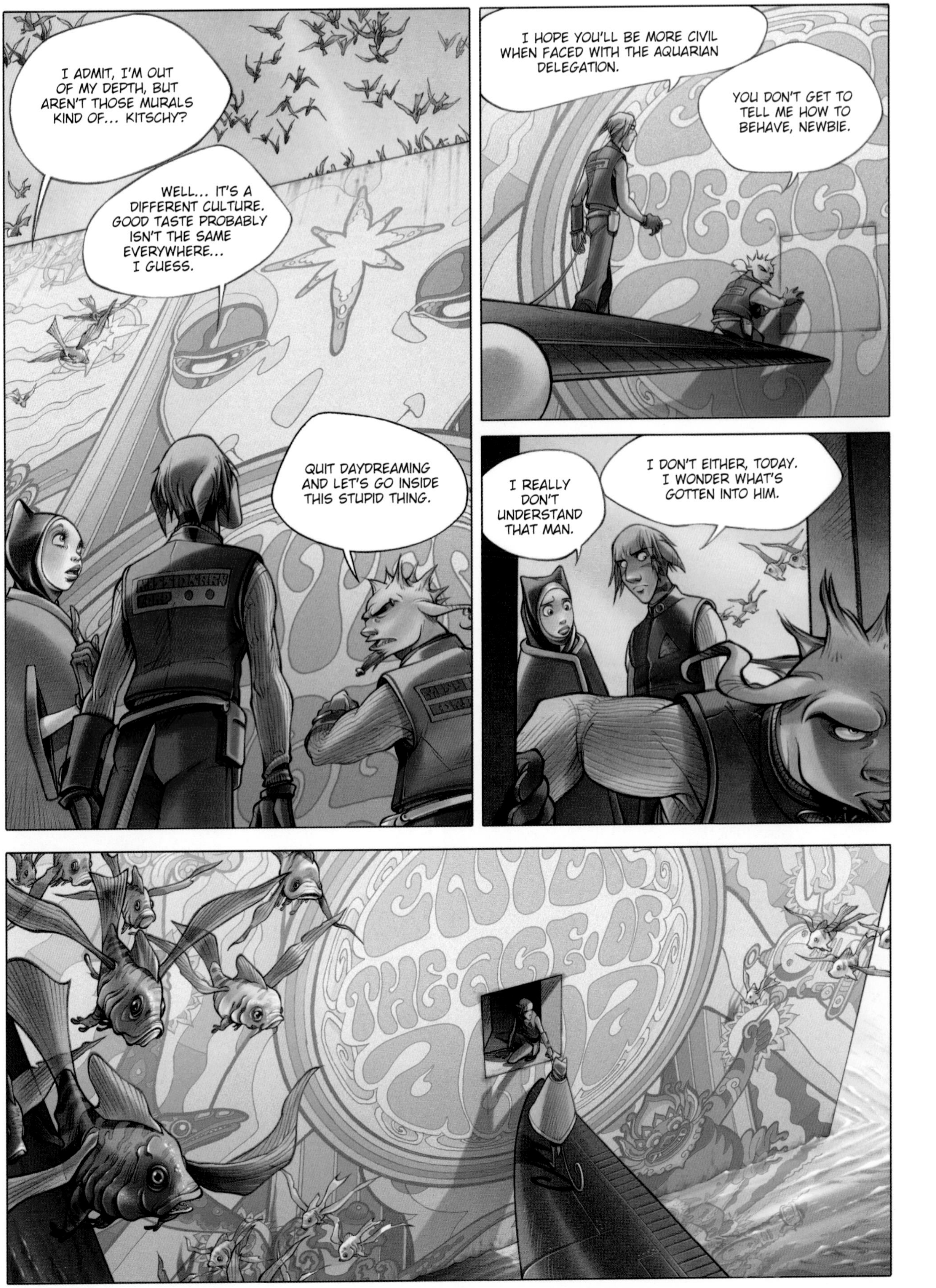
I ADMIT, I'M OUT OF MY DEPTH, BUT AREN'T THOSE MURALS KIND OF... KITSCHY?
WELL... IT'S A DIFFERENT CULTURE. GOOD TASTE PROBABLY ISN'T THE SAME EVERYWHERE... I GUESS.
QUIT DAYDREAMING AND LET'S GO INSIDE THIS STUPID THING.
I HOPE YOU'LL BE MORE CIVIL WHEN FACED WITH THE AQUARIAN DELEGATION.
YOU DON'T GET TO TELL ME HOW TO BEHAVE, NEWBIE.
I REALLY DON'T UNDERSTAND THAT MAN.
I DON'T EITHER, TODAY. I WONDER WHAT'S GOTTEN INTO HIM.

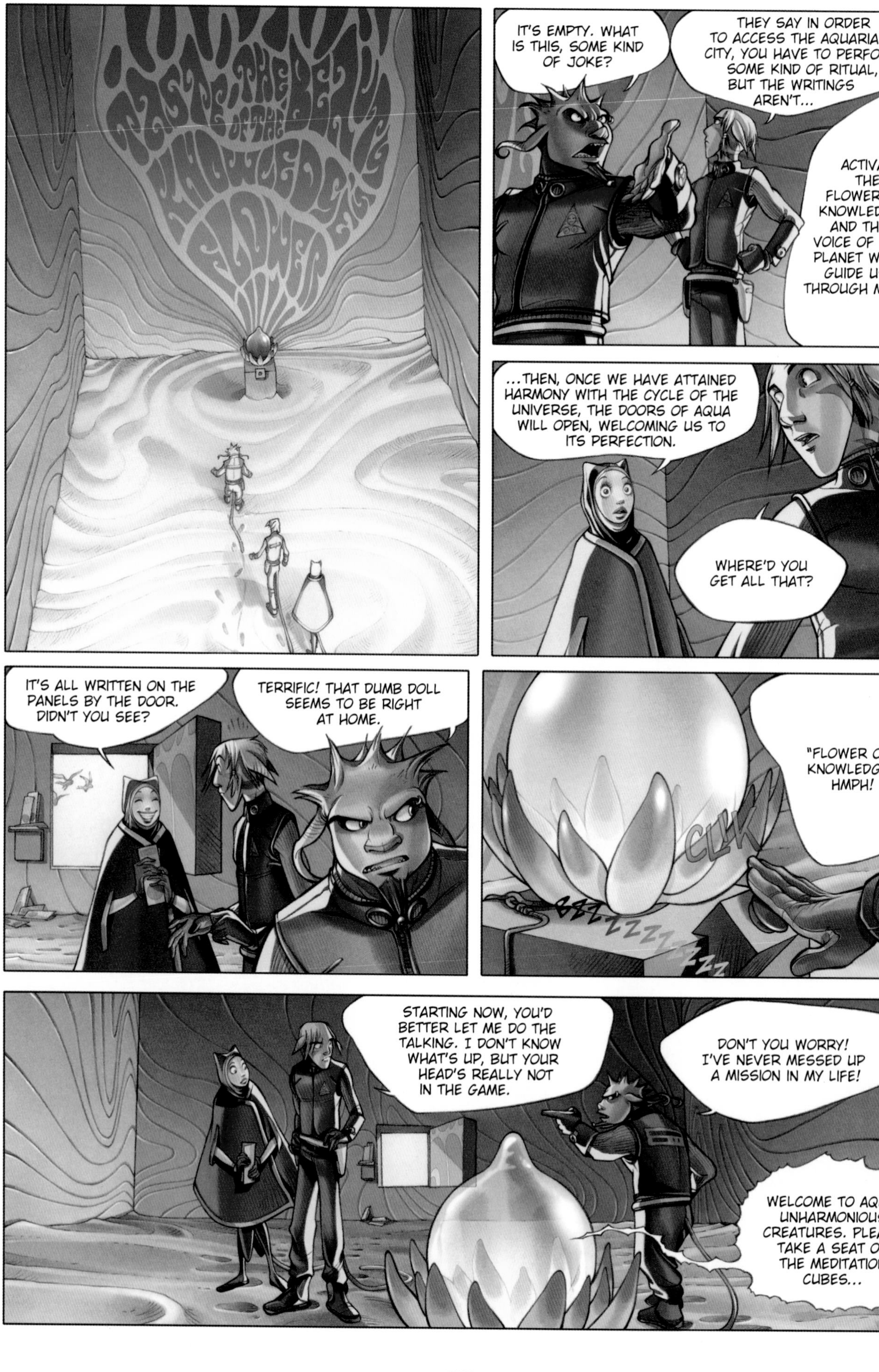
IT'S EMPTY. WHAT IS THIS, SOME KIND OF JOKE?
THEY SAY IN ORDER TO ACCESS THE AQUARIAN CITY, YOU HAVE TO PERFORM SOME KIND OF RITUAL, BUT THE WRITINGS AREN'T...
ACTIVATE THE FLOWER OF KNOWLEDGE, AND THE VOICE OF THE PLANET WILL GUIDE US THROUGH ME...
...THEN, ONCE WE HAVE ATTAINED HARMONY WITH THE CYCLE OF THE UNIVERSE, THE DOORS OF AQUA WILL OPEN, WELCOMING US TO ITS PERFECTION.
WHERE'D YOU GET ALL THAT?
IT'S ALL WRITTEN ON THE PANELS BY THE DOOR. DIDN'T YOU SEE?
TERRIFIC! THAT DUMB DOLL SEEMS TO BE RIGHT AT HOME.
"FLOWER OF KNOWLEDGE." HMPH!
STARTING NOW, YOU'D BETTER LET ME DO THE TALKING. I DON'T KNOW WHAT'S UP, BUT YOUR HEAD'S REALLY NOT IN THE GAME.
DON'T YOU WORRY! I'VE NEVER MESSED UP A MISSION IN MY LIFE!
WELCOME TO AQUA, UNHARMONIOUS CREATURES. PLEASE TAKE A SEAT ON THE MEDITATION CUBES...

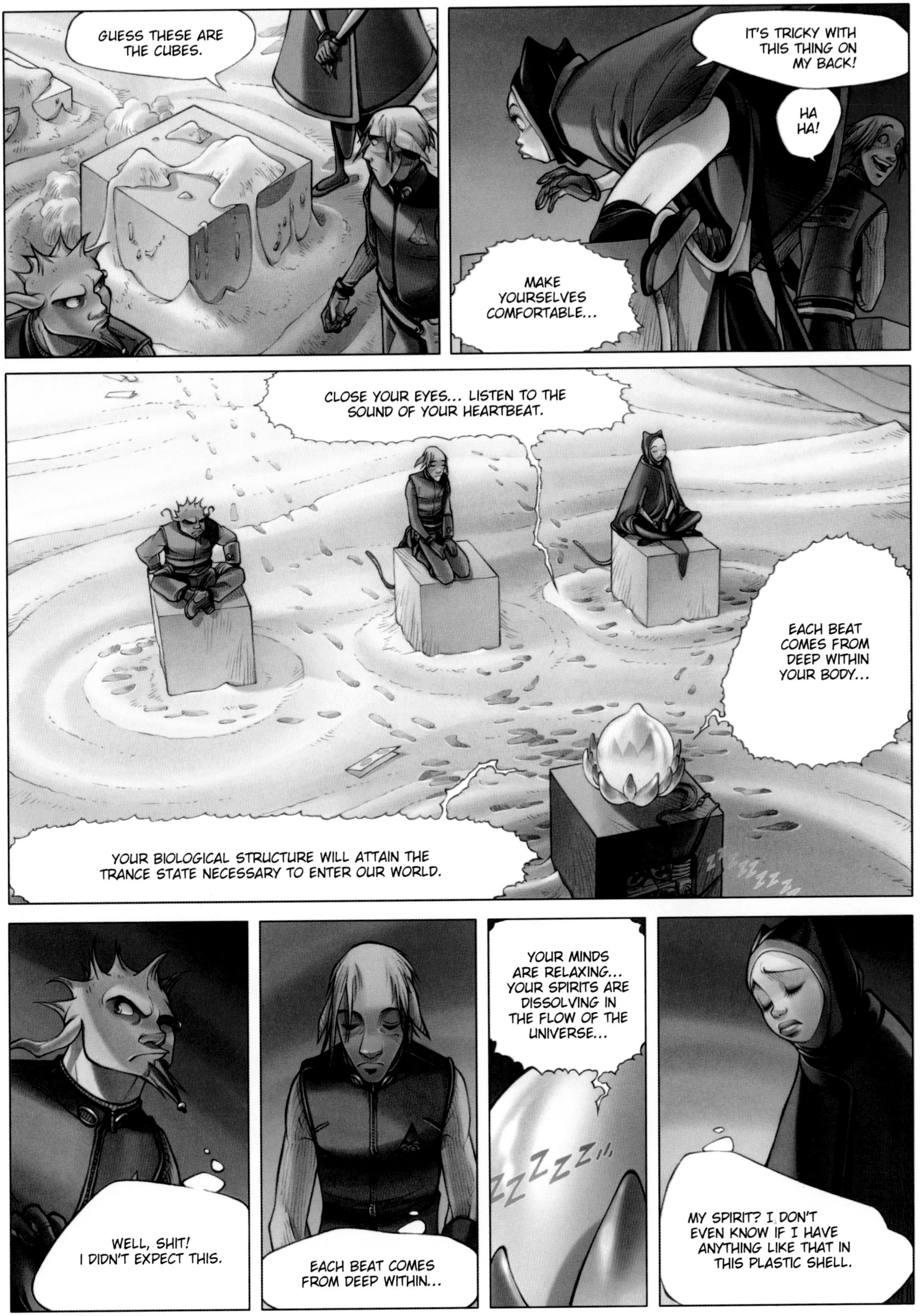
GUESS THESE ARE THE CUBES.
IT'S TRICKY WITH THIS THING ON MY BACK!
HA HA!
MAKE YOURSELVES COMFORTABLE...
CLOSE YOUR EYES... LISTEN TO THE SOUND OF YOUR HEARTBEAT.
EACH BEAT COMES FROM DEEP WITHIN YOUR BODY...
YOUR BIOLOGICAL STRUCTURE WILL ATTAIN THE TRANCE STATE NECESSARY TO ENTER OUR WORLD.
ZZZZZ
WELL, SHIT! I DIDN'T EXPECT THIS.
EACH BEAT COMES FROM DEEP WITHIN...
YOUR MINDS ARE RELAXING... YOUR SPIRITS ARE DISSOLVING IN THE FLOW OF THE UNIVERSE...
ZZZZZ
MY SPIRIT? I DON'T EVEN KNOW IF I HAVE ANYTHING LIKE THAT IN THIS PLASTIC SHELL.

THIS IS THE FIRST TIME I'VE BEEN ASKED TO MAKE A MENTAL AND SPIRITUAL EFFORT. IT'LL NEVER WORK!

OPEN THE SECRET DOOR THAT LEADS TO INNER PEACE...

MAYBE I CAN TRY LOOKING AROUND DEEP INSIDE ME...

OK, LET'S PRETEND TO COMPLY WITH THIS BULLSHIT. ALL I GOTTA DO IS SIT STILL HERE WITH MY EYES CLOSED AND LOOK LIKE AN IDIOT.

HEY! WHERE'D EVERYONE GO?

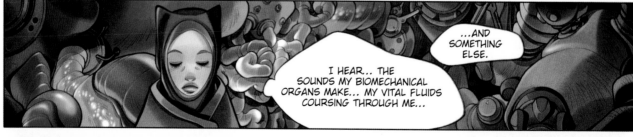

...AND SOMETHING ELSE.

I HEAR... THE SOUNDS MY BIOMECHANICAL ORGANS MAKE... MY VITAL FLUIDS COURSING THROUGH ME...

YOU HAVE ARRIVED. YOU MAY OPEN YOUR EYES NOW.

WELCOME TO AQUA.

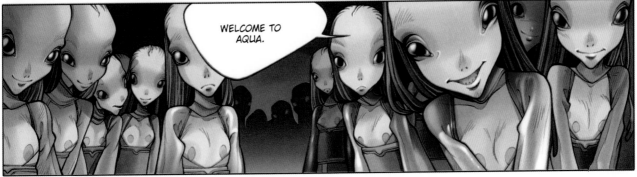

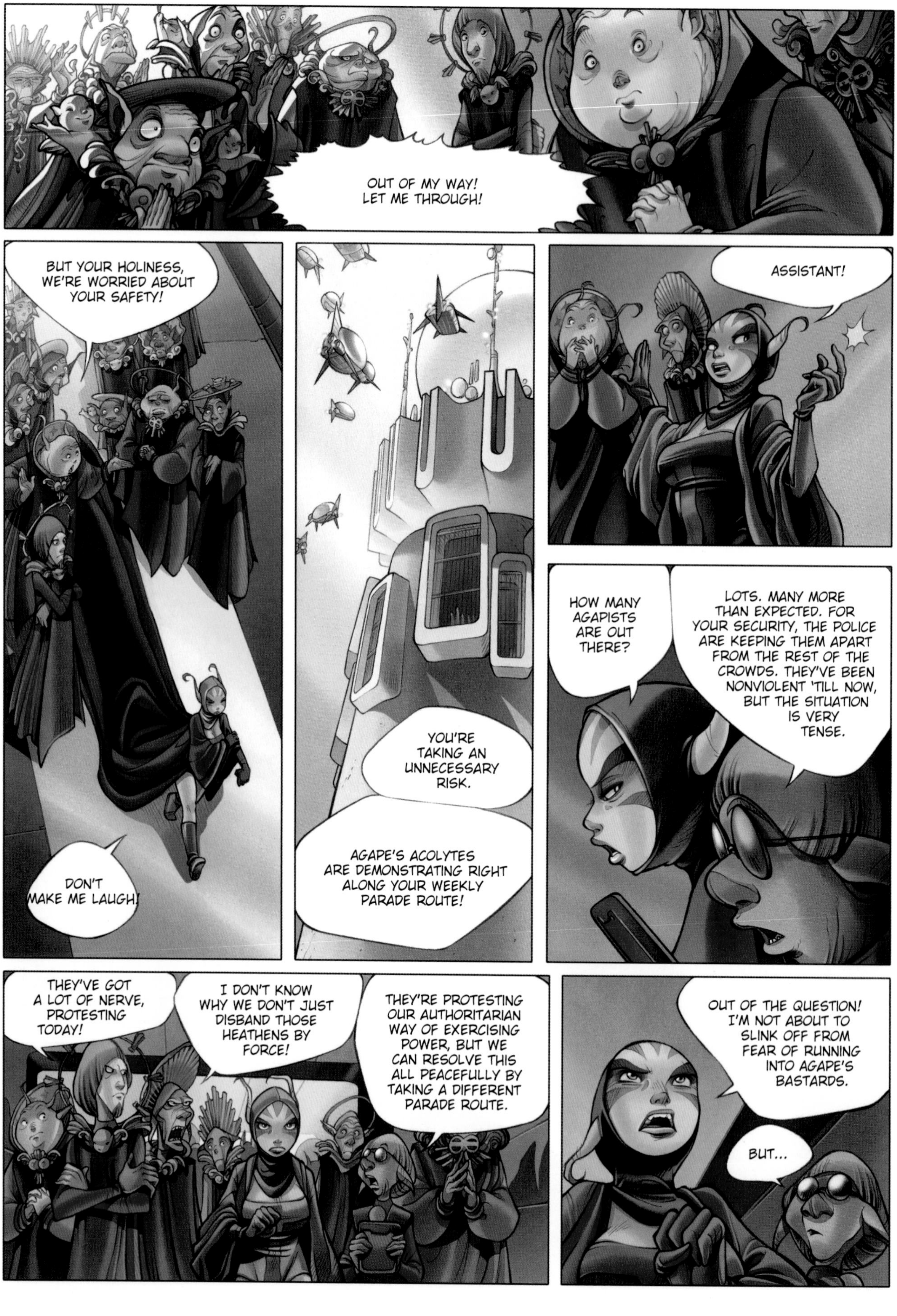
OUT OF MY WAY! LET ME THROUGH!
BUT YOUR HOLINESS, WE'RE WORRIED ABOUT YOUR SAFETY!
DON'T MAKE ME LAUGH!
YOU'RE TAKING AN UNNECESSARY RISK.
AGAPE'S ACOLYTES ARE DEMONSTRATING RIGHT ALONG YOUR WEEKLY PARADE ROUTE!
ASSISTANT!
HOW MANY AGAPISTS ARE OUT THERE?
LOTS. MANY MORE THAN EXPECTED. FOR YOUR SECURITY, THE POLICE ARE KEEPING THEM APART FROM THE REST OF THE CROWDS. THEY'VE BEEN NONVIOLENT 'TILL NOW, BUT THE SITUATION IS VERY TENSE.
THEY'VE GOT A LOT OF NERVE, PROTESTING TODAY!
I DON'T KNOW WHY WE DON'T JUST DISBAND THOSE HEATHENS BY FORCE!
THEY'RE PROTESTING OUR AUTHORITARIAN WAY OF EXERCISING POWER, BUT WE CAN RESOLVE THIS ALL PEACEFULLY BY TAKING A DIFFERENT PARADE ROUTE.
OUT OF THE QUESTION! I'M NOT ABOUT TO SLINK OFF FROM FEAR OF RUNNING INTO AGAPE'S BASTARDS.
BUT...

THE PARADE WILL TAKE PLACE AS PLANNED. NO CHANGES. EVERYONE TO YOUR POSTS.
ARE YOU QUITE CERTAIN?
HOW MANY DEMONSTRATORS DID YOU SAY?
PLUS, IT MIGHT RAIN TODAY. WHY DON'T WE PUSH IT BACK?
ENOUGH! ANYONE WHO DOESN'T GET IN THE PAPAL VESSEL WILL END UP IN THE INQUISITION'S IRONS. END OF DISCUSSION!
AGAPE AGAIN! EVEN DEAD, MY SISTER HAS MANAGED TO TARNISH MY BISHOP'S BLIND FAITH.
PAPAL BUBBLE, CHECK!
SHE INSINUATES HERSELF INTO EVERYTHING I DO, EATING AWAY AT THINGS FROM THE INSIDE, AND THEN TAKES IT ALL AWAY FROM ME, AS ALWAYS.
EPISCOPAL BUBBLE, CHECK.

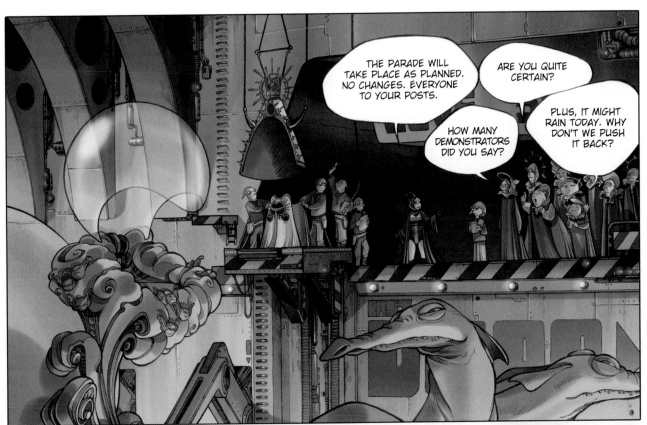

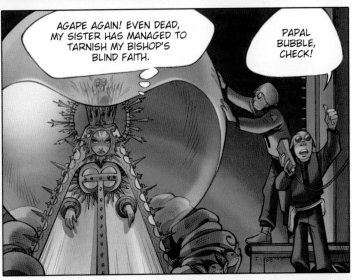

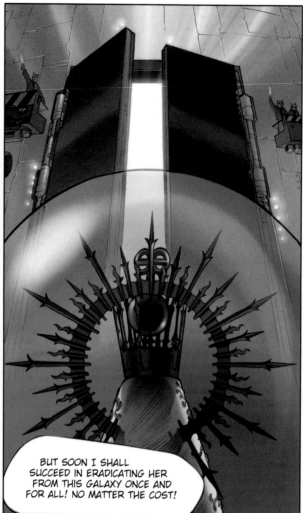

BUT SOON I SHALL SUCCEED IN ERADICATING HER FROM THIS GALAXY ONCE AND FOR ALL! NO MATTER THE COST!

GENIUS OF MIRACLES...WISH ME LUCK!

HERE WE ARE, BROTHERS! THE SACRED DOOR IS OPENING. IN A FEW SECONDS, LUDOVICA, THE HOLIEST OF HOLIES, WILL APPEAR FOR THE ADORATION OF THE MASSES.

THERE SHE IS! HALLELUJAH! HALLELUJAH!

THAT'S RIGHT... KEEP MOVING FORWARD, MY LITTLE SLUT...

I'VE BEEN WAITING FOR YOU TOO. WITH A NICE SURPRISE!

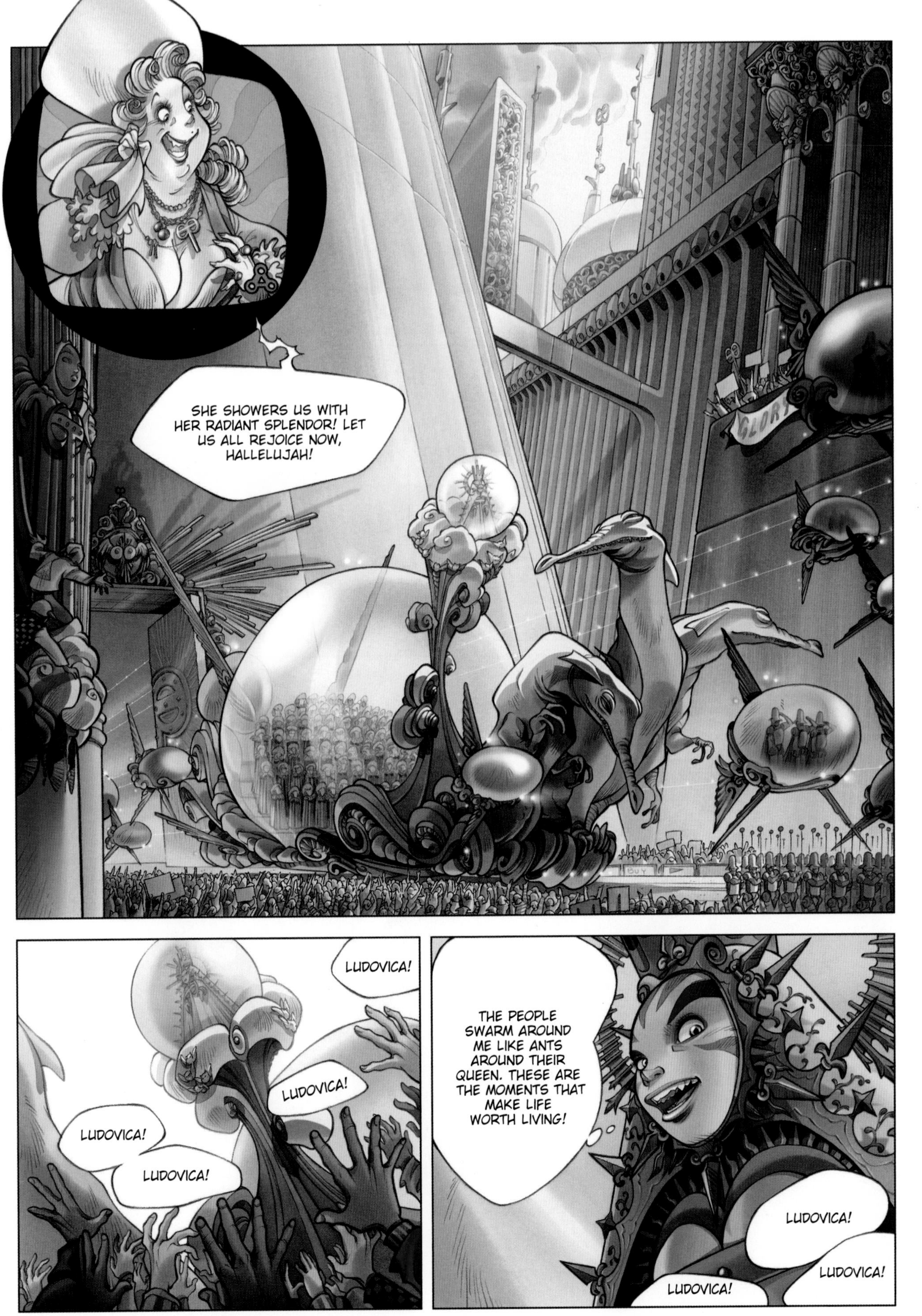
SHE SHOWERS US WITH HER RADIANT SPLENDOR! LET US ALL REJOICE NOW, HALLELUJAH!
LUDOVICA!
LUDOVICA!
LUDOVICA!
LUDOVICA!
THE PEOPLE SWARM AROUND ME LIKE ANTS AROUND THEIR QUEEN. THESE ARE THE MOMENTS THAT MAKE LIFE WORTH LIVING!
LUDOVICA!
LUDOVICA!
LUDOVICA!

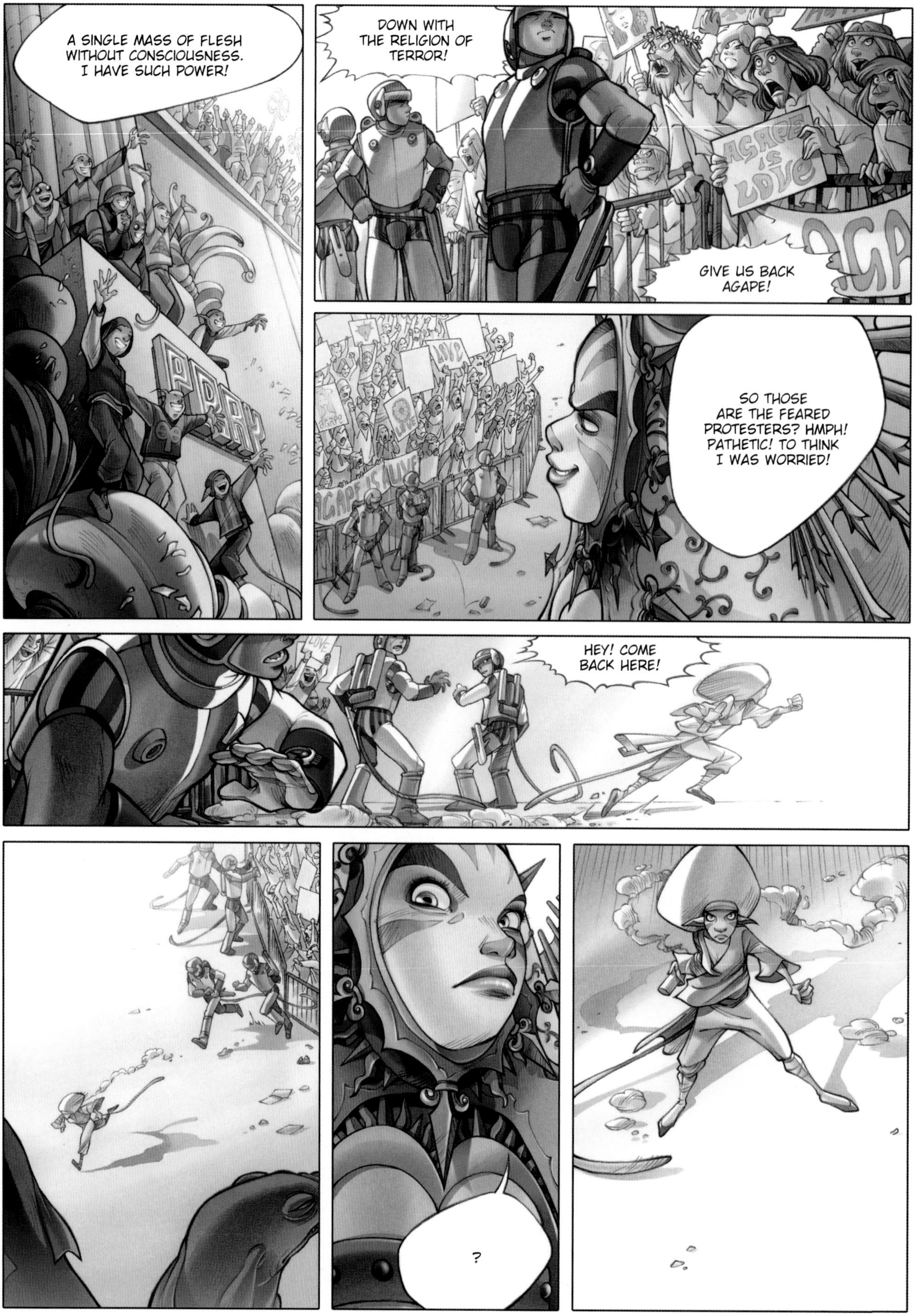
A SINGLE MASS OF FLESH WITHOUT CONSCIOUSNESS. I HAVE SUCH POWER!
DOWN WITH THE RELIGION OF TERROR!
AGAPE IS LOVE
GIVE US BACK AGAPE!
LOVE
AGAPE IS ALIVE
SO THOSE ARE THE FEARED PROTESTERS? HMPH! PATHETIC! TO THINK I WAS WORRIED!
LOVE
HEY! COME BACK HERE!
?

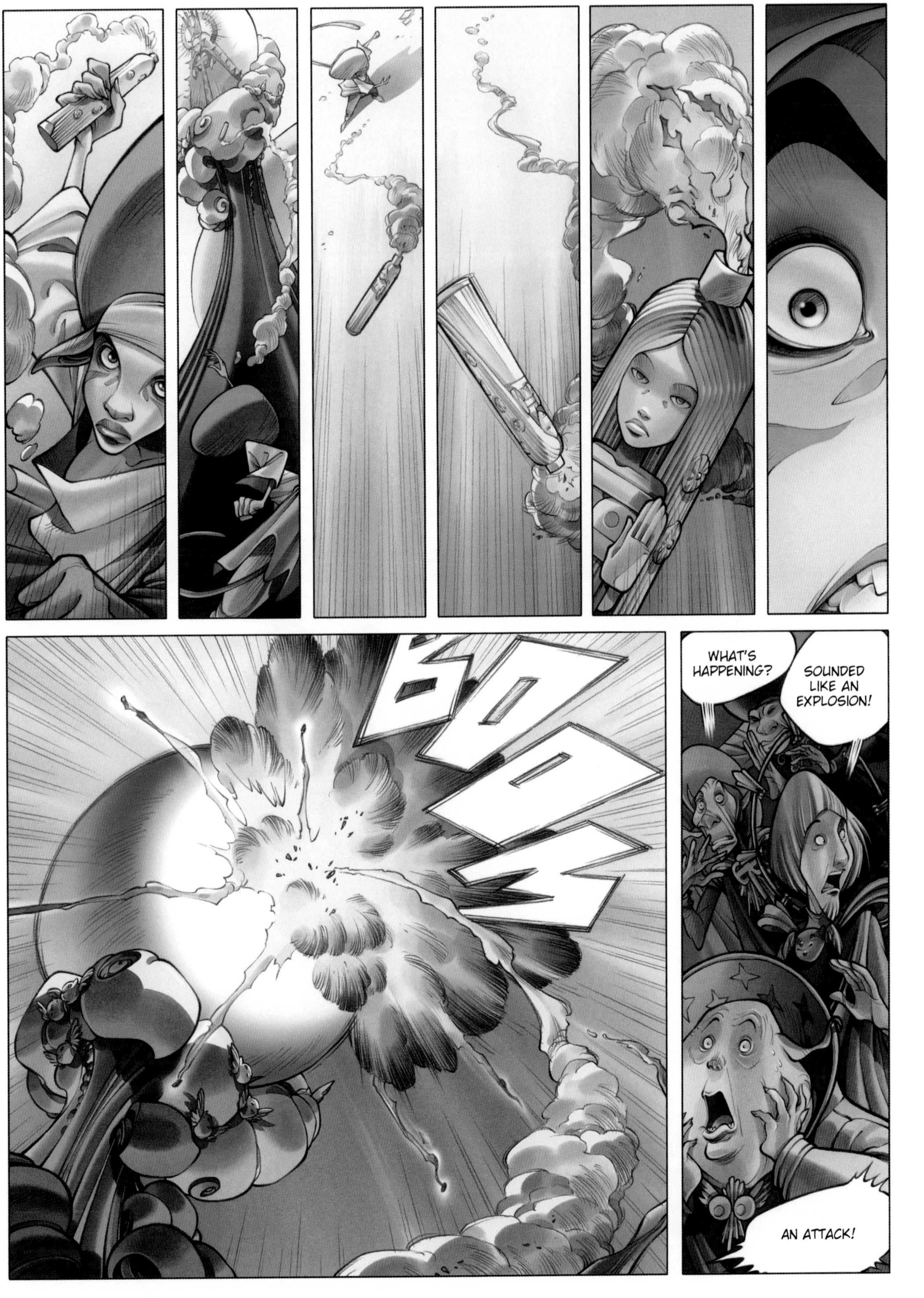
BOOM
WHAT'S HAPPENING?
SOUNDED LIKE AN EXPLOSION!
AN ATTACK!

THE SMOKE'S GETTING IN THE BUBBLE! HELP!

TAKE THIS!

WORM! HOW DARE YOU!

ZAP ZAP

ZAP

KILLERS! MURDERERS!

RRRUMBLE

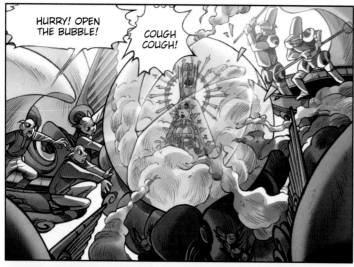

HURRY! OPEN THE BUBBLE!

COUGH COUGH!

DEAR LUDOVICA, WELCOME TO THE REIGN OF CHAOS!

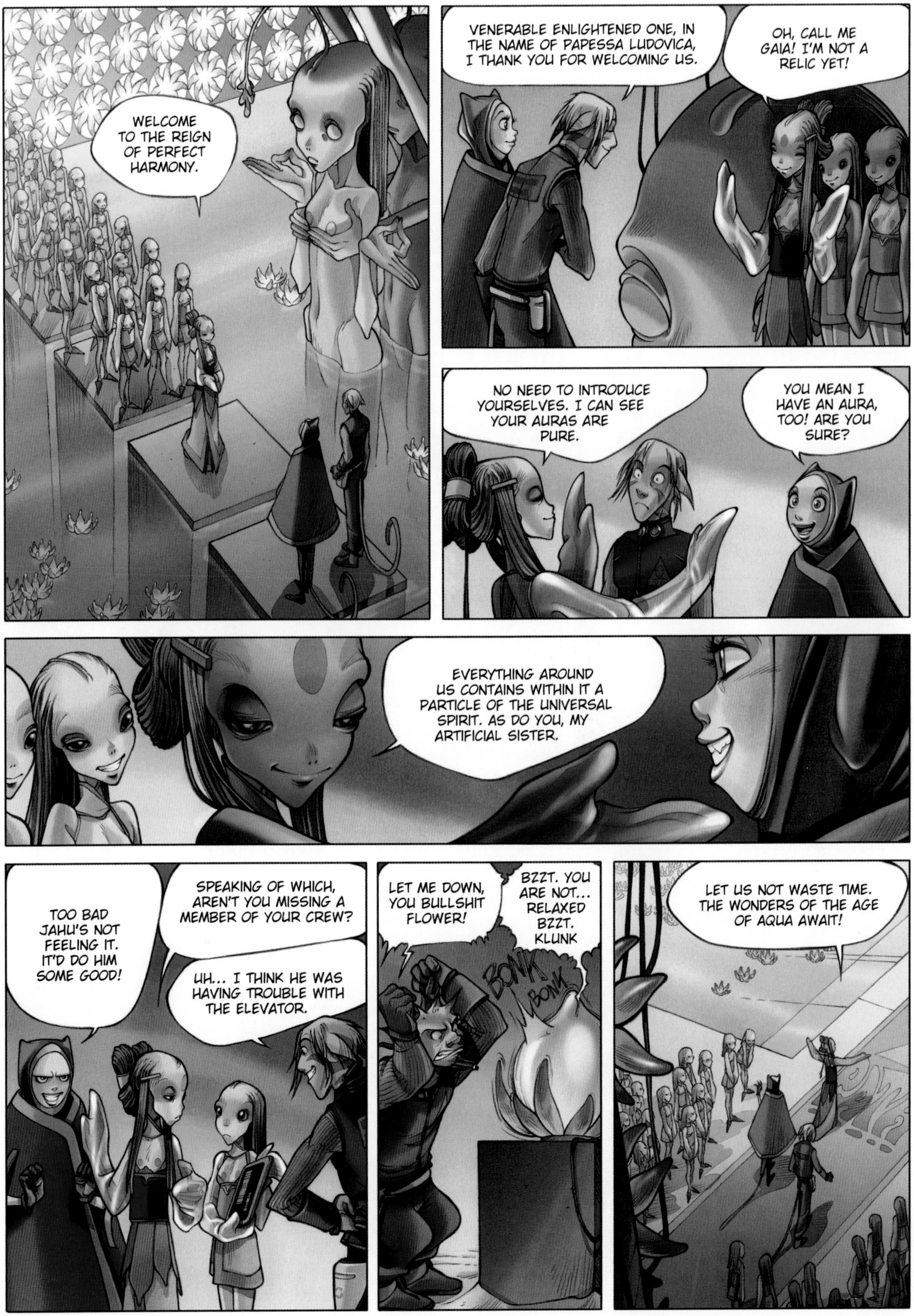
WELCOME TO THE REIGN OF PERFECT HARMONY.
VENERABLE ENLIGHTENED ONE, IN THE NAME OF PAPESSA LUDOVICA, I THANK YOU FOR WELCOMING US.
OH, CALL ME GAIA! I'M NOT A RELIC YET!
NO NEED TO INTRODUCE YOURSELVES. I CAN SEE YOUR AURAS ARE PURE.
YOU MEAN I HAVE AN AURA, TOO! ARE YOU SURE?
EVERYTHING AROUND US CONTAINS WITHIN IT A PARTICLE OF THE UNIVERSAL SPIRIT. AS DO YOU, MY ARTIFICIAL SISTER.
TOO BAD JAHU'S NOT FEELING IT. IT'D DO HIM SOME GOOD!
SPEAKING OF WHICH, AREN'T YOU MISSING A MEMBER OF YOUR CREW?
UH... I THINK HE WAS HAVING TROUBLE WITH THE ELEVATOR.
LET ME DOWN, YOU BULLSHIT FLOWER!
BZZT. YOU ARE NOT... RELAXED BZZT. KLUNK
BONK
BONK
LET US NOT WASTE TIME. THE WONDERS OF THE AGE OF AQUA AWAIT!

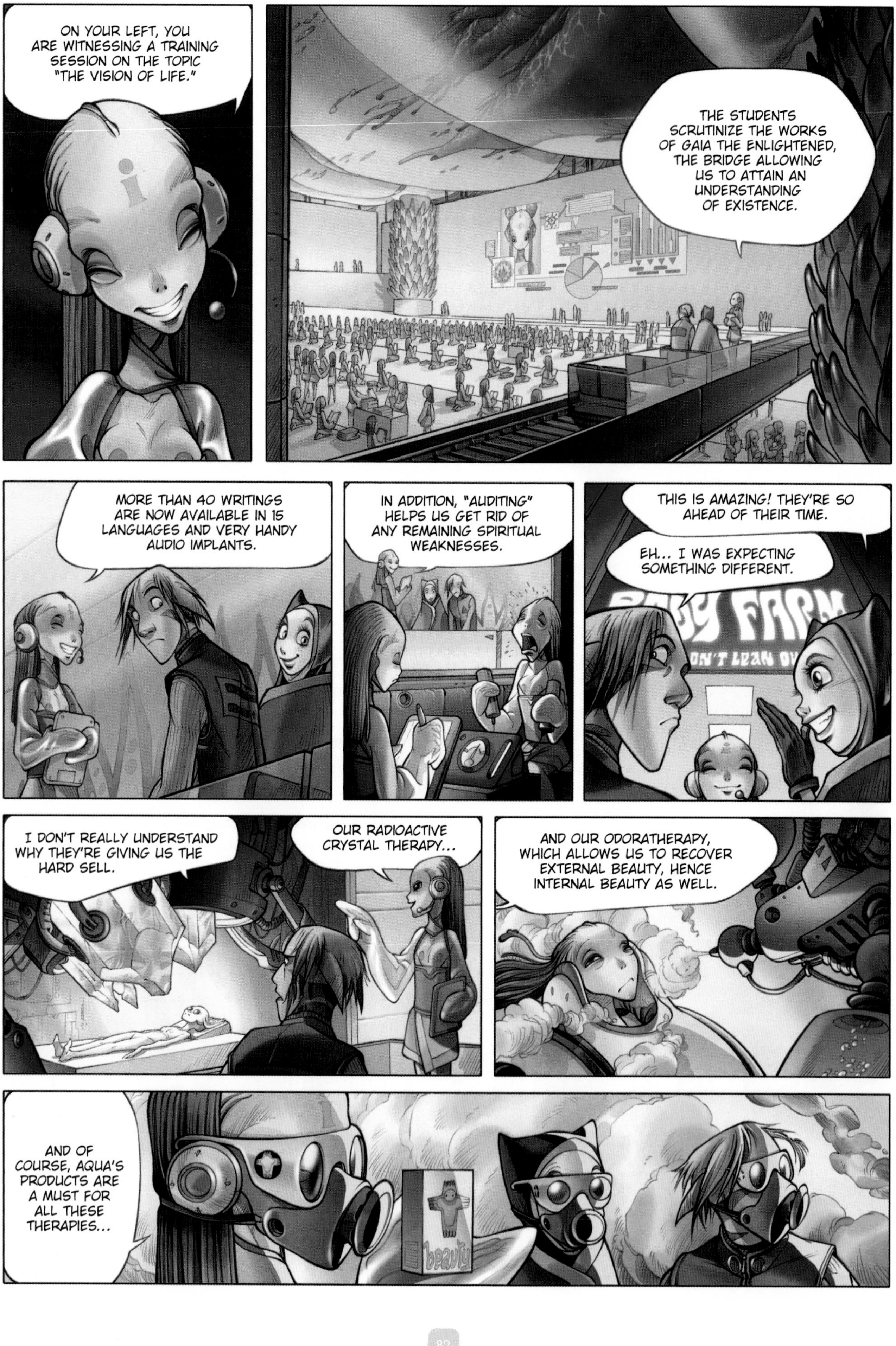
ON YOUR LEFT, YOU ARE WITNESSING A TRAINING SESSION ON THE TOPIC "THE VISION OF LIFE."
THE STUDENTS SCRUTINIZE THE WORKS OF GAIA THE ENLIGHTENED, THE BRIDGE ALLOWING US TO ATTAIN AN UNDERSTANDING OF EXISTENCE.
MORE THAN 40 WRITINGS ARE NOW AVAILABLE IN 15 LANGUAGES AND VERY HANDY AUDIO IMPLANTS.
IN ADDITION, "AUDITING" HELPS US GET RID OF ANY REMAINING SPIRITUAL WEAKNESSES.
THIS IS AMAZING! THEY'RE SO AHEAD OF THEIR TIME.
EH... I WAS EXPECTING SOMETHING DIFFERENT.
I DON'T REALLY UNDERSTAND WHY THEY'RE GIVING US THE HARD SELL.
OUR RADIOACTIVE CRYSTAL THERAPY...
AND OUR ODORATHERAPY, WHICH ALLOWS US TO RECOVER EXTERNAL BEAUTY, HENCE INTERNAL BEAUTY AS WELL.
AND OF COURSE, AQUA'S PRODUCTS ARE A MUST FOR ALL THESE THERAPIES...

...FOR THE WELL-BEING OF BODY AND SOUL!

OH, SCREW THIS! I CAN'T DO IT!

THIS MEDITATION CRAP IS THREATENING TO MESS UP THE WHOLE MISSION! GODDAMMIT, I'M HERE TO DO STUFF!

I HAVE TO FIGURE THIS OUT, AND FAST! I DON'T HAVE MUCH TIME LEFT.

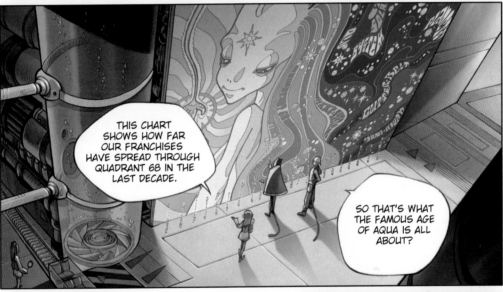

THIS CHART SHOWS HOW FAR OUR FRANCHISES HAVE SPREAD THROUGH QUADRANT 68 IN THE LAST DECADE.

SO THAT'S WHAT THE FAMOUS AGE OF AQUA IS ALL ABOUT?

JUST A CHAIN OF WELLNESS CENTERS SCATTERED THROUGH THE COSMOS?

THE SPIRITUAL PATH IS DRAWING MORE AND MORE FOLLOWERS!

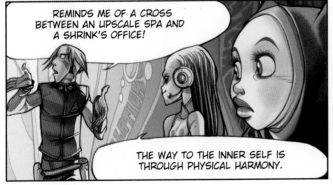

REMINDS ME OF A CROSS BETWEEN AN UPSCALE SPA AND A SHRINK'S OFFICE!

THE WAY TO THE INNER SELF IS THROUGH PHYSICAL HARMONY.

AQUA CENTERS PUT EVERYTHING YOU NEED AT YOUR DISPOSAL.

YEAH, IF YOU HAVE MONEY TO BLOW, SURE!

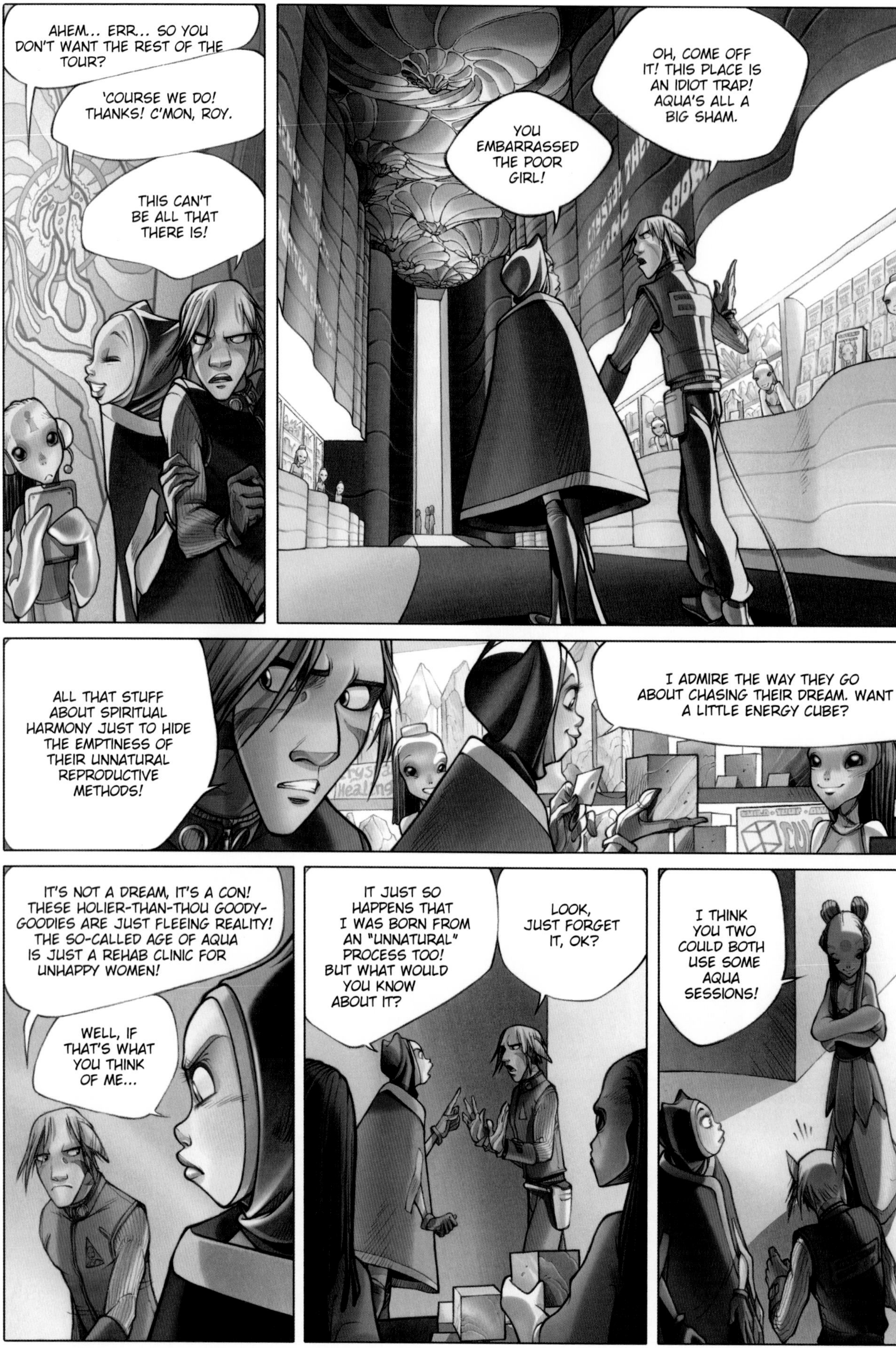
AHEM... ERR... SO YOU DON'T WANT THE REST OF THE TOUR?
'COURSE WE DO! THANKS! C'MON, ROY.
THIS CAN'T BE ALL THAT THERE IS!
YOU EMBARRASSED THE POOR GIRL!
OH, COME OFF IT! THIS PLACE IS AN IDIOT TRAP! AQUA'S ALL A BIG SHAM.
ALL THAT STUFF ABOUT SPIRITUAL HARMONY JUST TO HIDE THE EMPTINESS OF THEIR UNNATURAL REPRODUCTIVE METHODS!
I ADMIRE THE WAY THEY GO ABOUT CHASING THEIR DREAM. WANT A LITTLE ENERGY CUBE?
IT'S NOT A DREAM, IT'S A CON! THESE HOLIER-THAN-THOU GOODY-GOODIES ARE JUST FLEEING REALITY! THE SO-CALLED AGE OF AQUA IS JUST A REHAB CLINIC FOR UNHAPPY WOMEN!
WELL, IF THAT'S WHAT YOU THINK OF ME...
IT JUST SO HAPPENS THAT I WAS BORN FROM AN "UNNATURAL" PROCESS TOO! BUT WHAT WOULD YOU KNOW ABOUT IT?
LOOK, JUST FORGET IT, OK?
I THINK YOU TWO COULD BOTH USE SOME AQUA SESSIONS!

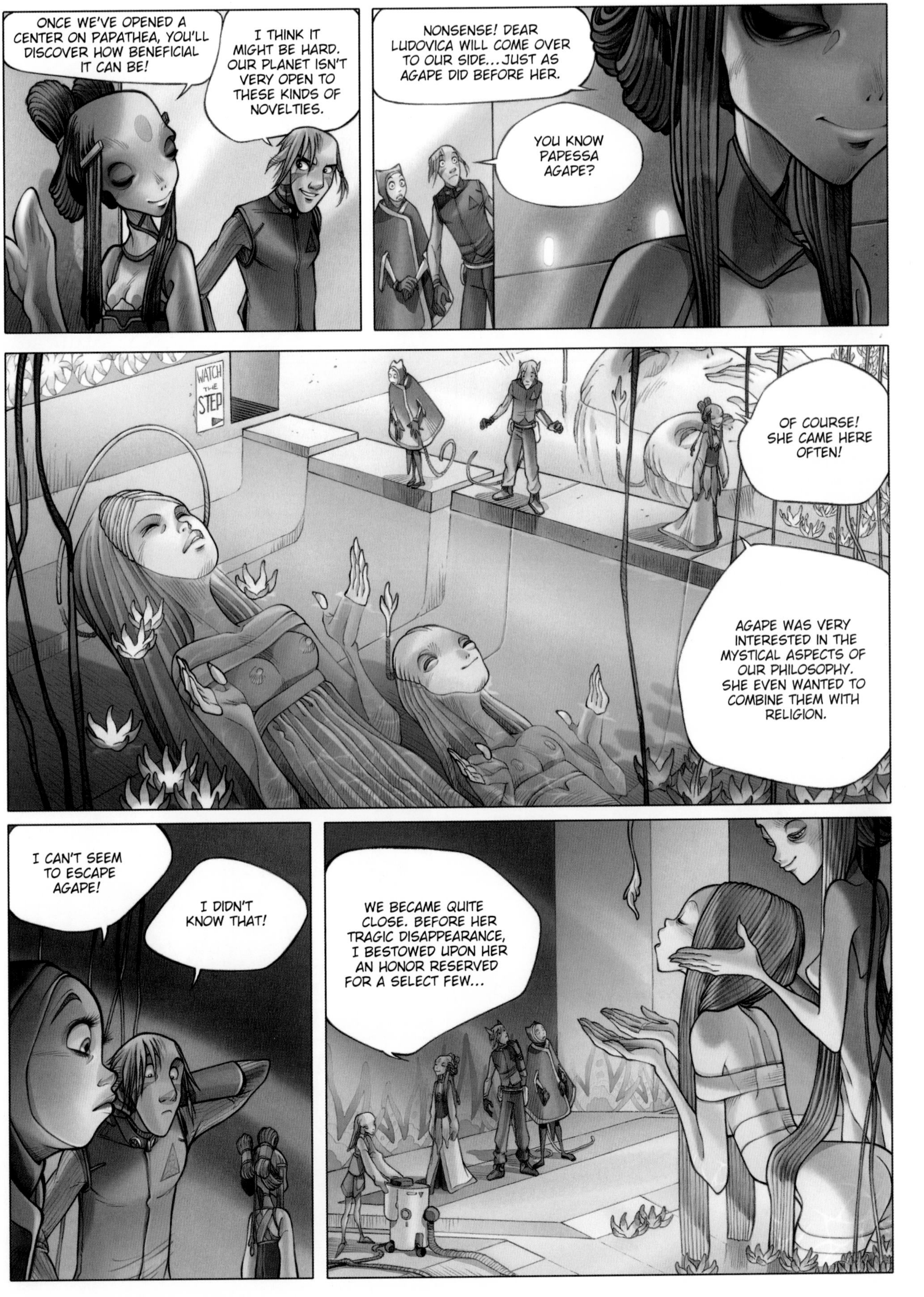
ONCE WE'VE OPENED A CENTER ON PAPATHEA, YOU'LL DISCOVER HOW BENEFICIAL IT CAN BE!
I THINK IT MIGHT BE HARD. OUR PLANET ISN'T VERY OPEN TO THESE KINDS OF NOVELTIES.
NONSENSE! DEAR LUDOVICA WILL COME OVER TO OUR SIDE... JUST AS AGAPE DID BEFORE HER.
YOU KNOW PAPESSA AGAPE?
WATCH THE STEP
OF COURSE! SHE CAME HERE OFTEN!
AGAPE WAS VERY INTERESTED IN THE MYSTICAL ASPECTS OF OUR PHILOSOPHY. SHE EVEN WANTED TO COMBINE THEM WITH RELIGION.
I CAN'T SEEM TO ESCAPE AGAPE!
I DIDN'T KNOW THAT!
WE BECAME QUITE CLOSE. BEFORE HER TRAGIC DISAPPEARANCE, I BESTOWED UPON HER AN HONOR RESERVED FOR A SELECT FEW...

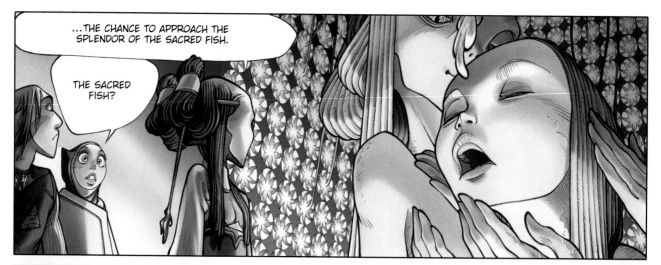

...THE CHANCE TO APPROACH THE SPLENDOR OF THE SACRED FISH.

THE SACRED FISH?

SEE THIS IMAGE? IT IS BUT ONE REPRESENTATION OF THE SACRED FISH: THE HEART OF COSMIC ENERGY.

IT CONTAINS THE ELEMENT THAT ALLOWS OUR SPECIES TO PROPAGATE.

INTERESTING! CAN WE SEE IT?

ABSOLUTELY NOT!

GO FIGURE...

BIP!

IT IS TIME NOW FOR OUR DAILY MEDITATION PHASE, DURING WHICH ALL ACTIVITY IS SUSPENDED.

YOU MAY TAKE PART, IF YOU WISH.

OH, COULD I?

NO THANKS! HAD ENOUGH SERENITY FOR TODAY!

IN THAT CASE, ROY, WE WILL ENTRUST YOU TO THE TUTOR DROIDS.

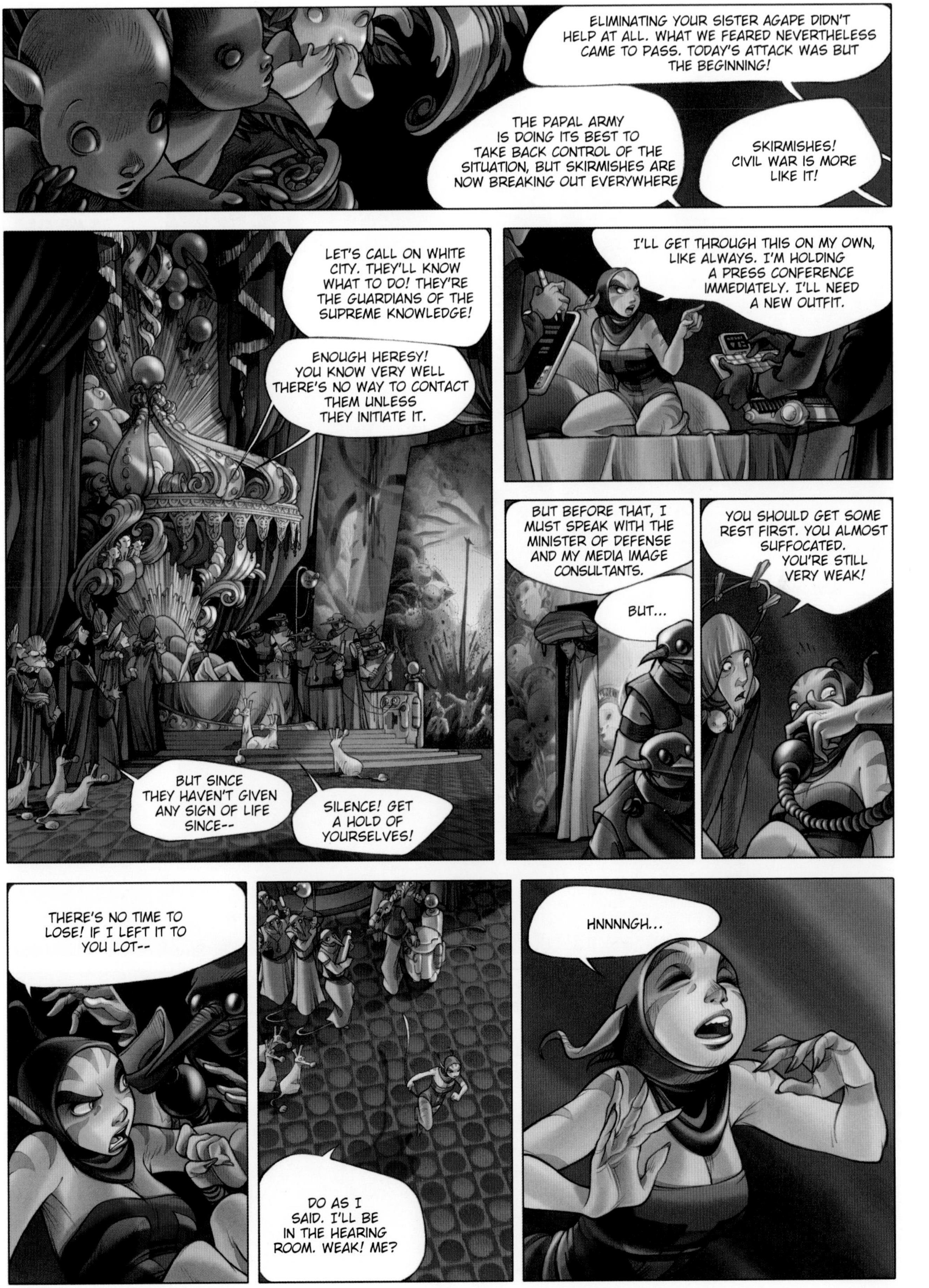
ELIMINATING YOUR SISTER AGAPE DIDN'T HELP AT ALL. WHAT WE FEARED NEVERTHELESS CAME TO PASS. TODAY'S ATTACK WAS BUT THE BEGINNING!
THE PAPAL ARMY IS DOING ITS BEST TO TAKE BACK CONTROL OF THE SITUATION, BUT SKIRMISHES ARE NOW BREAKING OUT EVERYWHERE
SKIRMISHES! CIVIL WAR IS MORE LIKE IT!
LET'S CALL ON WHITE CITY. THEY'LL KNOW WHAT TO DO! THEY'RE THE GUARDIANS OF THE SUPREME KNOWLEDGE!
ENOUGH HERESY! YOU KNOW VERY WELL THERE'S NO WAY TO CONTACT THEM UNLESS THEY INITIATE IT.
BUT SINCE THEY HAVEN'T GIVEN ANY SIGN OF LIFE SINCE--
SILENCE! GET A HOLD OF YOURSELVES!
I'LL GET THROUGH THIS ON MY OWN, LIKE ALWAYS. I'M HOLDING A PRESS CONFERENCE IMMEDIATELY. I'LL NEED A NEW OUTFIT.
BUT BEFORE THAT, I MUST SPEAK WITH THE MINISTER OF DEFENSE AND MY MEDIA IMAGE CONSULTANTS.
BUT...
YOU SHOULD GET SOME REST FIRST. YOU ALMOST SUFFOCATED. YOU'RE STILL VERY WEAK!
THERE'S NO TIME TO LOSE! IF I LEFT IT TO YOU LOT--
DO AS I SAID. I'LL BE IN THE HEARING ROOM. WEAK! ME?
HNNNNGH...

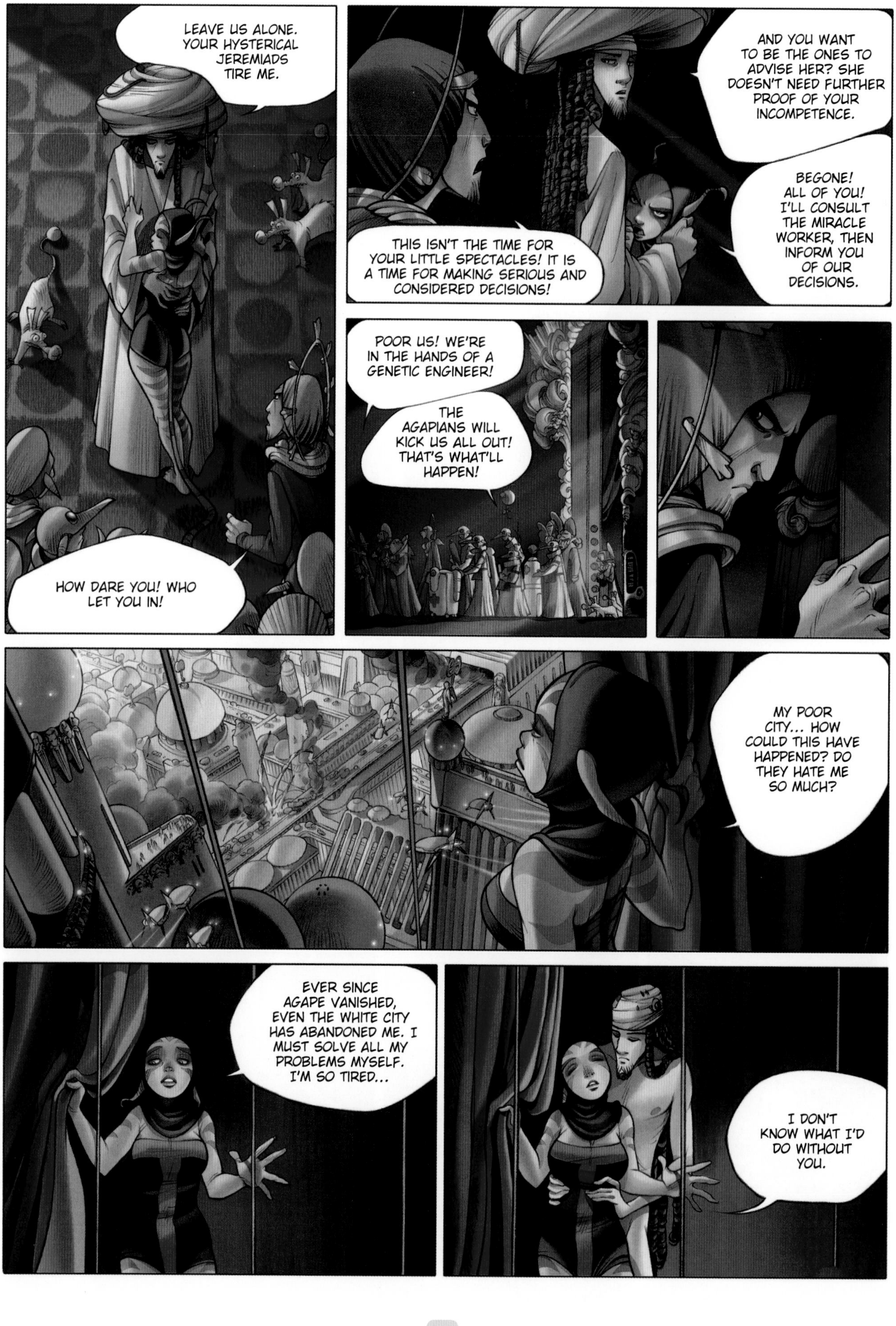
LEAVE US ALONE. YOUR HYSTERICAL JEREMIADS TIRE ME.
HOW DARE YOU! WHO LET YOU IN!
THIS ISN'T THE TIME FOR YOUR LITTLE SPECTACLES! IT IS A TIME FOR MAKING SERIOUS AND CONSIDERED DECISIONS!
AND YOU WANT TO BE THE ONES TO ADVISE HER? SHE DOESN'T NEED FURTHER PROOF OF YOUR INCOMPETENCE.
BEGONE! ALL OF YOU! I'LL CONSULT THE MIRACLE WORKER, THEN INFORM YOU OF OUR DECISIONS.
POOR US! WE'RE IN THE HANDS OF A GENETIC ENGINEER!
THE AGAPIANS WILL KICK US ALL OUT! THAT'S WHAT'LL HAPPEN!
MY POOR CITY... HOW COULD THIS HAVE HAPPENED? DO THEY HATE ME SO MUCH?
EVER SINCE AGAPE VANISHED, EVEN THE WHITE CITY HAS ABANDONED ME. I MUST SOLVE ALL MY PROBLEMS MYSELF. I'M SO TIRED...
I DON'T KNOW WHAT I'D DO WITHOUT YOU.

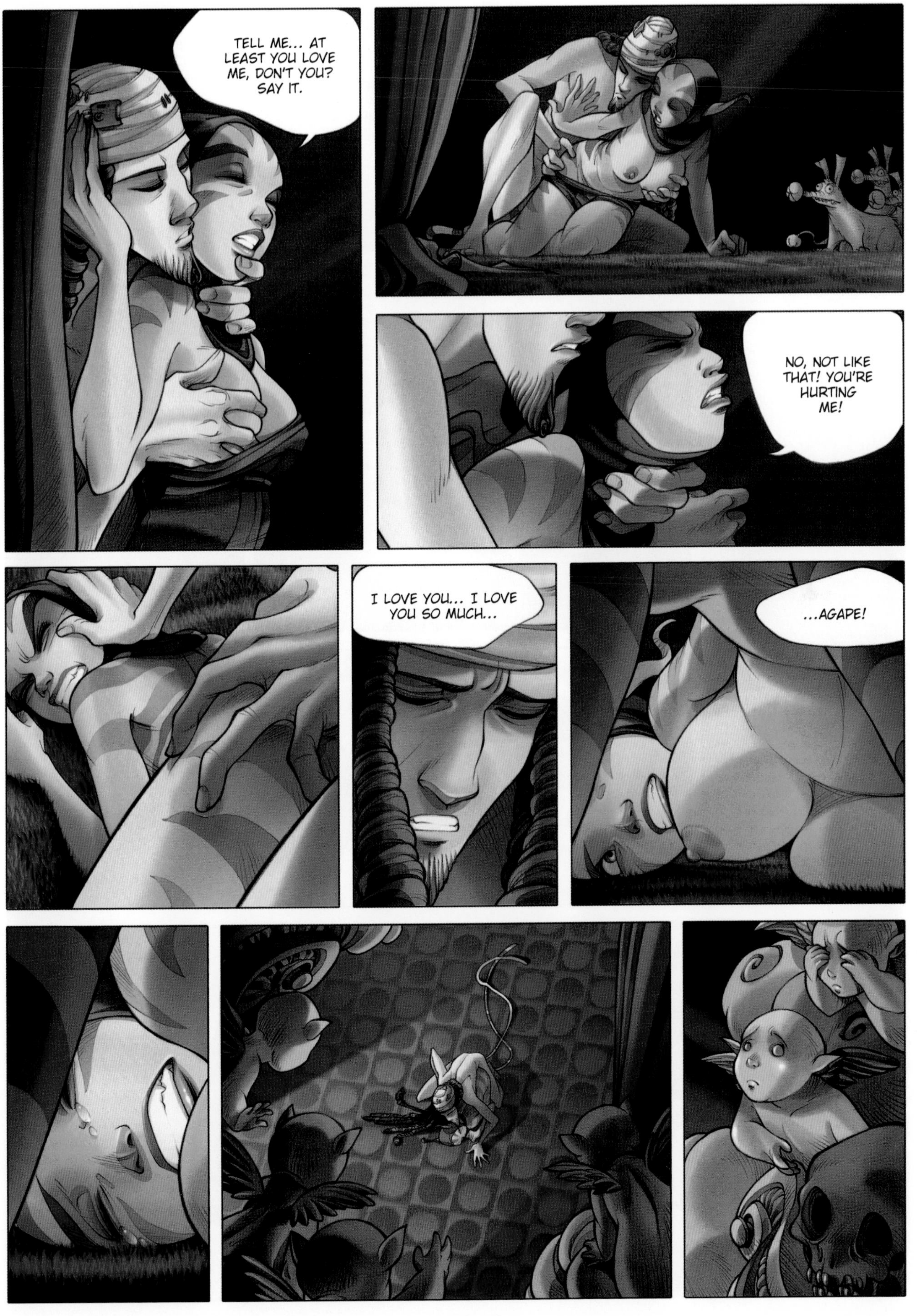
TELL ME... AT LEAST YOU LOVE ME, DON'T YOU? SAY IT.
NO, NOT LIKE THAT! YOU'RE HURTING ME!
I LOVE YOU... I LOVE YOU SO MUCH...
...AGAPE!

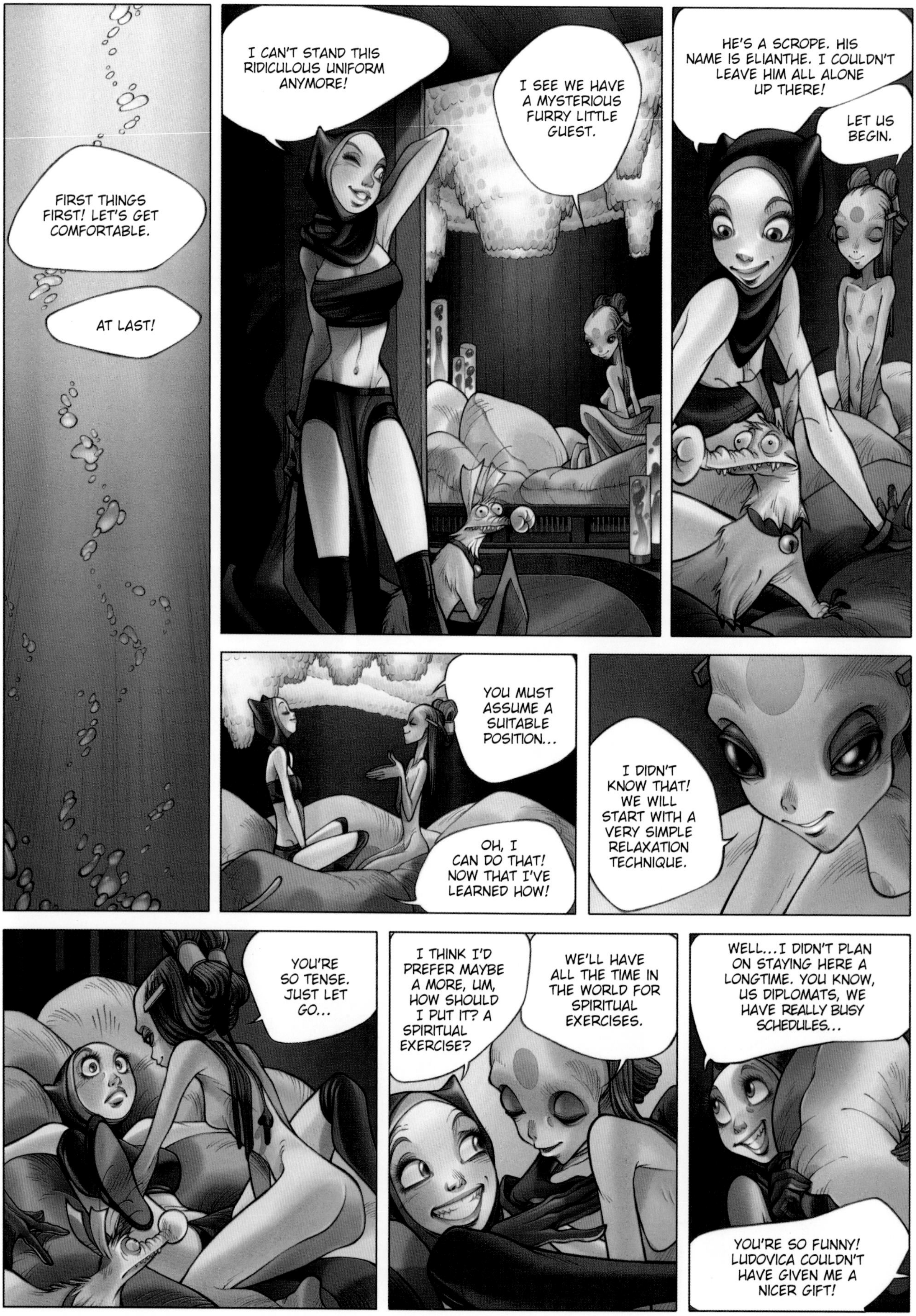
FIRST THINGS FIRST! LET'S GET COMFORTABLE.
AT LAST!
I CAN'T STAND THIS RIDICULOUS UNIFORM ANYMORE!
I SEE WE HAVE A MYSTERIOUS FURRY LITTLE GUEST.
HE'S A SCROPE. HIS NAME IS ELIANTHE. I COULDN'T LEAVE HIM ALL ALONE UP THERE!
LET US BEGIN.
YOU MUST ASSUME A SUITABLE POSITION...
OH, I CAN DO THAT! NOW THAT I'VE LEARNED HOW!
I DIDN'T KNOW THAT! WE WILL START WITH A VERY SIMPLE RELAXATION TECHNIQUE.
YOU'RE SO TENSE. JUST LET GO...
I THINK I'D PREFER MAYBE A MORE, UM, HOW SHOULD I PUT IT? A SPIRITUAL EXERCISE?
WE'LL HAVE ALL THE TIME IN THE WORLD FOR SPIRITUAL EXERCISES.
WELL...I DIDN'T PLAN ON STAYING HERE A LONGTIME. YOU KNOW, US DIPLOMATS, WE HAVE REALLY BUSY SCHEDULES...
YOU'RE SO FUNNY! LUDOVICA COULDN'T HAVE GIVEN ME A NICER GIFT!

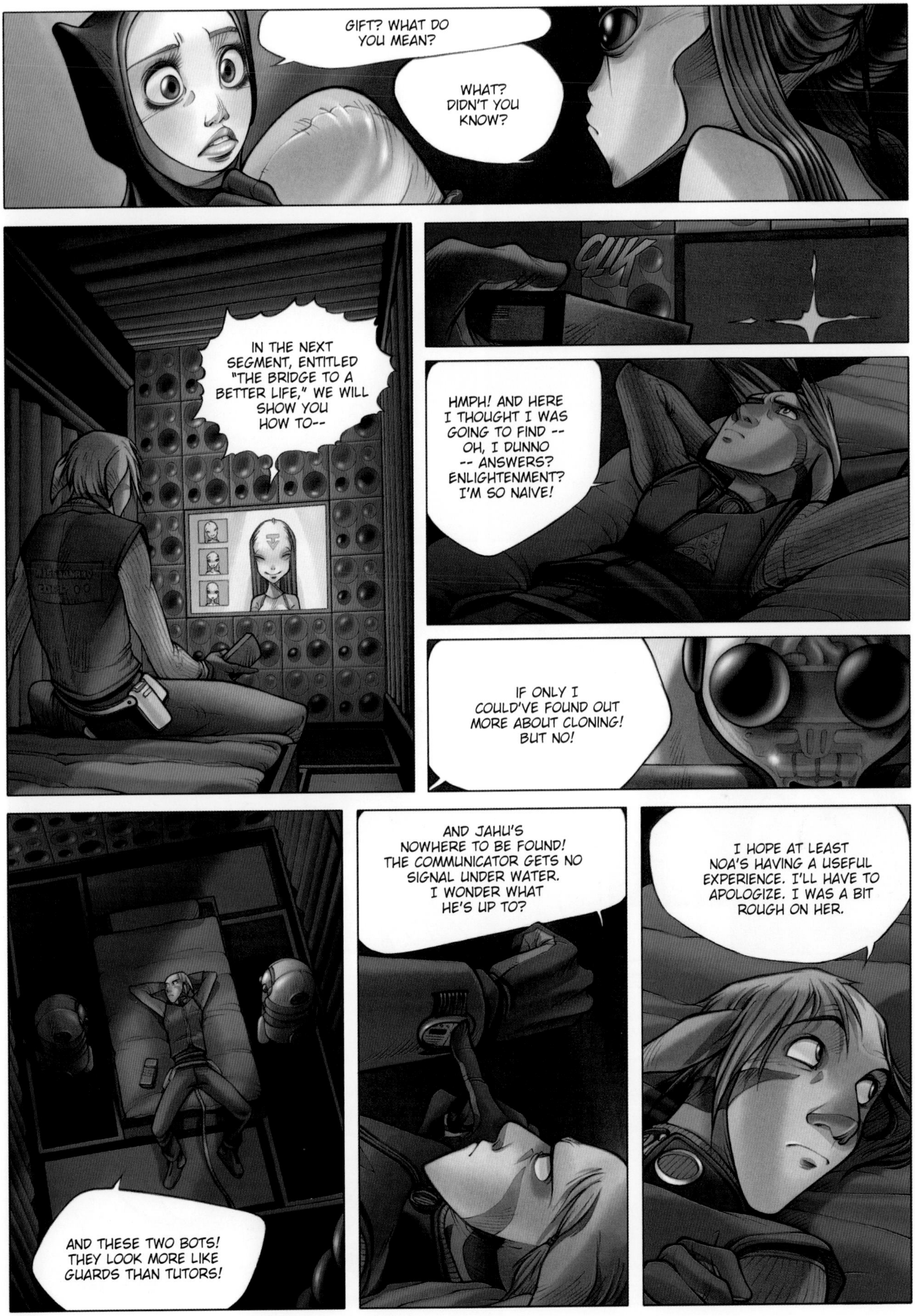
GIFT? WHAT DO YOU MEAN?
WHAT? DIDN'T YOU KNOW?
IN THE NEXT SEGMENT, ENTITLED "THE BRIDGE TO A BETTER LIFE," WE WILL SHOW YOU HOW TO--
CLIK
HMPH! AND HERE I THOUGHT I WAS GOING TO FIND -- OH, I DUNNO -- ANSWERS? ENLIGHTENMENT? I'M SO NAIVE!
IF ONLY I COULD'VE FOUND OUT MORE ABOUT CLONING! BUT NO!
AND THESE TWO BOTS! THEY LOOK MORE LIKE GUARDS THAN TUTORS!
AND JAHU'S NOWHERE TO BE FOUND! THE COMMUNICATOR GETS NO SIGNAL UNDER WATER. I WONDER WHAT HE'S UP TO?
I HOPE AT LEAST NOA'S HAVING A USEFUL EXPERIENCE. I'LL HAVE TO APOLOGIZE. I WAS A BIT ROUGH ON HER.

I UNDERSTAND HOW YOU MUST FEEL! I'LL LEAVE YOU ALONE NOW. WE'LL HAVE ALL THE TIME IN THE WORLD TO BE TOGETHER.

BASTARDS! THAT'S ALL I AM TO THEM! JUST A TOY!

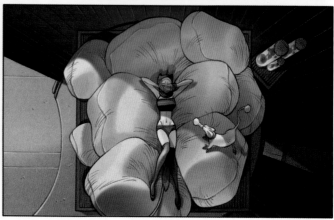

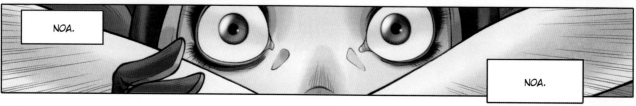

NOA.

NOA.

THE TIME HAS COME...

N-NO! NOT YET!

COME...

COME, AND REMEMBER!

NO!!

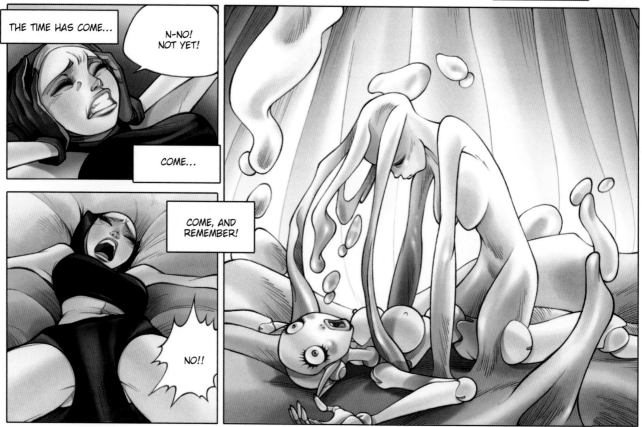

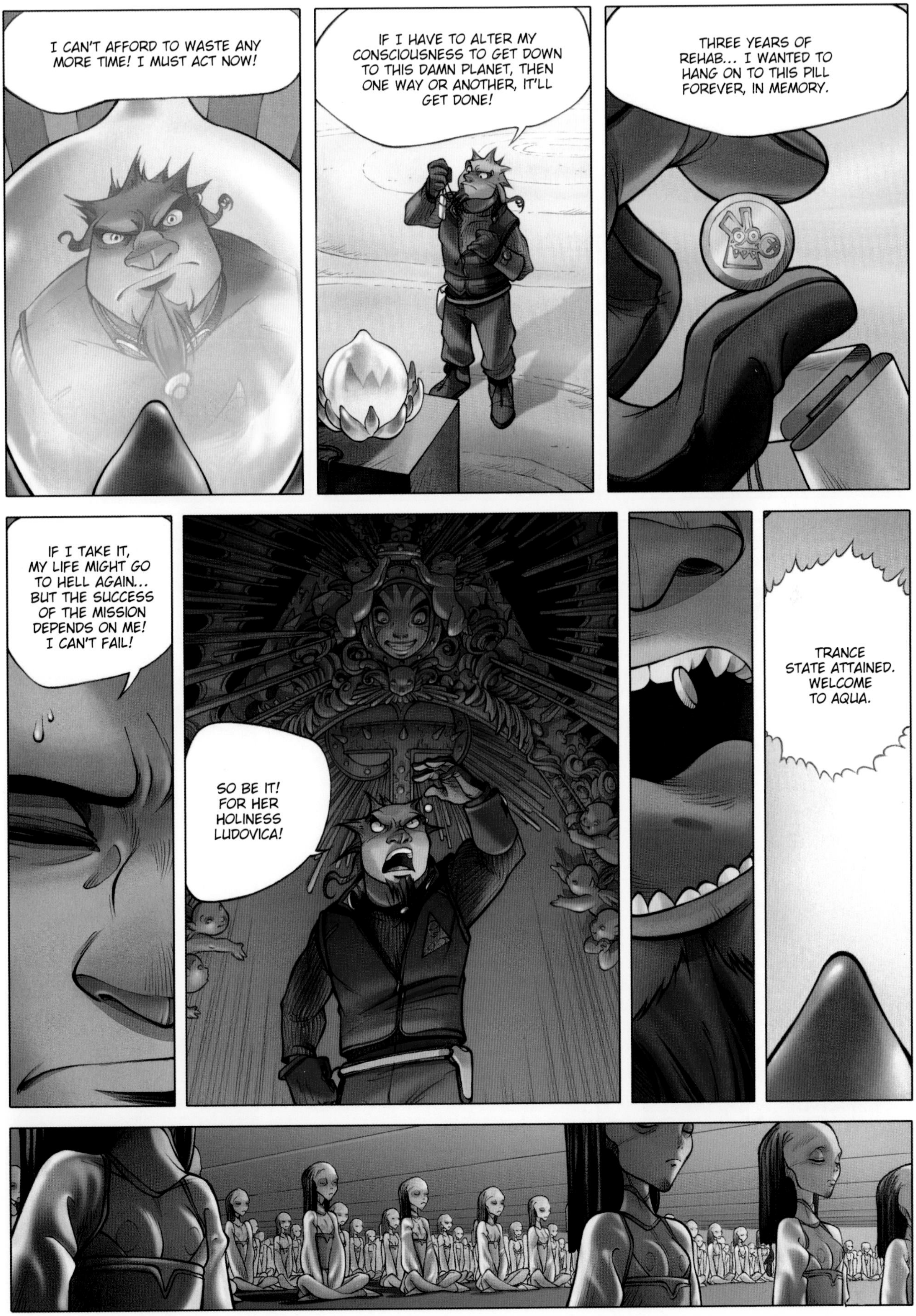
I CAN'T AFFORD TO WASTE ANY MORE TIME! I MUST ACT NOW!
IF I HAVE TO ALTER MY CONSCIOUSNESS TO GET DOWN TO THIS DAMN PLANET, THEN ONE WAY OR ANOTHER, IT'LL GET DONE!
THREE YEARS OF REHAB... I WANTED TO HANG ON TO THIS PILL FOREVER, IN MEMORY.
IF I TAKE IT, MY LIFE MIGHT GO TO HELL AGAIN... BUT THE SUCCESS OF THE MISSION DEPENDS ON ME! I CAN'T FAIL!
SO BE IT! FOR HER HOLINESS LUDOVICA!
TRANCE STATE ATTAINED. WELCOME TO AQUA.

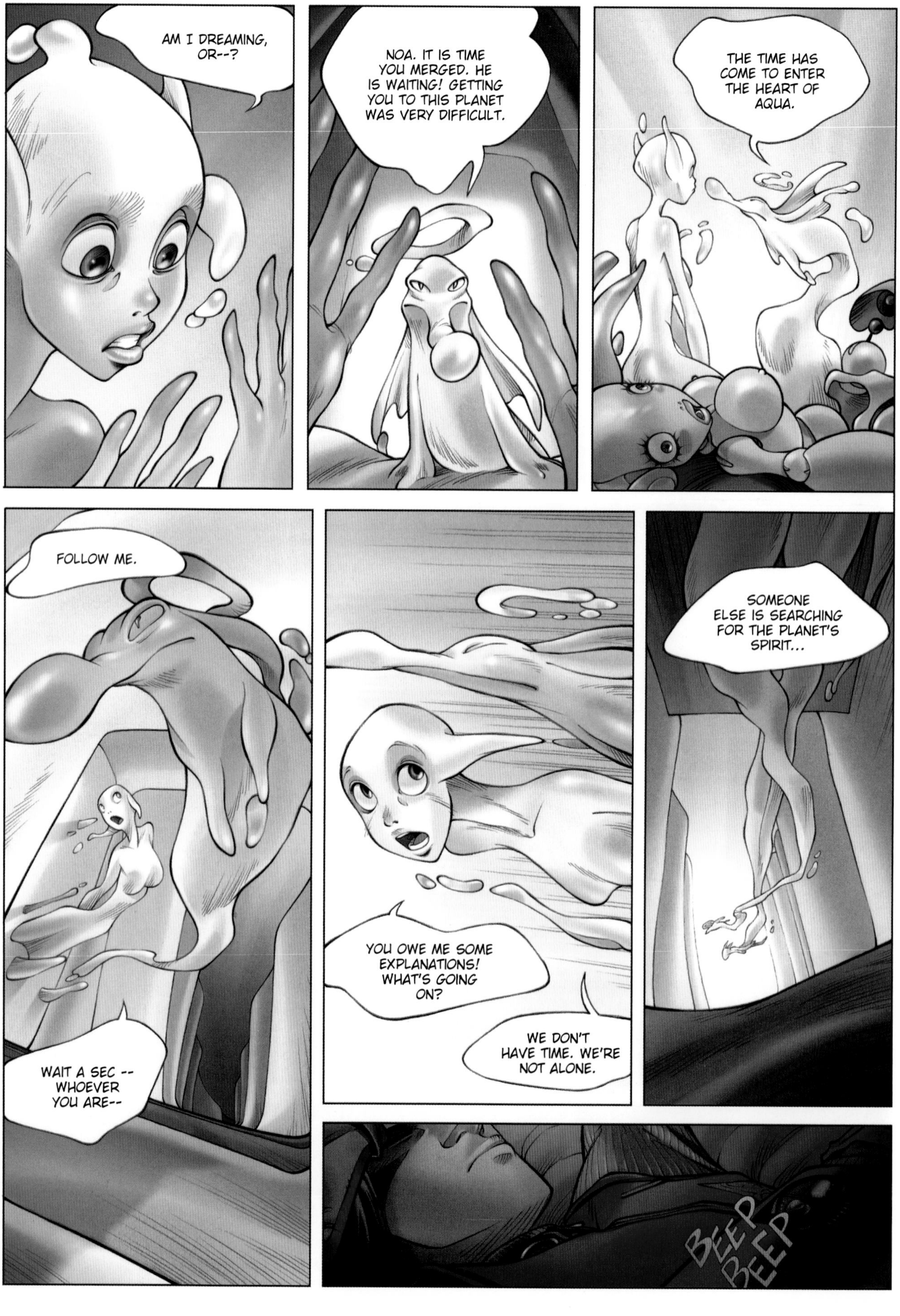

AM I DREAMING, OR--?
NOA. IT IS TIME YOU MERGED. HE IS WAITING! GETTING YOU TO THIS PLANET WAS VERY DIFFICULT.
THE TIME HAS COME TO ENTER THE HEART OF AQUA.
FOLLOW ME.
WAIT A SEC -- WHOEVER YOU ARE--
YOU OWE ME SOME EXPLANATIONS! WHAT'S GOING ON?
WE DON'T HAVE TIME. WE'RE NOT ALONE.
SOMEONE ELSE IS SEARCHING FOR THE PLANET'S SPIRIT...
BEEP BEEP

...IN ORDER TO RAPE IT.

AGENT JAHU REPORTING. I'VE ENTERED THE PLANET.

WELL DONE, MY FAITHFUL MISSIONARY! DO YOU NEED TO BE REMINDED OF THE WAY?

NO, MY LADY! FIRST HALLWAY ON THE RIGHT, THEN LEFT...

THEN ANOTHER RIGHT...

DOWN THE STAIRS...

I KNEW WE COULD COUNT ON YOU, JAHU!

NEVER DISAPPOINT US AGAIN!

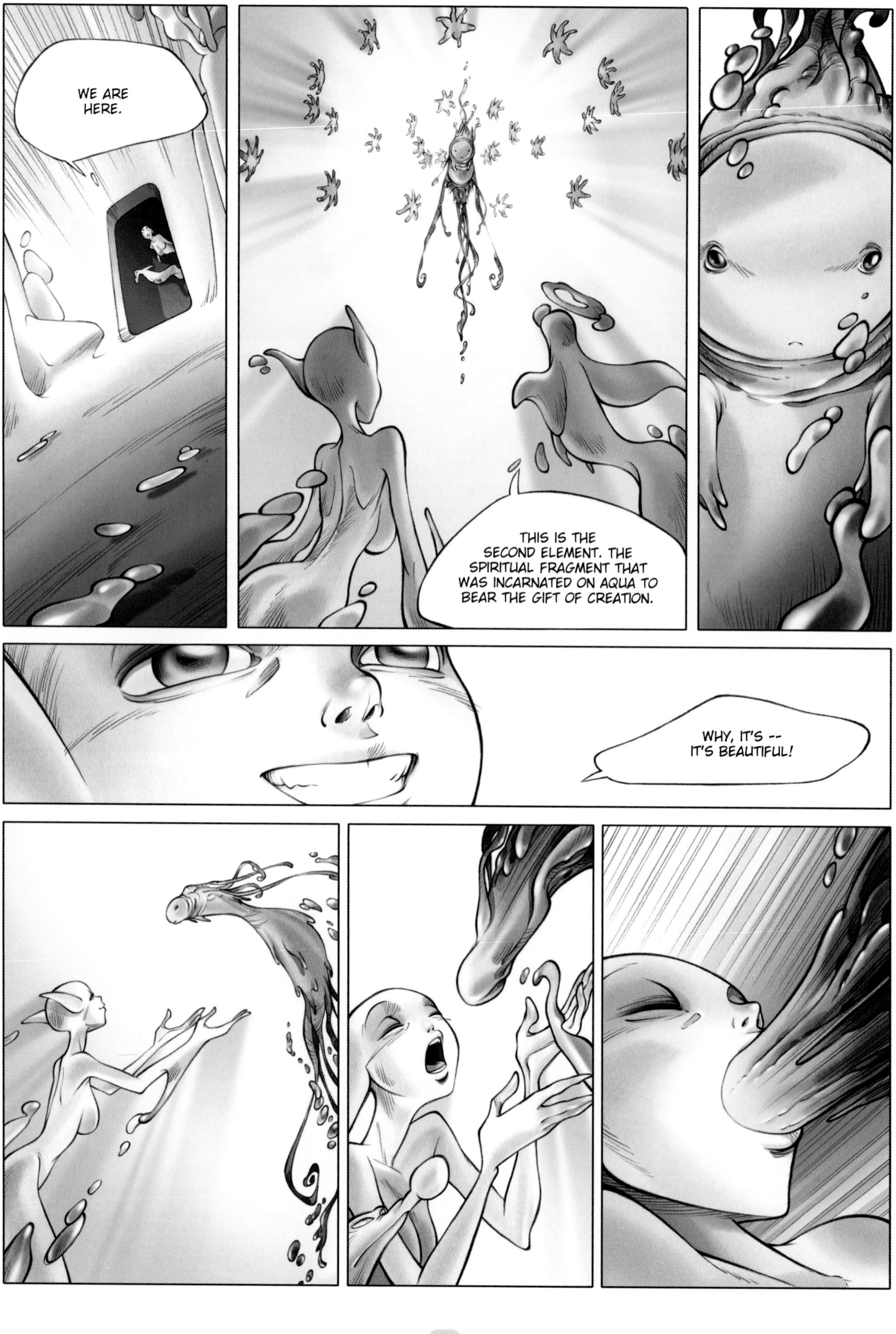
WE ARE
HERE.
THIS IS THE
SECOND ELEMENT. THE
SPIRITUAL FRAGMENT THAT
WAS INCARNATED ON AQUA TO
BEAR THE GIFT OF CREATION.
WHY, IT'S --
IT'S BEAUTIFUL!

PANT!
PANT!
PANT!

THERE IT IS.

THE KEY TO AQUARIAN CLONING IS THE DNA CONTAINED IN THAT SINGULAR SPECIMEN!

THE SACRED FISH.

SINGULAR!

DESTROY IT...

...FOR ME!

AAAARGH!

AAH!

WHAT -- WHAT'S GOING ON? WHAT JUST HAPPENED?

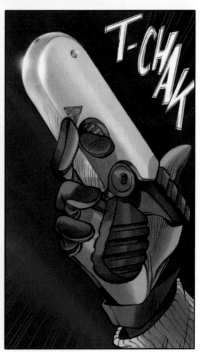

T-CHAK

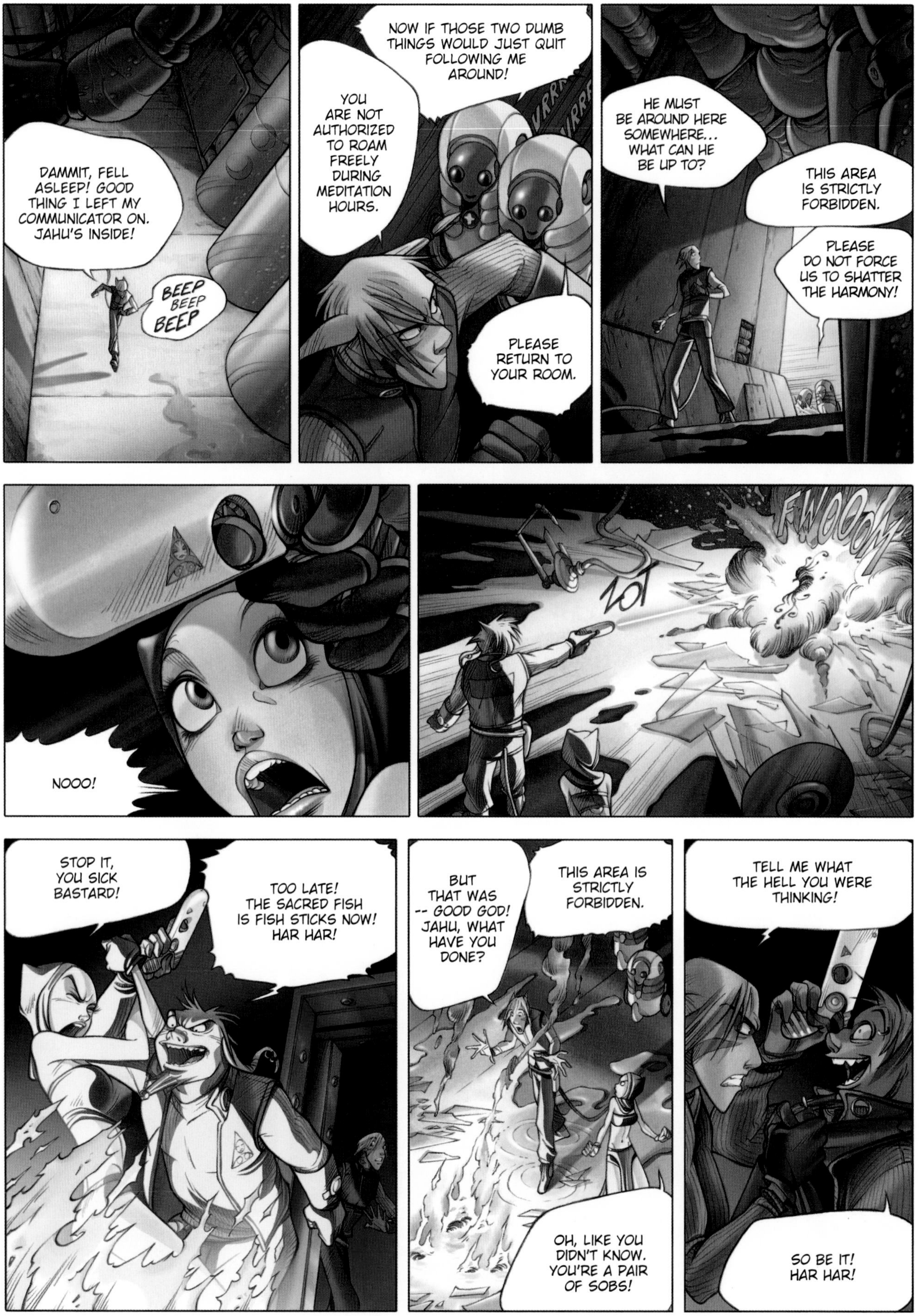
DAMMIT, FELL ASLEEP! GOOD THING I LEFT MY COMMUNICATOR ON. JAHU'S INSIDE!
BEEP BEEP BEEP
NOW IF THOSE TWO DUMB THINGS WOULD JUST QUIT FOLLOWING ME AROUND!
YOU ARE NOT AUTHORIZED TO ROAM FREELY DURING MEDITATION HOURS.
PLEASE RETURN TO YOUR ROOM.
HE MUST BE AROUND HERE SOMEWHERE... WHAT CAN HE BE UP TO?
THIS AREA IS STRICTLY FORBIDDEN.
PLEASE DO NOT FORCE US TO SHATTER THE HARMONY!
NOOO!
ZOT
FWOOOM
STOP IT, YOU SICK BASTARD!
TOO LATE! THE SACRED FISH IS FISH STICKS NOW! HAR HAR!
BUT THAT WAS -- GOOD GOD! JAHU, WHAT HAVE YOU DONE?
THIS AREA IS STRICTLY FORBIDDEN.
OH, LIKE YOU DIDN'T KNOW. YOU'RE A PAIR OF SOBS!
TELL ME WHAT THE HELL YOU WERE THINKING!
SO BE IT! HAR HAR!

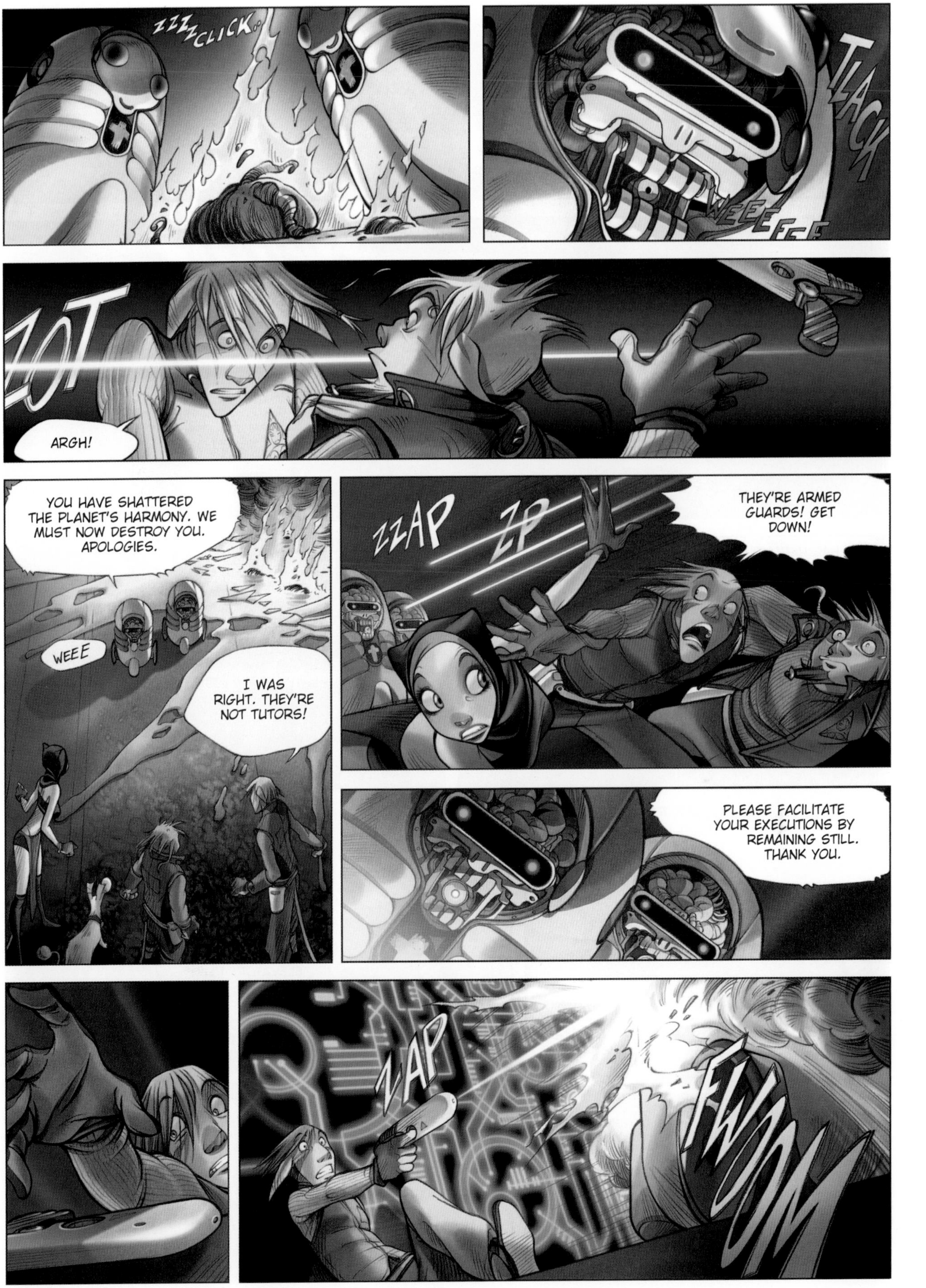
ZZZZCLICK
TLACK
WEEEEEEE
ZOT
ARGH!
YOU HAVE SHATTERED THE PLANET'S HARMONY. WE MUST NOW DESTROY YOU. APOLOGIES.
WEEE
I WAS RIGHT. THEY'RE NOT TUTORS!
ZZAP
ZP
THEY'RE ARMED GUARDS! GET DOWN!
PLEASE FACILITATE YOUR EXECUTIONS BY REMAINING STILL. THANK YOU.
ZAP
FWOOM

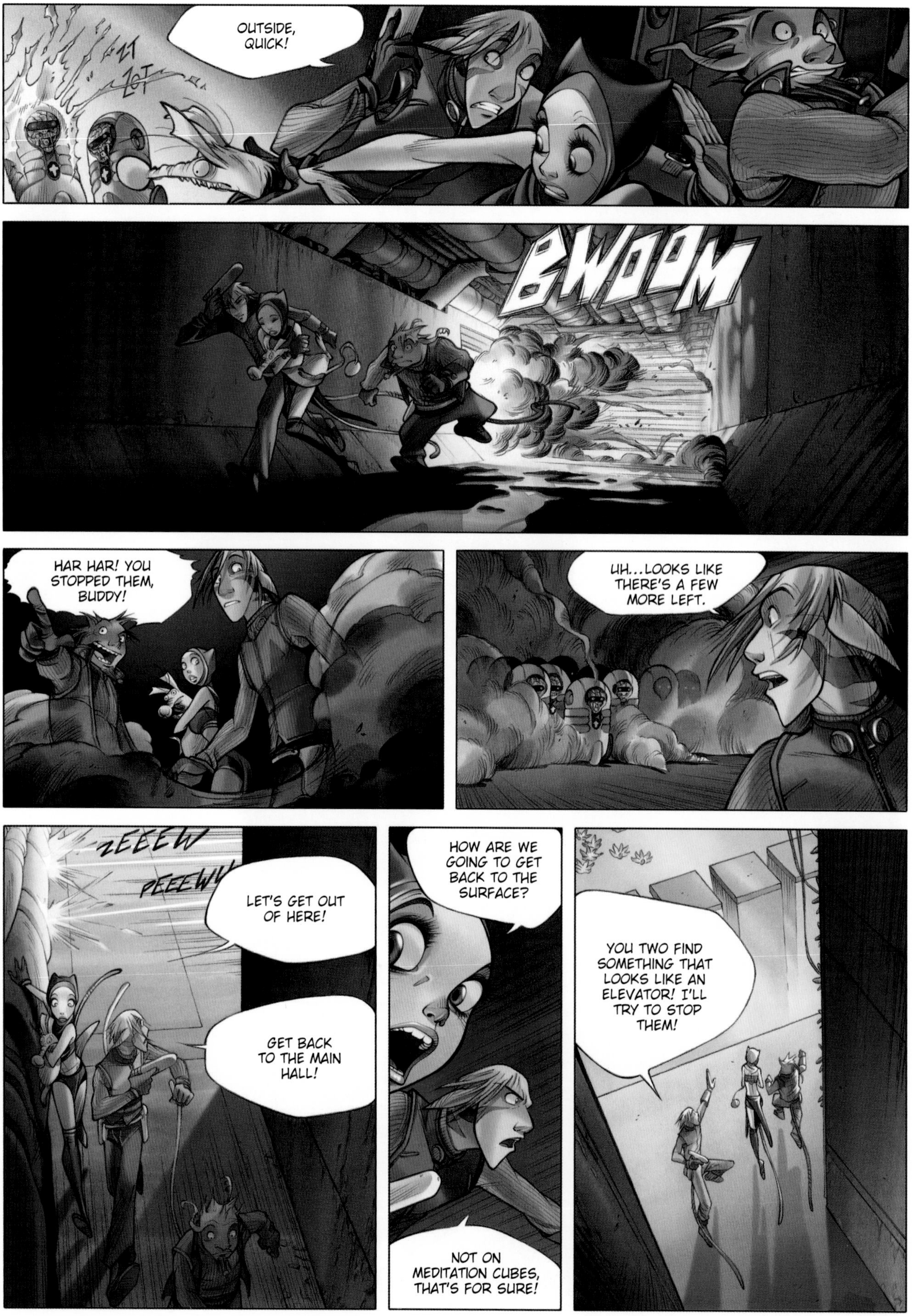
OUTSIDE, QUICK!
ZZT
ZOT
BWOOM
HAR HAR! YOU STOPPED THEM, BUDDY!
UH...LOOKS LIKE THERE'S A FEW MORE LEFT.
ZEEEW
PEEEWU
LET'S GET OUT OF HERE!
GET BACK TO THE MAIN HALL!
HOW ARE WE GOING TO GET BACK TO THE SURFACE?
NOT ON MEDITATION CUBES, THAT'S FOR SURE!
YOU TWO FIND SOMETHING THAT LOOKS LIKE AN ELEVATOR! I'LL TRY TO STOP THEM!

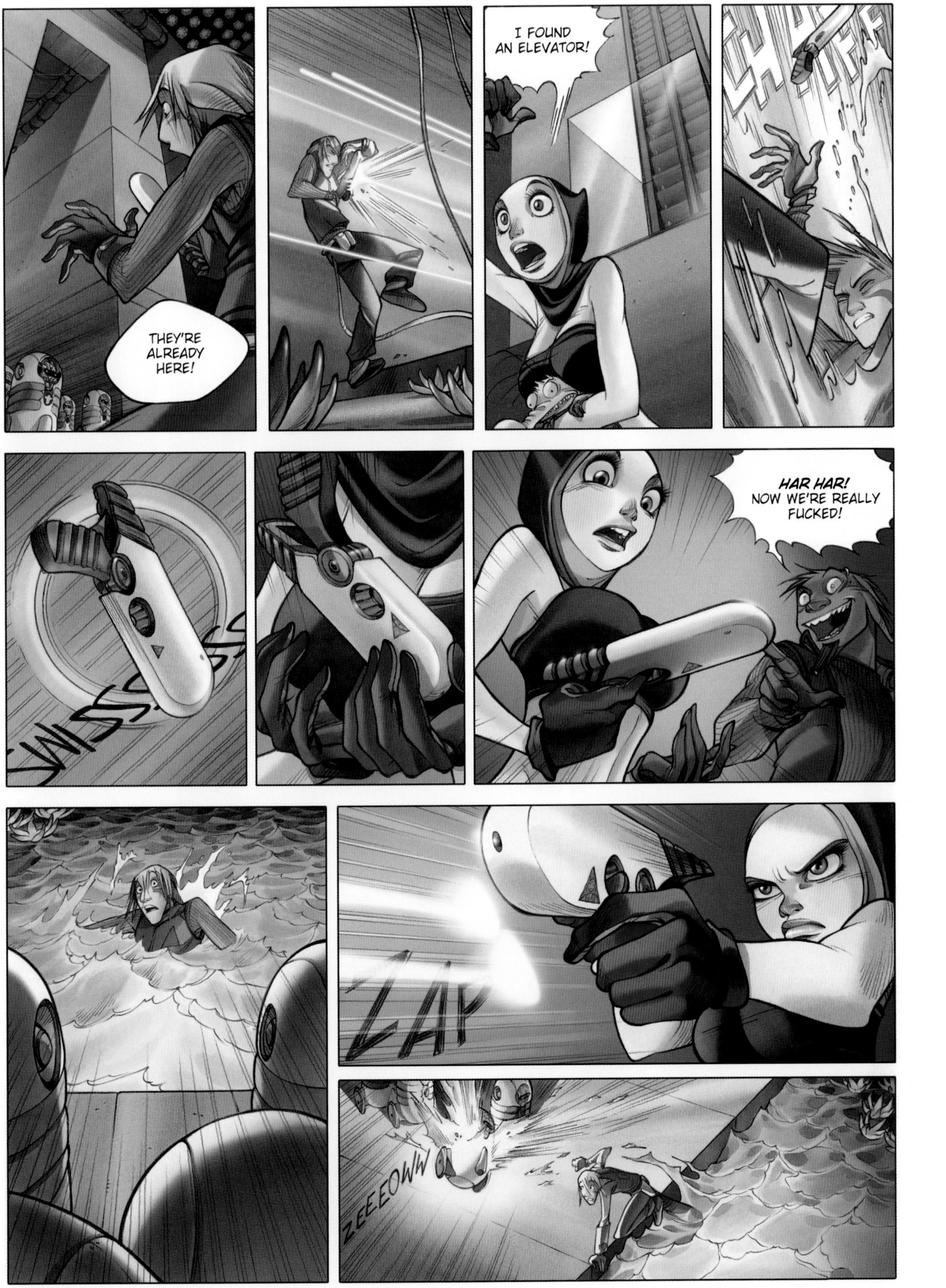
THEY'RE ALREADY HERE!
I FOUND AN ELEVATOR!
HAR HAR! NOW WE'RE REALLY FUCKED!
ZAP
ZEEEOWW

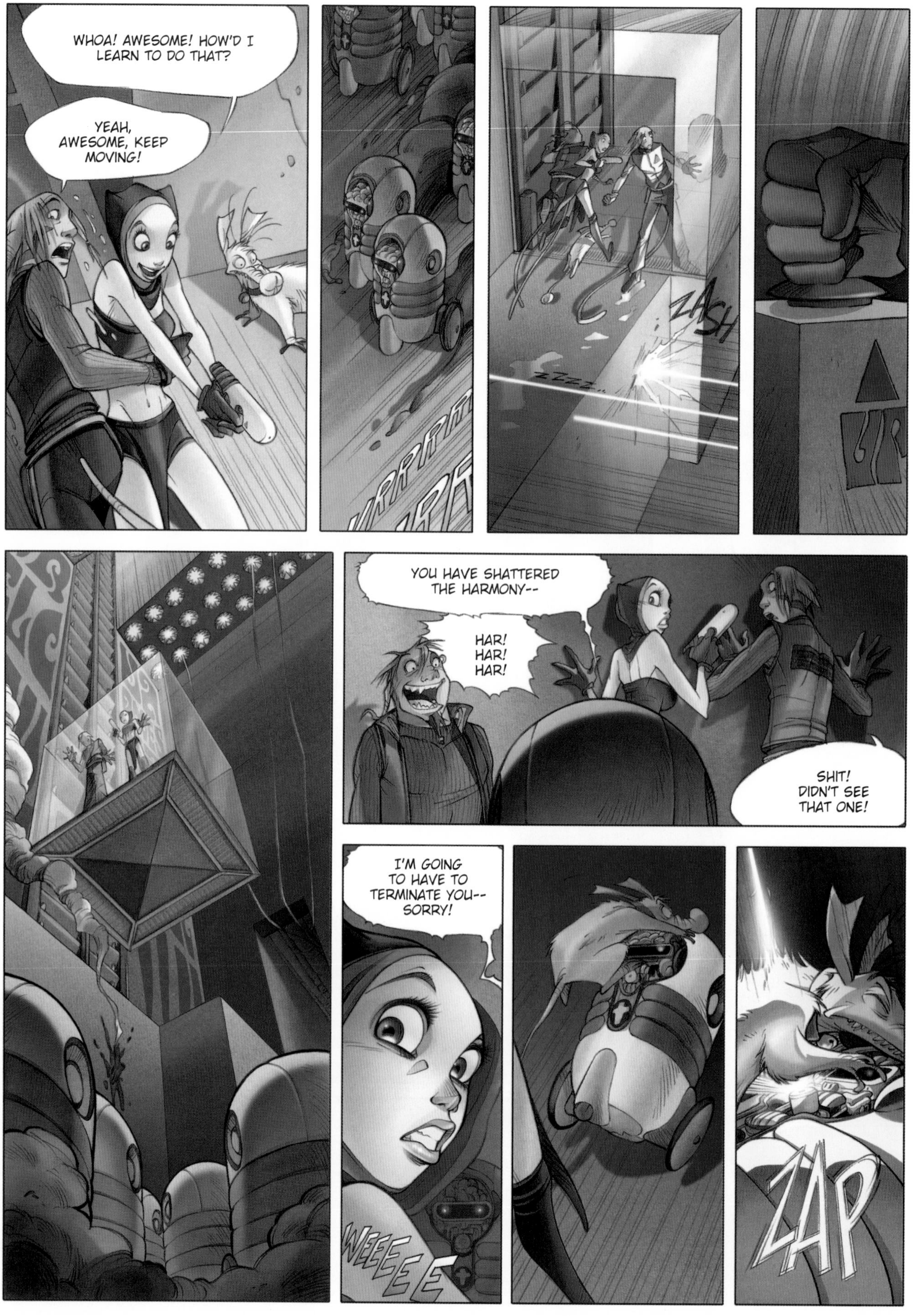

WHOA! AWESOME! HOW'D I LEARN TO DO THAT?
YEAH, AWESOME, KEEP MOVING!
VRRRRR
ZASH
ZZZZ...
YOU HAVE SHATTERED THE HARMONY--
HAR! HAR! HAR!
SHIT! DIDN'T SEE THAT ONE!
I'M GOING TO HAVE TO TERMINATE YOU-- SORRY!
WEEEEE
ZAP

CRASH

HAR! HAR! HAR!

WILL YOU QUIT LAUGHING ALREADY?

I CAN'T BELIEVE THIS! WHAT A FUCKING MESS!

YOU DISGUST ME! YOU'RE A PAIR OF MURDERERS! AND YOU WANTED TO LEAVE ME HERE!

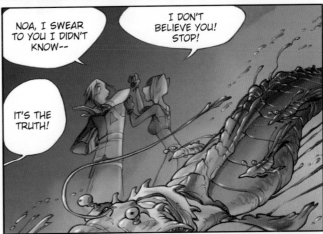

NOA, I SWEAR TO YOU I DIDN'T KNOW--

I DON'T BELIEVE YOU! STOP!

IT'S THE TRUTH!

HE DIDN'T KNOW I WAS SUPPOSED TO LEAVE YOU ON AQUA, OR THAT OUR MISSION WAS ACTUALLY TO SPREAD THE RELIGION OF PAPESSA LUDOVICA.

WE HID THE TRUTH FROM HIM BECAUSE HE WASN'T UP TO IT.

BUT, SUCKER THAT HE WAS, HE MADE FOR GOOD COVER WHILE I DID THE DIRTY WORK: EXTERMINATING THE HERETICS OF AQUA!

WITHOUT THE SACRED FISH, THEY'LL SLOWLY DIE AWAY...BUT ROY DIDN'T KNOW A THING! ALL THESE YEARS, AND HE STILL HAS NO IDEA WHAT THE SIDE HE'S WORKING FOR IS LIKE.

YOU'RE ALL INSANE! INSANE MURDERERS!

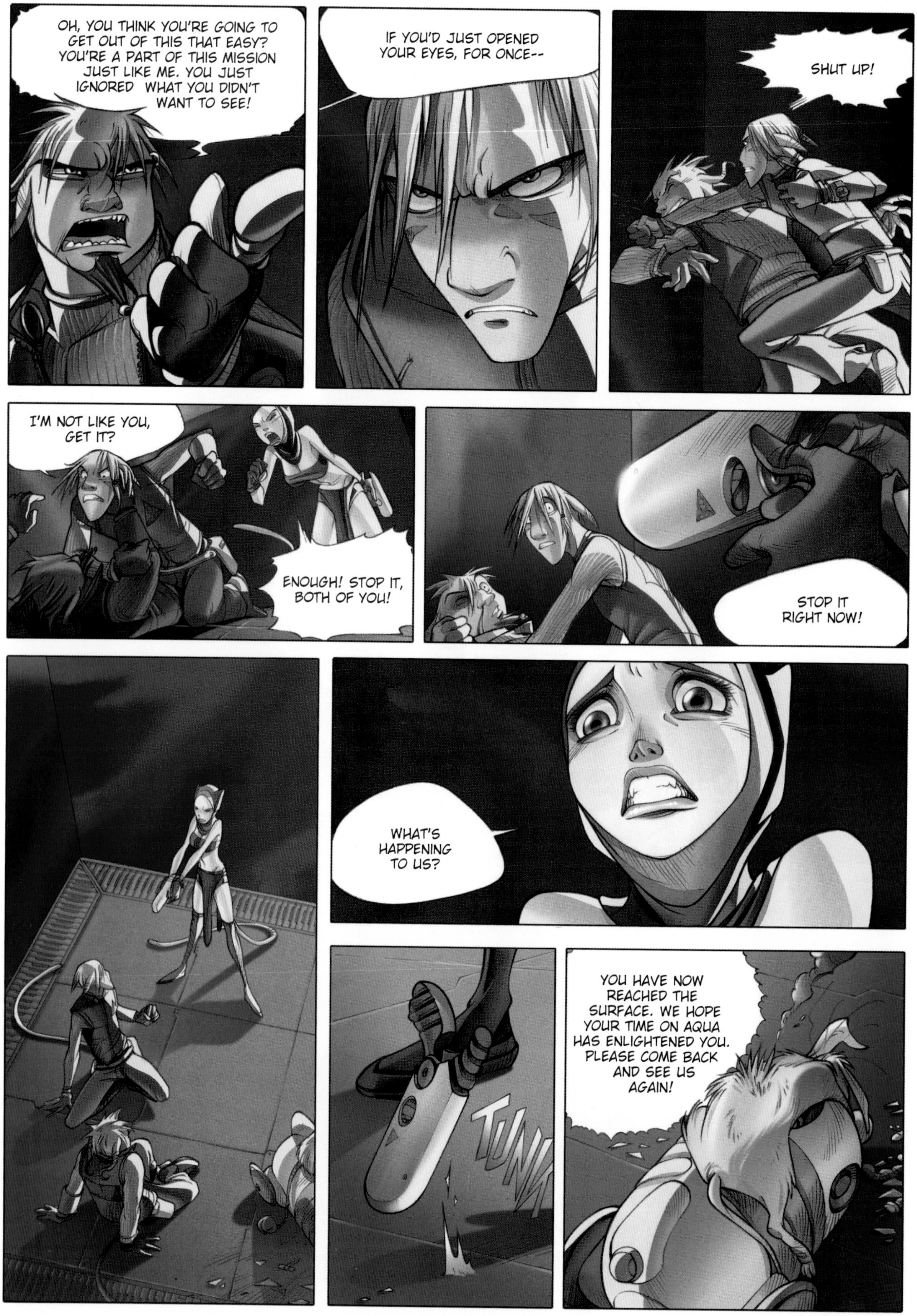
OH, YOU THINK YOU'RE GOING TO GET OUT OF THIS THAT EASY? YOU'RE A PART OF THIS MISSION JUST LIKE ME. YOU JUST IGNORED WHAT YOU DIDN'T WANT TO SEE!
IF YOU'D JUST OPENED YOUR EYES, FOR ONCE--
SHUT UP!
I'M NOT LIKE YOU, GET IT?
ENOUGH! STOP IT, BOTH OF YOU!
STOP IT RIGHT NOW!
WHAT'S HAPPENING TO US?
TUNK
YOU HAVE NOW REACHED THE SURFACE. WE HOPE YOUR TIME ON AQUA HAS ENLIGHTENED YOU. PLEASE COME BACK AND SEE US AGAIN!

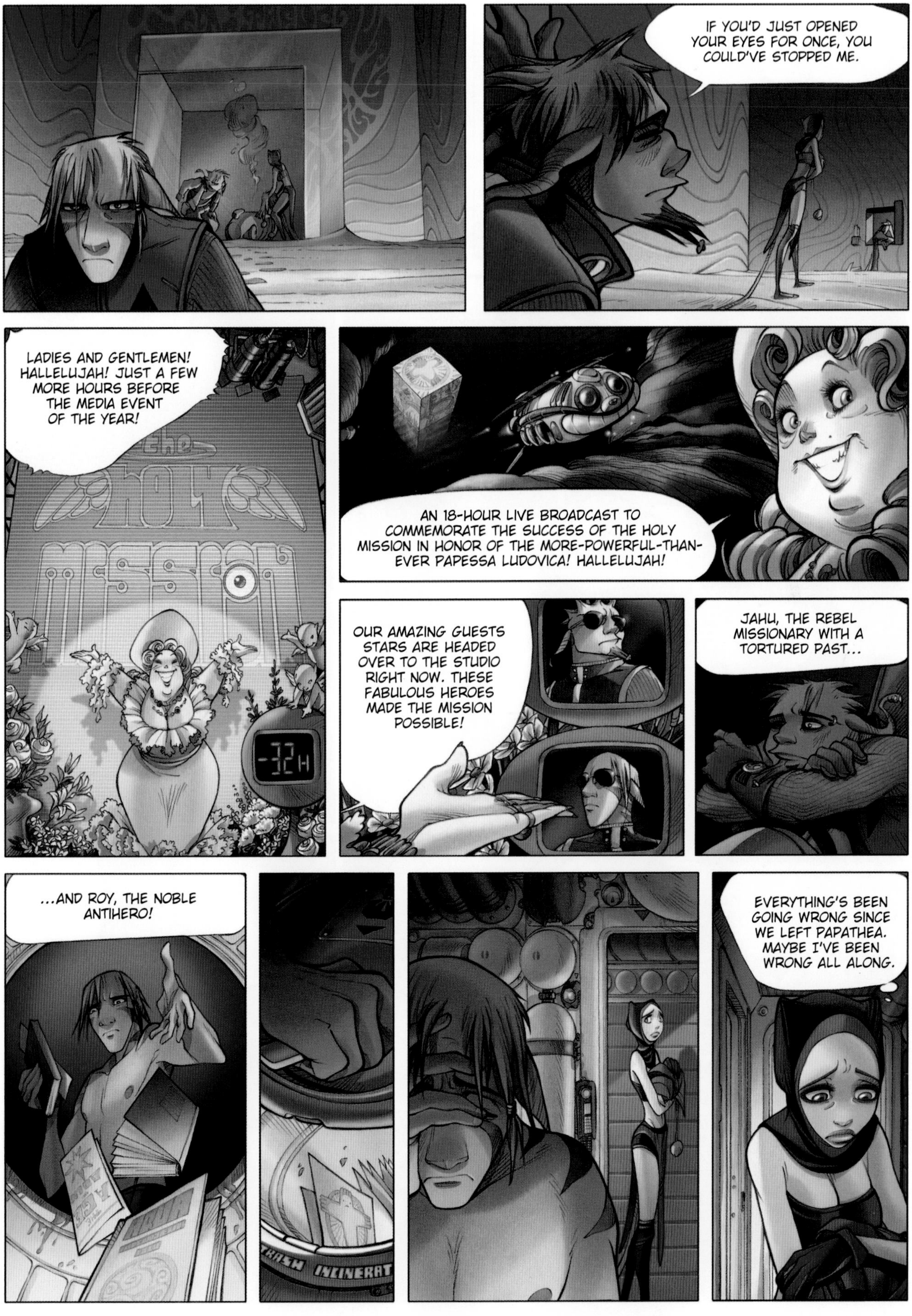
IF YOU'D JUST OPENED YOUR EYES FOR ONCE, YOU COULD'VE STOPPED ME.
LADIES AND GENTLEMEN! HALLELUJAH! JUST A FEW MORE HOURS BEFORE THE MEDIA EVENT OF THE YEAR!
AN 18-HOUR LIVE BROADCAST TO COMMEMORATE THE SUCCESS OF THE HOLY MISSION IN HONOR OF THE MORE-POWERFUL-THAN-EVER PAPESSA LUDOVICA! HALLELUJAH!
-32H
OUR AMAZING GUESTS STARS ARE HEADED OVER TO THE STUDIO RIGHT NOW. THESE FABULOUS HEROES MADE THE MISSION POSSIBLE!
JAHU, THE REBEL MISSIONARY WITH A TORTURED PAST...
...AND ROY, THE NOBLE ANTIHERO!
TRASH INCINERAT
EVERYTHING'S BEEN GOING WRONG SINCE WE LEFT PAPATHEA. MAYBE I'VE BEEN WRONG ALL ALONG.

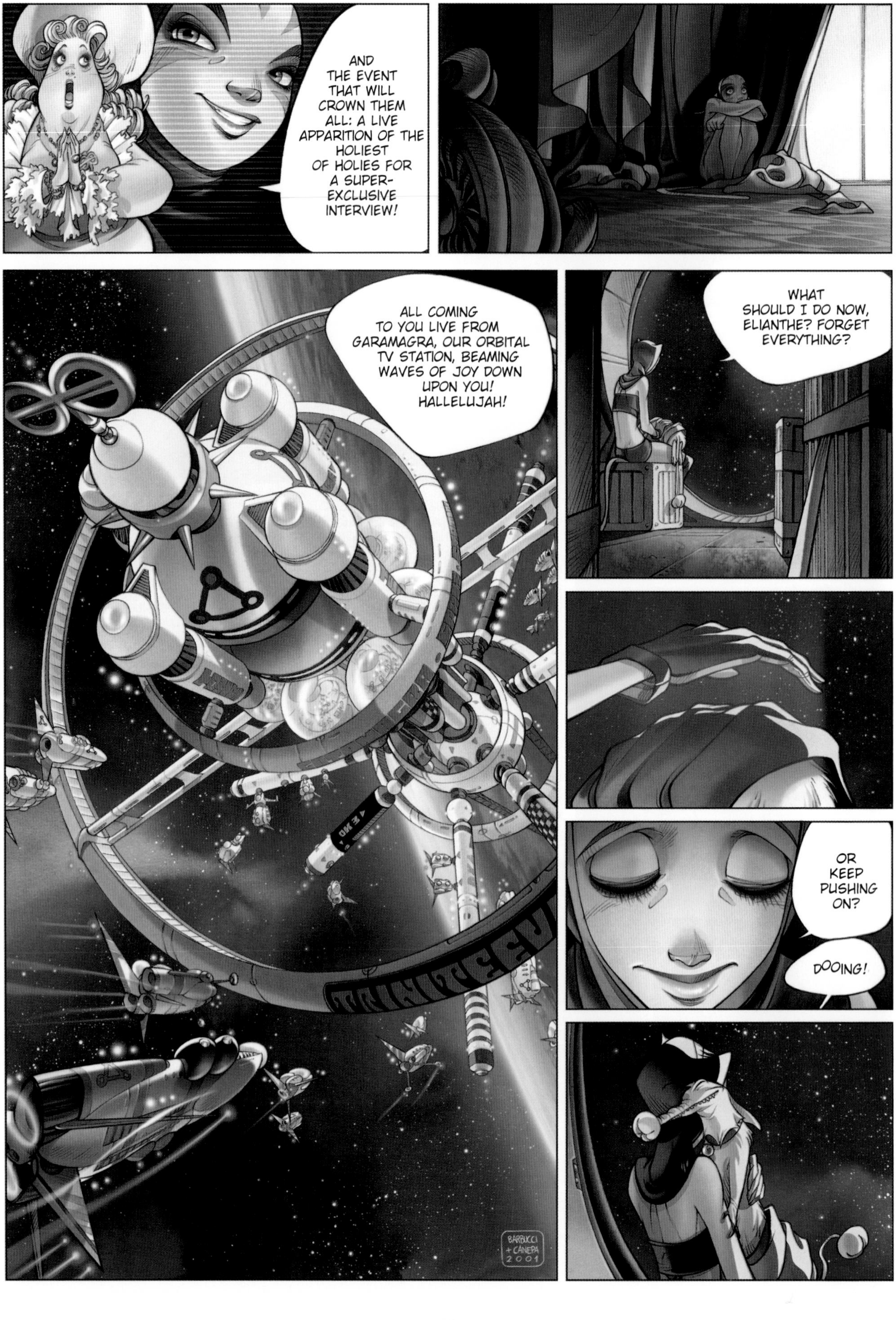
AND THE EVENT THAT WILL CROWN THEM ALL: A LIVE APPARITION OF THE HOLIEST OF HOLIES FOR A SUPER-EXCLUSIVE INTERVIEW!
ALL COMING TO YOU LIVE FROM GARAMAGRA, OUR ORBITAL TV STATION, BEAMING WAVES OF JOY DOWN UPON YOU! HALLELUJAH!
WHAT SHOULD I DO NOW, ELIANTHE? FORGET EVERYTHING?
OR KEEP PUSHING ON?
DOOING!
BARBUCCI + CANEPA 2001

SKYDOLL DECADE 00 > 10

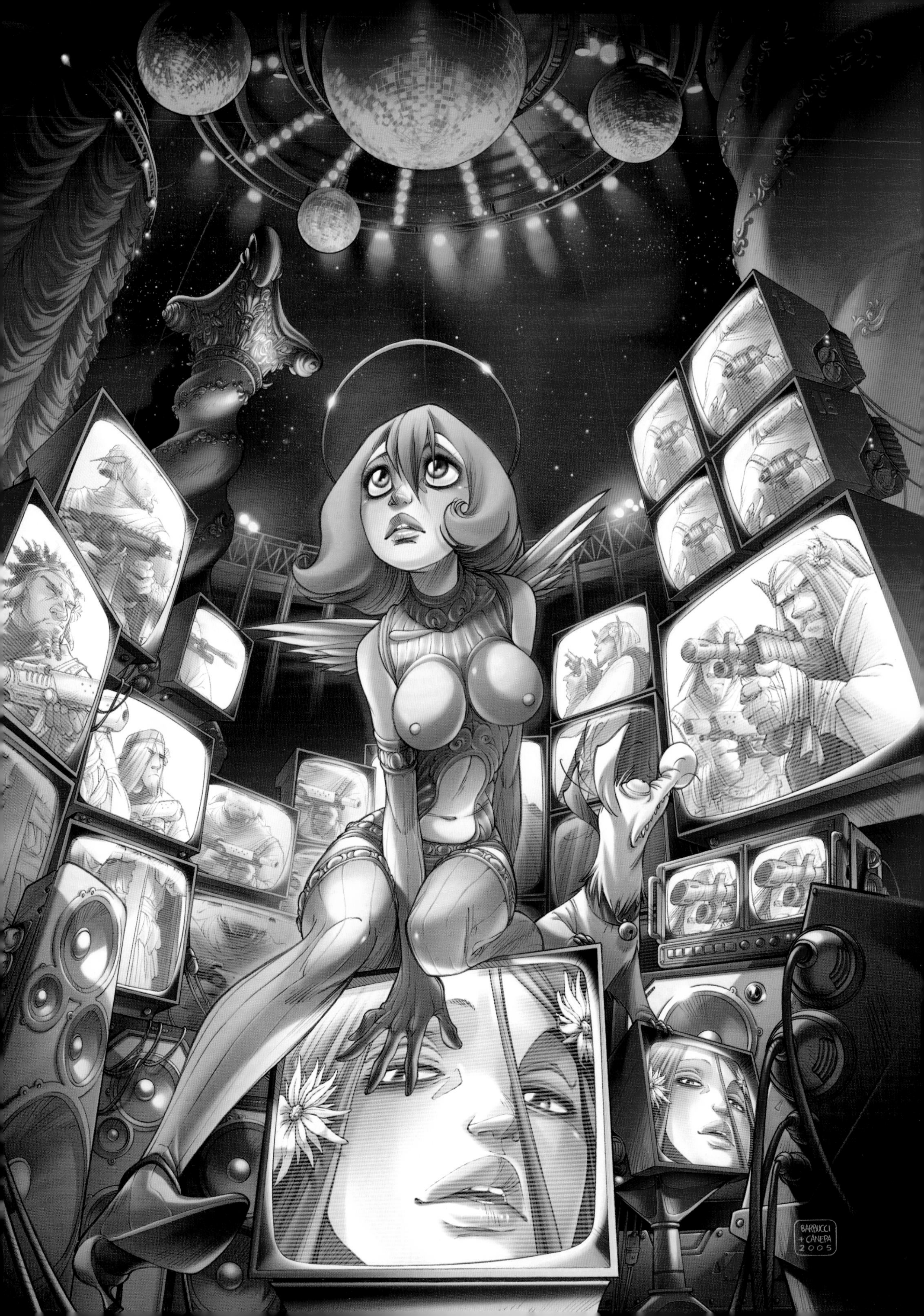
BARBUCCI
+ CANEPA
2005

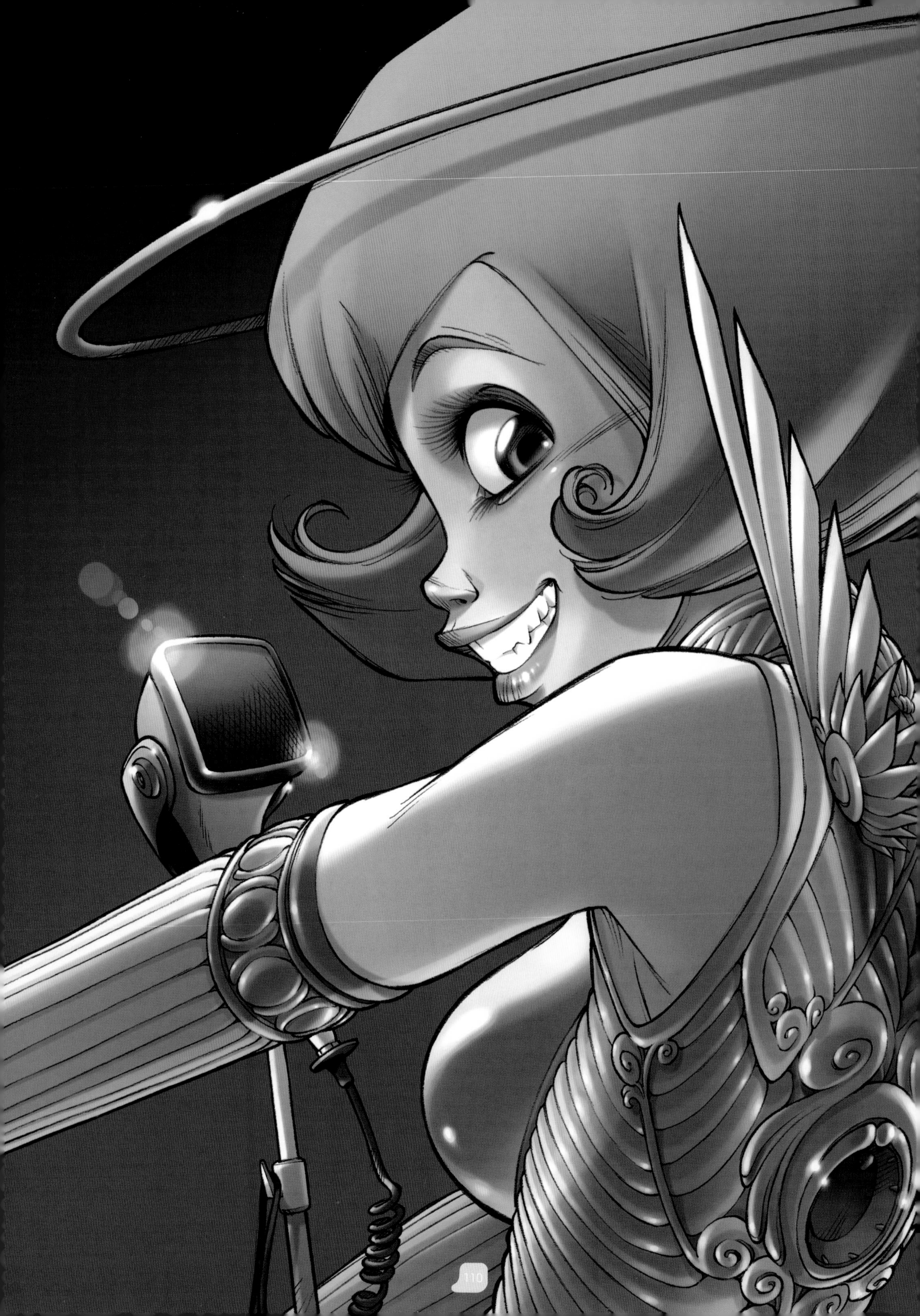

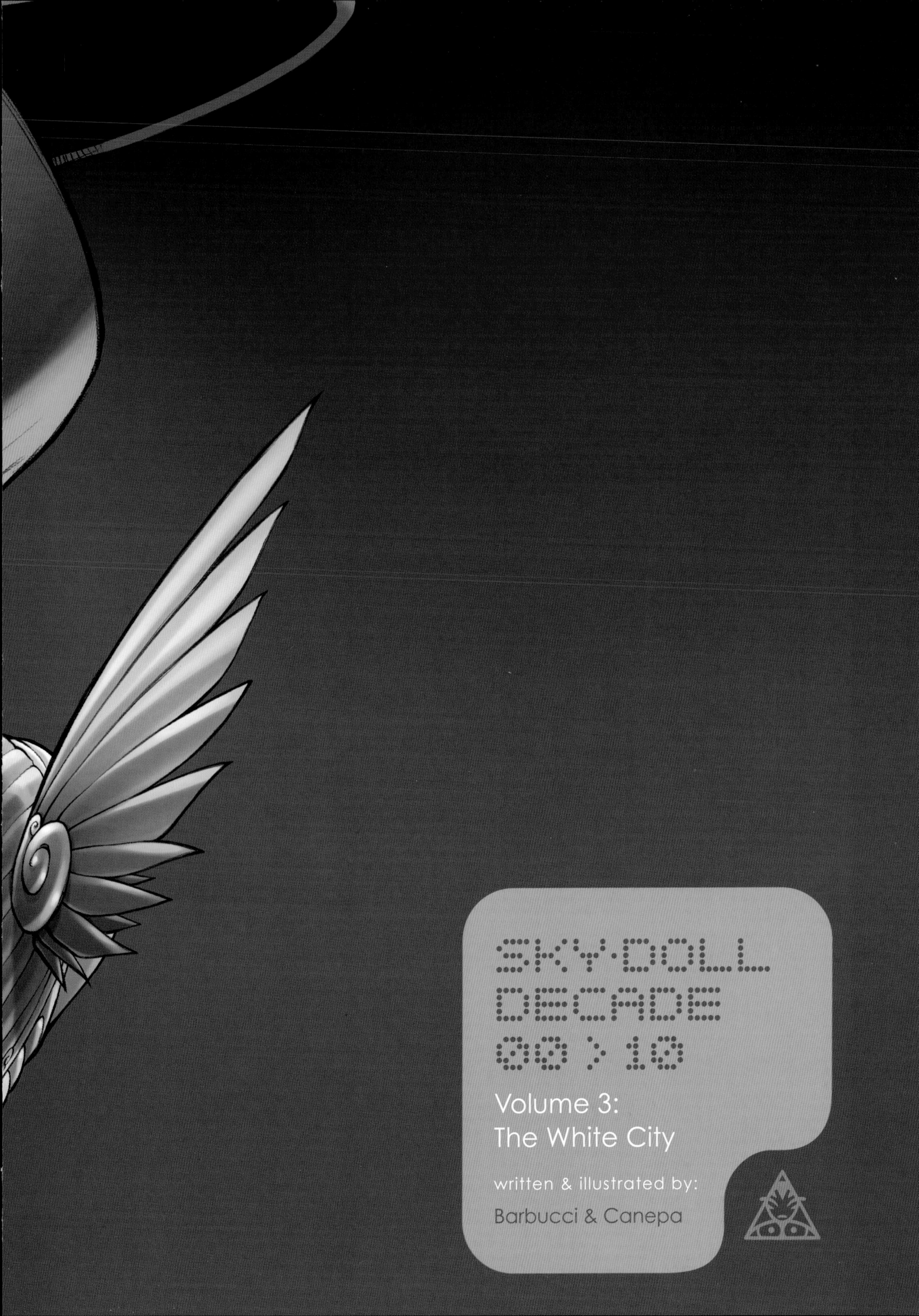

SKY·DOLL DECADE 00 > 10

Volume 3: The White City

written & illustrated by:
Barbucci & Canepa

"I have always had two obsessions: my thirst for justice, and the presumptuous conviction that I could change the world. Today, the latter has vanished."
~ Fabrizio de André

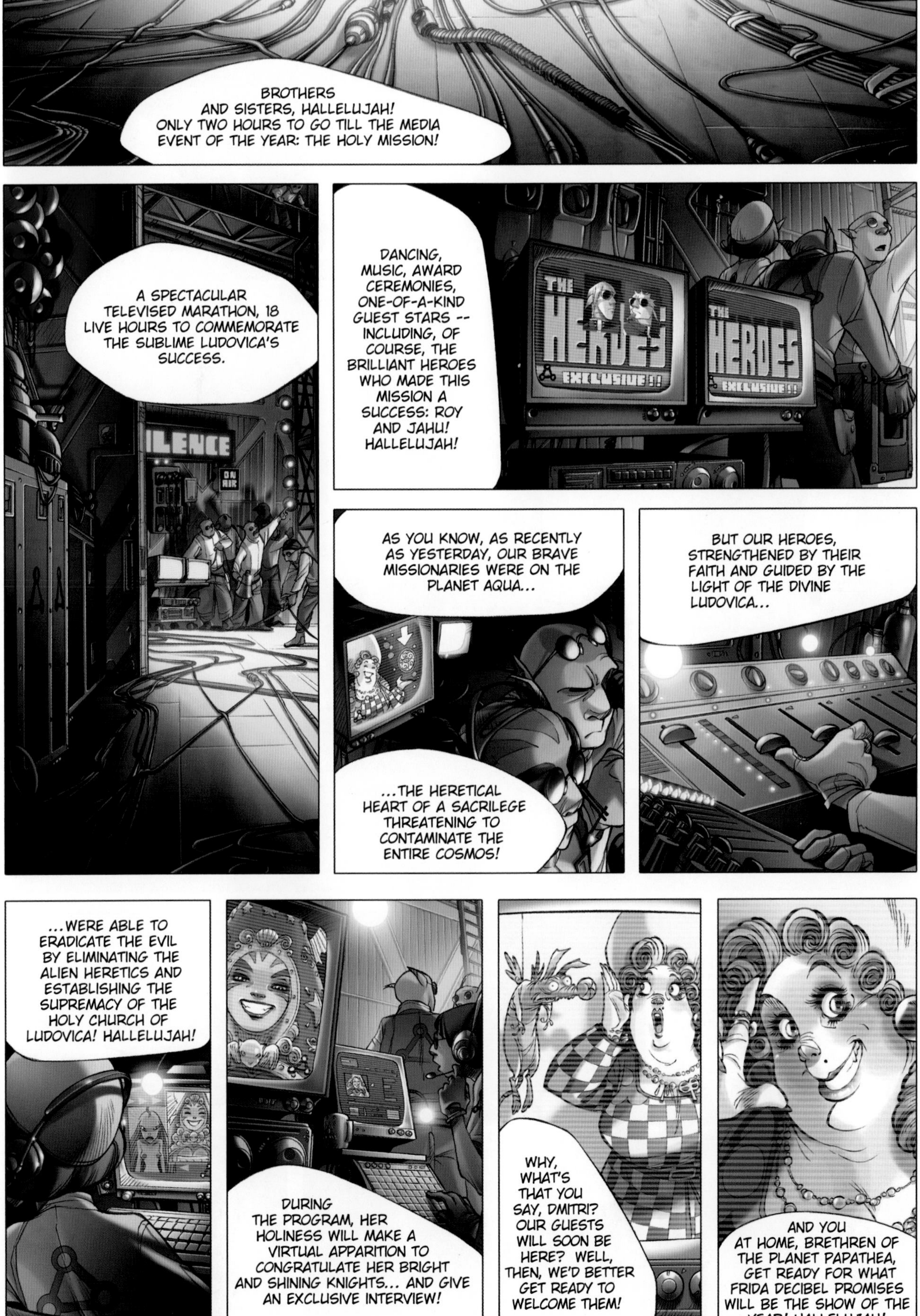
BROTHERS AND SISTERS, HALLELUJAH! ONLY TWO HOURS TO GO TILL THE MEDIA EVENT OF THE YEAR: THE HOLY MISSION!
A SPECTACULAR TELEVISED MARATHON, 18 LIVE HOURS TO COMMEMORATE THE SUBLIME LUDOVICA'S SUCCESS.
ILENCE
ON AIR
DANCING, MUSIC, AWARD CEREMONIES, ONE-OF-A-KIND GUEST STARS -- INCLUDING, OF COURSE, THE BRILLIANT HEROES WHO MADE THIS MISSION A SUCCESS: ROY AND JAHU! HALLELUJAH!
THE HEROES EXCLUSIVE!!
THE HEROES EXCLUSIVE!!
AS YOU KNOW, AS RECENTLY AS YESTERDAY, OUR BRAVE MISSIONARIES WERE ON THE PLANET AQUA...
...THE HERETICAL HEART OF A SACRILEGE THREATENING TO CONTAMINATE THE ENTIRE COSMOS!
BUT OUR HEROES, STRENGTHENED BY THEIR FAITH AND GUIDED BY THE LIGHT OF THE DIVINE LUDOVICA...
...WERE ABLE TO ERADICATE THE EVIL BY ELIMINATING THE ALIEN HERETICS AND ESTABLISHING THE SUPREMACY OF THE HOLY CHURCH OF LUDOVICA! HALLELUJAH!
DURING THE PROGRAM, HER HOLINESS WILL MAKE A VIRTUAL APPARITION TO CONGRATULATE HER BRIGHT AND SHINING KNIGHTS... AND GIVE AN EXCLUSIVE INTERVIEW!
WHY, WHAT'S THAT YOU SAY, DMITRI? OUR GUESTS WILL SOON BE HERE? WELL, THEN, WE'D BETTER GET READY TO WELCOME THEM!
AND YOU AT HOME, BRETHREN OF THE PLANET PAPATHEA, GET READY FOR WHAT FRIDA DECIBEL PROMISES WILL BE THE SHOW OF THE YEAR! HALLELUJAH!

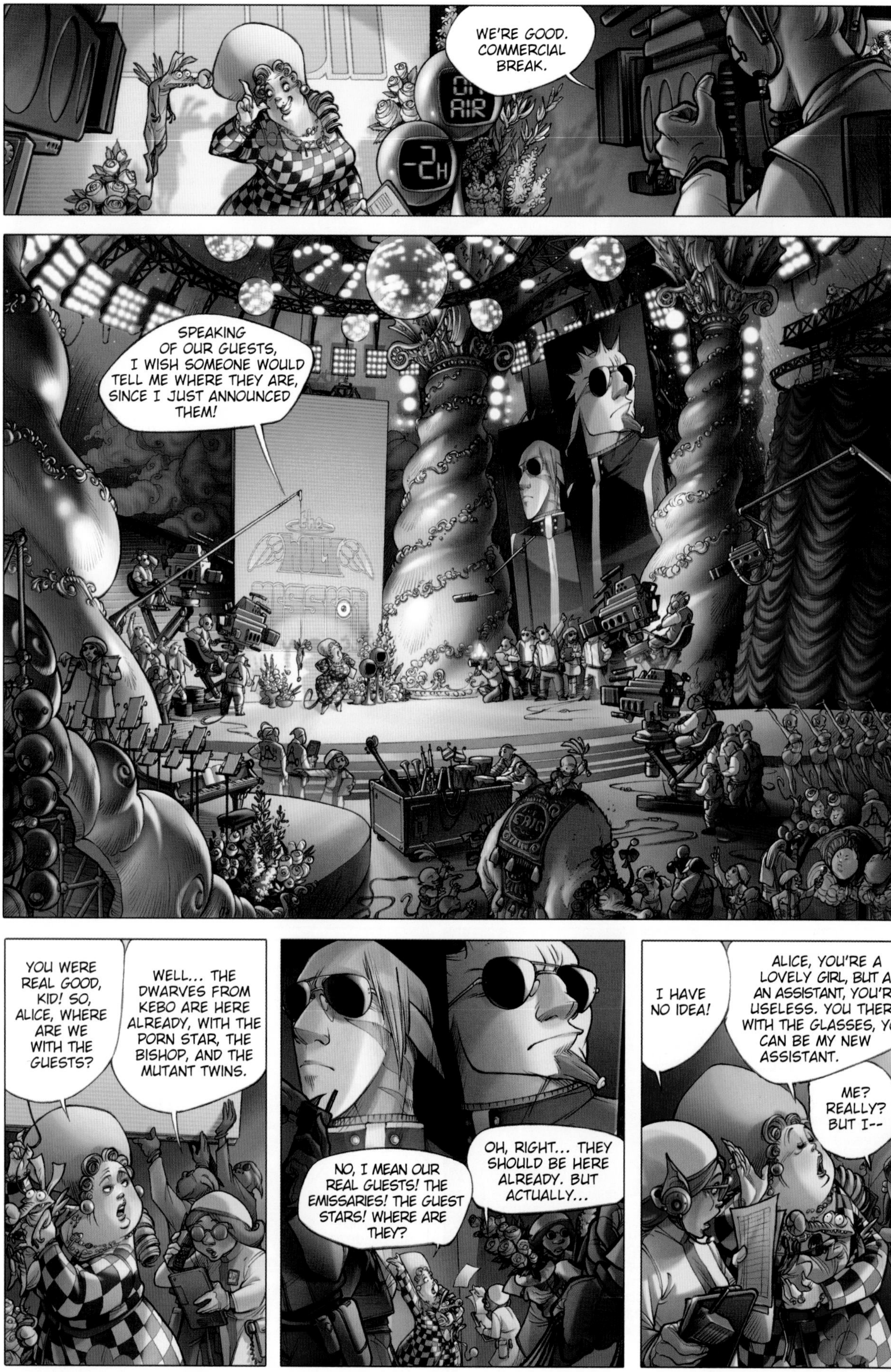
WE'RE GOOD. COMMERCIAL BREAK.
SPEAKING OF OUR GUESTS, I WISH SOMEONE WOULD TELL ME WHERE THEY ARE, SINCE I JUST ANNOUNCED THEM!
YOU WERE REAL GOOD, KID! SO, ALICE, WHERE ARE WE WITH THE GUESTS?
WELL... THE DWARVES FROM KEBO ARE HERE ALREADY, WITH THE PORN STAR, THE BISHOP, AND THE MUTANT TWINS.
NO, I MEAN OUR REAL GUESTS! THE EMISSARIES! THE GUEST STARS! WHERE ARE THEY?
OH, RIGHT... THEY SHOULD BE HERE ALREADY. BUT ACTUALLY...
I HAVE NO IDEA!
ALICE, YOU'RE A LOVELY GIRL, BUT AS AN ASSISTANT, YOU'RE USELESS. YOU THERE, WITH THE GLASSES, YOU CAN BE MY NEW ASSISTANT.
ME? REALLY? BUT I--

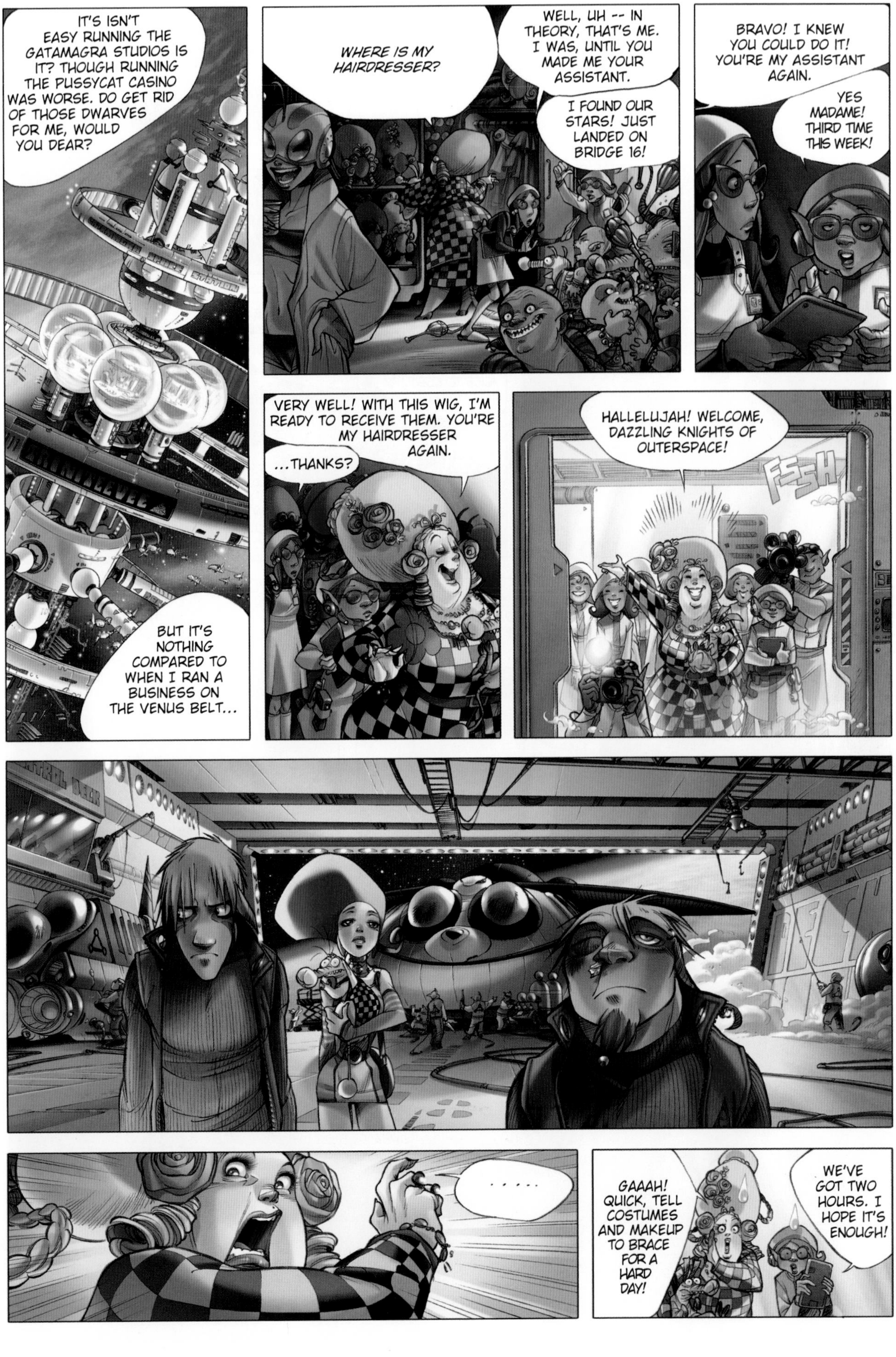
IT'S ISN'T EASY RUNNING THE GATAMAGRA STUDIOS IS IT? THOUGH RUNNING THE PUSSYCAT CASINO WAS WORSE. DO GET RID OF THOSE DWARVES FOR ME, WOULD YOU DEAR?
BUT IT'S NOTHING COMPARED TO WHEN I RAN A BUSINESS ON THE VENUS BELT...
WHERE IS MY HAIRDRESSER?
WELL, UH -- IN THEORY, THAT'S ME. I WAS, UNTIL YOU MADE ME YOUR ASSISTANT.
I FOUND OUR STARS! JUST LANDED ON BRIDGE 16!
BRAVO! I KNEW YOU COULD DO IT! YOU'RE MY ASSISTANT AGAIN.
YES MADAME! THIRD TIME THIS WEEK!
VERY WELL! WITH THIS WIG, I'M READY TO RECEIVE THEM. YOU'RE MY HAIRDRESSER AGAIN.
...THANKS?
HALLELUJAH! WELCOME, DAZZLING KNIGHTS OF OUTERSPACE!
FSSH
. . . . .
GAAAH! QUICK, TELL COSTUMES AND MAKEUP TO BRACE FOR A HARD DAY!
WE'VE GOT TWO HOURS. I HOPE IT'S ENOUGH!

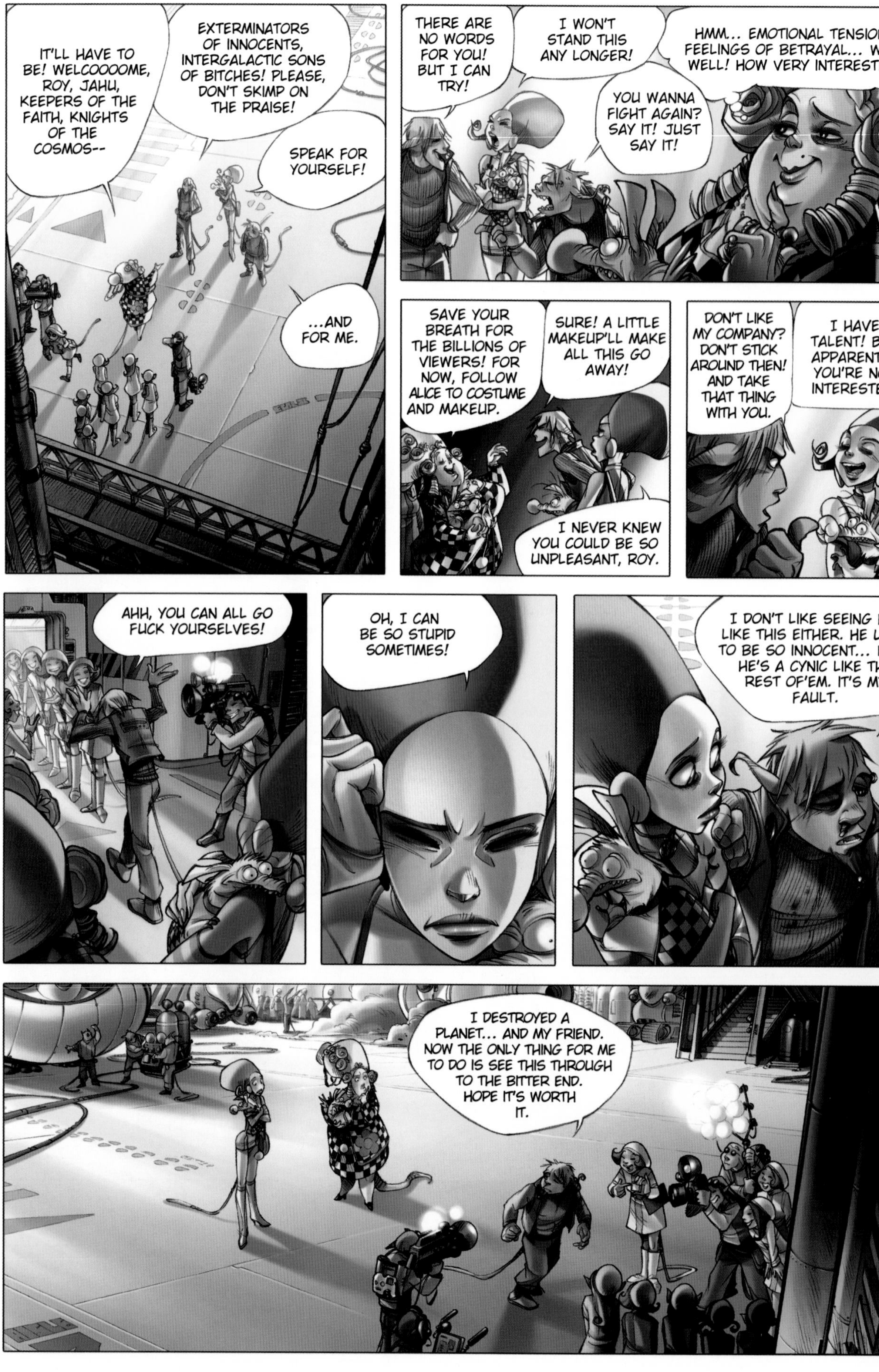
IT'LL HAVE TO BE! WELCOOOOME, ROY, JAHU, KEEPERS OF THE FAITH, KNIGHTS OF THE COSMOS--
EXTERMINATORS OF INNOCENTS, INTERGALACTIC SONS OF BITCHES! PLEASE, DON'T SKIMP ON THE PRAISE!
SPEAK FOR YOURSELF!
...AND FOR ME.
THERE ARE NO WORDS FOR YOU! BUT I CAN TRY!
I WON'T STAND THIS ANY LONGER!
YOU WANNA FIGHT AGAIN? SAY IT! JUST SAY IT!
HMM... EMOTIONAL TENSIONS, FEELINGS OF BETRAYAL... WELL, WELL! HOW VERY INTERESTING!
SAVE YOUR BREATH FOR THE BILLIONS OF VIEWERS! FOR NOW, FOLLOW ALICE TO COSTUME AND MAKEUP.
SURE! A LITTLE MAKEUP'LL MAKE ALL THIS GO AWAY!
I NEVER KNEW YOU COULD BE SO UNPLEASANT, ROY.
DON'T LIKE MY COMPANY? DON'T STICK AROUND THEN! AND TAKE THAT THING WITH YOU.
I HAVE TALENT! BUT APPARENTLY YOU'RE NOT INTERESTED.
AHH, YOU CAN ALL GO FUCK YOURSELVES!
OH, I CAN BE SO STUPID SOMETIMES!
I DON'T LIKE SEEING HIM LIKE THIS EITHER. HE USED TO BE SO INNOCENT... NOW, HE'S A CYNIC LIKE THE REST OF'EM. IT'S MY FAULT.
I DESTROYED A PLANET... AND MY FRIEND. NOW THE ONLY THING FOR ME TO DO IS SEE THIS THROUGH TO THE BITTER END. HOPE IT'S WORTH IT.

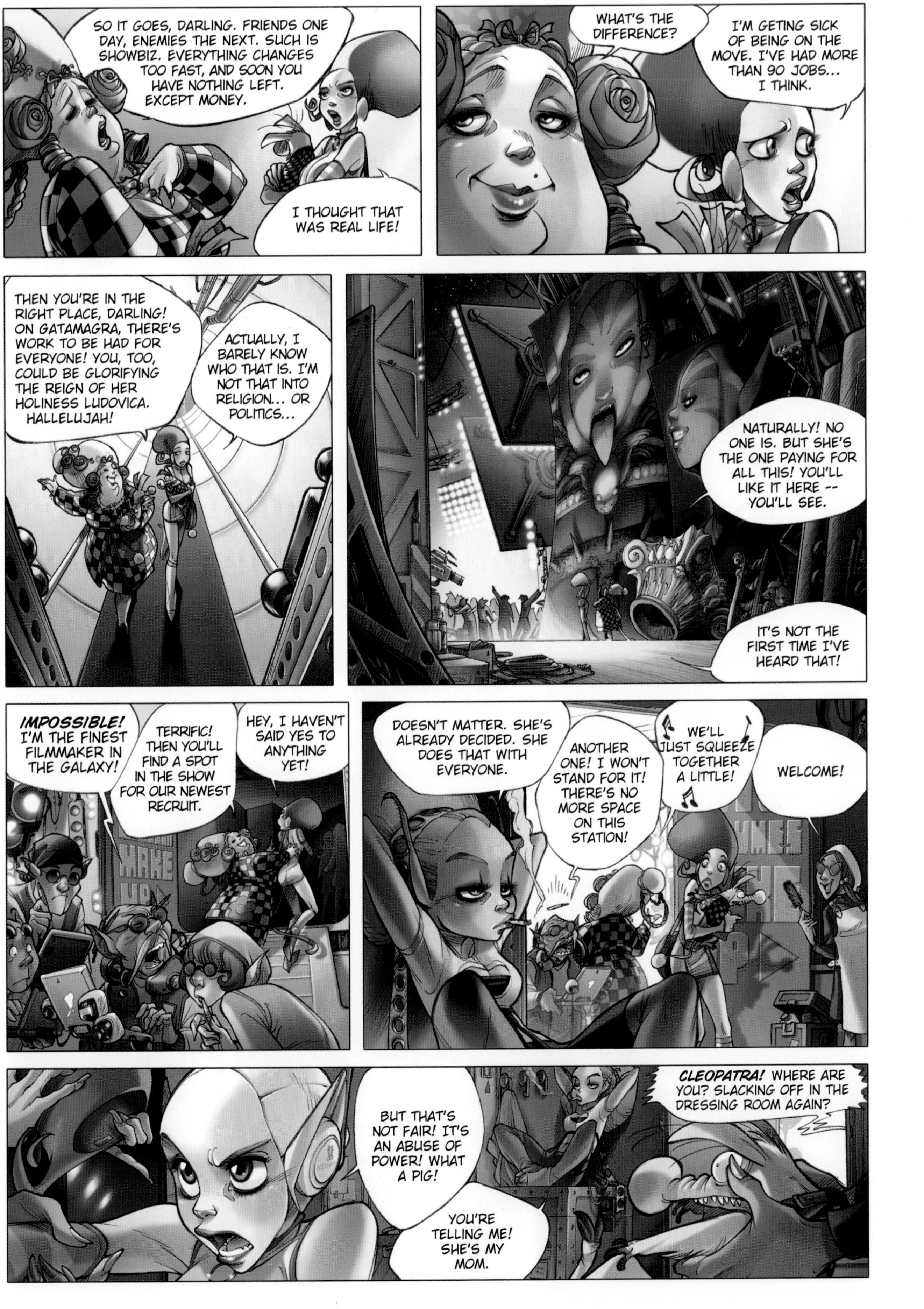

SO IT GOES, DARLING. FRIENDS ONE DAY, ENEMIES THE NEXT. SUCH IS SHOWBIZ. EVERYTHING CHANGES TOO FAST, AND SOON YOU HAVE NOTHING LEFT. EXCEPT MONEY.
I THOUGHT THAT WAS REAL LIFE!
WHAT'S THE DIFFERENCE?
I'M GETING SICK OF BEING ON THE MOVE. I'VE HAD MORE THAN 90 JOBS... I THINK.
THEN YOU'RE IN THE RIGHT PLACE, DARLING! ON GATAMAGRA, THERE'S WORK TO BE HAD FOR EVERYONE! YOU, TOO, COULD BE GLORIFYING THE REIGN OF HER HOLINESS LUDOVICA. HALLELUJAH!
ACTUALLY, I BARELY KNOW WHO THAT IS. I'M NOT THAT INTO RELIGION... OR POLITICS...
NATURALLY! NO ONE IS. BUT SHE'S THE ONE PAYING FOR ALL THIS! YOU'LL LIKE IT HERE -- YOU'LL SEE.
IT'S NOT THE FIRST TIME I'VE HEARD THAT!
IMPOSSIBLE! I'M THE FINEST FILMMAKER IN THE GALAXY!
TERRIFIC! THEN YOU'LL FIND A SPOT IN THE SHOW FOR OUR NEWEST RECRUIT.
HEY, I HAVEN'T SAID YES TO ANYTHING YET!
MAKE UP
DOESN'T MATTER. SHE'S ALREADY DECIDED. SHE DOES THAT WITH EVERYONE.
ANOTHER ONE! I WON'T STAND FOR IT! THERE'S NO MORE SPACE ON THIS STATION!
WE'LL JUST SQUEEZE TOGETHER A LITTLE!
WELCOME!
BUT THAT'S NOT FAIR! IT'S AN ABUSE OF POWER! WHAT A PIG!
YOU'RE TELLING ME! SHE'S MY MOM.
CLEOPATRA! WHERE ARE YOU? SLACKING OFF IN THE DRESSING ROOM AGAIN?

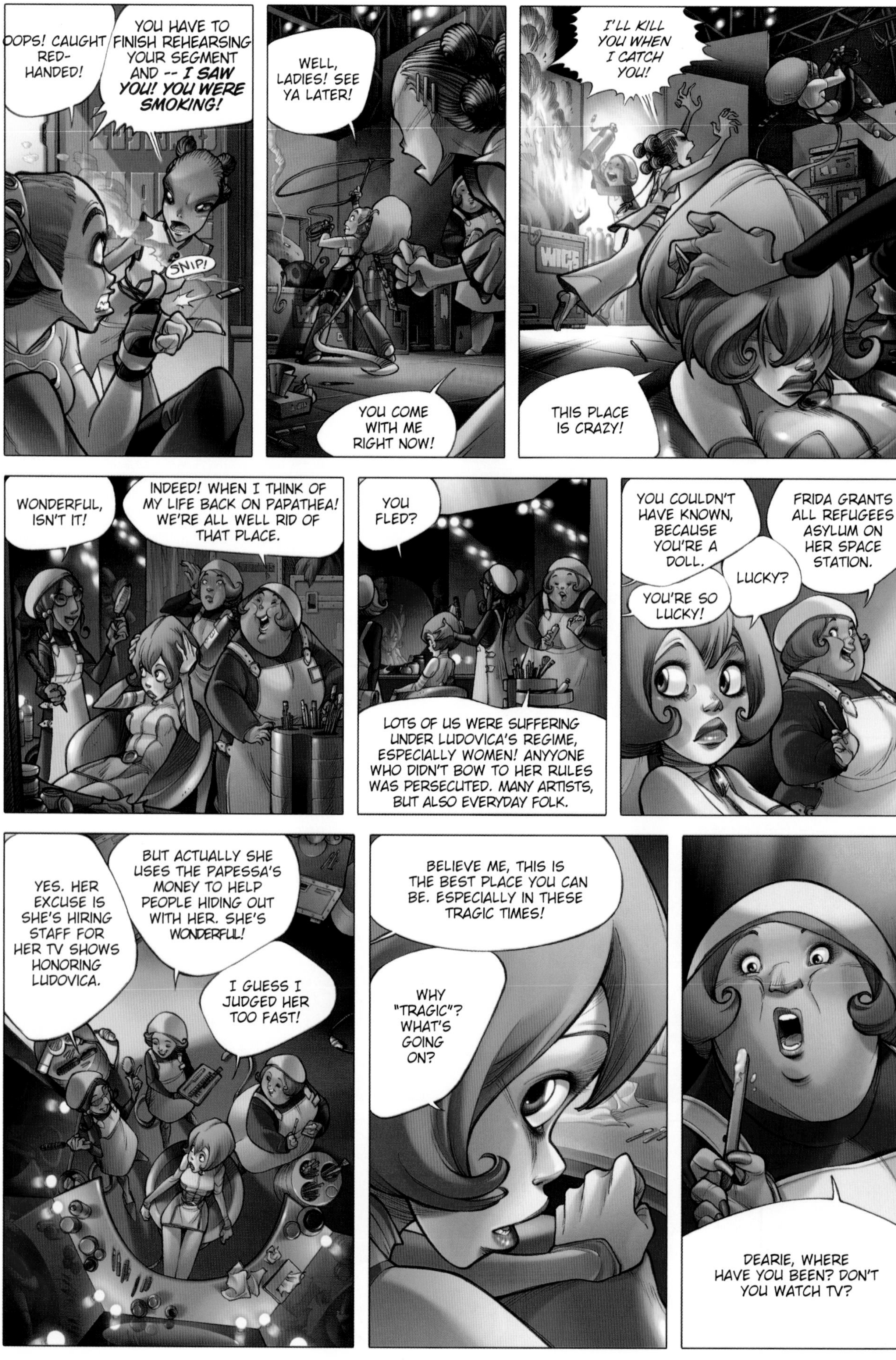
OOPS! CAUGHT RED-HANDED!
YOU HAVE TO FINISH REHEARSING YOUR SEGMENT AND -- I SAW YOU! YOU WERE SMOKING!
SNIP!
WELL, LADIES! SEE YA LATER!
YOU COME WITH ME RIGHT NOW!
I'LL KILL YOU WHEN I CATCH YOU!
WIGS
THIS PLACE IS CRAZY!
WONDERFUL, ISN'T IT!
INDEED! WHEN I THINK OF MY LIFE BACK ON PAPATHEA! WE'RE ALL WELL RID OF THAT PLACE.
YOU FLED?
LOTS OF US WERE SUFFERING UNDER LUDOVICA'S REGIME, ESPECIALLY WOMEN! ANYYONE WHO DIDN'T BOW TO HER RULES WAS PERSECUTED. MANY ARTISTS, BUT ALSO EVERYDAY FOLK.
YOU COULDN'T HAVE KNOWN, BECAUSE YOU'RE A DOLL.
YOU'RE SO LUCKY!
LUCKY?
FRIDA GRANTS ALL REFUGEES ASYLUM ON HER SPACE STATION.
YES. HER EXCUSE IS SHE'S HIRING STAFF FOR HER TV SHOWS HONORING LUDOVICA.
BUT ACTUALLY SHE USES THE PAPESSA'S MONEY TO HELP PEOPLE HIDING OUT WITH HER. SHE'S WONDERFUL!
I GUESS I JUDGED HER TOO FAST!
BELIEVE ME, THIS IS THE BEST PLACE YOU CAN BE. ESPECIALLY IN THESE TRAGIC TIMES!
WHY "TRAGIC"? WHAT'S GOING ON?
DEARIE, WHERE HAVE YOU BEEN? DON'T YOU WATCH TV?

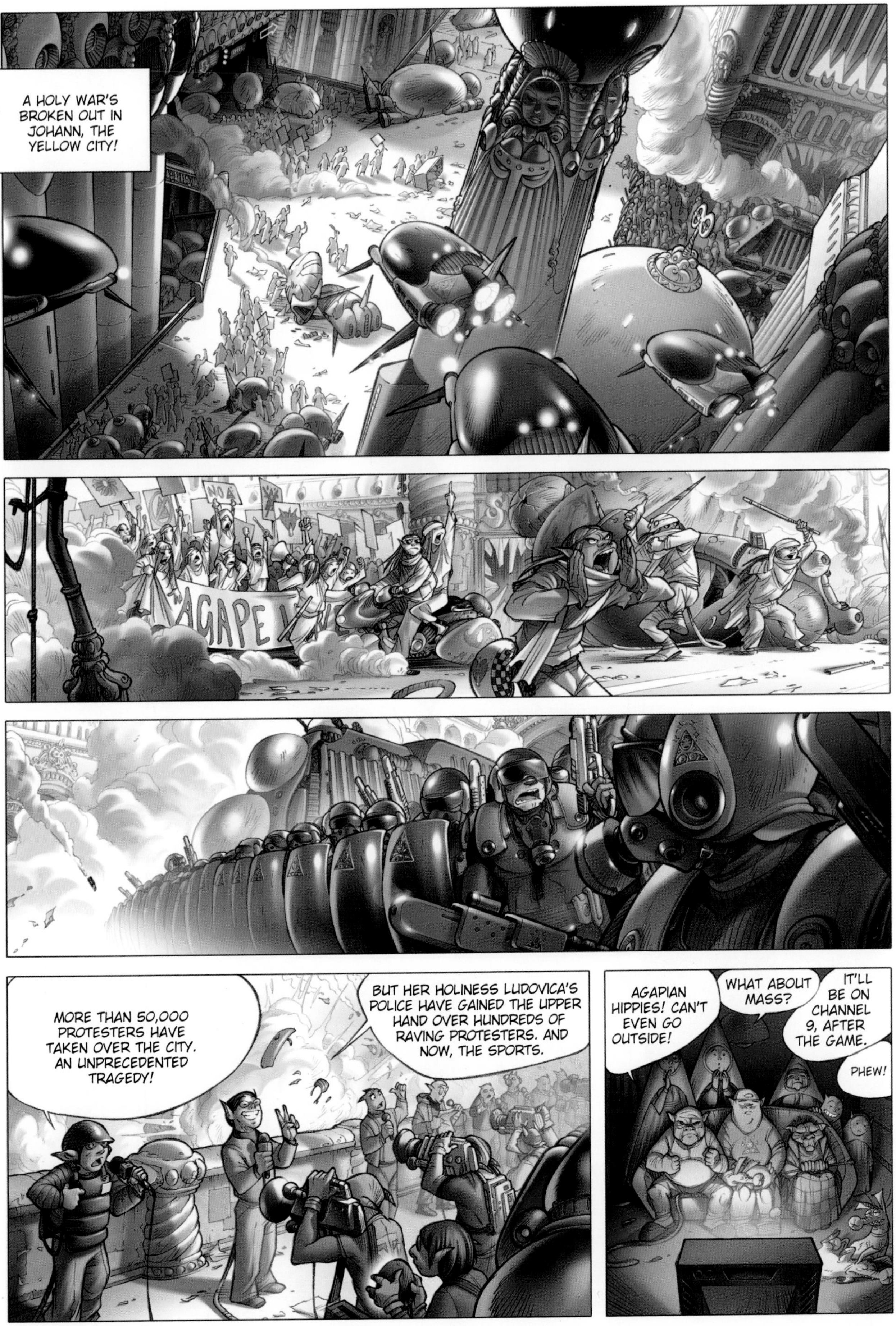
A HOLY WAR'S BROKEN OUT IN JOHANN, THE YELLOW CITY!
AGAPE
MORE THAN 50,000 PROTESTERS HAVE TAKEN OVER THE CITY. AN UNPRECEDENTED TRAGEDY!
BUT HER HOLINESS LUDOVICA'S POLICE HAVE GAINED THE UPPER HAND OVER HUNDREDS OF RAVING PROTESTERS. AND NOW, THE SPORTS.
AGAPIAN HIPPIES! CAN'T EVEN GO OUTSIDE!
WHAT ABOUT MASS?
IT'LL BE ON CHANNEL 9, AFTER THE GAME.
PHEW!

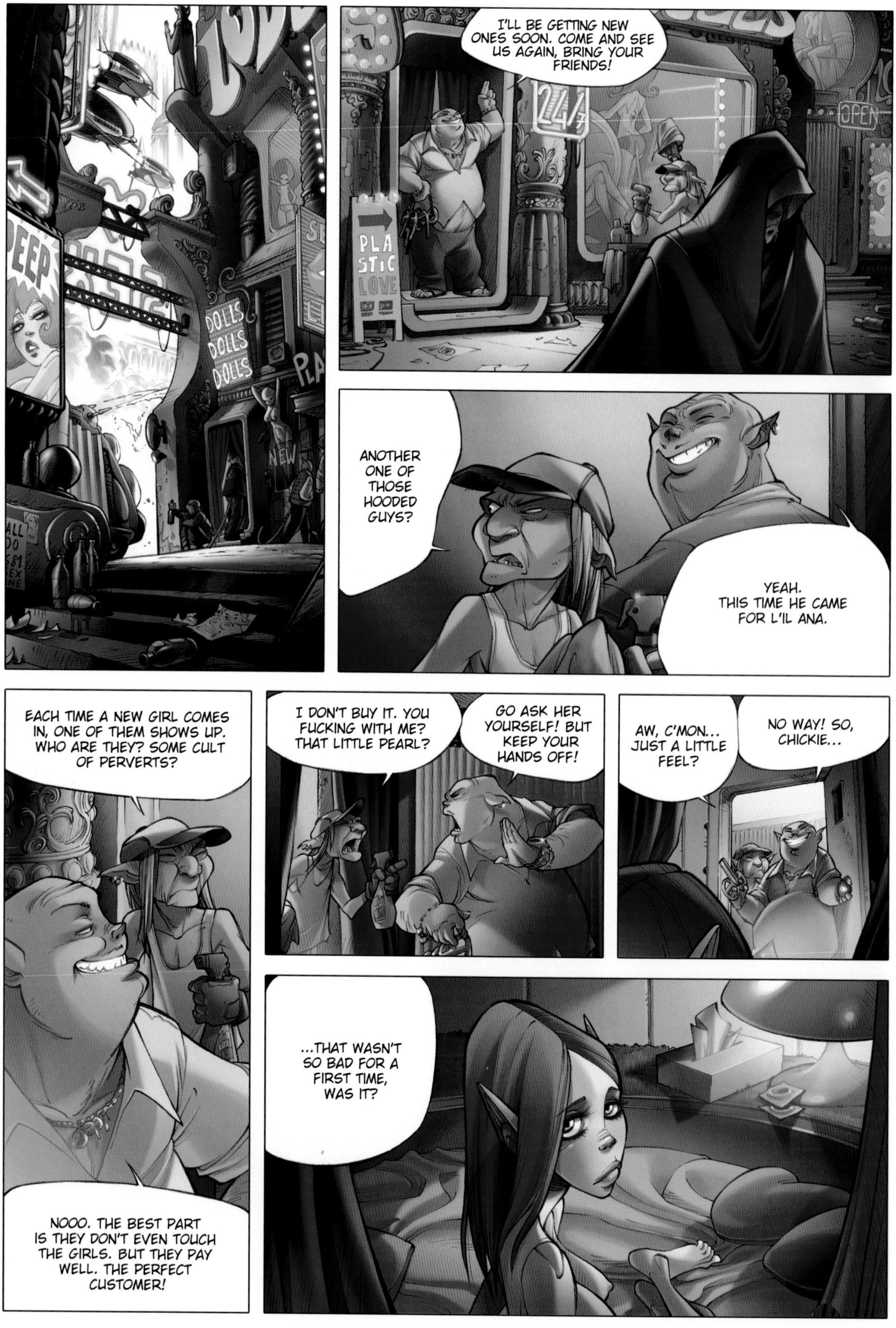

PLA STiC LOVE
DOLLS DOLLS DOLLS
NEW
24/7
OPEN
I'LL BE GETTING NEW ONES SOON. COME AND SEE US AGAIN, BRING YOUR FRIENDS!
ANOTHER ONE OF THOSE HOODED GUYS?
YEAH. THIS TIME HE CAME FOR L'IL ANA.
EACH TIME A NEW GIRL COMES IN, ONE OF THEM SHOWS UP. WHO ARE THEY? SOME CULT OF PERVERTS?
NOOO. THE BEST PART IS THEY DON'T EVEN TOUCH THE GIRLS. BUT THEY PAY WELL. THE PERFECT CUSTOMER!
I DON'T BUY IT. YOU FUCKING WITH ME? THAT LITTLE PEARL?
GO ASK HER YOURSELF! BUT KEEP YOUR HANDS OFF!
AW, C'MON... JUST A LITTLE FEEL?
NO WAY! SO, CHICKIE...
...THAT WASN'T SO BAD FOR A FIRST TIME, WAS IT?

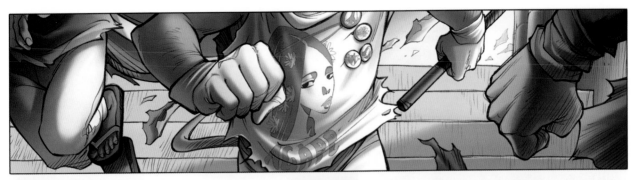

LUDOVICAN PIGS! GO FUCK YOURSELVES! HA HAA!

HEY! YOU LUDOVICAN SCUM! YOU MADE A BIG MISTAKE COMING OUT HERE!

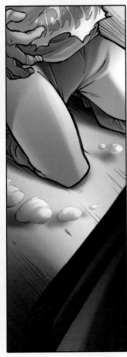

FORGIVE ME, YOUR HOLINESS!

HEY, WHAT'S WRONG? YOU LOOK LIKE YOU JUST SAW A GHOST!

ALMOST! A... SEEKER! AN ARCHBISHOP OF OUR HOLY AGAPE!

OR KEEP A YOU'LL SEE -- WE WON'T MAKE IT OUT OF HERE ALIVE! I CAN FEEL IT. ON?

THEY'RE NOT JUST NOSTALGIC DEMONSTRATORS. SOMETHING BIG IS ABOUT TO HAPPEN.

I CAN FEEL IT RIGHT HERE.

MAYBE IT'S SOMETHING YOU ATE?

DRIVER! YOU IMBECILE! WHY IS THIS TAKING SO LONG! WE SHOULD BE BACK AT THE PALACE ALREADY!

I HAD TO MAKE A DETOUR. PROTESTERS ARE BLOCKING THE MAIN BOULEVARD.

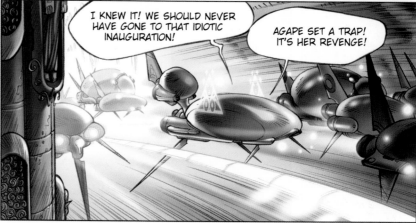

I KNEW IT! WE SHOULD NEVER HAVE GONE TO THAT IDIOTIC INAUGURATION!

AGAPE SET A TRAP! IT'S HER REVENGE!

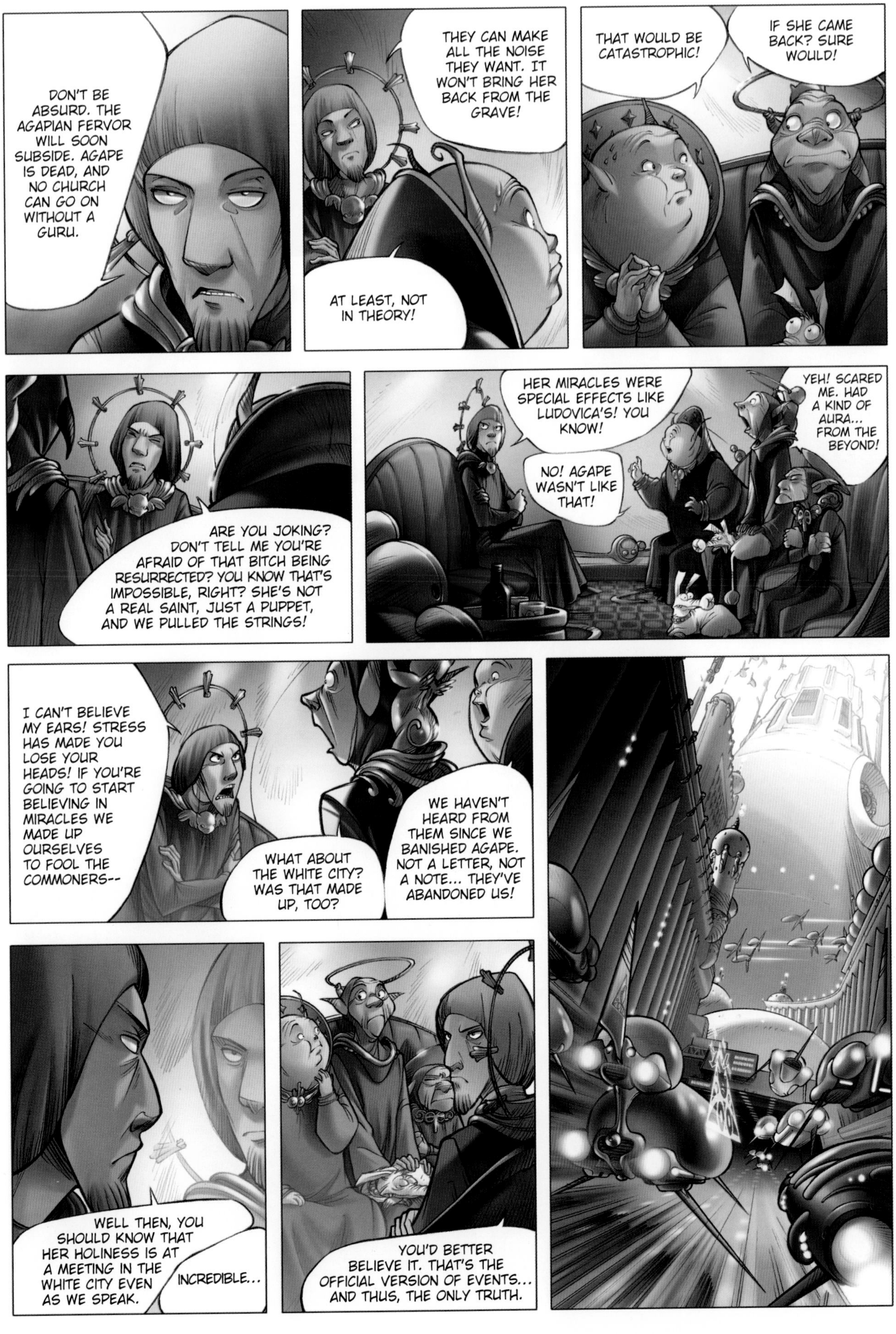
DON'T BE ABSURD. THE AGAPIAN FERVOR WILL SOON SUBSIDE. AGAPE IS DEAD, AND NO CHURCH CAN GO ON WITHOUT A GURU.
THEY CAN MAKE ALL THE NOISE THEY WANT. IT WON'T BRING HER BACK FROM THE GRAVE!
AT LEAST, NOT IN THEORY!
THAT WOULD BE CATASTROPHIC!
IF SHE CAME BACK? SURE WOULD!
ARE YOU JOKING? DON'T TELL ME YOU'RE AFRAID OF THAT BITCH BEING RESURRECTED? YOU KNOW THAT'S IMPOSSIBLE, RIGHT? SHE'S NOT A REAL SAINT, JUST A PUPPET, AND WE PULLED THE STRINGS!
HER MIRACLES WERE SPECIAL EFFECTS LIKE LUDOVICA'S! YOU KNOW!
NO! AGAPE WASN'T LIKE THAT!
YEH! SCARED ME. HAD A KIND OF AURA... FROM THE BEYOND!
I CAN'T BELIEVE MY EARS! STRESS HAS MADE YOU LOSE YOUR HEADS! IF YOU'RE GOING TO START BELIEVING IN MIRACLES WE MADE UP OURSELVES TO FOOL THE COMMONERS--
WHAT ABOUT THE WHITE CITY? WAS THAT MADE UP, TOO?
WE HAVEN'T HEARD FROM THEM SINCE WE BANISHED AGAPE. NOT A LETTER, NOT A NOTE... THEY'VE ABANDONED US!
WELL THEN, YOU SHOULD KNOW THAT HER HOLINESS IS AT A MEETING IN THE WHITE CITY EVEN AS WE SPEAK.
INCREDIBLE...
YOU'D BETTER BELIEVE IT. THAT'S THE OFFICIAL VERSION OF EVENTS... AND THUS, THE ONLY TRUTH.

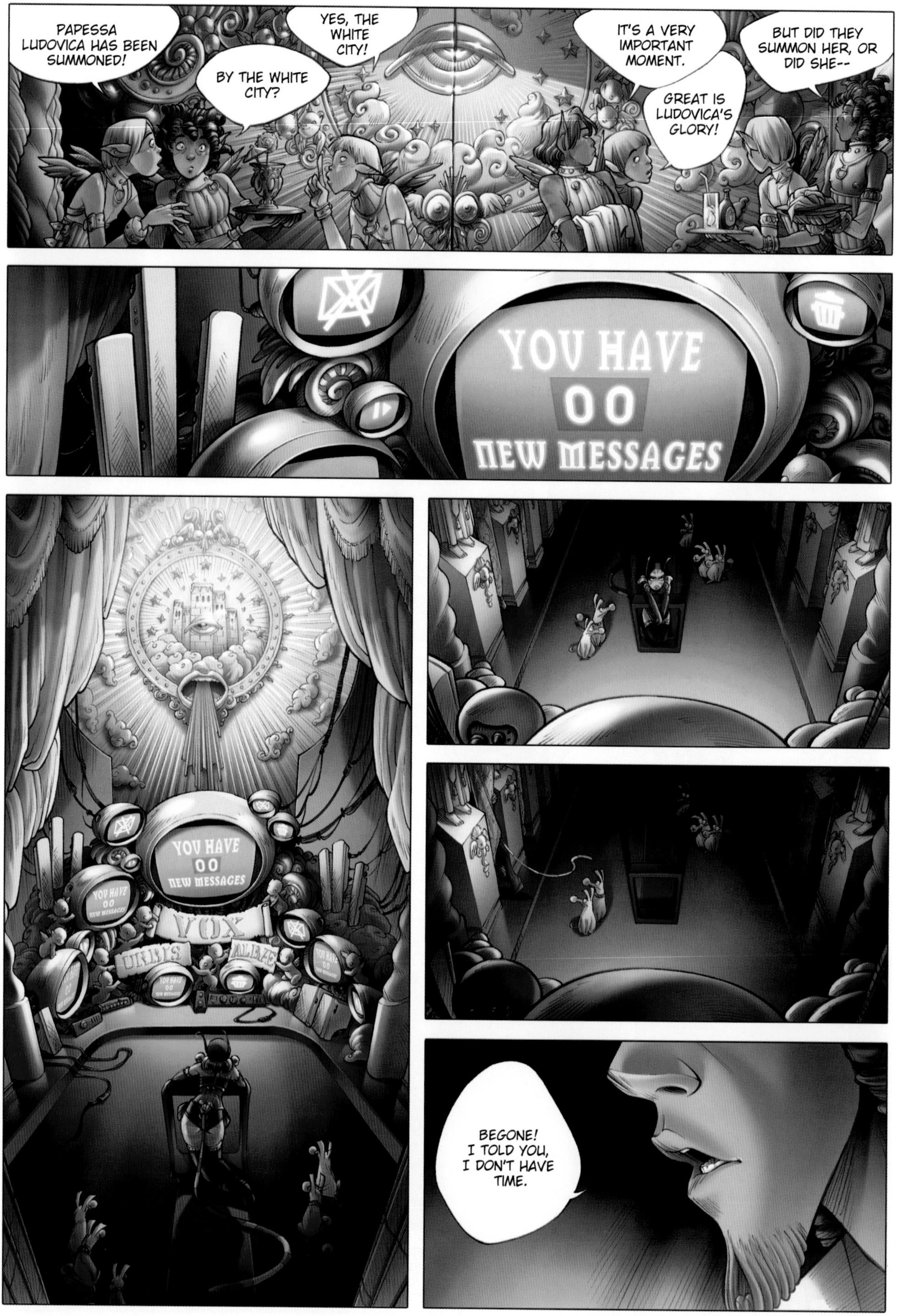
PAPESSA LUDOVICA HAS BEEN SUMMONED!
BY THE WHITE CITY?
YES, THE WHITE CITY!
IT'S A VERY IMPORTANT MOMENT.
GREAT IS LUDOVICA'S GLORY!
BUT DID THEY SUMMON HER, OR DID SHE--
YOU HAVE
00
NEW MESSAGES
YOU HAVE
00
NEW MESSAGES
VOX
URBIS
BEGONE! I TOLD YOU, I DON'T HAVE TIME.

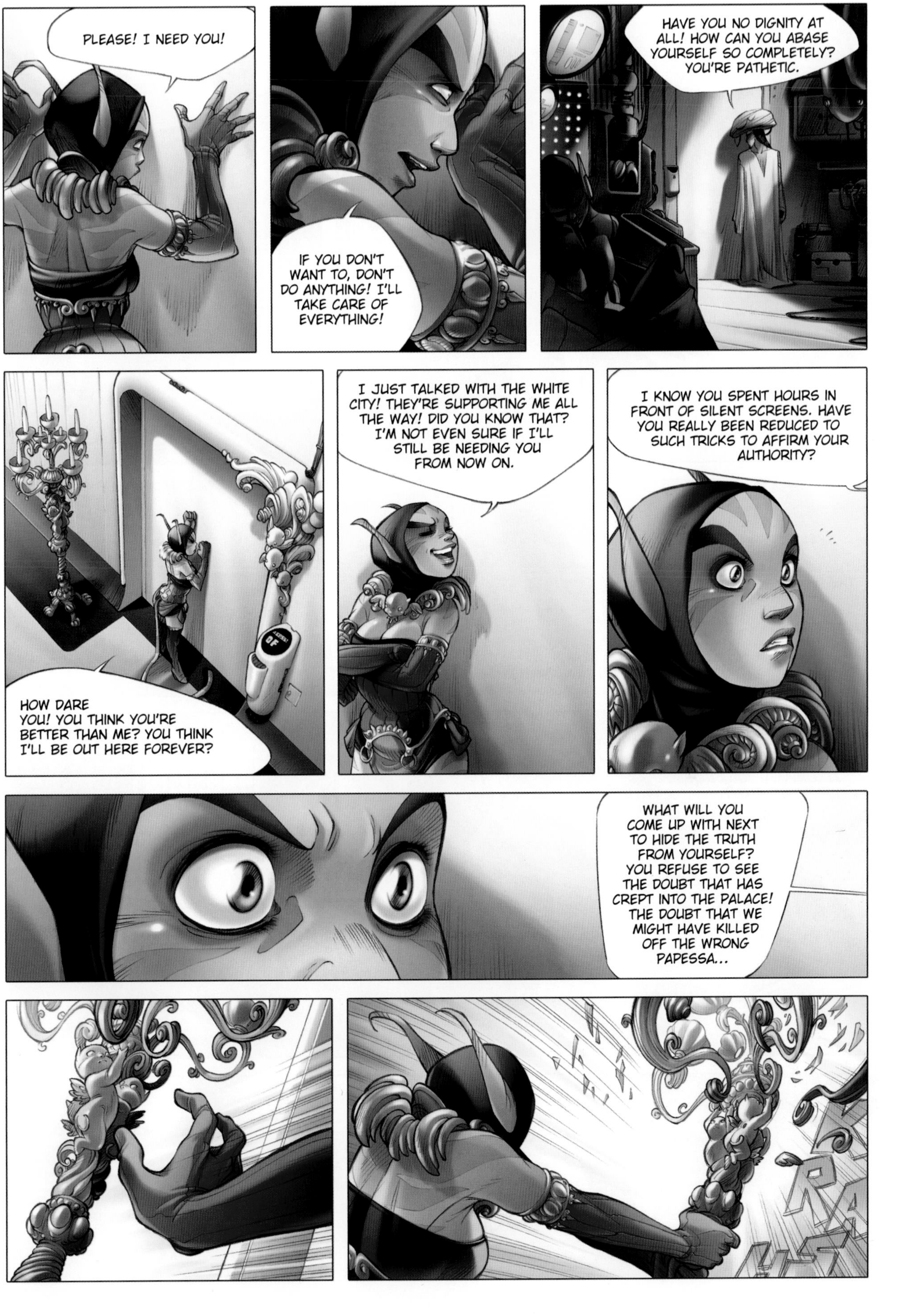
PLEASE! I NEED YOU!
IF YOU DON'T WANT TO, DON'T DO ANYTHING! I'LL TAKE CARE OF EVERYTHING!
HAVE YOU NO DIGNITY AT ALL! HOW CAN YOU ABASE YOURSELF SO COMPLETELY? YOU'RE PATHETIC.
HOW DARE YOU! YOU THINK YOU'RE BETTER THAN ME? YOU THINK I'LL BE OUT HERE FOREVER?
I JUST TALKED WITH THE WHITE CITY! THEY'RE SUPPORTING ME ALL THE WAY! DID YOU KNOW THAT? I'M NOT EVEN SURE IF I'LL STILL BE NEEDING YOU FROM NOW ON.
I KNOW YOU SPENT HOURS IN FRONT OF SILENT SCREENS. HAVE YOU REALLY BEEN REDUCED TO SUCH TRICKS TO AFFIRM YOUR AUTHORITY?
WHAT WILL YOU COME UP WITH NEXT TO HIDE THE TRUTH FROM YOURSELF? YOU REFUSE TO SEE THE DOUBT THAT HAS CREPT INTO THE PALACE! THE DOUBT THAT WE MIGHT HAVE KILLED OFF THE WRONG PAPESSA...

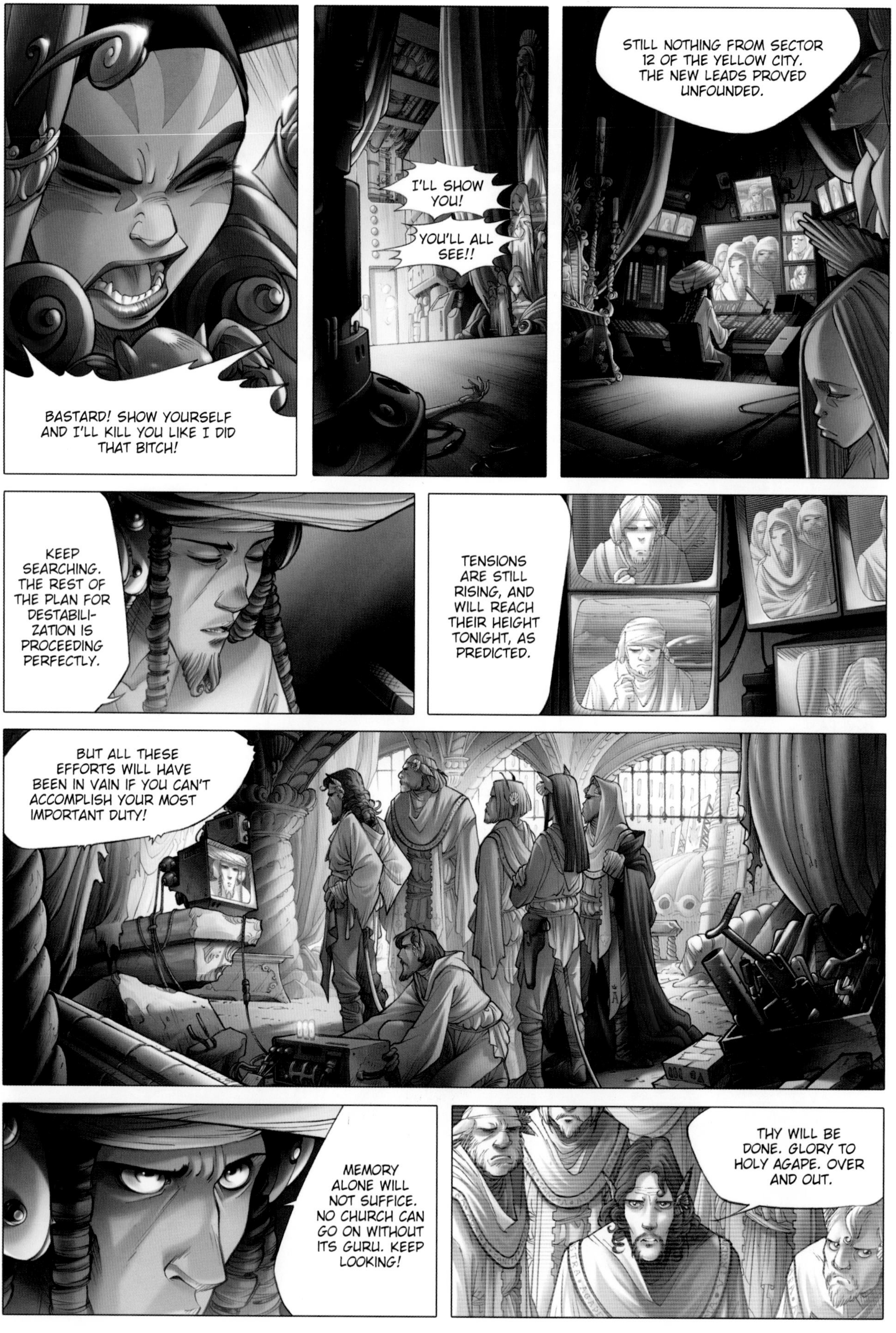
BASTARD! SHOW YOURSELF AND I'LL KILL YOU LIKE I DID THAT BITCH!
I'LL SHOW YOU!
YOU'LL ALL SEE!!
STILL NOTHING FROM SECTOR 12 OF THE YELLOW CITY. THE NEW LEADS PROVED UNFOUNDED.
KEEP SEARCHING. THE REST OF THE PLAN FOR DESTABILI-ZATION IS PROCEEDING PERFECTLY.
TENSIONS ARE STILL RISING, AND WILL REACH THEIR HEIGHT TONIGHT, AS PREDICTED.
BUT ALL THESE EFFORTS WILL HAVE BEEN IN VAIN IF YOU CAN'T ACCOMPLISH YOUR MOST IMPORTANT DUTY!
MEMORY ALONE WILL NOT SUFFICE. NO CHURCH CAN GO ON WITHOUT ITS GURU. KEEP LOOKING!
THY WILL BE DONE. GLORY TO HOLY AGAPE. OVER AND OUT.

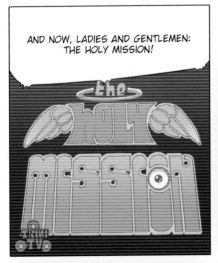

AND NOW, LADIES AND GENTLEMEN: THE HOLY MISSION!

LIVE FROM SUTDIO 5 ON ORBITAL STATION GATAMAGRA...

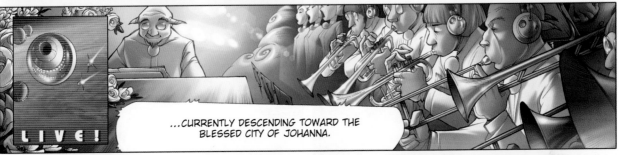

...CURRENTLY DESCENDING TOWARD THE BLESSED CITY OF JOHANNA.

YOU STILL HAVE TIME BEFORE WE GO ON AIR. WHILE YOU WAIT, PLEASE READ OVER THE QUESTIONS WE'LL BE ASKING. YOUR REPLIES ARE IN RED.

YOU GOING TO STICK A HAND UP OUR ASSES AND MOVE US AROUND LIKE PUPPETS, TOO?

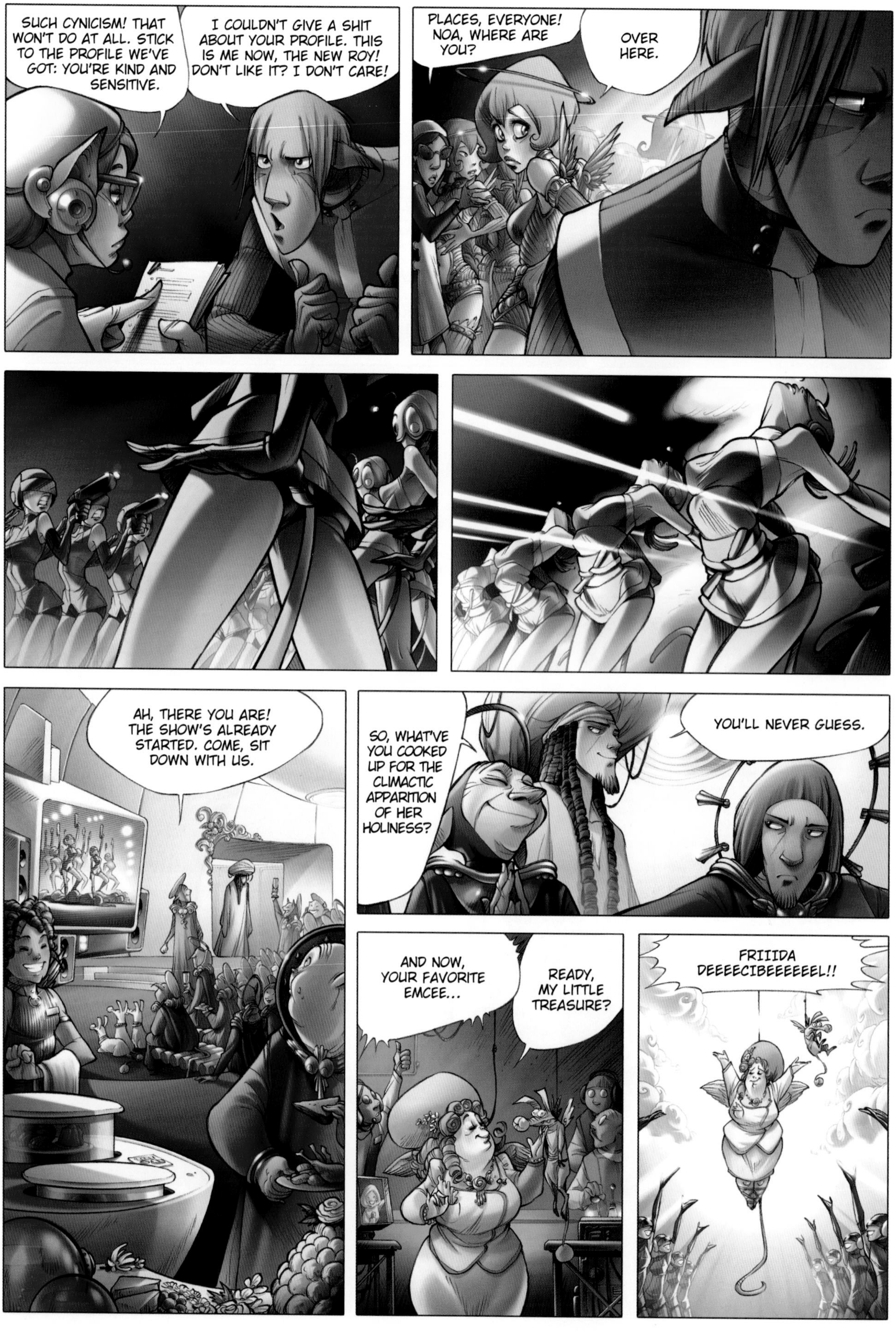
SUCH CYNICISM! THAT WON'T DO AT ALL. STICK TO THE PROFILE WE'VE GOT: YOU'RE KIND AND SENSITIVE.
I COULDN'T GIVE A SHIT ABOUT YOUR PROFILE. THIS IS ME NOW, THE NEW ROY! DON'T LIKE IT? I DON'T CARE!
PLACES, EVERYONE! NOA, WHERE ARE YOU?
OVER HERE.
AH, THERE YOU ARE! THE SHOW'S ALREADY STARTED. COME, SIT DOWN WITH US.
SO, WHAT'VE YOU COOKED UP FOR THE CLIMACTIC APPARITION OF HER HOLINESS?
YOU'LL NEVER GUESS.
AND NOW, YOUR FAVORITE EMCEE...
READY, MY LITTLE TREASURE?
FRIIIDA DEEEECIBEEEEEEL!!

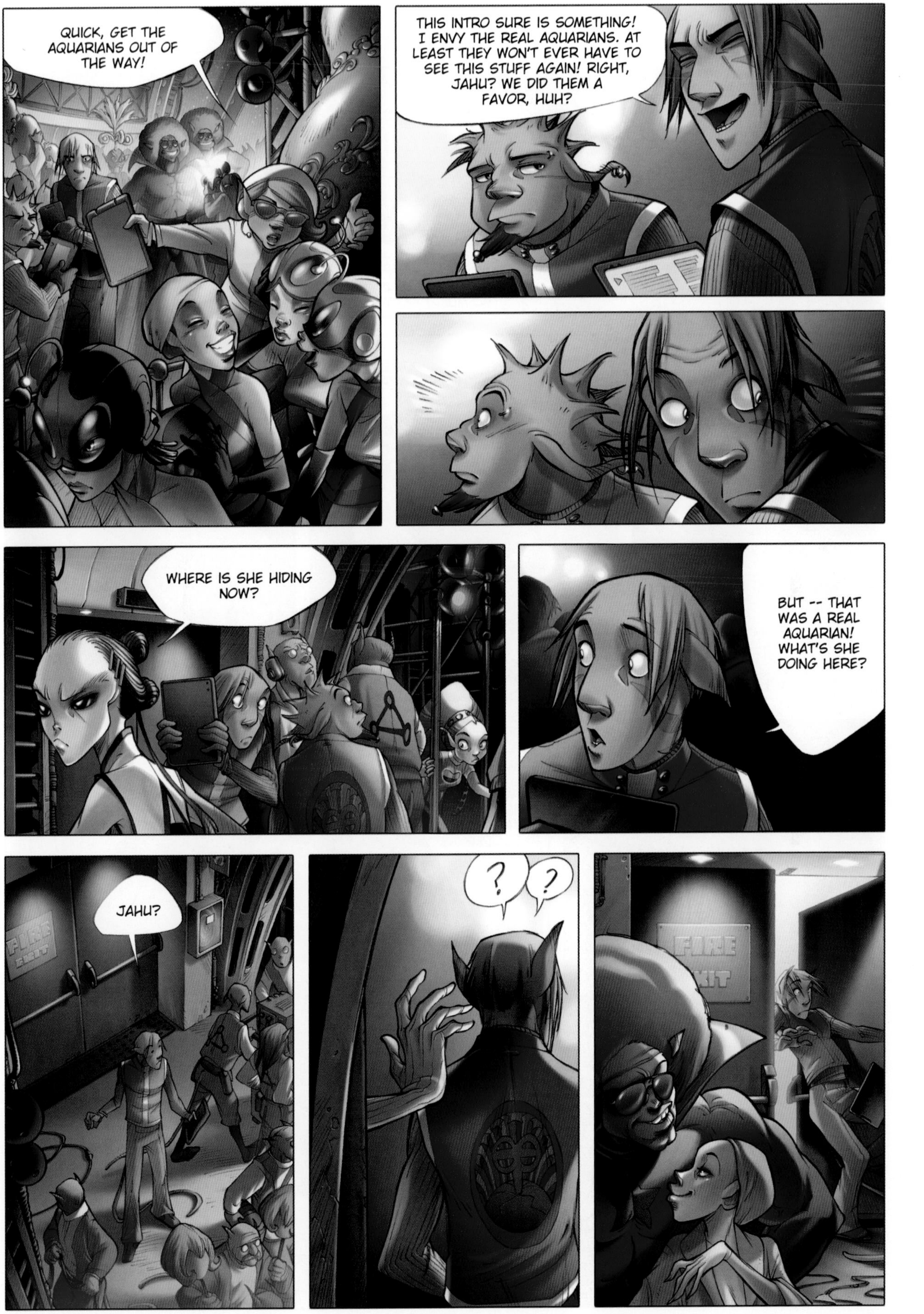
QUICK, GET THE AQUARIANS OUT OF THE WAY!
THIS INTRO SURE IS SOMETHING! I ENVY THE REAL AQUARIANS. AT LEAST THEY WON'T EVER HAVE TO SEE THIS STUFF AGAIN! RIGHT, JAHU? WE DID THEM A FAVOR, HUH?
WHERE IS SHE HIDING NOW?
BUT -- THAT WAS A REAL AQUARIAN! WHAT'S SHE DOING HERE?
JAHU?
?
?

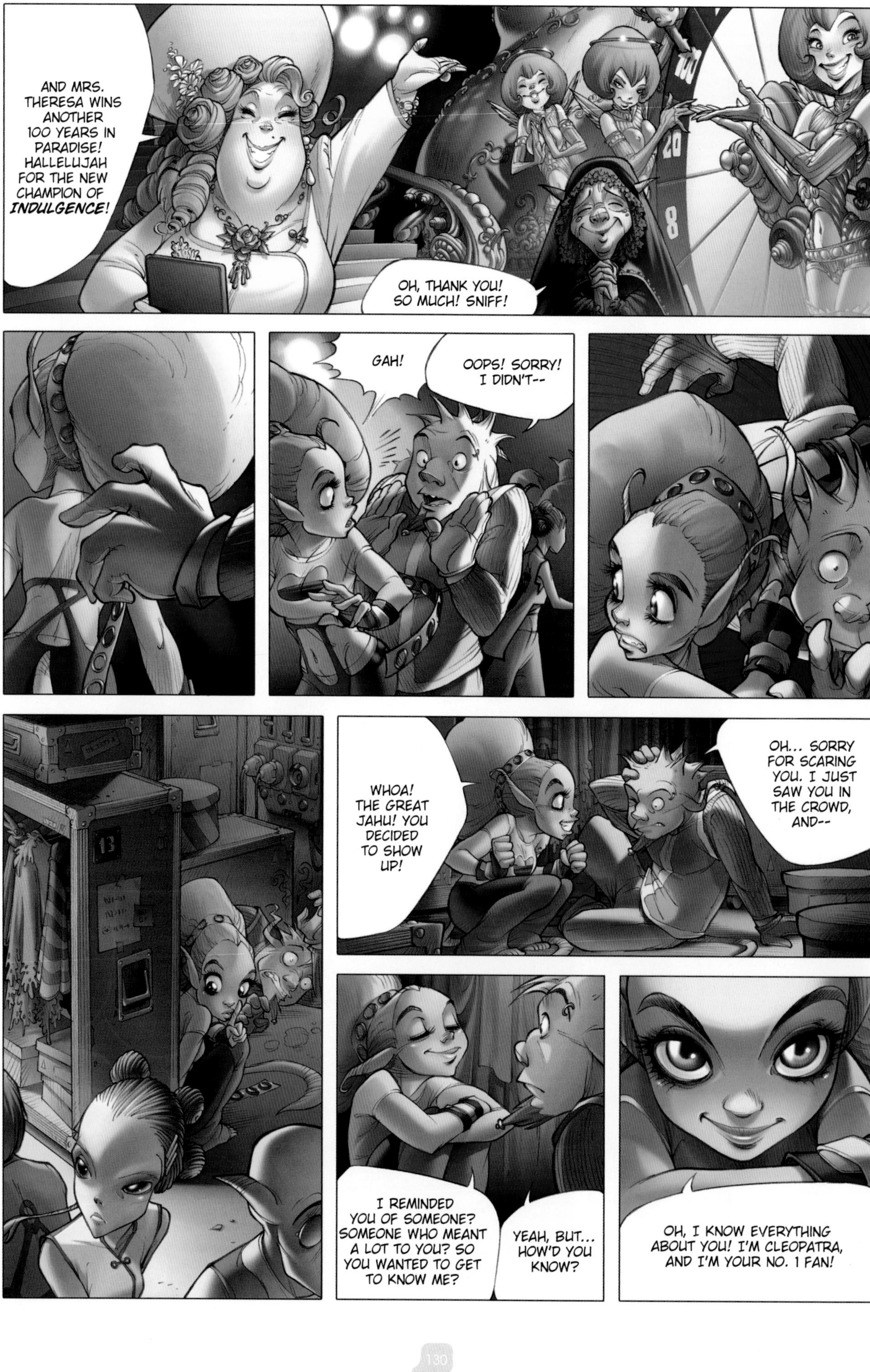

AND MRS. THERESA WINS ANOTHER 100 YEARS IN PARADISE! HALLELUJAH FOR THE NEW CHAMPION OF **INDULGENCE**!
OH, THANK YOU! SO MUCH! SNIFF!
GAH!
OOPS! SORRY! I DIDN'T--
WHOA! THE GREAT JAHU! YOU DECIDED TO SHOW UP!
OH... SORRY FOR SCARING YOU. I JUST SAW YOU IN THE CROWD, AND--
I REMINDED YOU OF SOMEONE? SOMEONE WHO MEANT A LOT TO YOU? SO YOU WANTED TO GET TO KNOW ME?
YEAH, BUT... HOW'D YOU KNOW?
OH, I KNOW EVERYTHING ABOUT YOU! I'M CLEOPATRA, AND I'M YOUR NO. 1 FAN!

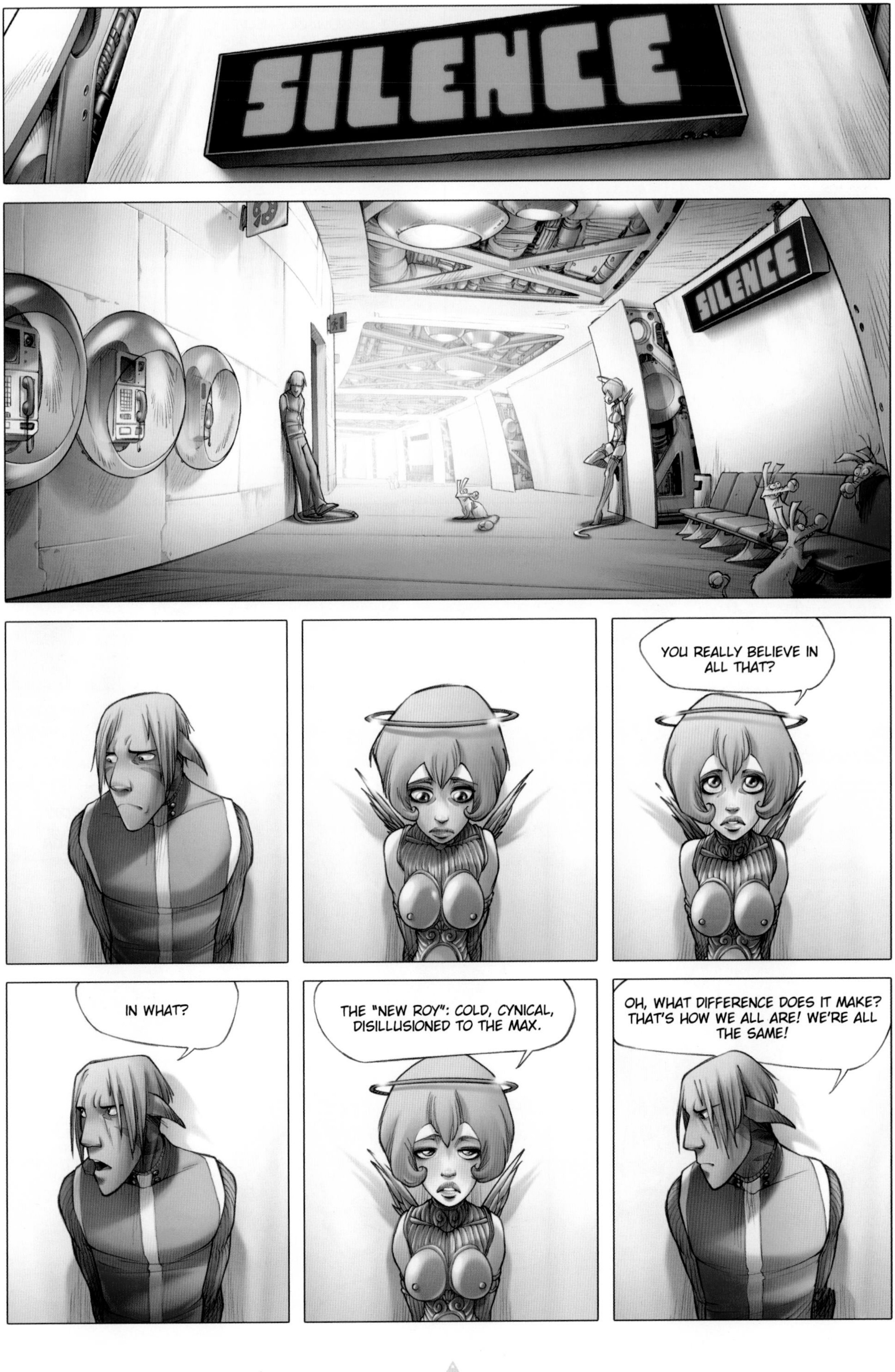
SILENCE
SILENCE
YOU REALLY BELIEVE IN ALL THAT?
IN WHAT?
THE "NEW ROY": COLD, CYNICAL, DISILLUSIONED TO THE MAX.
OH, WHAT DIFFERENCE DOES IT MAKE? THAT'S HOW WE ALL ARE! WE'RE ALL THE SAME!

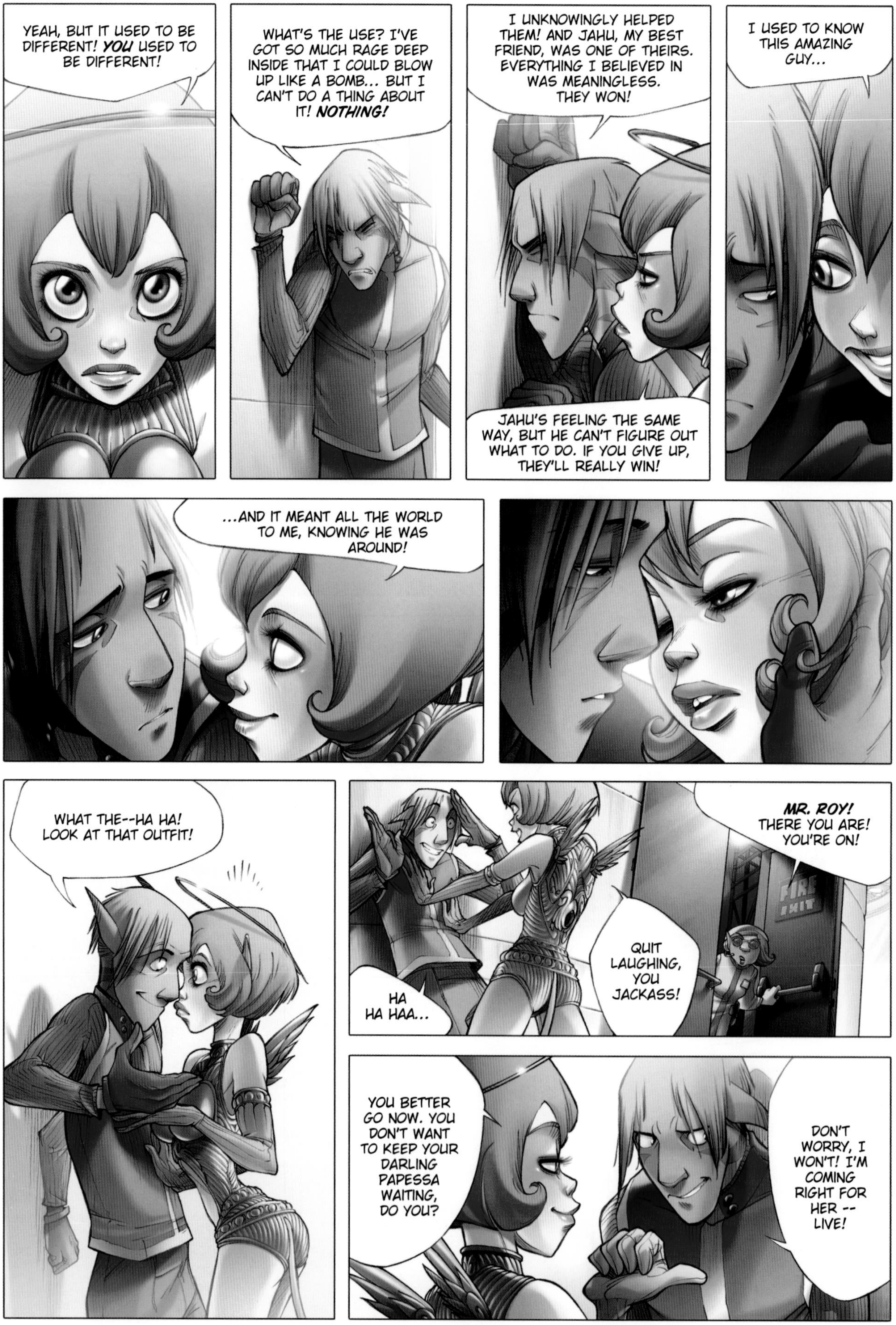

YEAH, BUT IT USED TO BE DIFFERENT! YOU USED TO BE DIFFERENT!
WHAT'S THE USE? I'VE GOT SO MUCH RAGE DEEP INSIDE THAT I COULD BLOW UP LIKE A BOMB... BUT I CAN'T DO A THING ABOUT IT! NOTHING!
I UNKNOWINGLY HELPED THEM! AND JAHU, MY BEST FRIEND, WAS ONE OF THEIRS. EVERYTHING I BELIEVED IN WAS MEANINGLESS. THEY WON!
JAHU'S FEELING THE SAME WAY, BUT HE CAN'T FIGURE OUT WHAT TO DO. IF YOU GIVE UP, THEY'LL REALLY WIN!
I USED TO KNOW THIS AMAZING GUY...
...AND IT MEANT ALL THE WORLD TO ME, KNOWING HE WAS AROUND!
WHAT THE--HA HA! LOOK AT THAT OUTFIT!
HA HA HAA...
QUIT LAUGHING, YOU JACKASS!
MR. ROY! THERE YOU ARE! YOU'RE ON!
FIRE EXIT
YOU BETTER GO NOW. YOU DON'T WANT TO KEEP YOUR DARLING PAPESSA WAITING, DO YOU?
DON'T WORRY, I WON'T! I'M COMING RIGHT FOR HER -- LIVE!

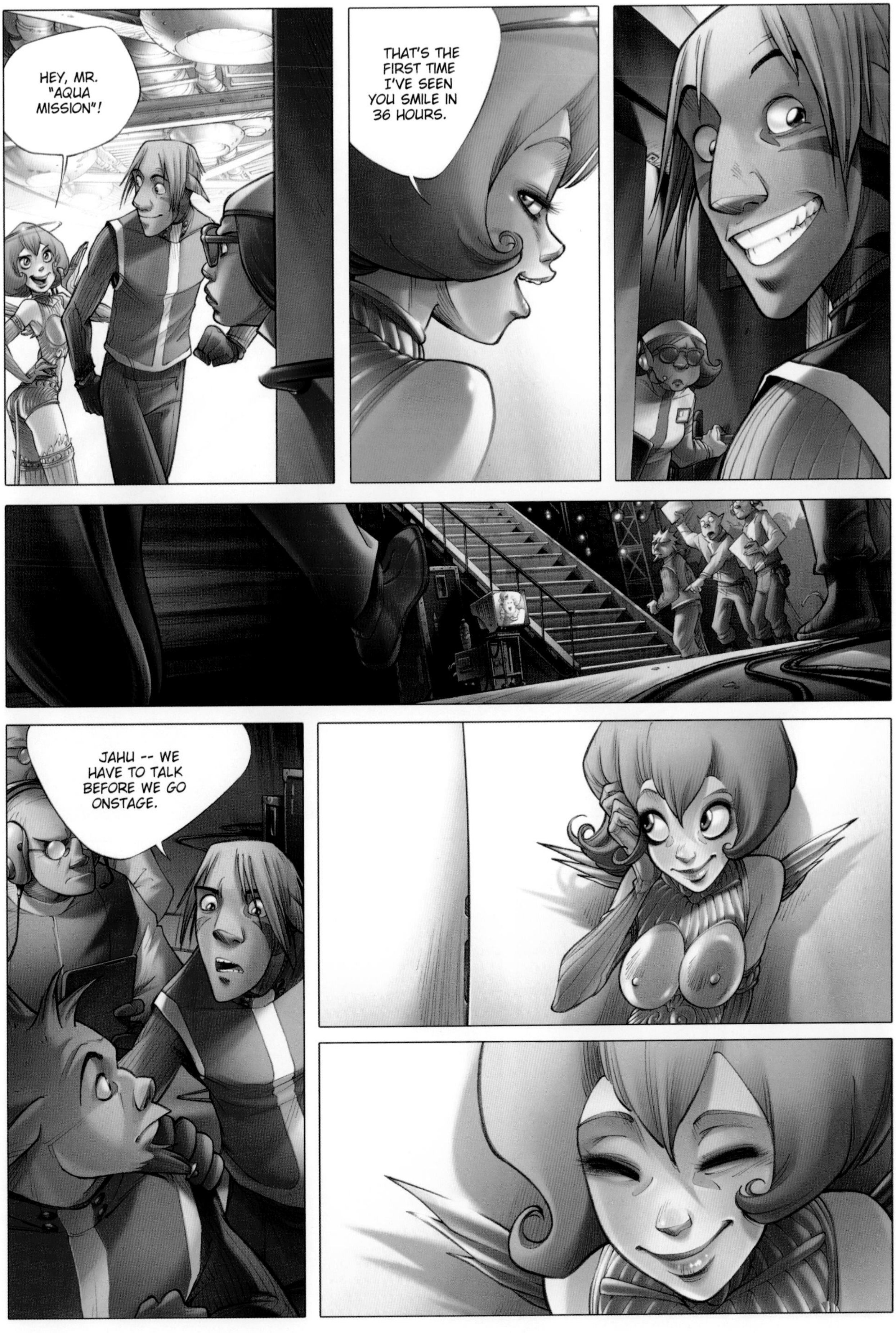
HEY, MR. "AQUA MISSION"!
THAT'S THE FIRST TIME I'VE SEEN YOU SMILE IN 36 HOURS.
JAHU -- WE HAVE TO TALK BEFORE WE GO ONSTAGE.

VERY MOVING! THERE MUST BE SOMEONE WHO CAN INTERCEDE ON YOUR BEHALF WITH THE HOLY MOTHER!

AND NOW FOR HER FAVORITE HEROES, TODAY'S SUPERSTAR GUESTS...

ROY AND JAHU!!

?

CRRR...

FSSs

DON'T WORRY! WE'RE RIGHT HERE!

AND WE'VE GOT A LOT OF THINGS TO SAY!

WELL, WELL. THIS IS MORE THAN I COULD'VE HOPED FOR. MY SHOW JUST KEEPS GETTING MORE INTERESTING...

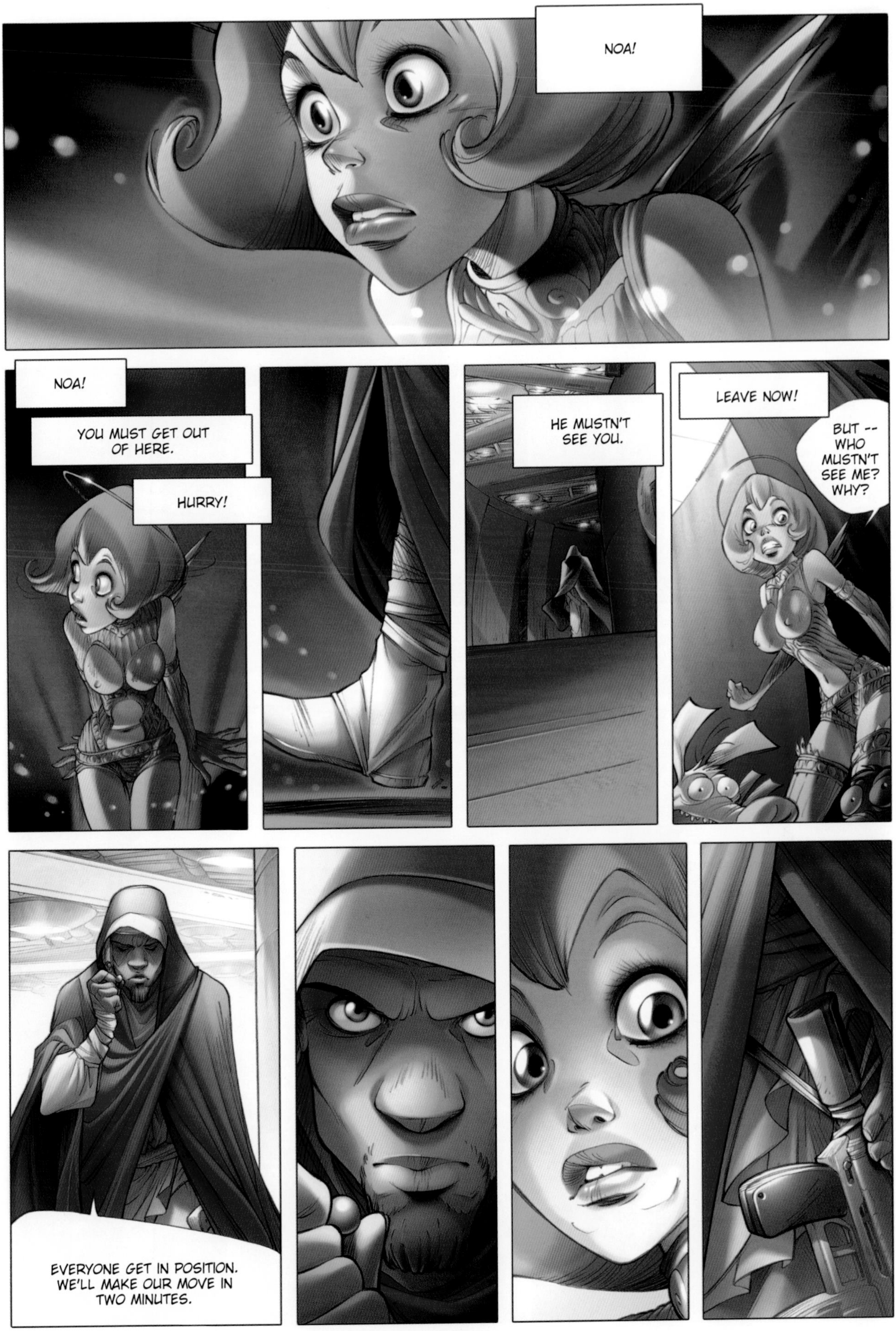

NOA!
NOA!
YOU MUST GET OUT OF HERE.
HURRY!
HE MUSTN'T SEE YOU.
LEAVE NOW!
BUT -- WHO MUSTN'T SEE ME? WHY?
EVERYONE GET IN POSITION. WE'LL MAKE OUR MOVE IN TWO MINUTES.

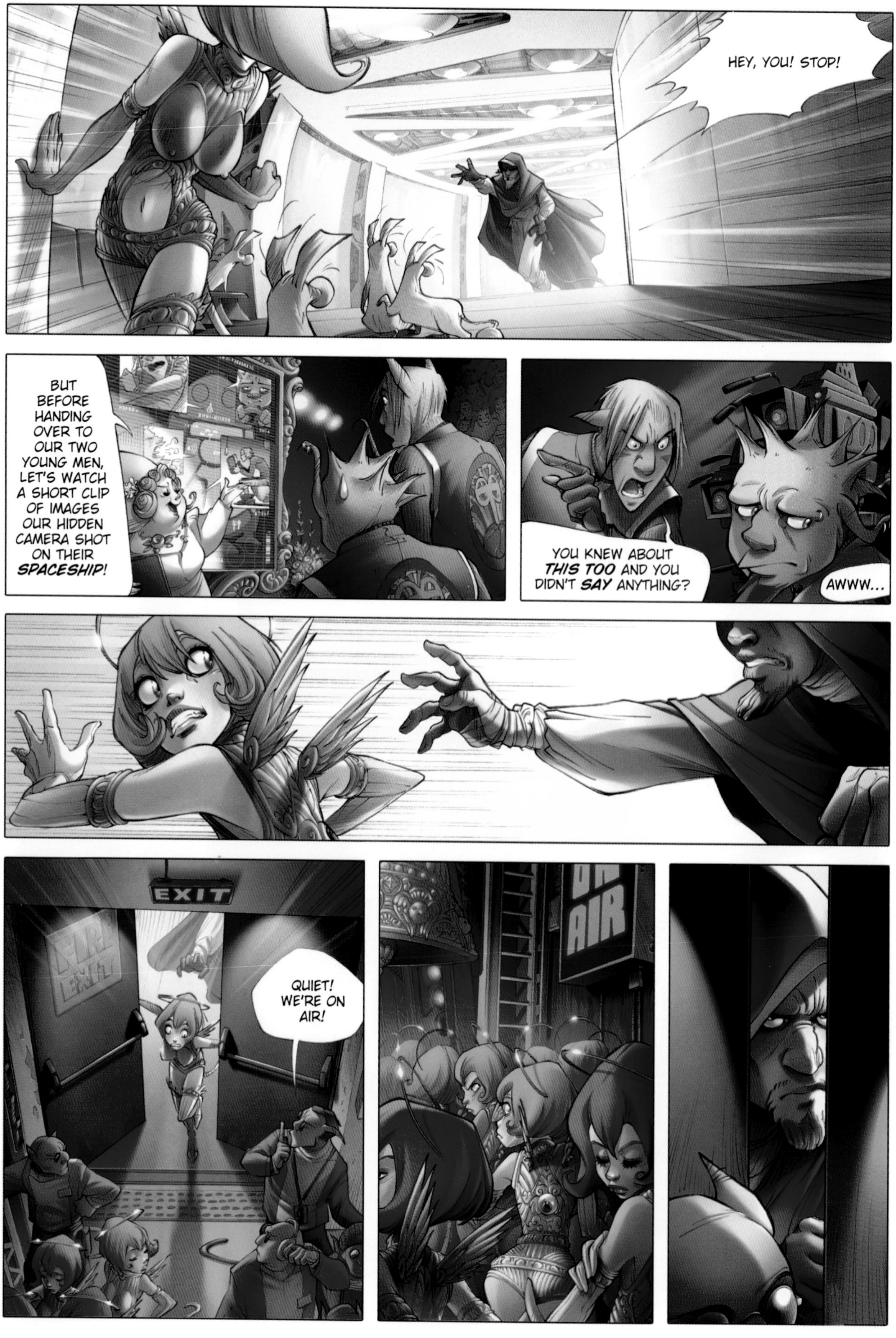
HEY, YOU! STOP!
BUT BEFORE HANDING OVER TO OUR TWO YOUNG MEN, LET'S WATCH A SHORT CLIP OF IMAGES OUR HIDDEN CAMERA SHOT ON THEIR SPACESHIP!
YOU KNEW ABOUT THIS TOO AND YOU DIDN'T SAY ANYTHING?
AWWW...
EXIT
QUIET! WE'RE ON AIR!
AIR

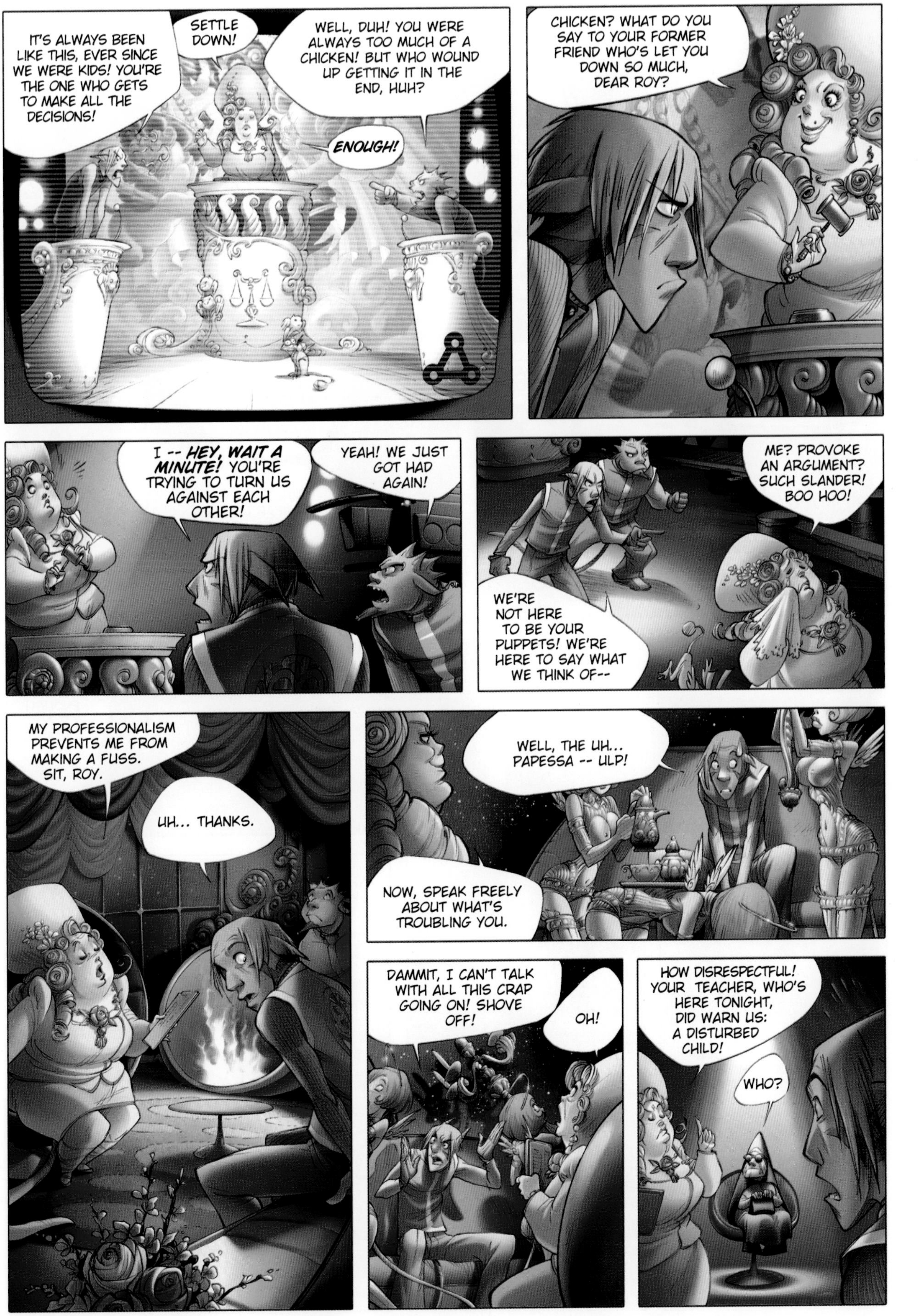

IT'S ALWAYS BEEN LIKE THIS, EVER SINCE WE WERE KIDS! YOU'RE THE ONE WHO GETS TO MAKE ALL THE DECISIONS!
SETTLE DOWN!
WELL, DUH! YOU WERE ALWAYS TOO MUCH OF A CHICKEN! BUT WHO WOUND UP GETTING IT IN THE END, HUH?
ENOUGH!
CHICKEN? WHAT DO YOU SAY TO YOUR FORMER FRIEND WHO'S LET YOU DOWN SO MUCH, DEAR ROY?
I -- HEY, WAIT A MINUTE! YOU'RE TRYING TO TURN US AGAINST EACH OTHER!
YEAH! WE JUST GOT HAD AGAIN!
ME? PROVOKE AN ARGUMENT? SUCH SLANDER! BOO HOO!
WE'RE NOT HERE TO BE YOUR PUPPETS! WE'RE HERE TO SAY WHAT WE THINK OF--
MY PROFESSIONALISM PREVENTS ME FROM MAKING A FUSS. SIT, ROY.
UH... THANKS.
WELL, THE UH... PAPESSA -- ULP!
NOW, SPEAK FREELY ABOUT WHAT'S TROUBLING YOU.
DAMMIT, I CAN'T TALK WITH ALL THIS CRAP GOING ON! SHOVE OFF!
OH!
HOW DISRESPECTFUL! YOUR TEACHER, WHO'S HERE TONIGHT, DID WARN US: A DISTURBED CHILD!
WHO?

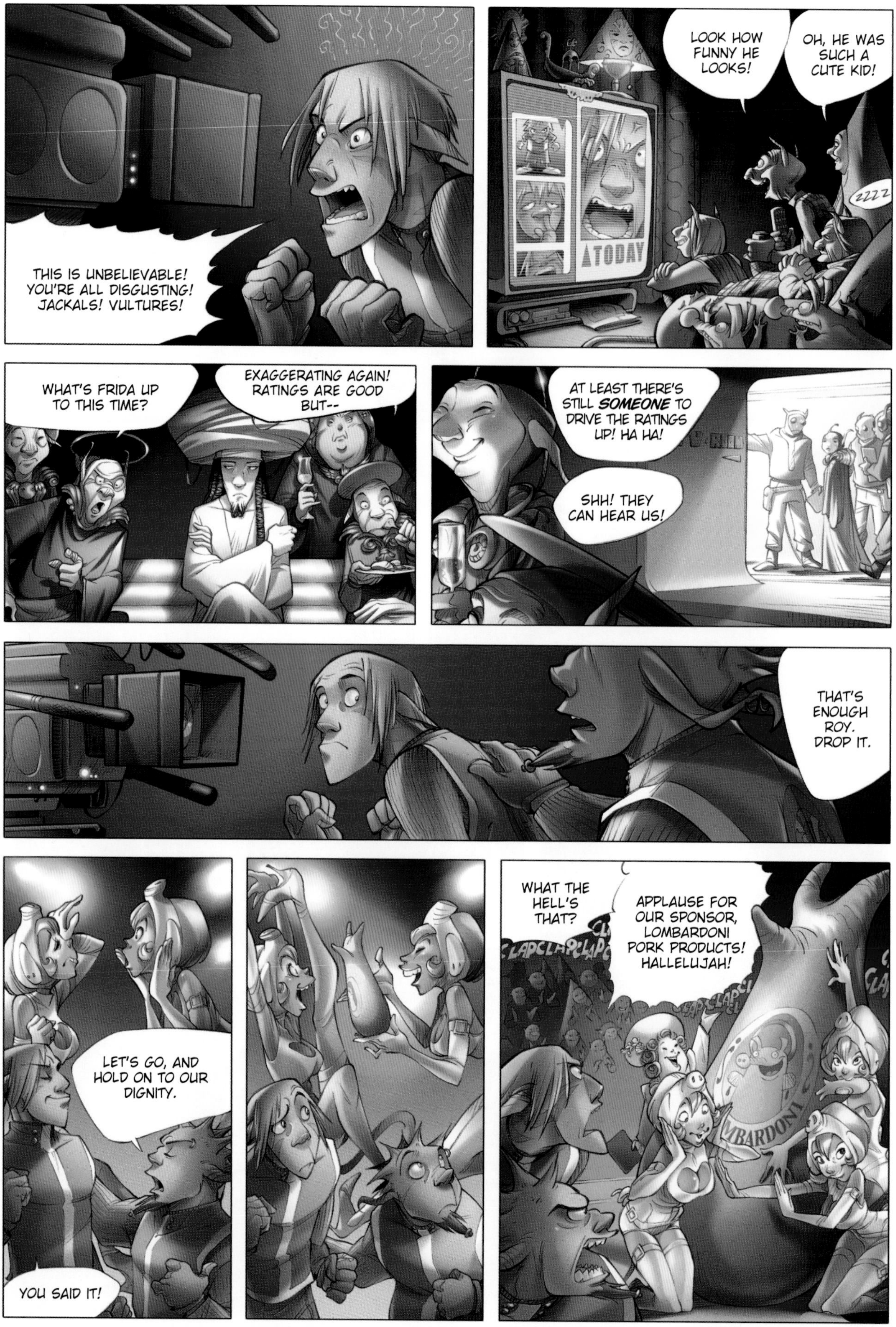
THIS IS UNBELIEVABLE! YOU'RE ALL DISGUSTING! JACKALS! VULTURES!
LOOK HOW FUNNY HE LOOKS!
OH, HE WAS SUCH A CUTE KID!
TODAY
ZZZZ
WHAT'S FRIDA UP TO THIS TIME?
EXAGGERATING AGAIN! RATINGS ARE GOOD BUT--
AT LEAST THERE'S STILL **SOMEONE** TO DRIVE THE RATINGS UP! HA HA!
SHH! THEY CAN HEAR US!
THAT'S ENOUGH ROY. DROP IT.
LET'S GO, AND HOLD ON TO OUR DIGNITY.
YOU SAID IT!
WHAT THE HELL'S THAT?
APPLAUSE FOR OUR SPONSOR, LOMBARDONI PORK PRODUCTS! HALLELUJAH!
CLAP CLAP CLAP
MBARDONI

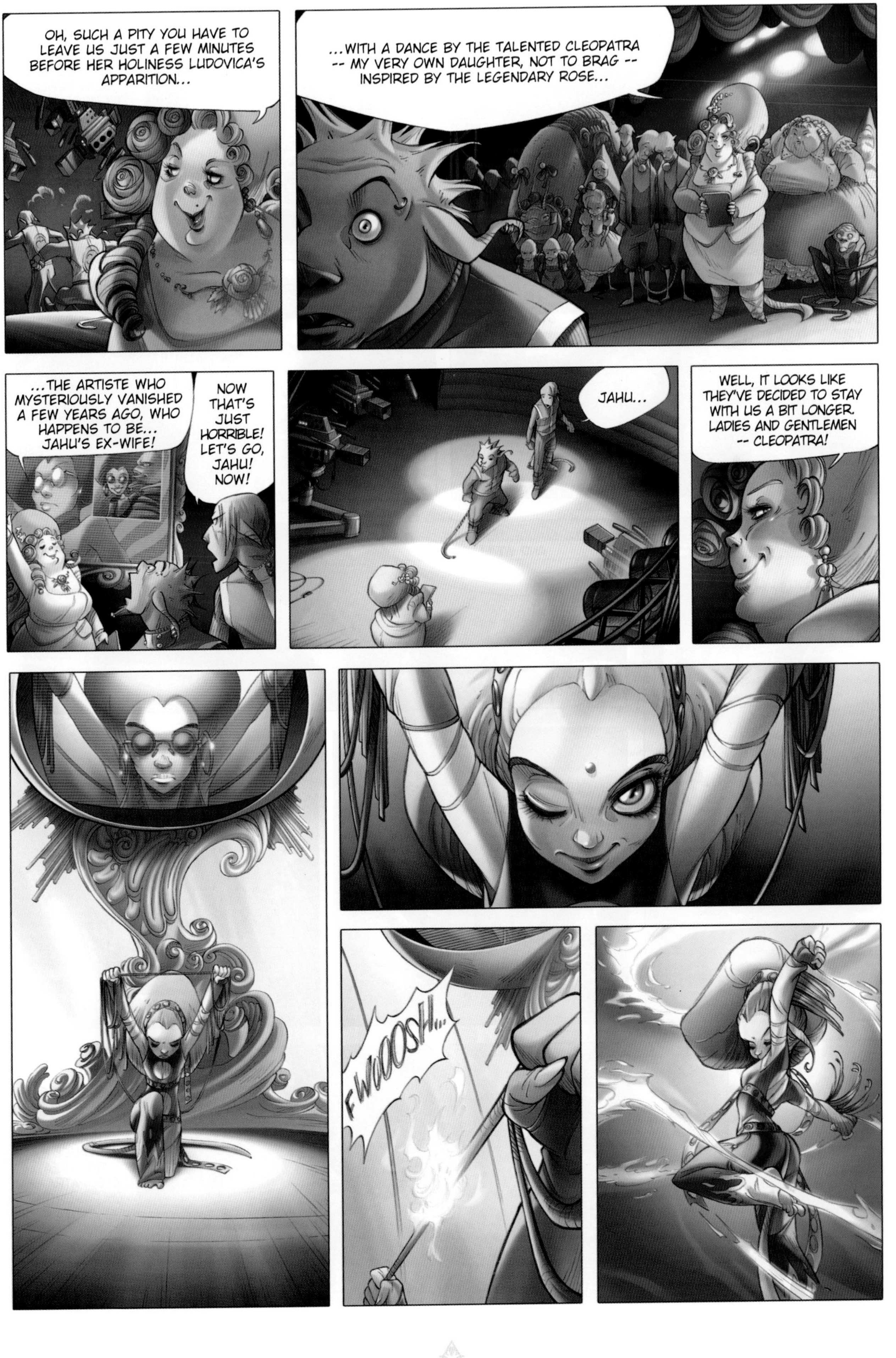
OH, SUCH A PITY YOU HAVE TO LEAVE US JUST A FEW MINUTES BEFORE HER HOLINESS LUDOVICA'S APPARITION...
...WITH A DANCE BY THE TALENTED CLEOPATRA -- MY VERY OWN DAUGHTER, NOT TO BRAG -- INSPIRED BY THE LEGENDARY ROSE...
...THE ARTISTE WHO MYSTERIOUSLY VANISHED A FEW YEARS AGO, WHO HAPPENS TO BE... JAHU'S EX-WIFE!
NOW THAT'S JUST HORRIBLE! LET'S GO, JAHU! NOW!
JAHU...
WELL, IT LOOKS LIKE THEY'VE DECIDED TO STAY WITH US A BIT LONGER. LADIES AND GENTLEMEN -- CLEOPATRA!
FWOOOSH...

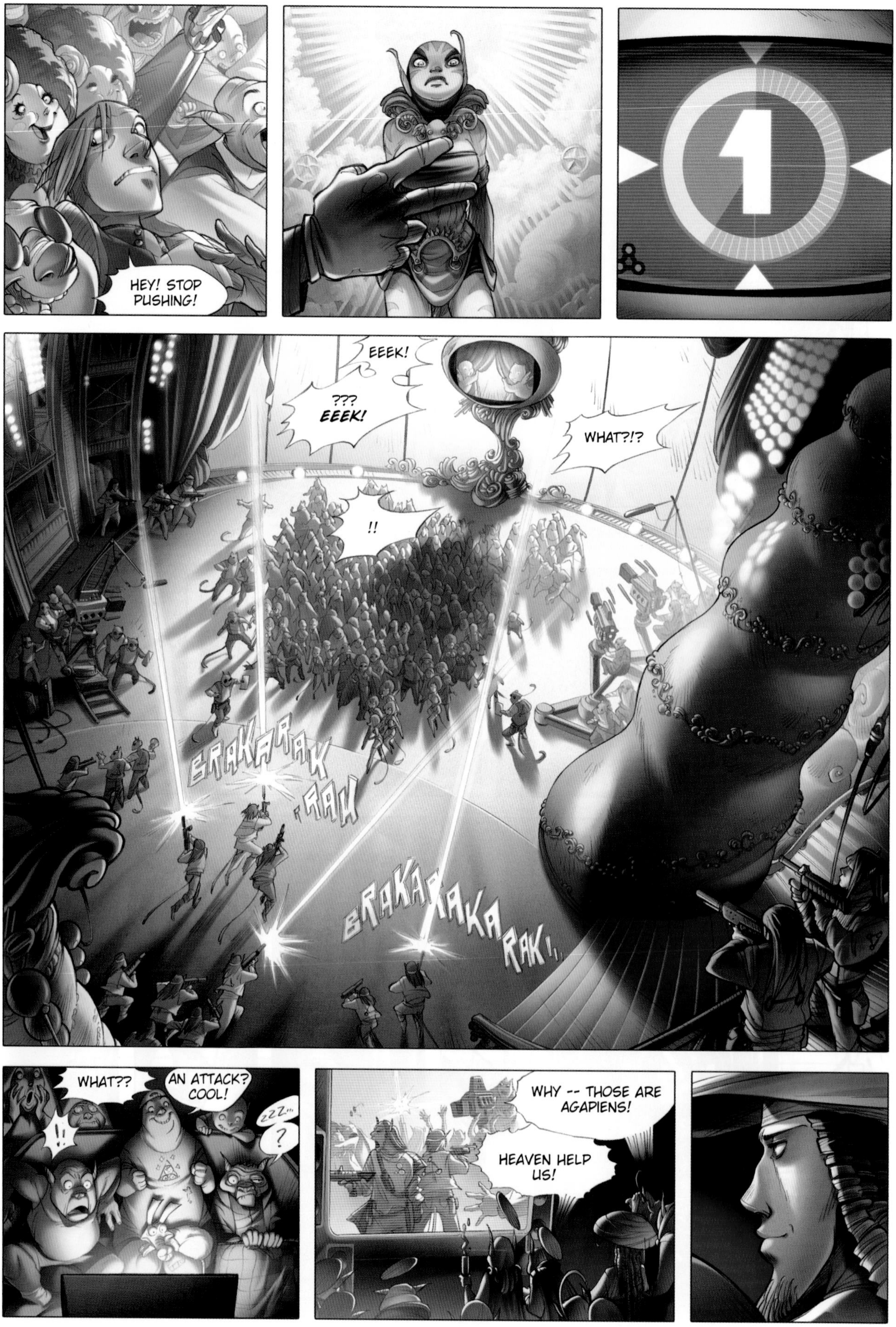

HEY! STOP PUSHING!
1
EEEK!
??? EEEK!
WHAT?!?
!!
BRAKARAK RAK
BRAKARAKAKARAK!
WHAT??
AN ATTACK? COOL!
!!
ZZZ...
?
WHY -- THOSE ARE AGAPIENS!
HEAVEN HELP US!

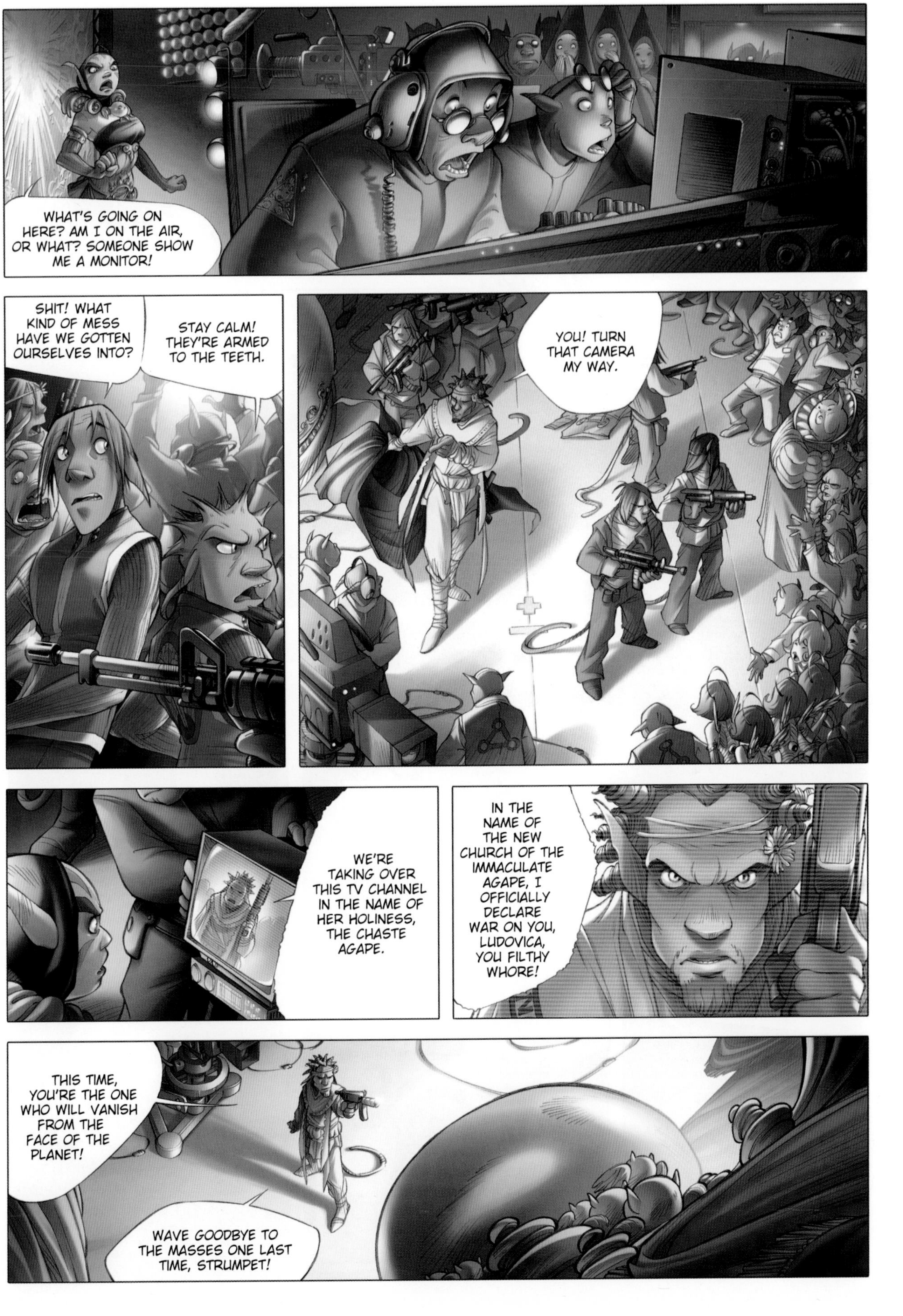
WHAT'S GOING ON HERE? AM I ON THE AIR, OR WHAT? SOMEONE SHOW ME A MONITOR!
SHIT! WHAT KIND OF MESS HAVE WE GOTTEN OURSELVES INTO?
STAY CALM! THEY'RE ARMED TO THE TEETH.
YOU! TURN THAT CAMERA MY WAY.
WE'RE TAKING OVER THIS TV CHANNEL IN THE NAME OF HER HOLINESS, THE CHASTE AGAPE.
IN THE NAME OF THE NEW CHURCH OF THE IMMACULATE AGAPE, I OFFICIALLY DECLARE WAR ON YOU, LUDOVICA, YOU FILTHY WHORE!
THIS TIME, YOU'RE THE ONE WHO WILL VANISH FROM THE FACE OF THE PLANET!
WAVE GOODBYE TO THE MASSES ONE LAST TIME, STRUMPET!

NOOOOO!

THEY BROKE THE CONNECTION!

WE CAN'T SEE A THING!

DAMMIT! THIS ISN'T RIGHT!

OH, NO!

LET'S HEAD STRAIGHT FOR THE STUDIO!

DAMNED IMBECILES! THIS WASN'T IN THE PLAN!

YOUR HOLINESS!

COME NOW!

AAAARGH!! RAAAWWRR!

THE EXPLOSION MUST'VE SHORT-CIRCUITED THEIR EQUIPMENT!

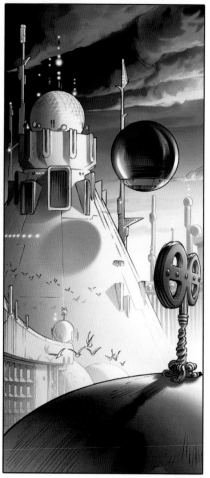

WAIT! I'M GETTING IMAGES AGAIN! THEY'RE ON THE EMERGENCY CHANNEL!

BZZZT! ARE WE BACK ON THE AIR? GOOD. WHATEVER YOU DO, FILM EVERYTHING.

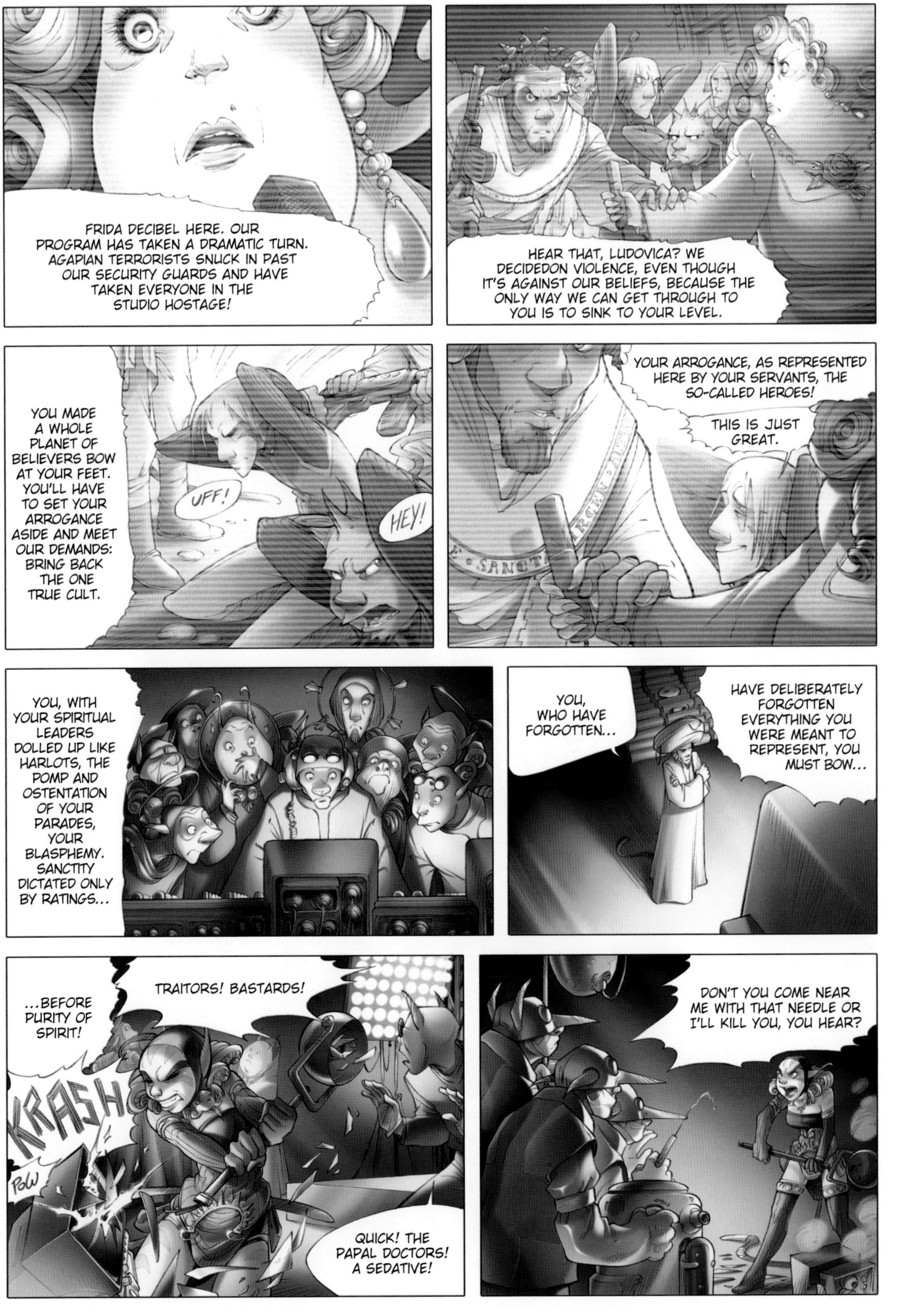
FRIDA DECIBEL HERE. OUR PROGRAM HAS TAKEN A DRAMATIC TURN. AGAPIAN TERRORISTS SNUCK IN PAST OUR SECURITY GUARDS AND HAVE TAKEN EVERYONE IN THE STUDIO HOSTAGE!
HEAR THAT, LUDOVICA? WE DECIDEDON VIOLENCE, EVEN THOUGH IT'S AGAINST OUR BELIEFS, BECAUSE THE ONLY WAY WE CAN GET THROUGH TO YOU IS TO SINK TO YOUR LEVEL.
YOU MADE A WHOLE PLANET OF BELIEVERS BOW AT YOUR FEET. YOU'LL HAVE TO SET YOUR ARROGANCE ASIDE AND MEET OUR DEMANDS: BRING BACK THE ONE TRUE CULT.
UFF!
HEY!
YOUR ARROGANCE, AS REPRESENTED HERE BY YOUR SERVANTS, THE SO-CALLED HEROES!
THIS IS JUST GREAT.
YOU, WITH YOUR SPIRITUAL LEADERS DOLLED UP LIKE HARLOTS, THE POMP AND OSTENTATION OF YOUR PARADES, YOUR BLASPHEMY. SANCTITY DICTATED ONLY BY RATINGS...
YOU, WHO HAVE FORGOTTEN...
HAVE DELIBERATELY FORGOTTEN EVERYTHING YOU WERE MEANT TO REPRESENT, YOU MUST BOW...
...BEFORE PURITY OF SPIRIT!
TRAITORS! BASTARDS!
KRASH
POW
QUICK! THE PAPAL DOCTORS! A SEDATIVE!
DON'T YOU COME NEAR ME WITH THAT NEEDLE OR I'LL KILL YOU, YOU HEAR?

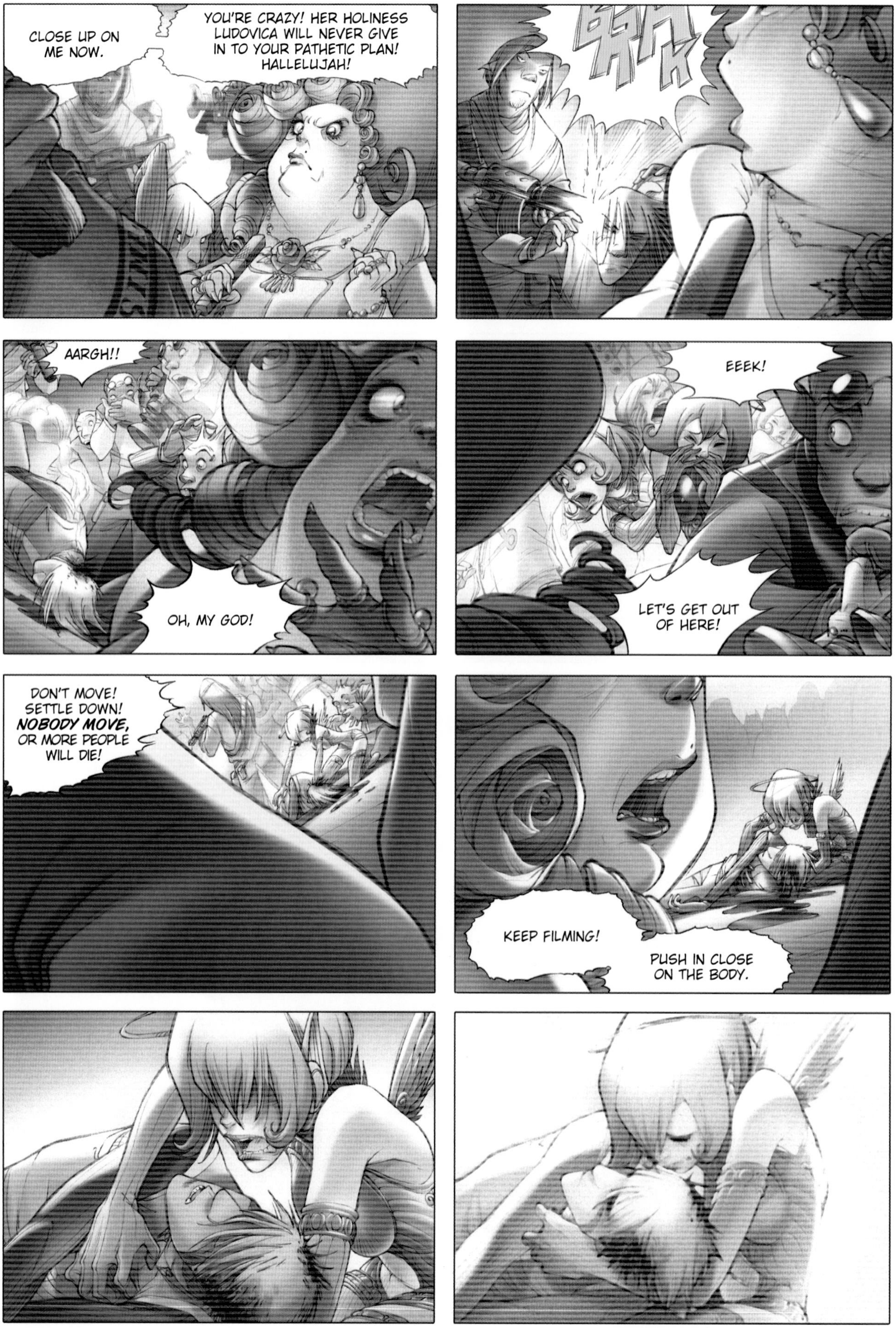
CLOSE UP ON ME NOW.
YOU'RE CRAZY! HER HOLINESS LUDOVICA WILL NEVER GIVE IN TO YOUR PATHETIC PLAN! HALLELUJAH!
AARGH!!
OH, MY GOD!
EEEK!
LET'S GET OUT OF HERE!
DON'T MOVE! SETTLE DOWN! **NOBODY MOVE,** OR MORE PEOPLE WILL DIE!
KEEP FILMING!
PUSH IN CLOSE ON THE BODY.

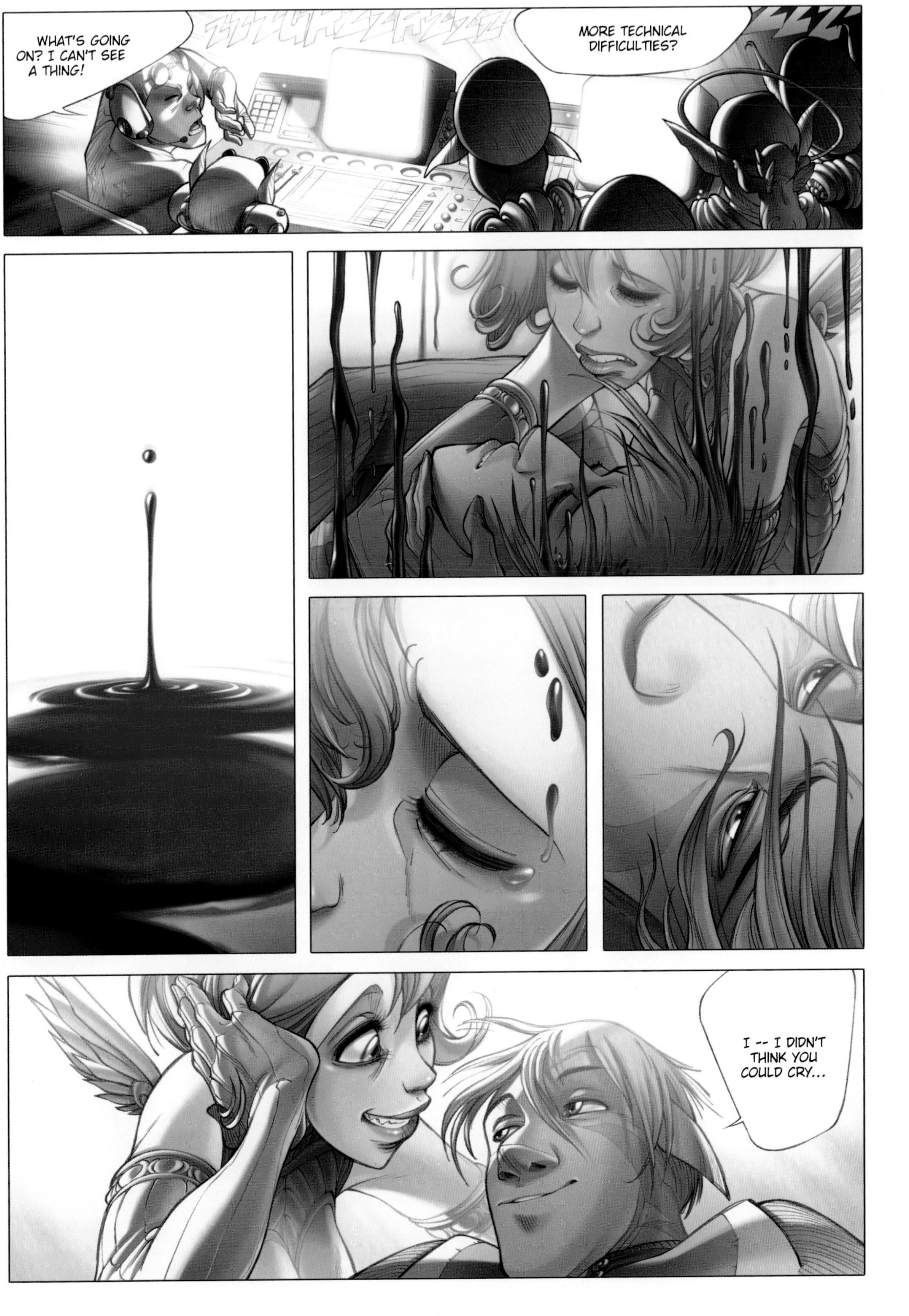
WHAT'S GOING ON? I CAN'T SEE A THING!
MORE TECHNICAL DIFFICULTIES?
I -- I DIDN'T THINK YOU COULD CRY...

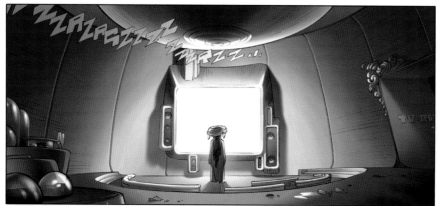

GENIUS OF MIRACLES... I NEED YOU...

WHAT -- WHAT THE DEVIL'S GOING ON? HE'S NOT DEAD?

I DON'T KNOW. I--

BREEP

BREEP

BREEP

DO YOU READ ME? THIS IS INCREDIBLE! AFTER SO LONG! I THINK--

YES, I SAW EVERYTHING. THERE CAN BE NO DOUBT.

BRING HER UP HERE RIGHT AWAY. NO, PASS ME TO HER FIRST. I WANT TO SPEAK TO HER.

HEAVENS! NO!

I HAVE FOUND YOU AT LAST, MY LOVE. I'VE LOOKED FOR YOU EVERYWHERE. DO YOU RECOGNIZE MY VOICE?

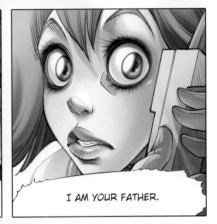

I AM YOUR FATHER.

COME WITH ME. COME BACK HOME. LET THEM BRING YOU HERE. I WILL BE WAITING.

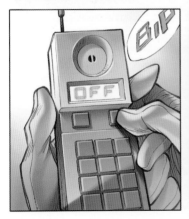

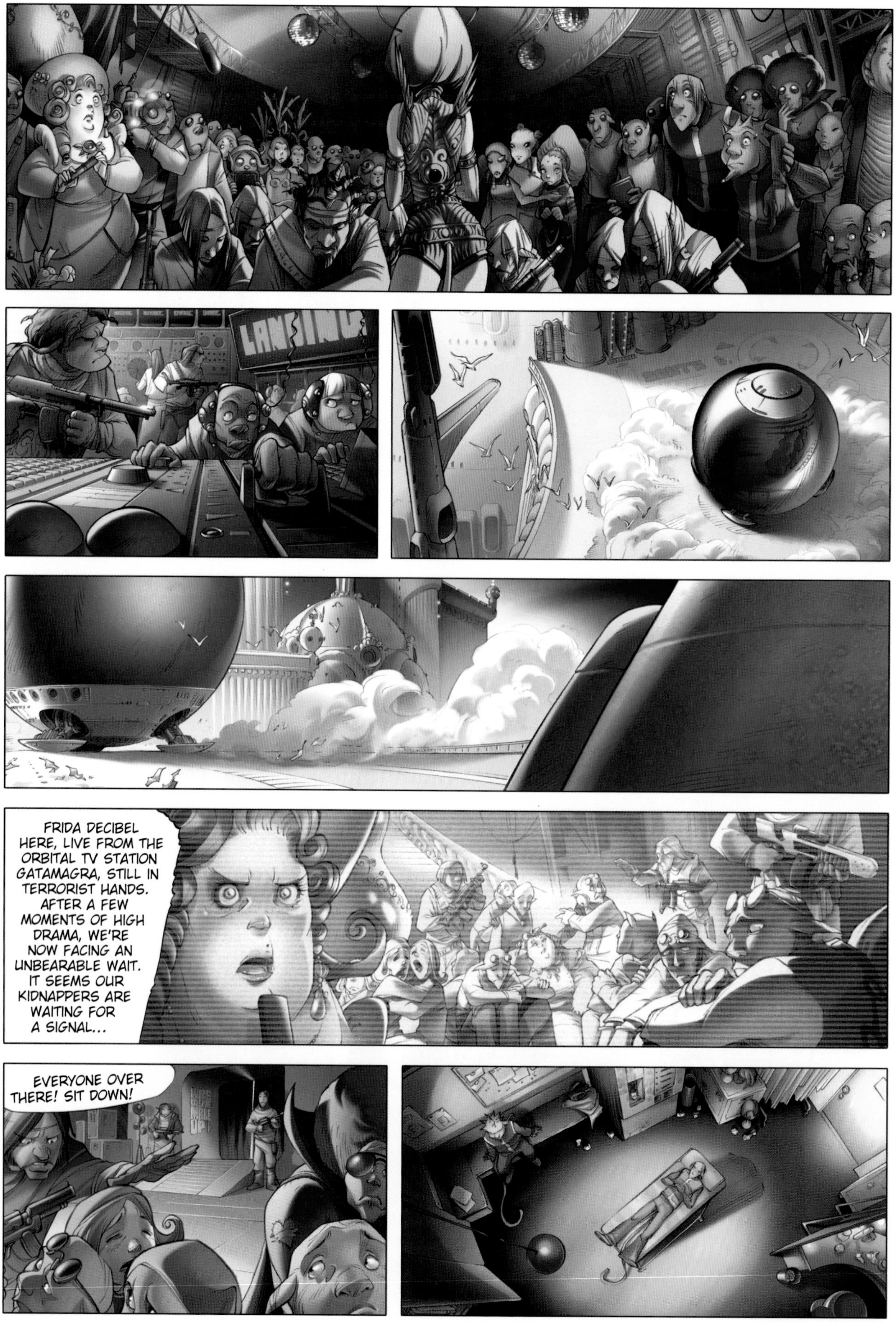
LANDING
FRIDA DECIBEL HERE, LIVE FROM THE ORBITAL TV STATION GATAMAGRA, STILL IN TERRORIST HANDS. AFTER A FEW MOMENTS OF HIGH DRAMA, WE'RE NOW FACING AN UNBEARABLE WAIT. IT SEEMS OUR KIDNAPPERS ARE WAITING FOR A SIGNAL...
EVERYONE OVER THERE! SIT DOWN!

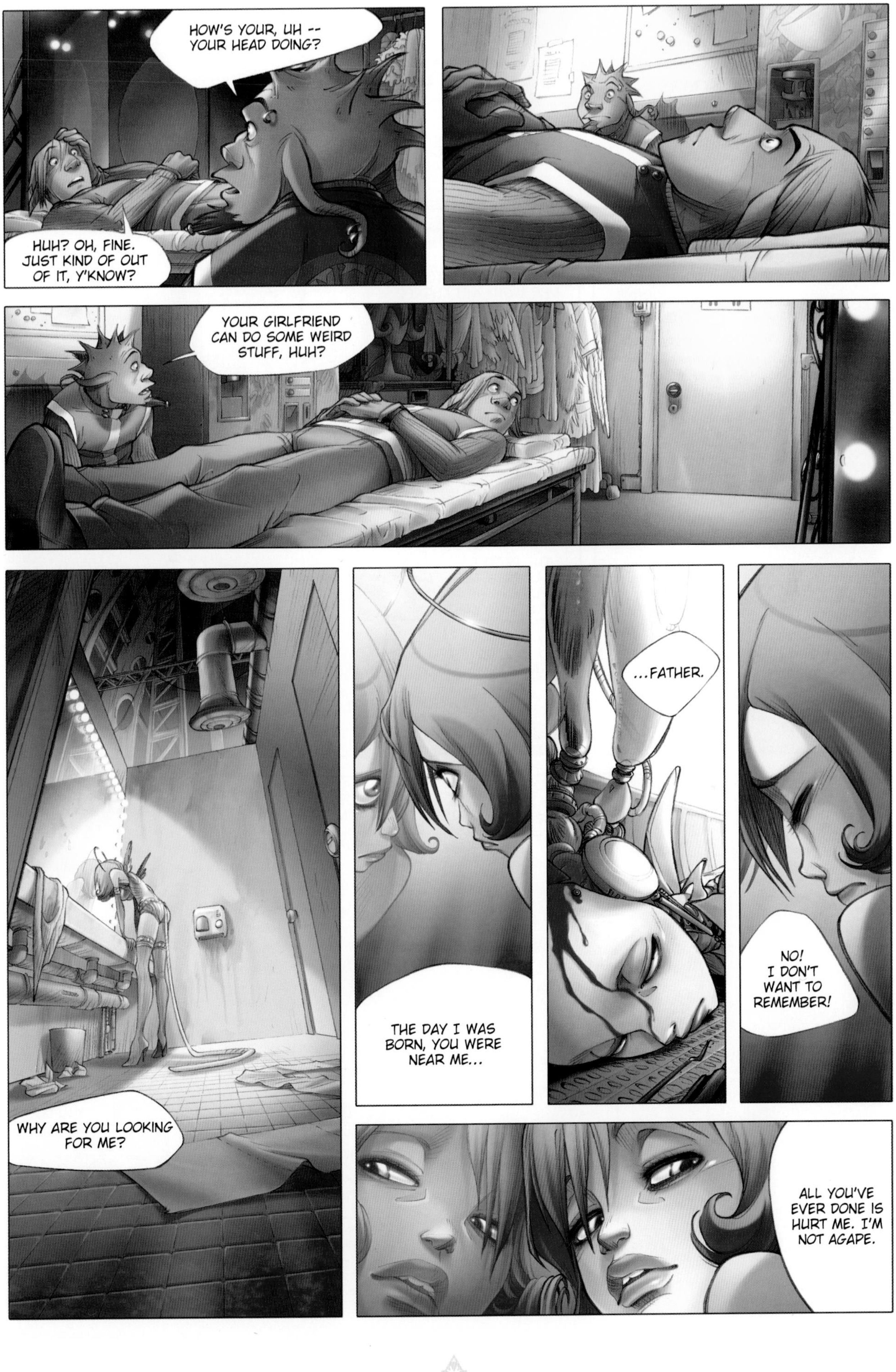
HOW'S YOUR, UH -- YOUR HEAD DOING?
HUH? OH, FINE. JUST KIND OF OUT OF IT, Y'KNOW?
YOUR GIRLFRIEND CAN DO SOME WEIRD STUFF, HUH?
WHY ARE YOU LOOKING FOR ME?
THE DAY I WAS BORN, YOU WERE NEAR ME...
...FATHER.
NO! I DON'T WANT TO REMEMBER!
ALL YOU'VE EVER DONE IS HURT ME. I'M NOT AGAPE.

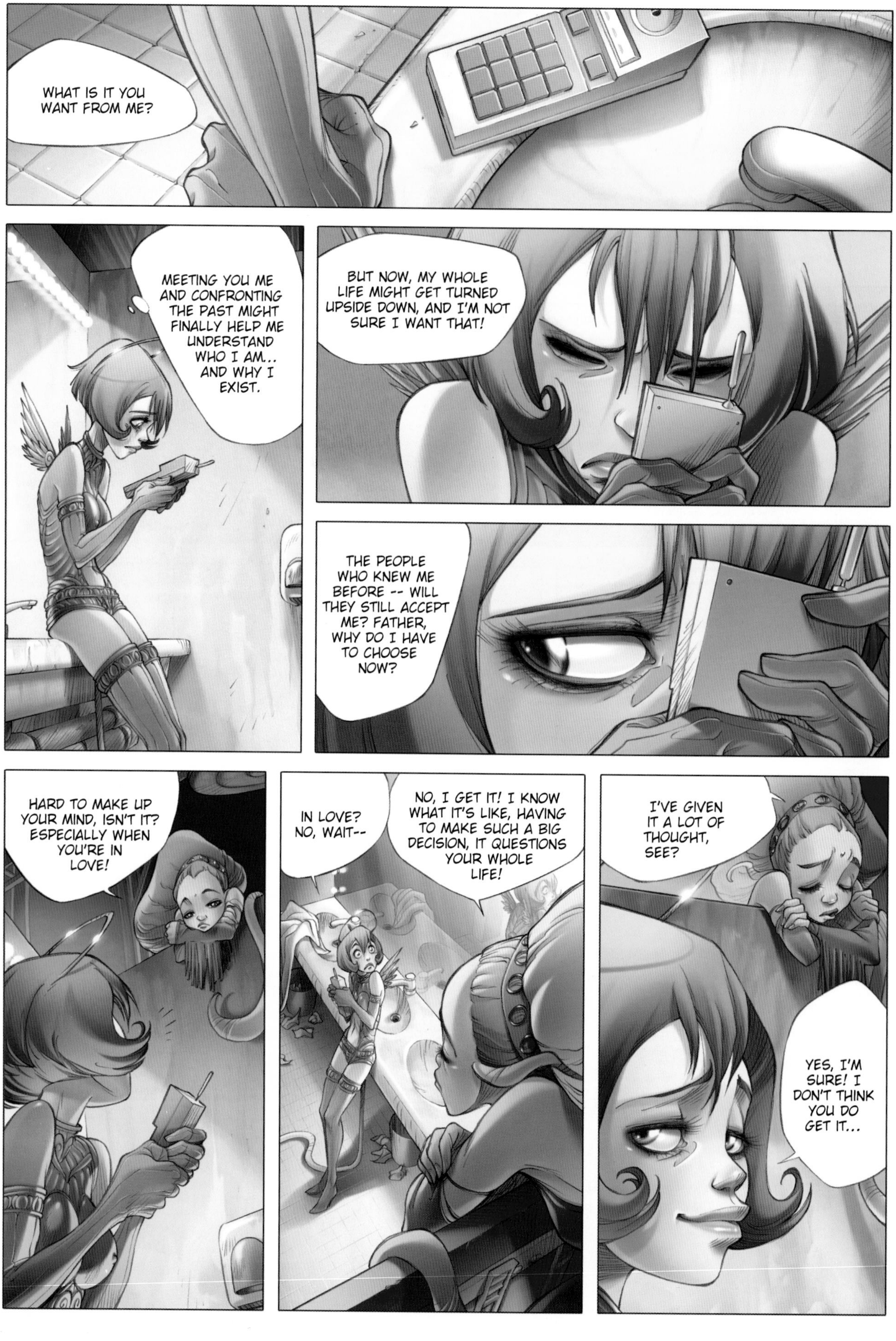
WHAT IS IT YOU WANT FROM ME?
MEETING YOU ME AND CONFRONTING THE PAST MIGHT FINALLY HELP ME UNDERSTAND WHO I AM... AND WHY I EXIST.
BUT NOW, MY WHOLE LIFE MIGHT GET TURNED UPSIDE DOWN, AND I'M NOT SURE I WANT THAT!
THE PEOPLE WHO KNEW ME BEFORE -- WILL THEY STILL ACCEPT ME? FATHER, WHY DO I HAVE TO CHOOSE NOW?
HARD TO MAKE UP YOUR MIND, ISN'T IT? ESPECIALLY WHEN YOU'RE IN LOVE!
IN LOVE? NO, WAIT--
NO, I GET IT! I KNOW WHAT IT'S LIKE, HAVING TO MAKE SUCH A BIG DECISION, IT QUESTIONS YOUR WHOLE LIFE!
I'VE GIVEN IT A LOT OF THOUGHT, SEE?
YES, I'M SURE! I DON'T THINK YOU DO GET IT...

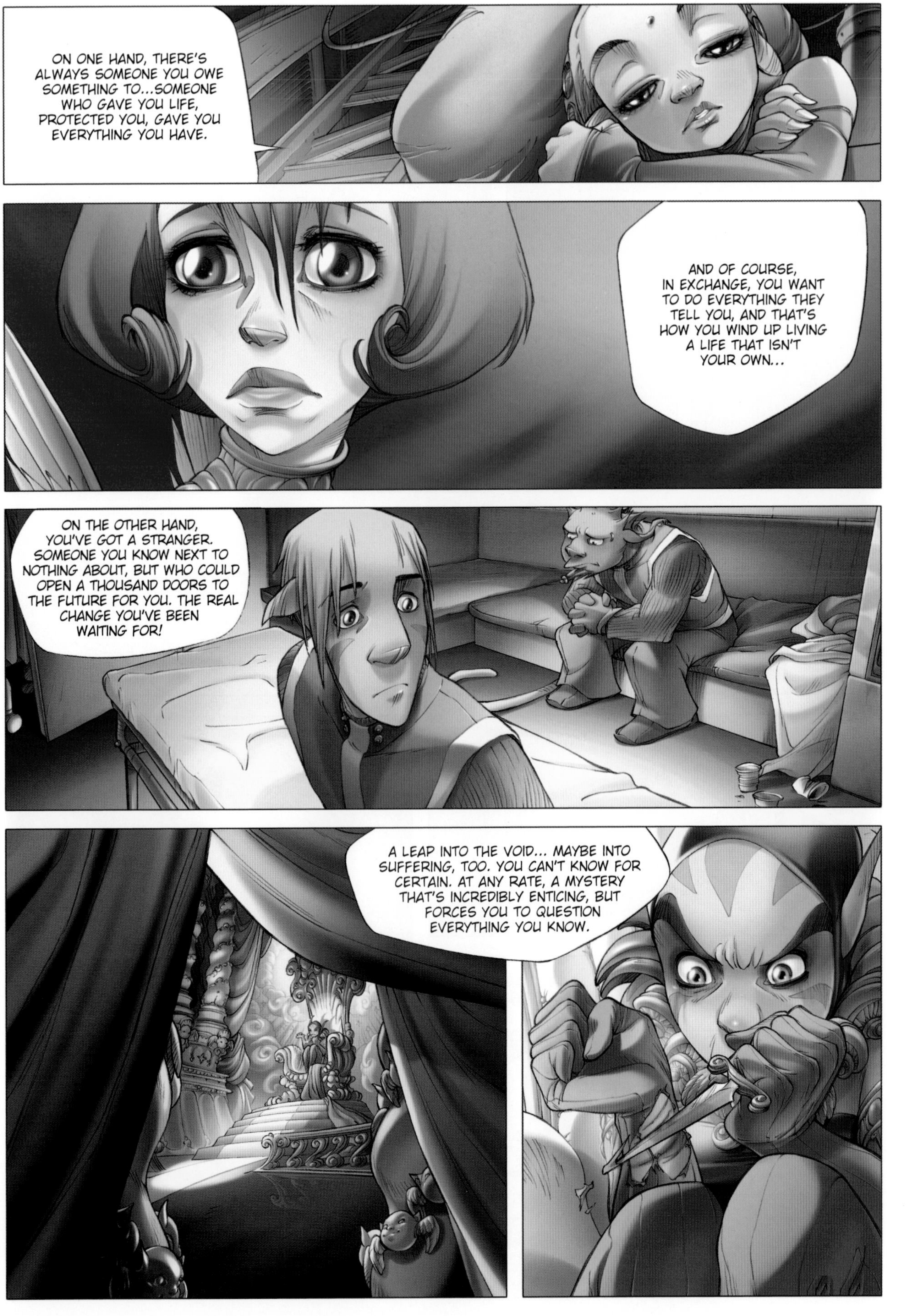
ON ONE HAND, THERE'S ALWAYS SOMEONE YOU OWE SOMETHING TO...SOMEONE WHO GAVE YOU LIFE, PROTECTED YOU, GAVE YOU EVERYTHING YOU HAVE.
AND OF COURSE, IN EXCHANGE, YOU WANT TO DO EVERYTHING THEY TELL YOU, AND THAT'S HOW YOU WIND UP LIVING A LIFE THAT ISN'T YOUR OWN...
ON THE OTHER HAND, YOU'VE GOT A STRANGER. SOMEONE YOU KNOW NEXT TO NOTHING ABOUT, BUT WHO COULD OPEN A THOUSAND DOORS TO THE FUTURE FOR YOU. THE REAL CHANGE YOU'VE BEEN WAITING FOR!
A LEAP INTO THE VOID... MAYBE INTO SUFFERING, TOO. YOU CAN'T KNOW FOR CERTAIN. AT ANY RATE, A MYSTERY THAT'S INCREDIBLY ENTICING, BUT FORCES YOU TO QUESTION EVERYTHING YOU KNOW.

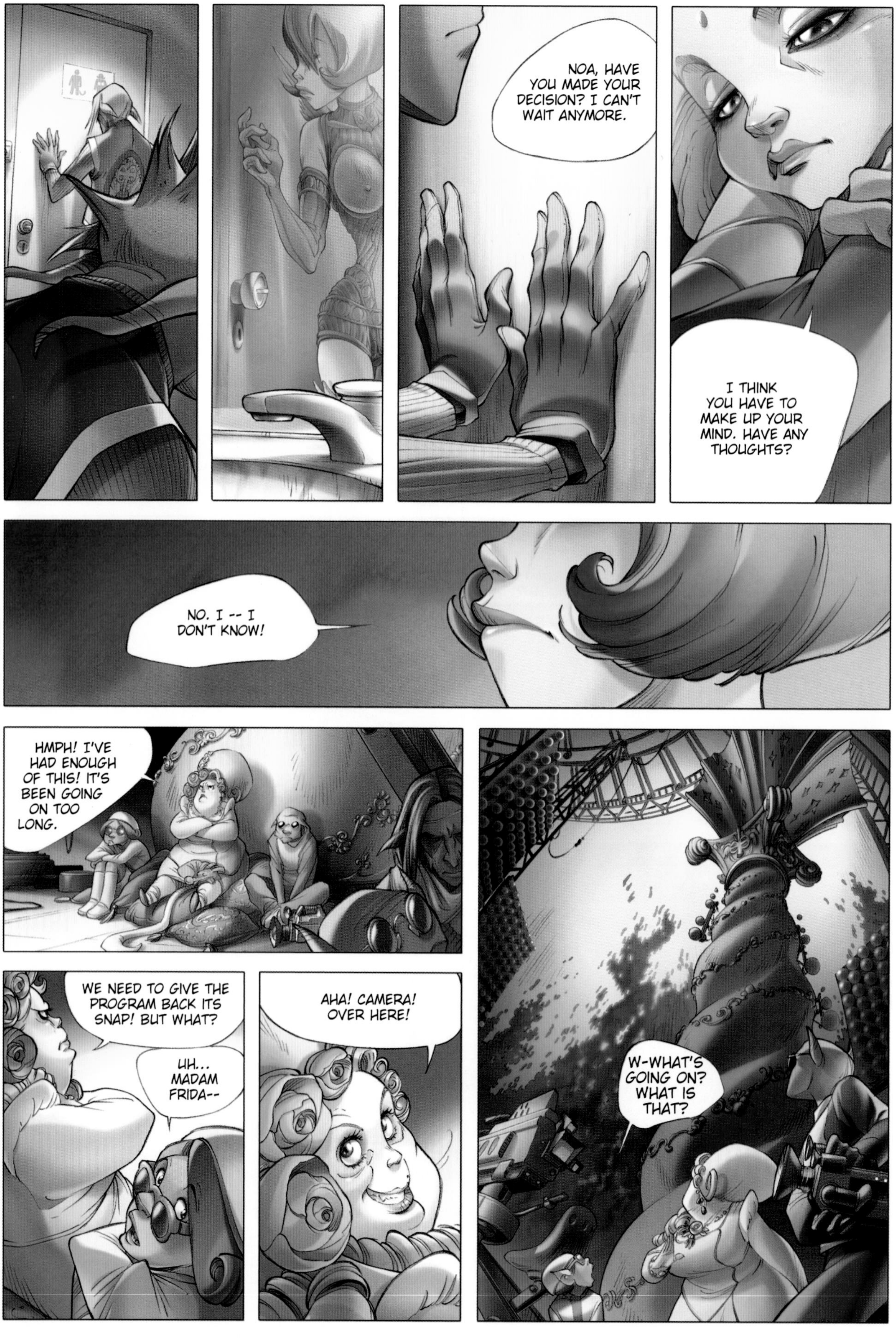
NOA, HAVE YOU MADE YOUR DECISION? I CAN'T WAIT ANYMORE.
I THINK YOU HAVE TO MAKE UP YOUR MIND. HAVE ANY THOUGHTS?
NO. I -- I DON'T KNOW!
HMPH! I'VE HAD ENOUGH OF THIS! IT'S BEEN GOING ON TOO LONG.
WE NEED TO GIVE THE PROGRAM BACK ITS SNAP! BUT WHAT?
UH... MADAM FRIDA--
AHA! CAMERA! OVER HERE!
W-WHAT'S GOING ON? WHAT IS THAT?

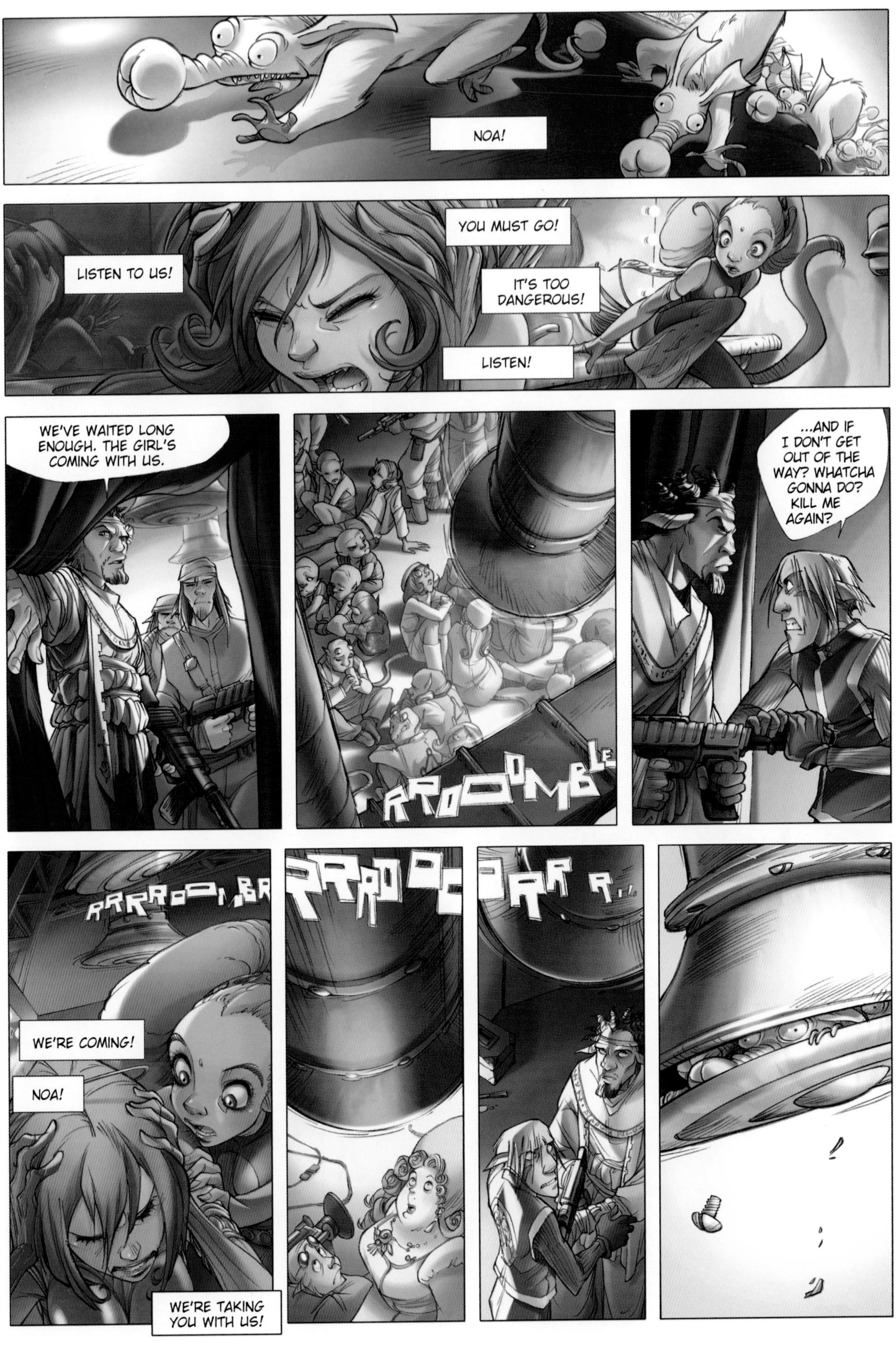
NOA!
LISTEN TO US!
YOU MUST GO!
IT'S TOO DANGEROUS!
LISTEN!
WE'VE WAITED LONG ENOUGH. THE GIRL'S COMING WITH US.
RRROOOMBLE
...AND IF I DON'T GET OUT OF THE WAY? WHATCHA GONNA DO? KILL ME AGAIN?
RRRROOOMBR
RRRROOOORRR R...
WE'RE COMING!
NOA!
WE'RE TAKING YOU WITH US!

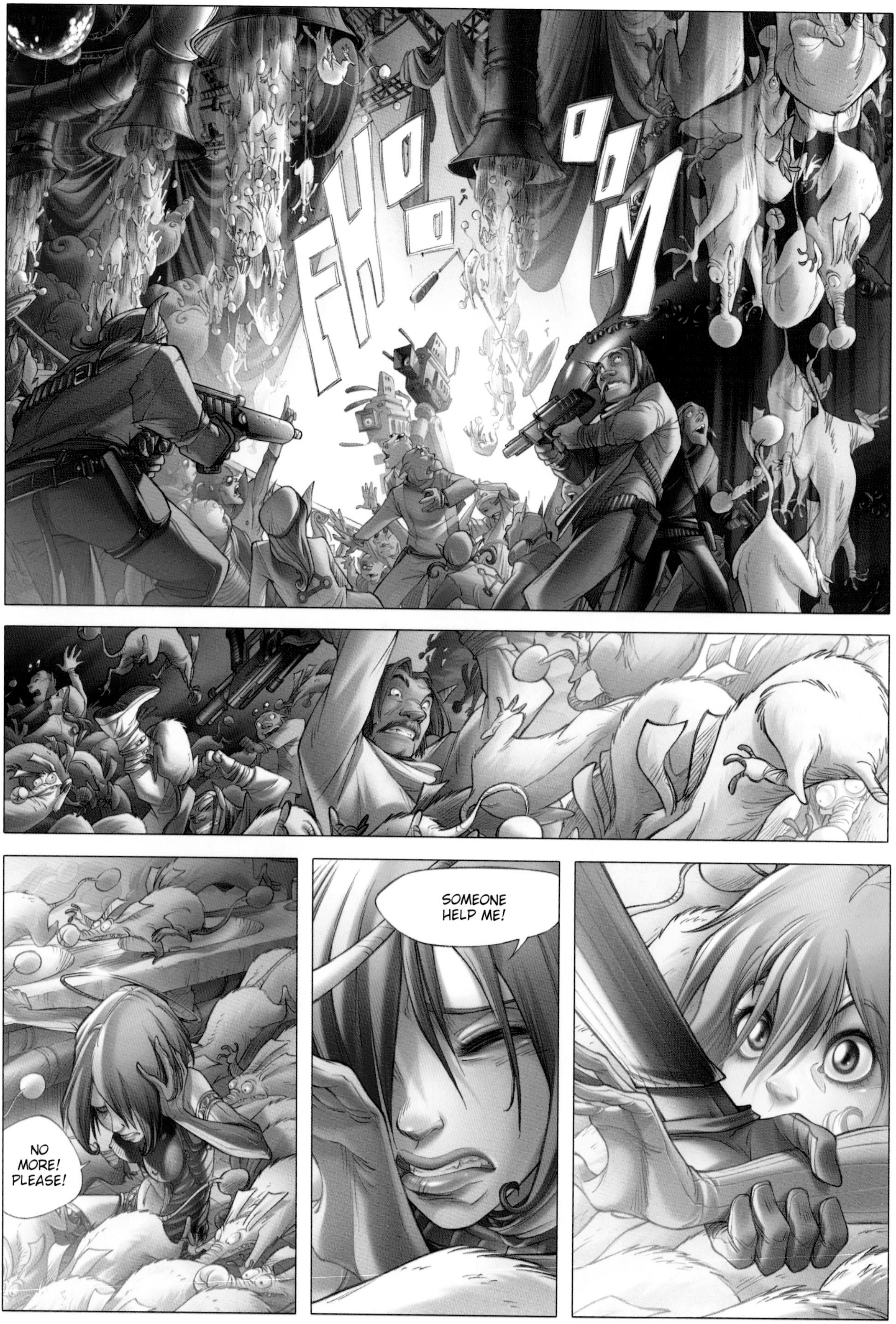
FHOOOOM
NO MORE! PLEASE!
SOMEONE HELP ME!

HA HA! WONDERFUL! FILM! FILM IT ALL!

MADAM FRIDA, I THINK YOUR DAUGHTER'S RUNNING AWAY.

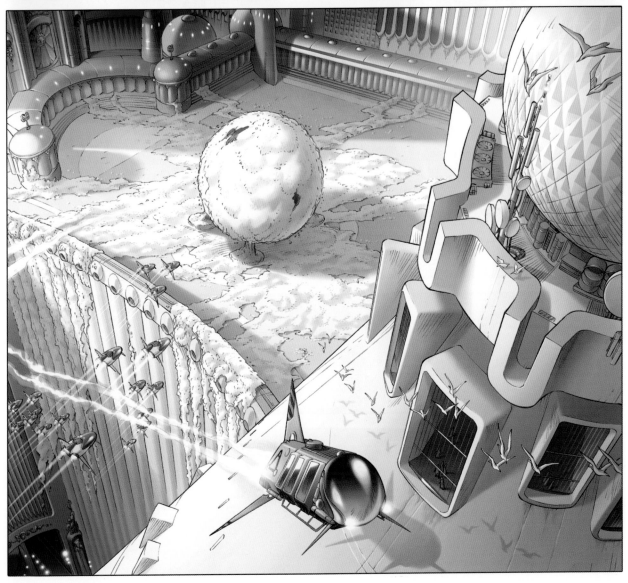

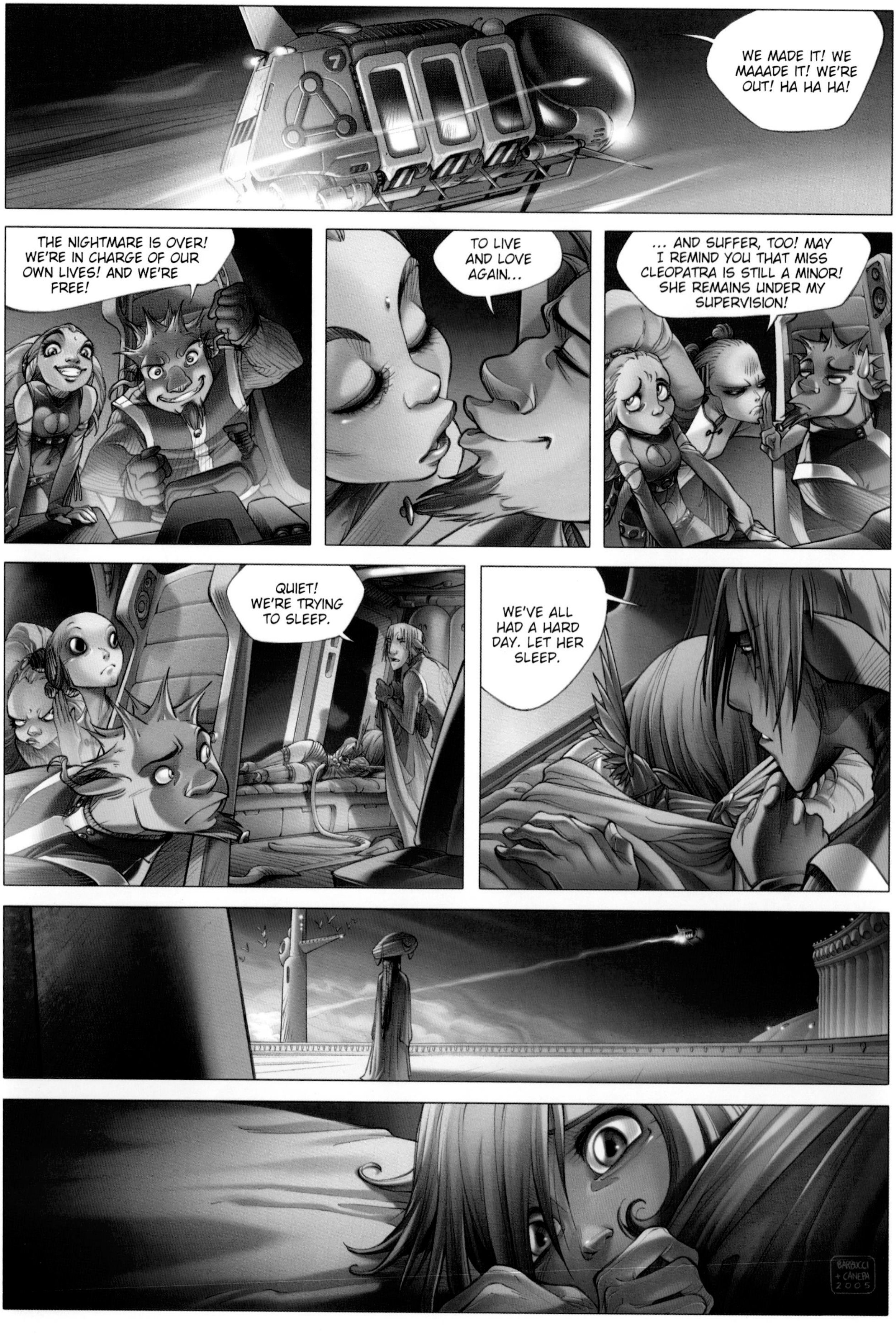

WE MADE IT! WE MAAADE IT! WE'RE OUT! HA HA HA!
THE NIGHTMARE IS OVER! WE'RE IN CHARGE OF OUR OWN LIVES! AND WE'RE FREE!
TO LIVE AND LOVE AGAIN...
... AND SUFFER, TOO! MAY I REMIND YOU THAT MISS CLEOPATRA IS STILL A MINOR! SHE REMAINS UNDER MY SUPERVISION!
QUIET! WE'RE TRYING TO SLEEP.
WE'VE ALL HAD A HARD DAY. LET HER SLEEP.
BARBUCCI + CANEPA 2005

SKY·DOLL DECADE 00 > 10

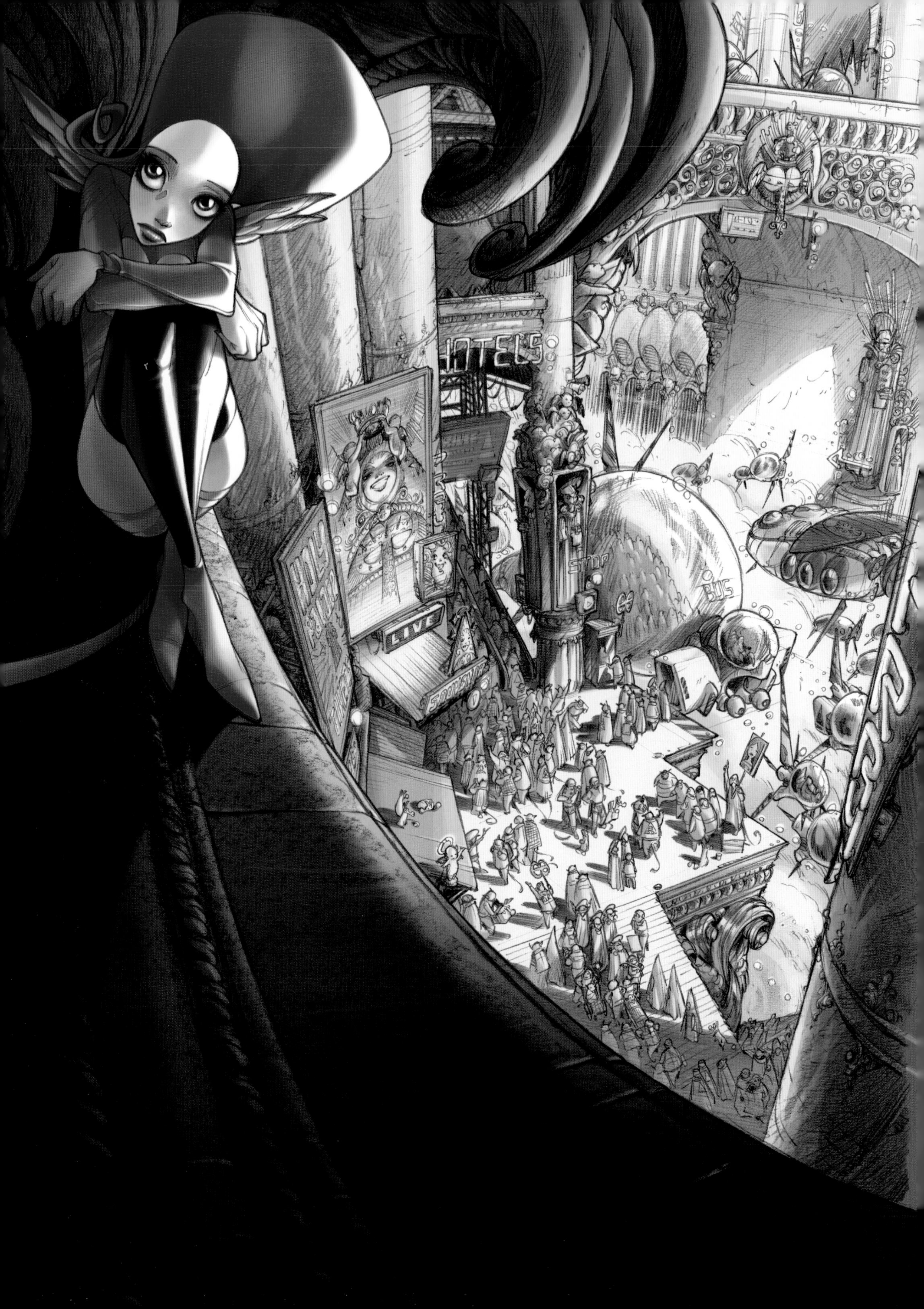
HOTELS
LIVE
STOP
BUS

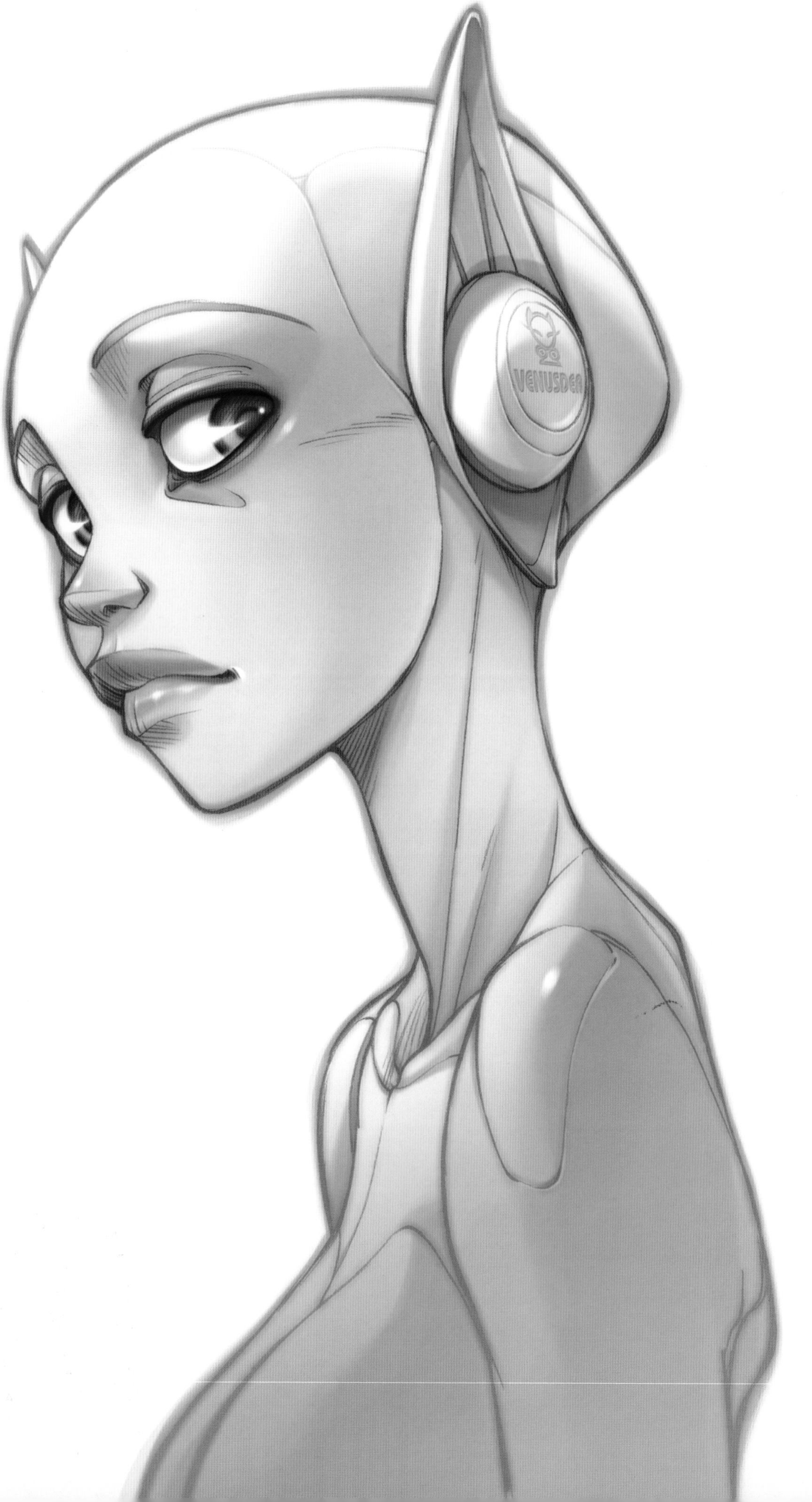
VENUSDEA

SKY·DOLL
DECADE 00 > 10
Volume 0: Doll Factory

written & illustrated by:
Barbucci & Canepa

*"Anything that happens, happens.
Anything that, in happening, causes something else to happen,
causes something else to happen.
Anything that, in happening, causes itself to happen again, happens again.
It doesn't necessarily do it in chronological order, though."*
~ Douglas Adams

I REMEMBER...

...THE DAY I WAS BORN.

MY MIND EMPTY OF ALL THOUGHT, NO DREAMS, JUST SENSATIONS...

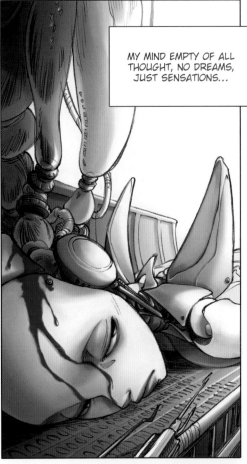

FOR ME, THAT'S ALL IN THE PAST.

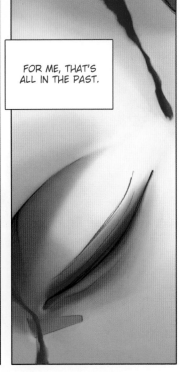

AND THE MAN WHO GAVE ME LIFE...

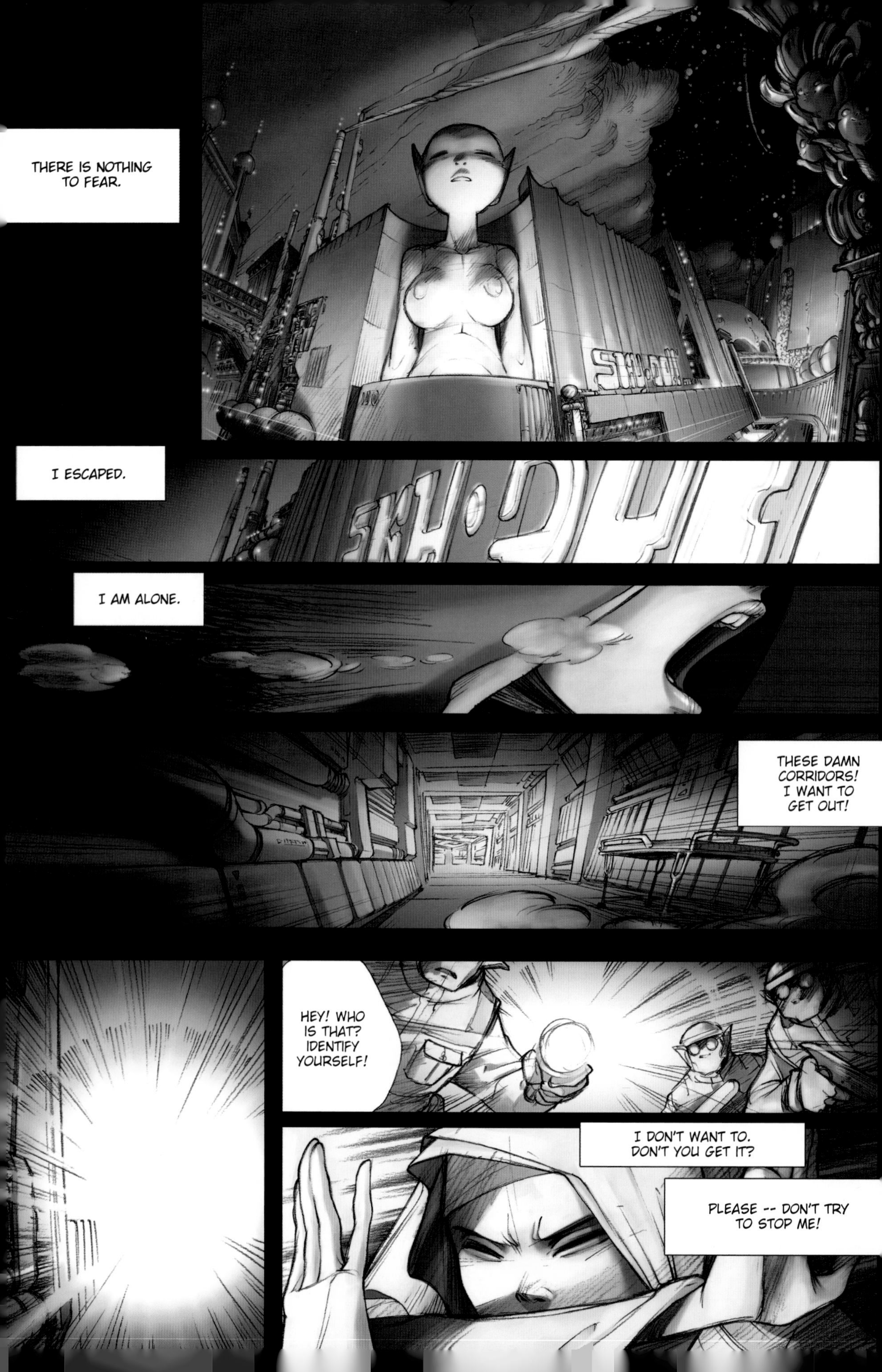
THERE IS NOTHING TO FEAR.
I ESCAPED.
I AM ALONE.
THESE DAMN CORRIDORS! I WANT TO GET OUT!
HEY! WHO IS THAT? IDENTIFY YOURSELF!
I DON'T WANT TO. DON'T YOU GET IT?
PLEASE -- DON'T TRY TO STOP ME!

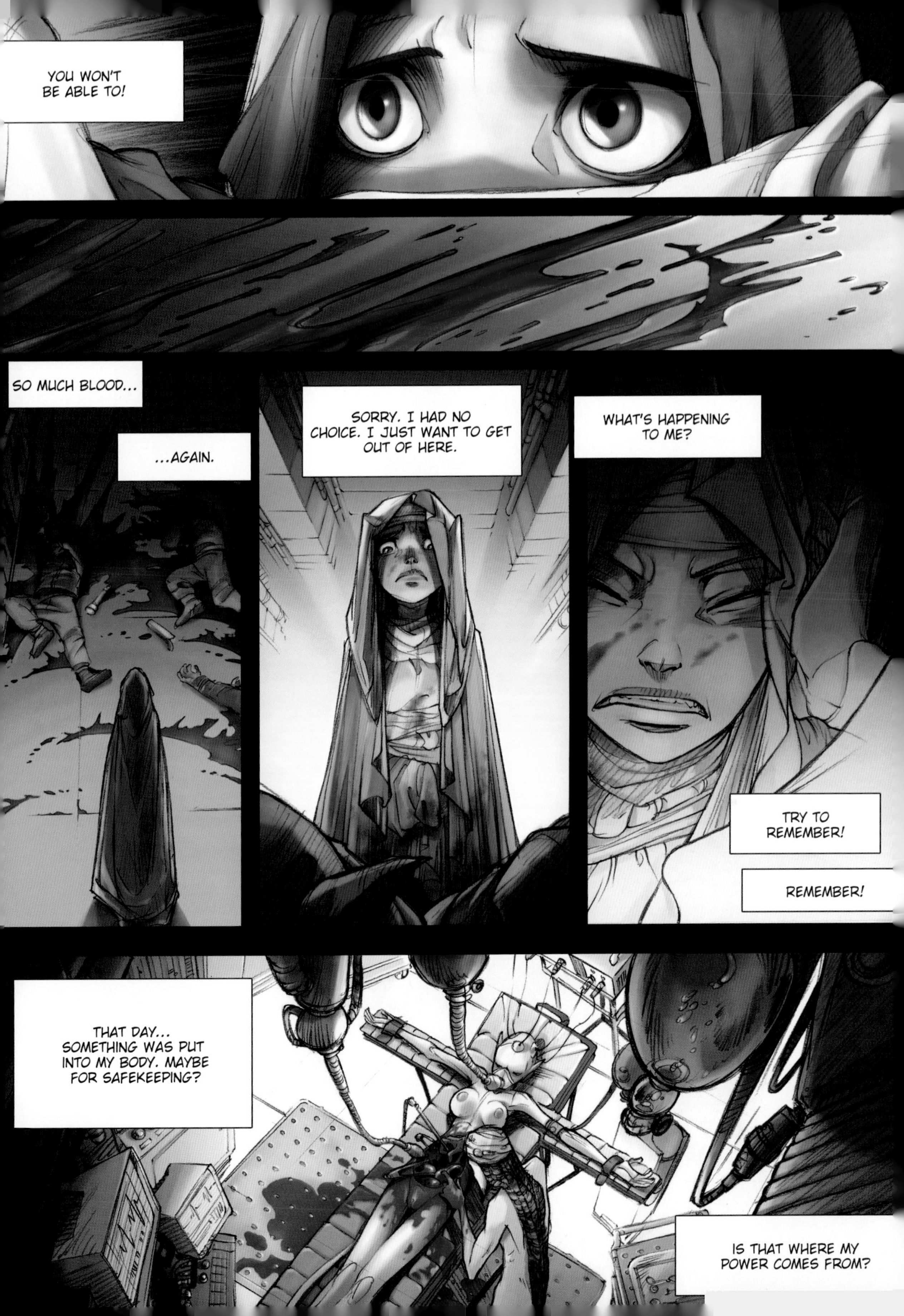
YOU WON'T BE ABLE TO!
SO MUCH BLOOD...
...AGAIN.
SORRY. I HAD NO CHOICE. I JUST WANT TO GET OUT OF HERE.
WHAT'S HAPPENING TO ME?
TRY TO REMEMBER!
REMEMBER!
THAT DAY... SOMETHING WAS PUT INTO MY BODY. MAYBE FOR SAFEKEEPING?
IS THAT WHERE MY POWER COMES FROM?

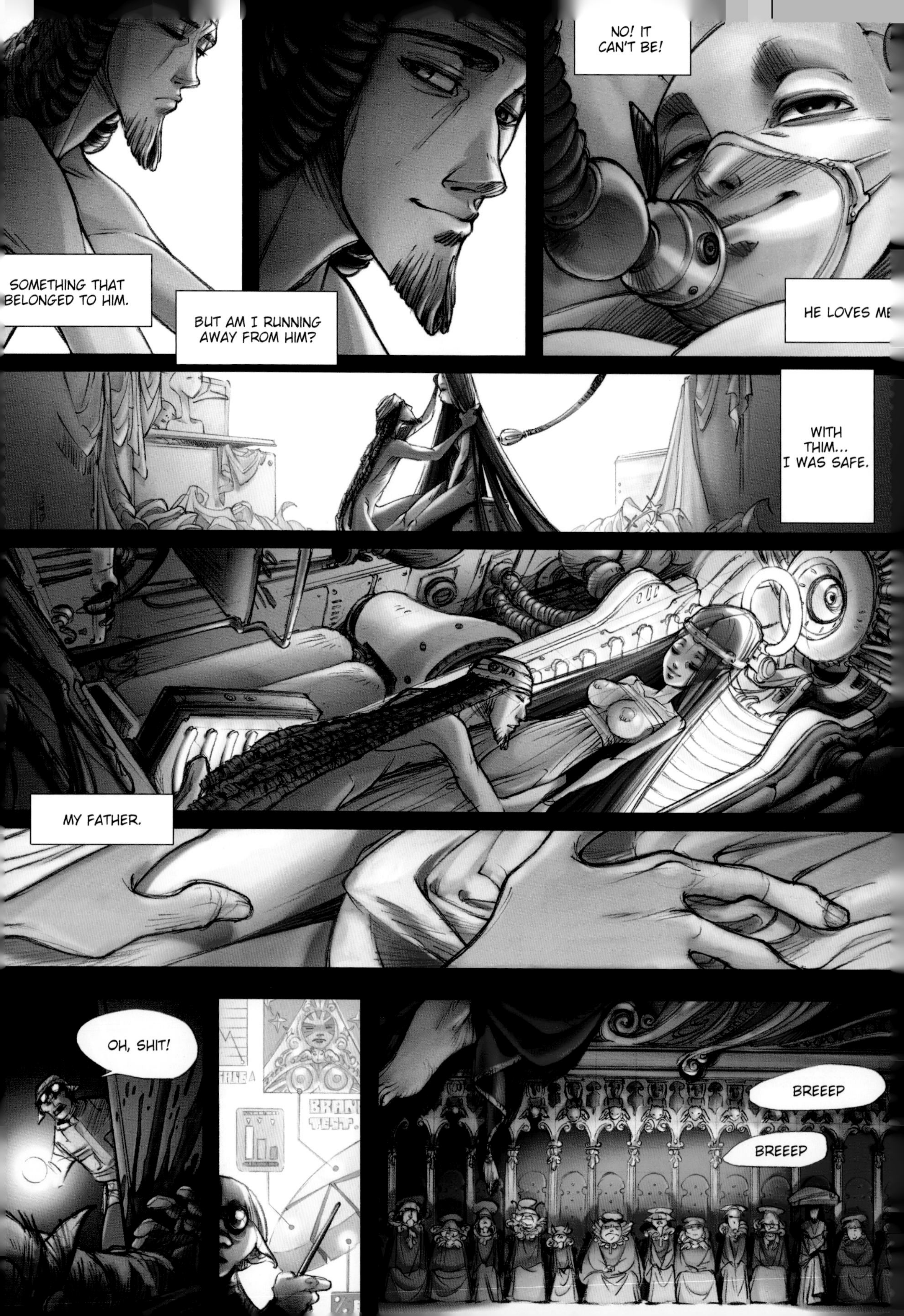
SOMETHING THAT BELONGED TO HIM.
BUT AM I RUNNING AWAY FROM HIM?
NO! IT CAN'T BE!
HE LOVES ME
WITH THIM... I WAS SAFE.
MY FATHER.
OH, SHIT!
BREEEP
BREEEP

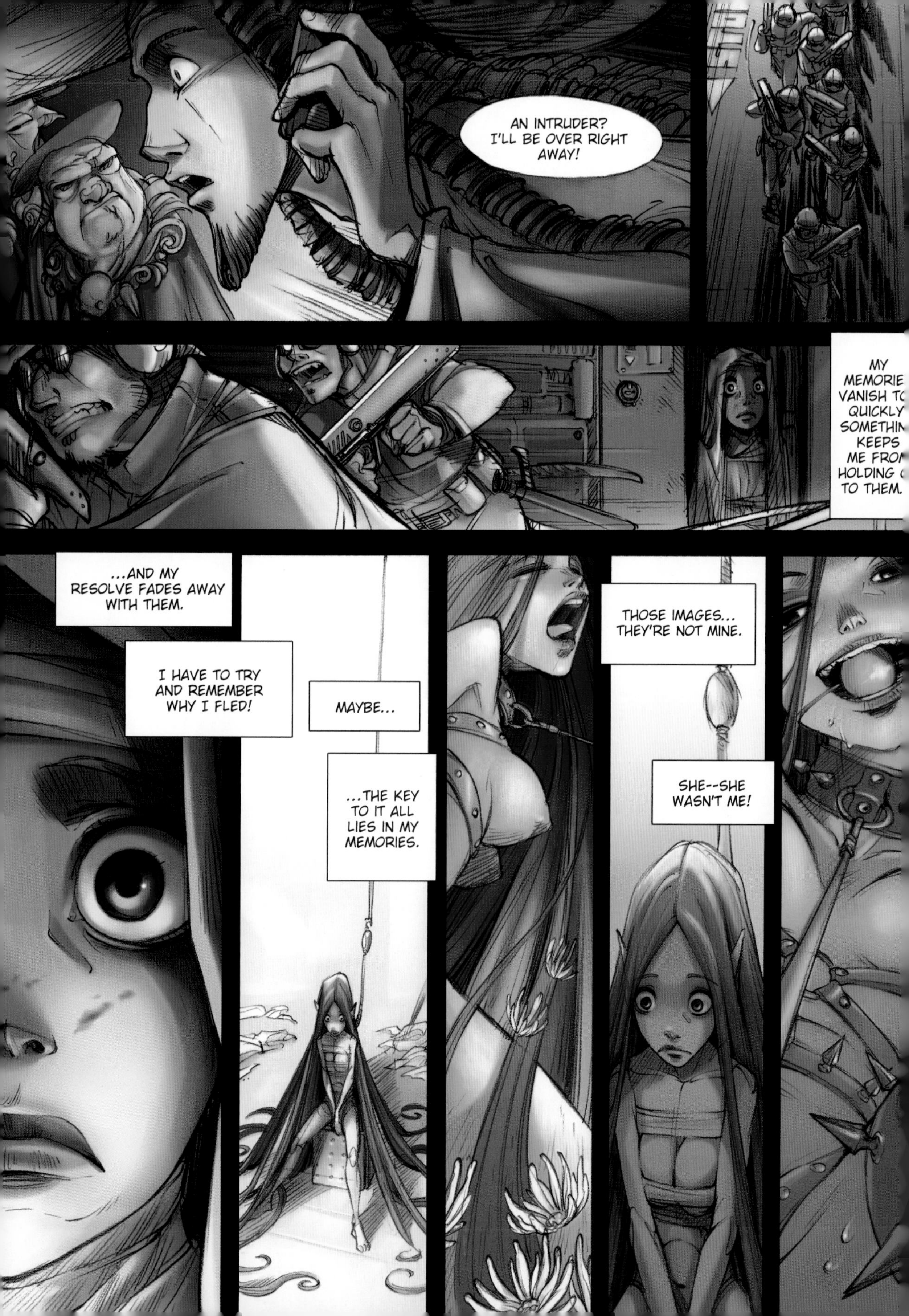
AN INTRUDER? I'LL BE OVER RIGHT AWAY!
MY MEMORIE VANISH TO QUICKLY SOMETHIN KEEPS ME FROM HOLDING TO THEM.
...AND MY RESOLVE FADES AWAY WITH THEM.
I HAVE TO TRY AND REMEMBER WHY I FLED!
MAYBE...
...THE KEY TO IT ALL LIES IN MY MEMORIES.
THOSE IMAGES... THEY'RE NOT MINE.
SHE--SHE WASN'T ME!

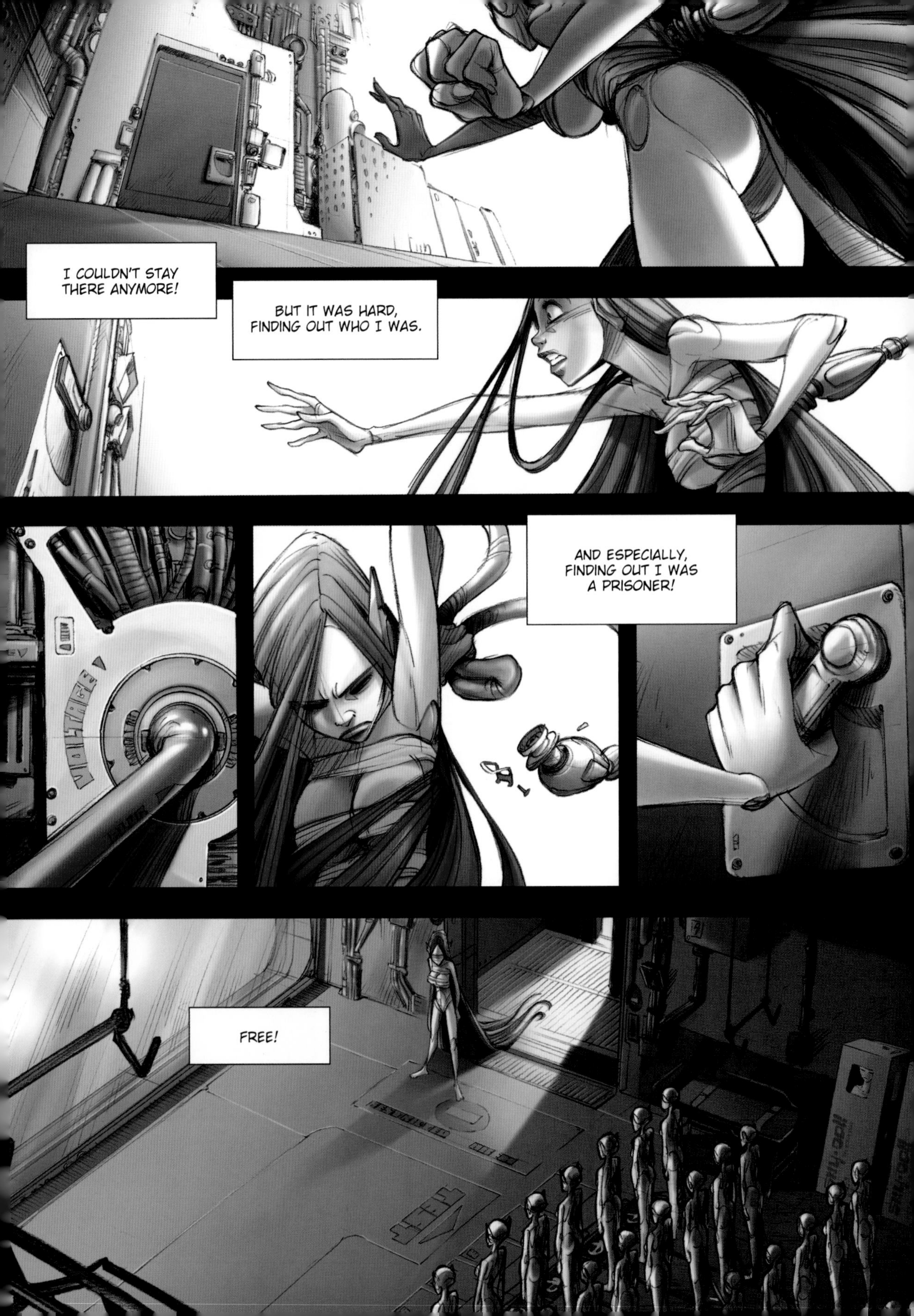
I COULDN'T STAY THERE ANYMORE!
BUT IT WAS HARD, FINDING OUT WHO I WAS.
AND ESPECIALLY, FINDING OUT I WAS A PRISONER!
FREE!

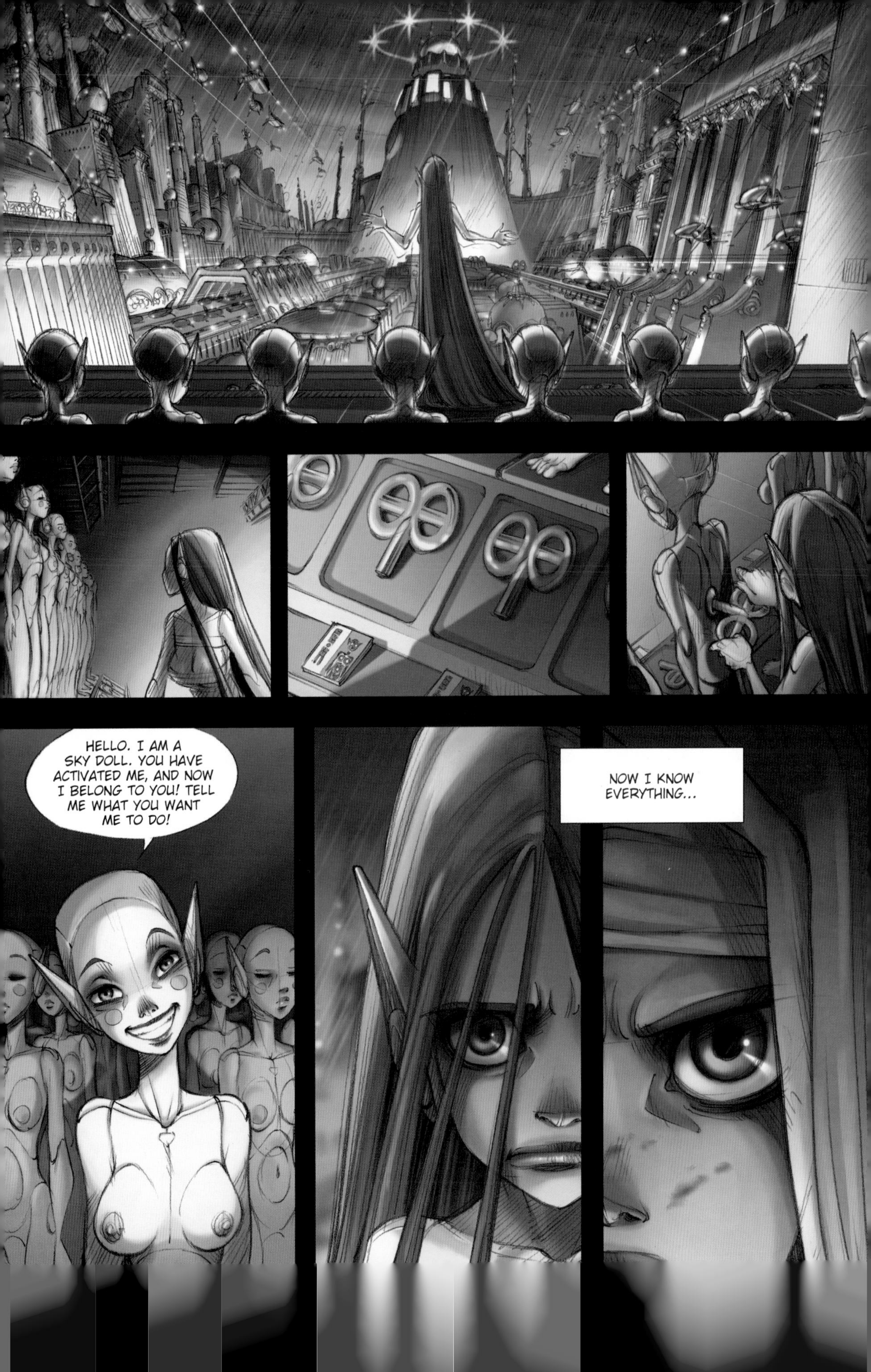
HELLO. I AM A SKY DOLL. YOU HAVE ACTIVATED ME, AND NOW I BELONG TO YOU! TELL ME WHAT YOU WANT ME TO DO!
NOW I KNOW EVERYTHING...

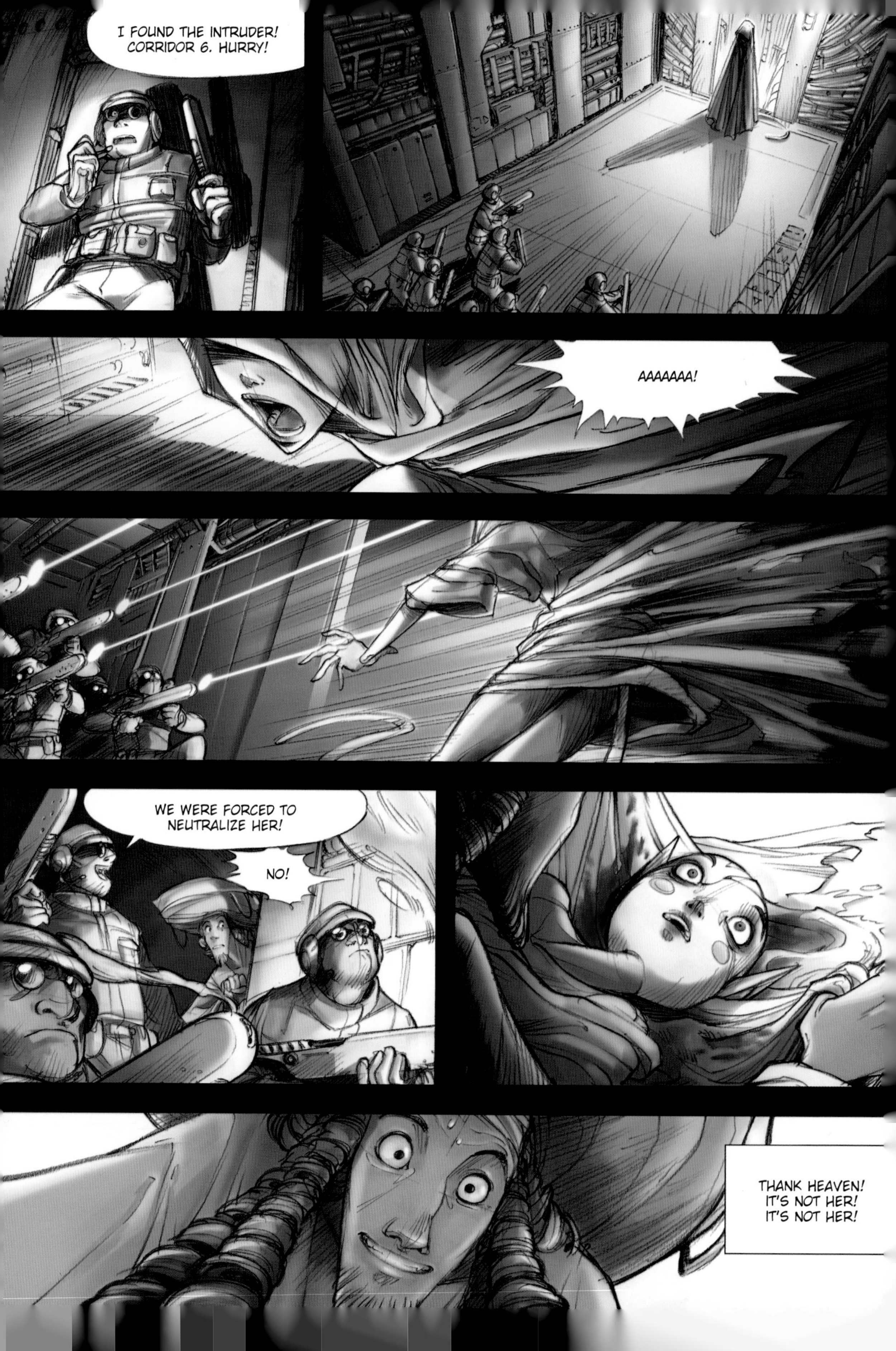
I FOUND THE INTRUDER! CORRIDOR 6. HURRY!
AAAAAAA!
WE WERE FORCED TO NEUTRALIZE HER!
NO!
THANK HEAVEN! IT'S NOT HER! IT'S NOT HER!

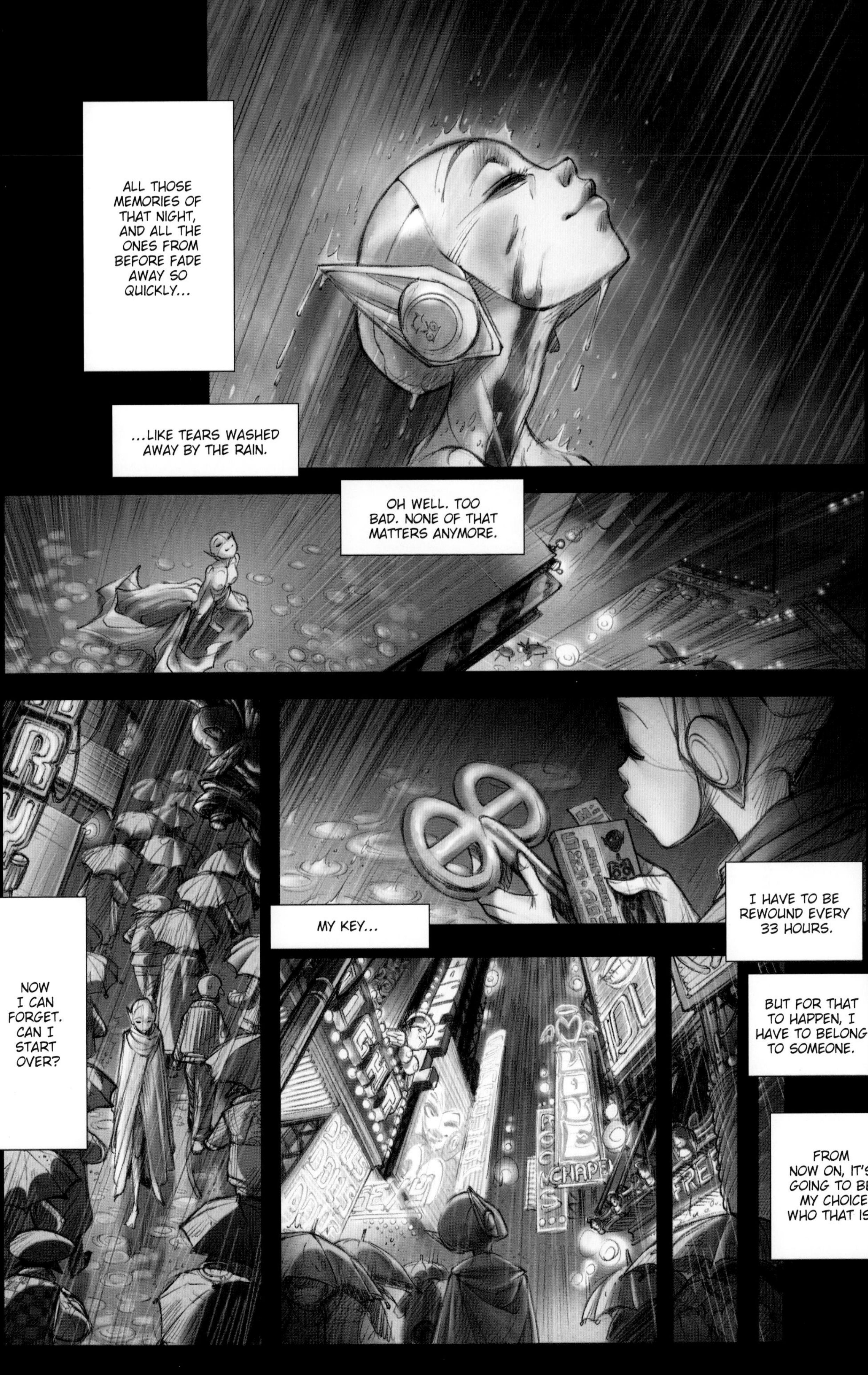
ALL THOSE MEMORIES OF THAT NIGHT, AND ALL THE ONES FROM BEFORE FADE AWAY SO QUICKLY...
...LIKE TEARS WASHED AWAY BY THE RAIN.
OH WELL. TOO BAD. NONE OF THAT MATTERS ANYMORE.
NOW I CAN FORGET. CAN I START OVER?
MY KEY...
I HAVE TO BE REWOUND EVERY 33 HOURS.
BUT FOR THAT TO HAPPEN, I HAVE TO BELONG TO SOMEONE.
FROM NOW ON, IT'S GOING TO BE MY CHOICE WHO THAT IS.

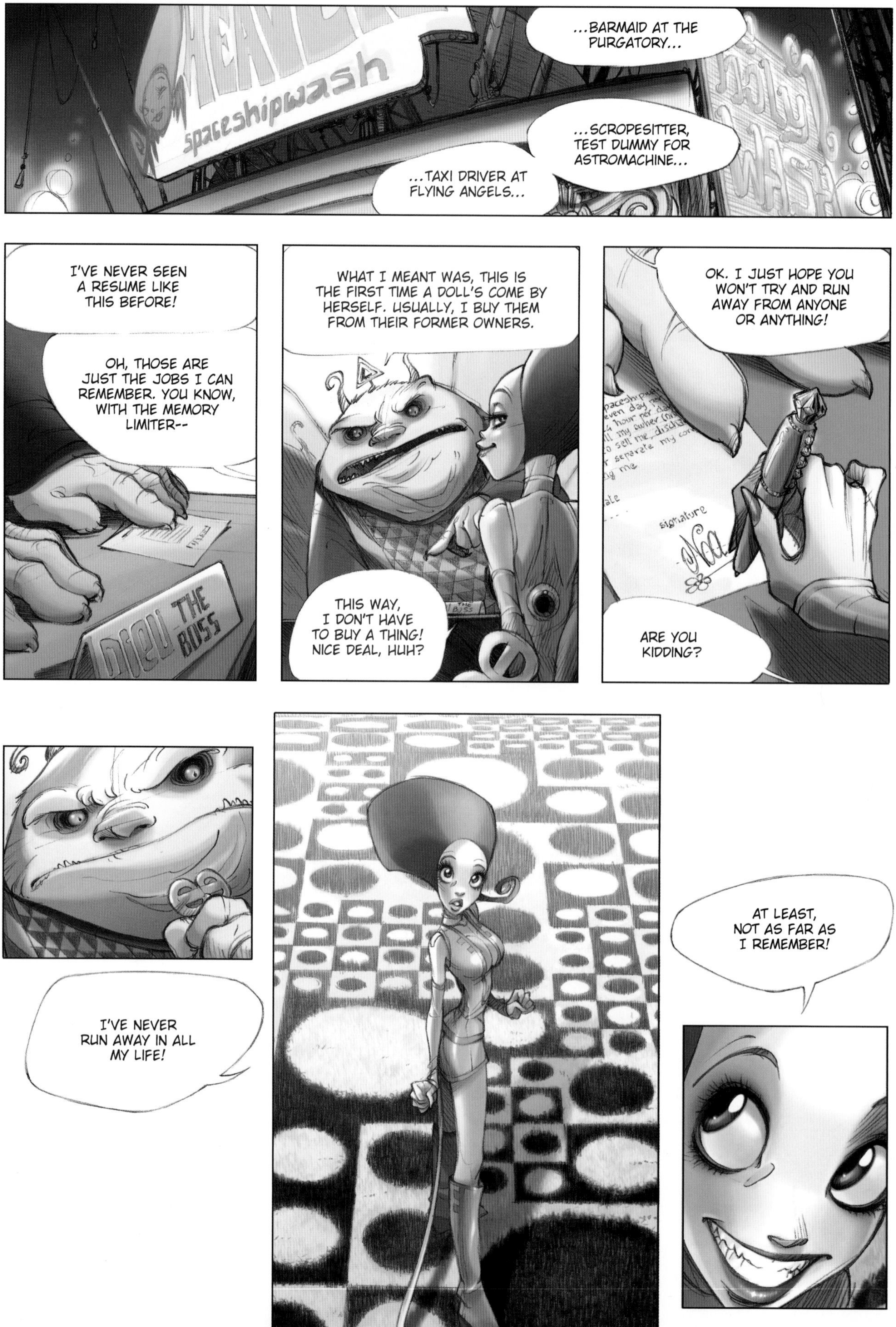
HEAVEN spaceshipwash
...BARMAID AT THE PURGATORY...
...SCROPESITTER, TEST DUMMY FOR ASTROMACHINE...
...TAXI DRIVER AT FLYING ANGELS...
I'VE NEVER SEEN A RESUME LIKE THIS BEFORE!
OH, THOSE ARE JUST THE JOBS I CAN REMEMBER. YOU KNOW, WITH THE MEMORY LIMITER--
THE BOSS
WHAT I MEANT WAS, THIS IS THE FIRST TIME A DOLL'S COME BY HERSELF. USUALLY, I BUY THEM FROM THEIR FORMER OWNERS.
THIS WAY, I DON'T HAVE TO BUY A THING! NICE DEAL, HUH?
OK. I JUST HOPE YOU WON'T TRY AND RUN AWAY FROM ANYONE OR ANYTHING!
signature
ARE YOU KIDDING?
I'VE NEVER RUN AWAY IN ALL MY LIFE!
AT LEAST, NOT AS FAR AS I REMEMBER!

SKY·DOLL DECADE 00 > 10

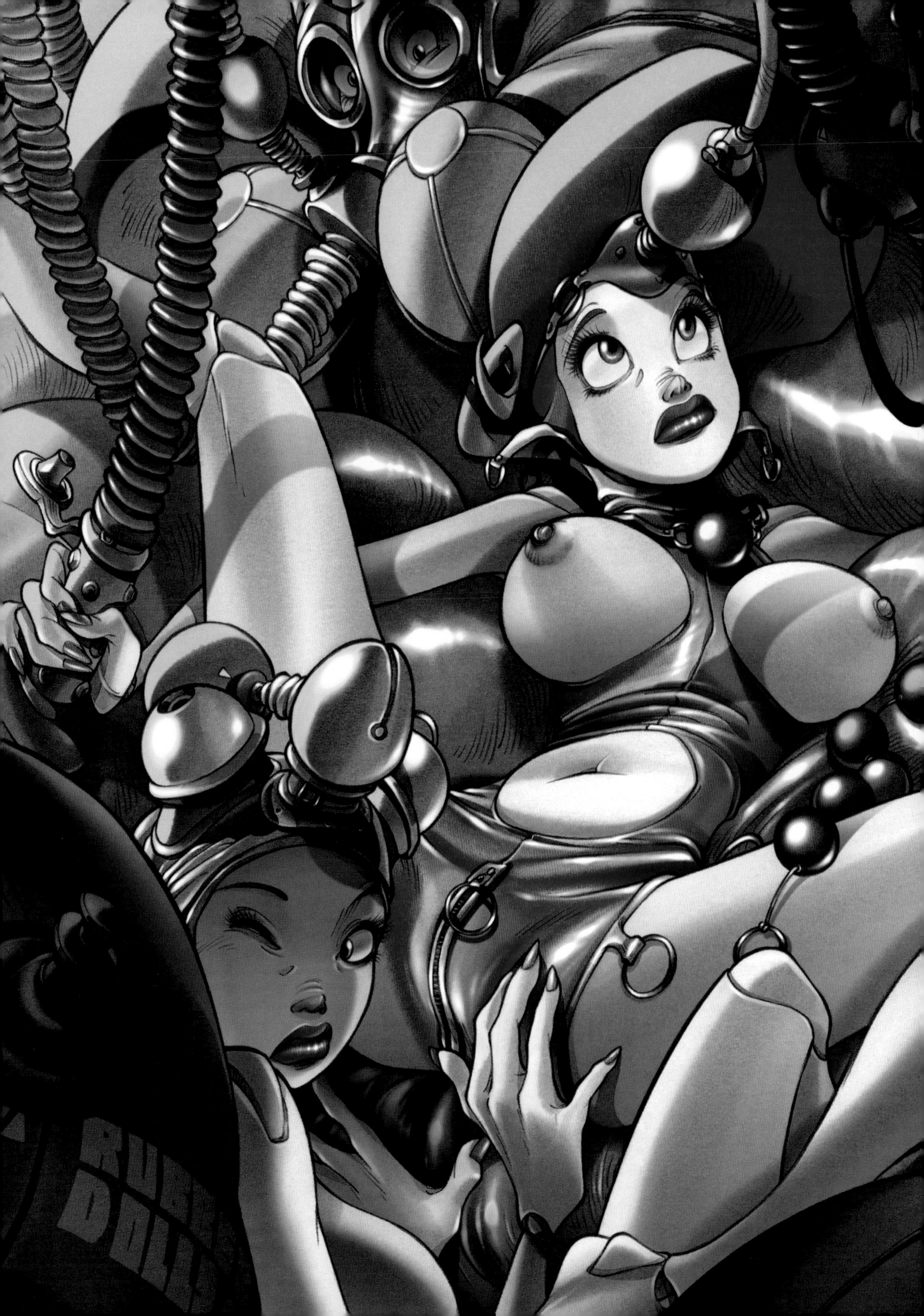

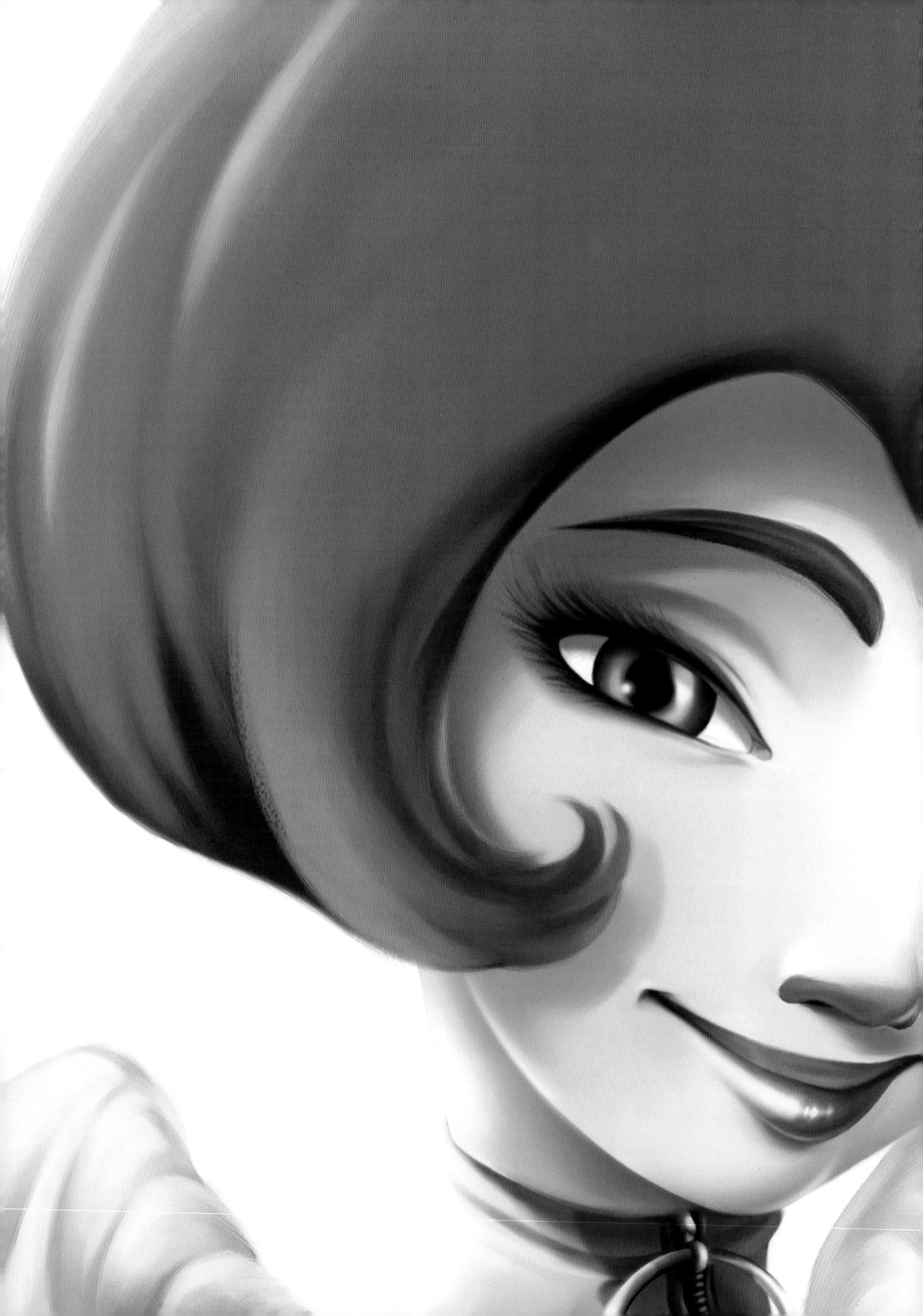

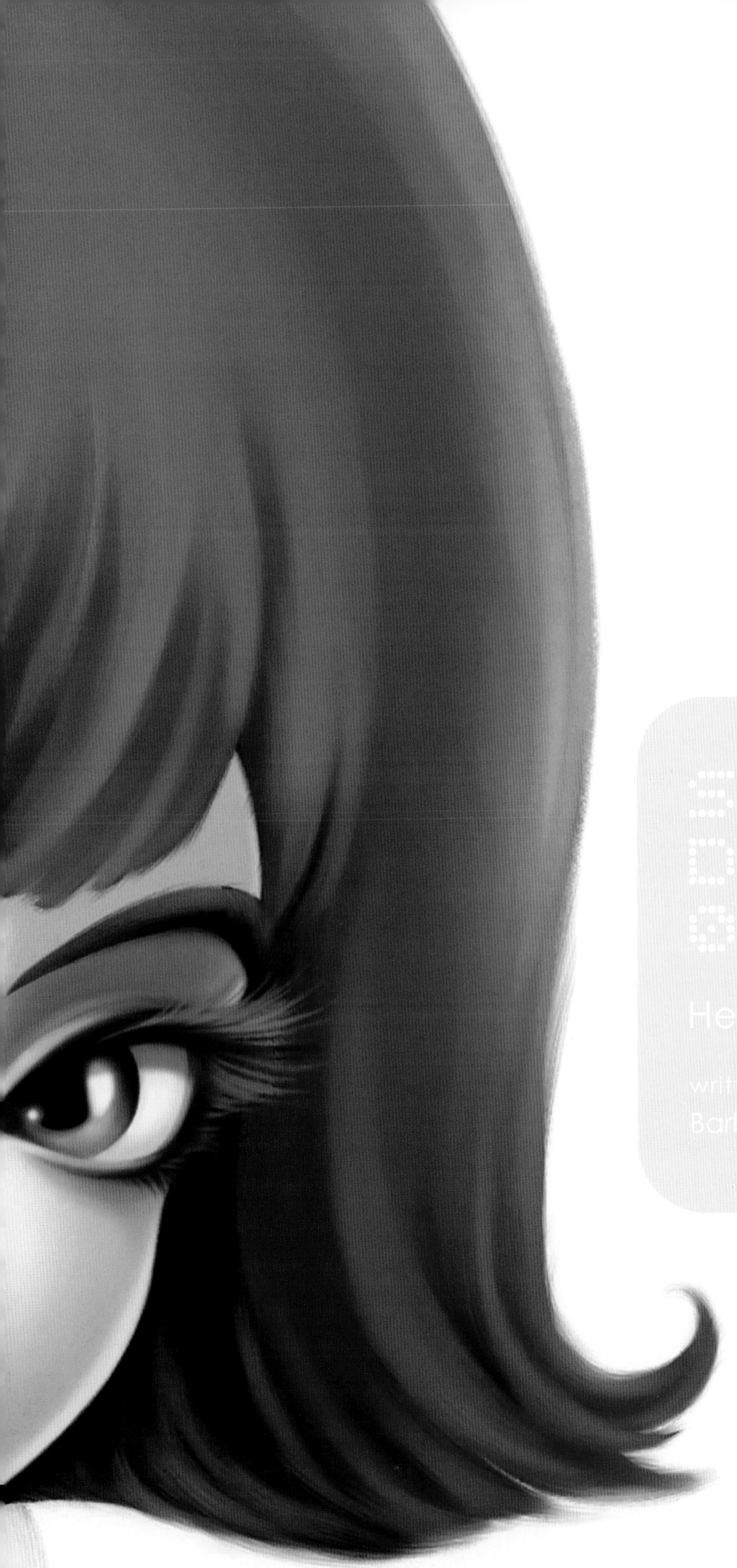

SKY·DOLL
DECADE
00 > 10

Heaven Dolls

written & illustrated by:
Barbucci & Canepa

"For ours is the kingdom of joy… especially now that our Holy Mother, in her infinite bounty, has brought back indulgences for anyone who's sinned with a doll! Remember, the only real doll is an original Skydoll ©… like the ones waiting for you at Heaven Astrowash to buff up your rocketship! Hallelujah, brothers! It's no sin!"
~ ~ Frida Decibel

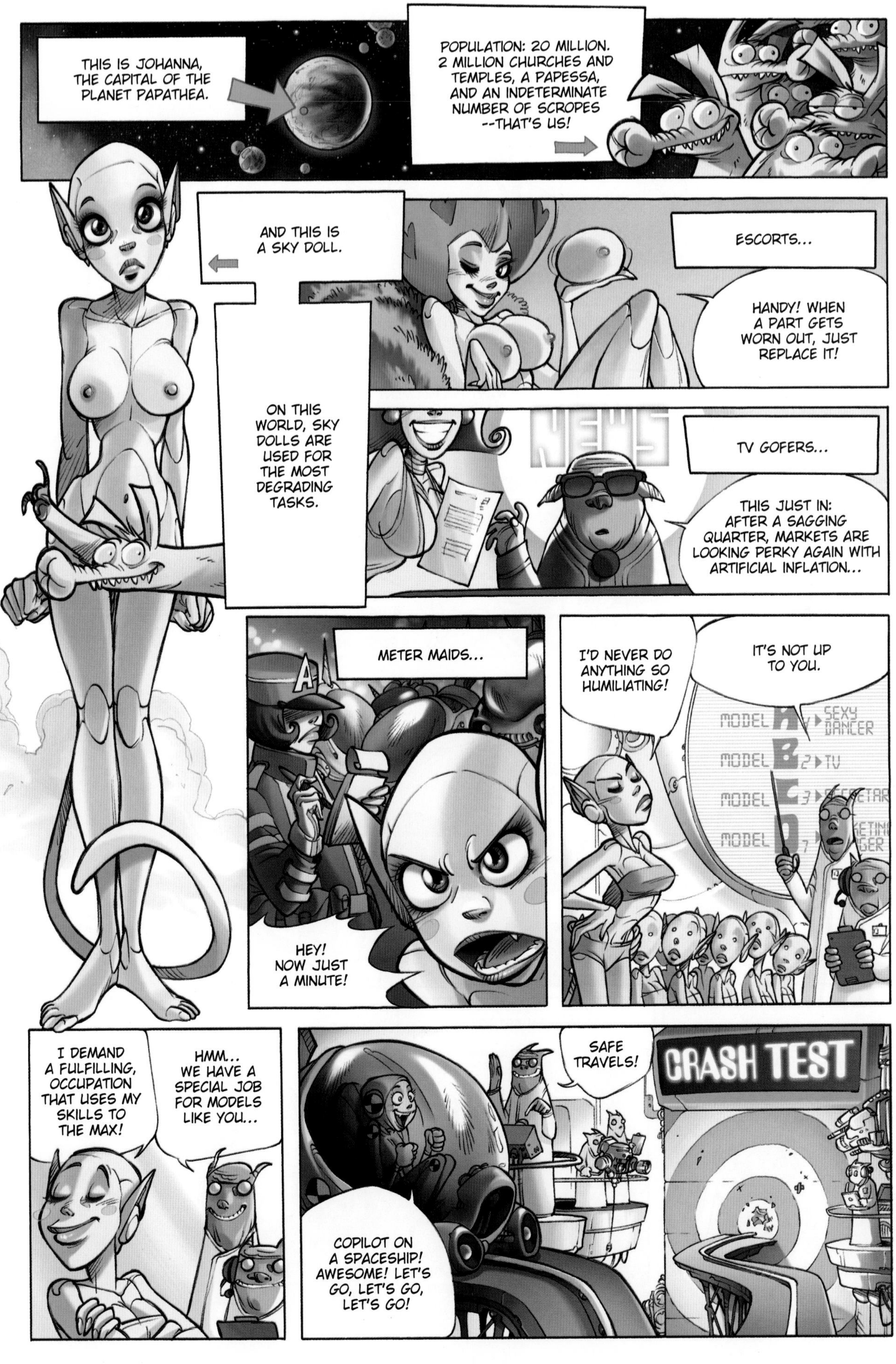
THIS IS JOHANNA, THE CAPITAL OF THE PLANET PAPATHEA.
POPULATION: 20 MILLION. 2 MILLION CHURCHES AND TEMPLES, A PAPESSA, AND AN INDETERMINATE NUMBER OF SCROPES --THAT'S US!
AND THIS IS A SKY DOLL.
ON THIS WORLD, SKY DOLLS ARE USED FOR THE MOST DEGRADING TASKS.
ESCORTS...
HANDY! WHEN A PART GETS WORN OUT, JUST REPLACE IT!
TV GOFERS...
THIS JUST IN: AFTER A SAGGING QUARTER, MARKETS ARE LOOKING PERKY AGAIN WITH ARTIFICIAL INFLATION...
METER MAIDS...
HEY! NOW JUST A MINUTE!
I'D NEVER DO ANYTHING SO HUMILIATING!
IT'S NOT UP TO YOU.
MODEL
SEXY DANCER
MODEL
TV
MODEL
MODEL
I DEMAND A FULFILLING, OCCUPATION THAT USES MY SKILLS TO THE MAX!
HMM... WE HAVE A SPECIAL JOB FOR MODELS LIKE YOU...
COPILOT ON A SPACESHIP! AWESOME! LET'S GO, LET'S GO, LET'S GO!
SAFE TRAVELS!
CRASH TEST

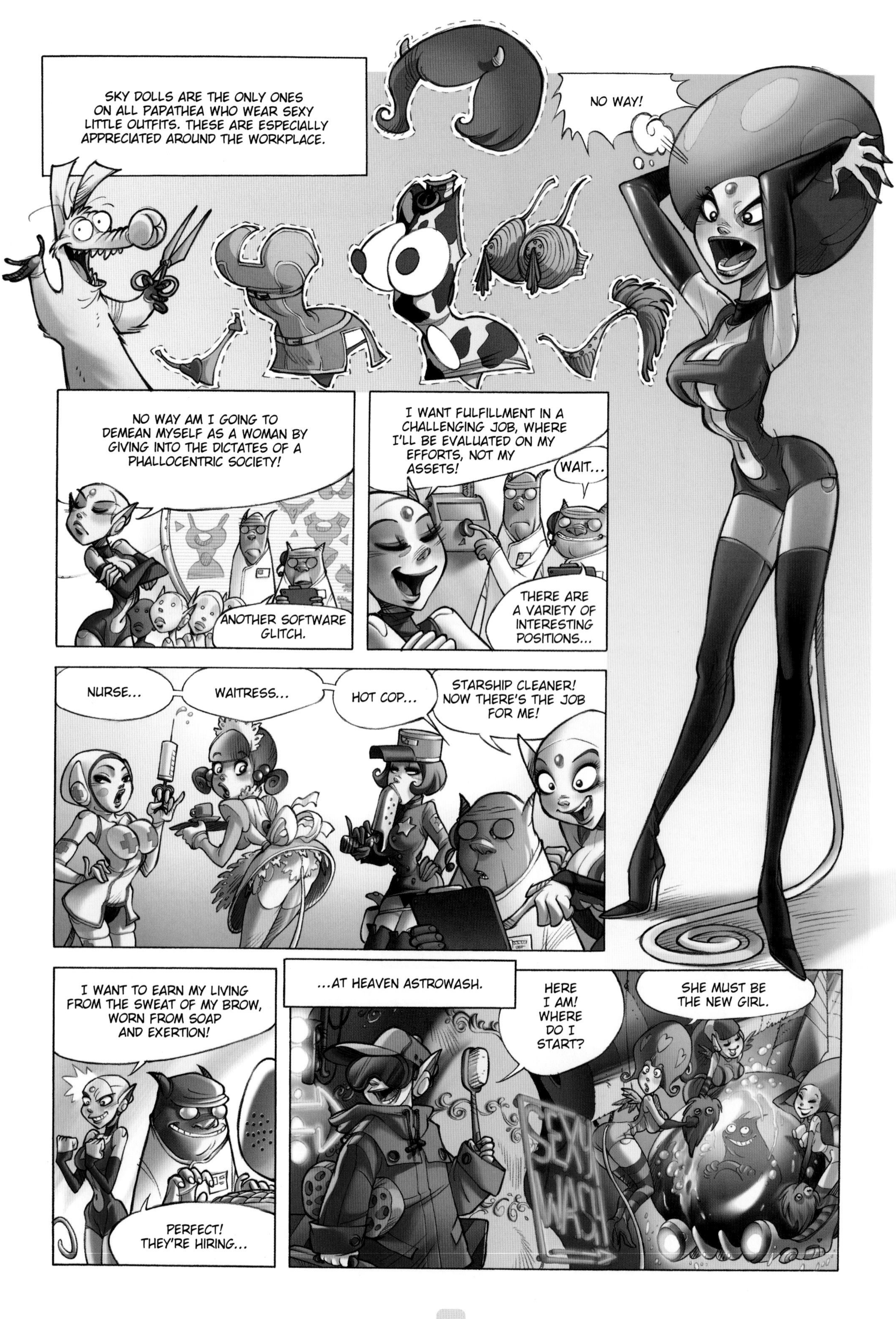
SKY DOLLS ARE THE ONLY ONES ON ALL PAPATHEA WHO WEAR SEXY LITTLE OUTFITS. THESE ARE ESPECIALLY APPRECIATED AROUND THE WORKPLACE.
NO WAY!
NO WAY AM I GOING TO DEMEAN MYSELF AS A WOMAN BY GIVING INTO THE DICTATES OF A PHALLOCENTRIC SOCIETY!
ANOTHER SOFTWARE GLITCH.
I WANT FULFILLMENT IN A CHALLENGING JOB, WHERE I'LL BE EVALUATED ON MY EFFORTS, NOT MY ASSETS!
WAIT...
THERE ARE A VARIETY OF INTERESTING POSITIONS...
NURSE...
WAITRESS...
HOT COP...
STARSHIP CLEANER! NOW THERE'S THE JOB FOR ME!
I WANT TO EARN MY LIVING FROM THE SWEAT OF MY BROW, WORN FROM SOAP AND EXERTION!
PERFECT! THEY'RE HIRING...
...AT HEAVEN ASTROWASH.
HERE I AM! WHERE DO I START?
SHE MUST BE THE NEW GIRL.
SEXY WASH

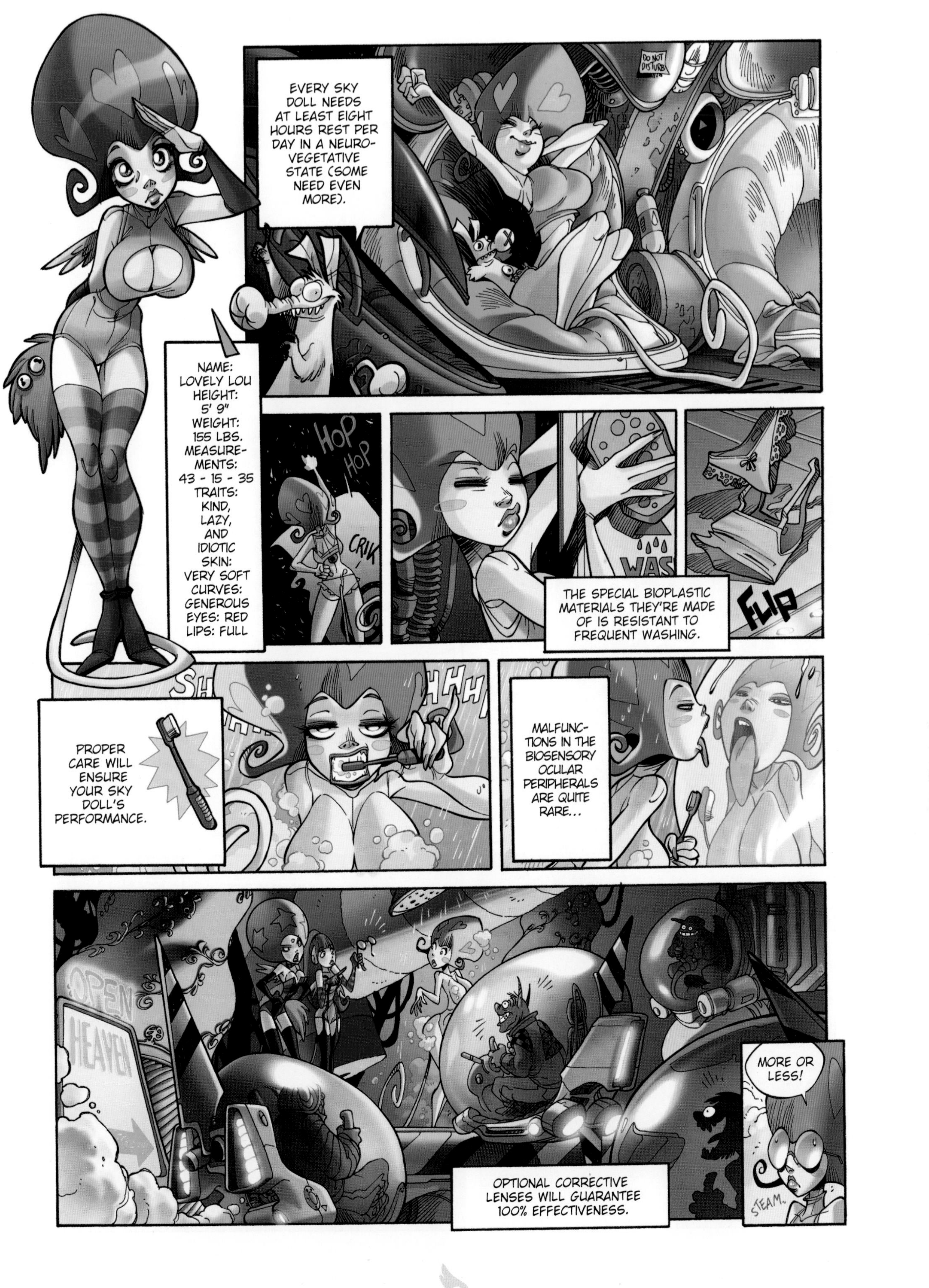
NAME: LOVELY LOU HEIGHT: 5' 9" WEIGHT: 155 LBS. MEASUREMENTS: 43 - 15 - 35 TRAITS: KIND, LAZY, AND IDIOTIC SKIN: VERY SOFT CURVES: GENEROUS EYES: RED LIPS: FULL
EVERY SKY DOLL NEEDS AT LEAST EIGHT HOURS REST PER DAY IN A NEURO-VEGETATIVE STATE (SOME NEED EVEN MORE).
DO NOT DISTURB
HOP HOP
CRIK
FLIP
THE SPECIAL BIOPLASTIC MATERIALS THEY'RE MADE OF IS RESISTANT TO FREQUENT WASHING.
PROPER CARE WILL ENSURE YOUR SKY DOLL'S PERFORMANCE.
MALFUNCTIONS IN THE BIOSENSORY OCULAR PERIPHERALS ARE QUITE RARE...
OPEN
HEAVEN
MORE OR LESS!
OPTIONAL CORRECTIVE LENSES WILL GUARANTEE 100% EFFECTIVENESS.
STEAM..

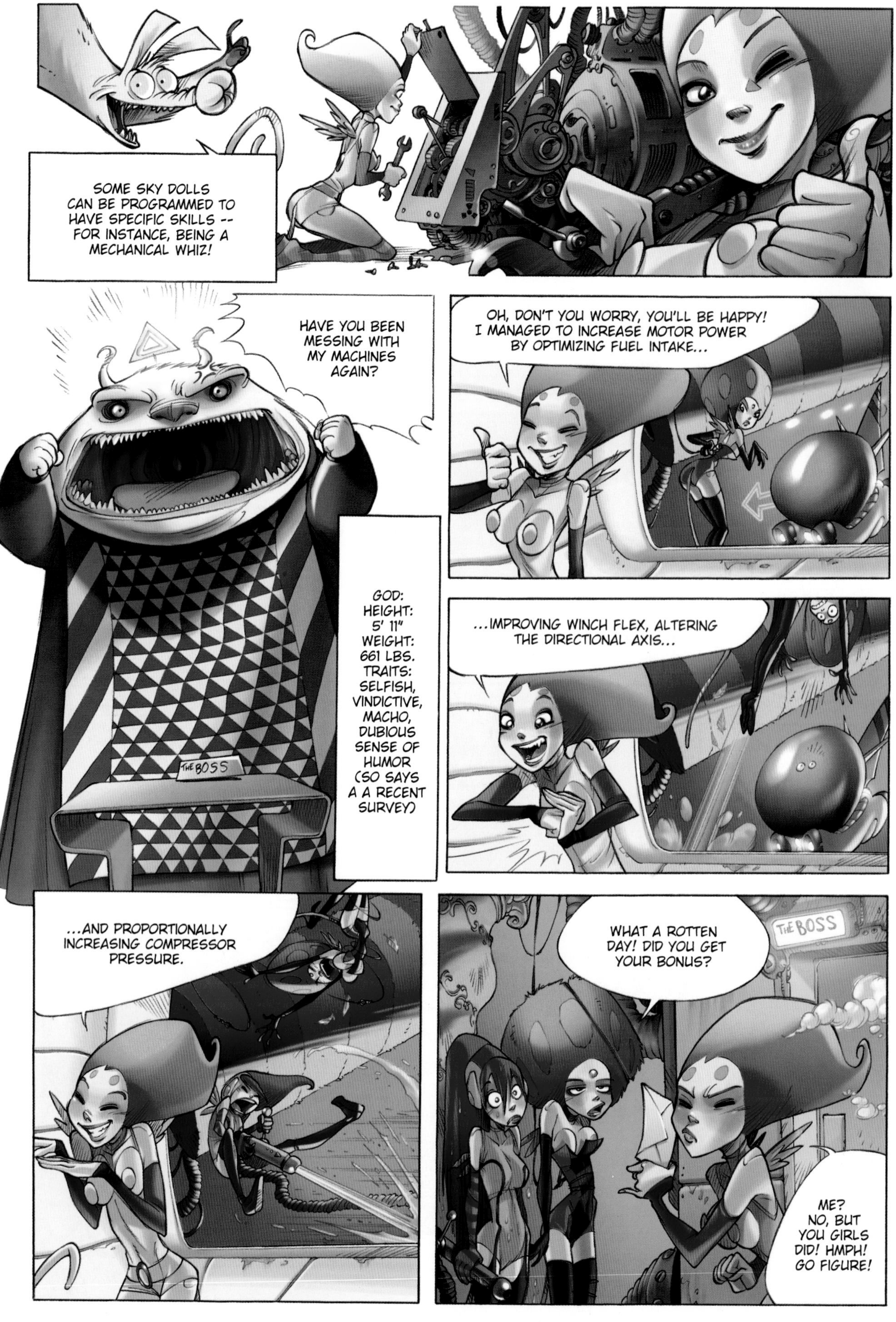
SOME SKY DOLLS CAN BE PROGRAMMED TO HAVE SPECIFIC SKILLS -- FOR INSTANCE, BEING A MECHANICAL WHIZ!
HAVE YOU BEEN MESSING WITH MY MACHINES AGAIN?
GOD: HEIGHT: 5' 11" WEIGHT: 661 LBS. TRAITS: SELFISH, VINDICTIVE, MACHO, DUBIOUS SENSE OF HUMOR (SO SAYS A A RECENT SURVEY)
THE BOSS
OH, DON'T YOU WORRY, YOU'LL BE HAPPY! I MANAGED TO INCREASE MOTOR POWER BY OPTIMIZING FUEL INTAKE...
...IMPROVING WINCH FLEX, ALTERING THE DIRECTIONAL AXIS...
...AND PROPORTIONALLY INCREASING COMPRESSOR PRESSURE.
WHAT A ROTTEN DAY! DID YOU GET YOUR BONUS?
THE BOSS
ME? NO, BUT YOU GIRLS DID! HMPH! GO FIGURE!

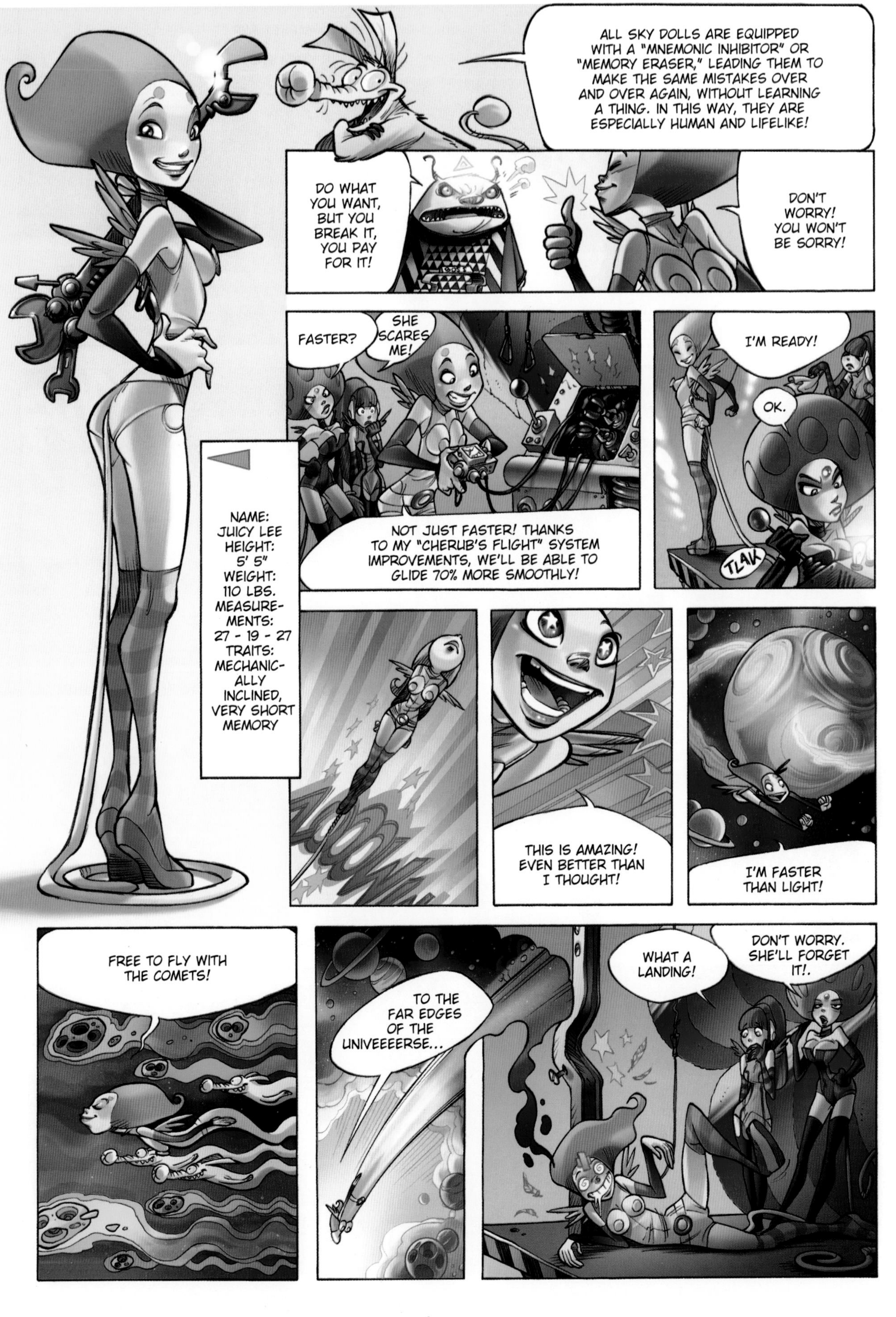

ALL SKY DOLLS ARE EQUIPPED WITH A "MNEMONIC INHIBITOR" OR "MEMORY ERASER," LEADING THEM TO MAKE THE SAME MISTAKES OVER AND OVER AGAIN, WITHOUT LEARNING A THING. IN THIS WAY, THEY ARE ESPECIALLY HUMAN AND LIFELIKE!
NAME: JUICY LEE HEIGHT: 5' 5" WEIGHT: 110 LBS. MEASURE-MENTS: 27 - 19 - 27 TRAITS: MECHANIC-ALLY INCLINED, VERY SHORT MEMORY
DO WHAT YOU WANT, BUT YOU BREAK IT, YOU PAY FOR IT!
DON'T WORRY! YOU WON'T BE SORRY!
FASTER?
SHE SCARES ME!
NOT JUST FASTER! THANKS TO MY "CHERUB'S FLIGHT" SYSTEM IMPROVEMENTS, WE'LL BE ABLE TO GLIDE 70% MORE SMOOTHLY!
I'M READY!
OK.
TLAK
THIS IS AMAZING! EVEN BETTER THAN I THOUGHT!
I'M FASTER THAN LIGHT!
FREE TO FLY WITH THE COMETS!
TO THE FAR EDGES OF THE UNIVEEEERSE...
WHAT A LANDING!
DON'T WORRY. SHE'LL FORGET IT!.

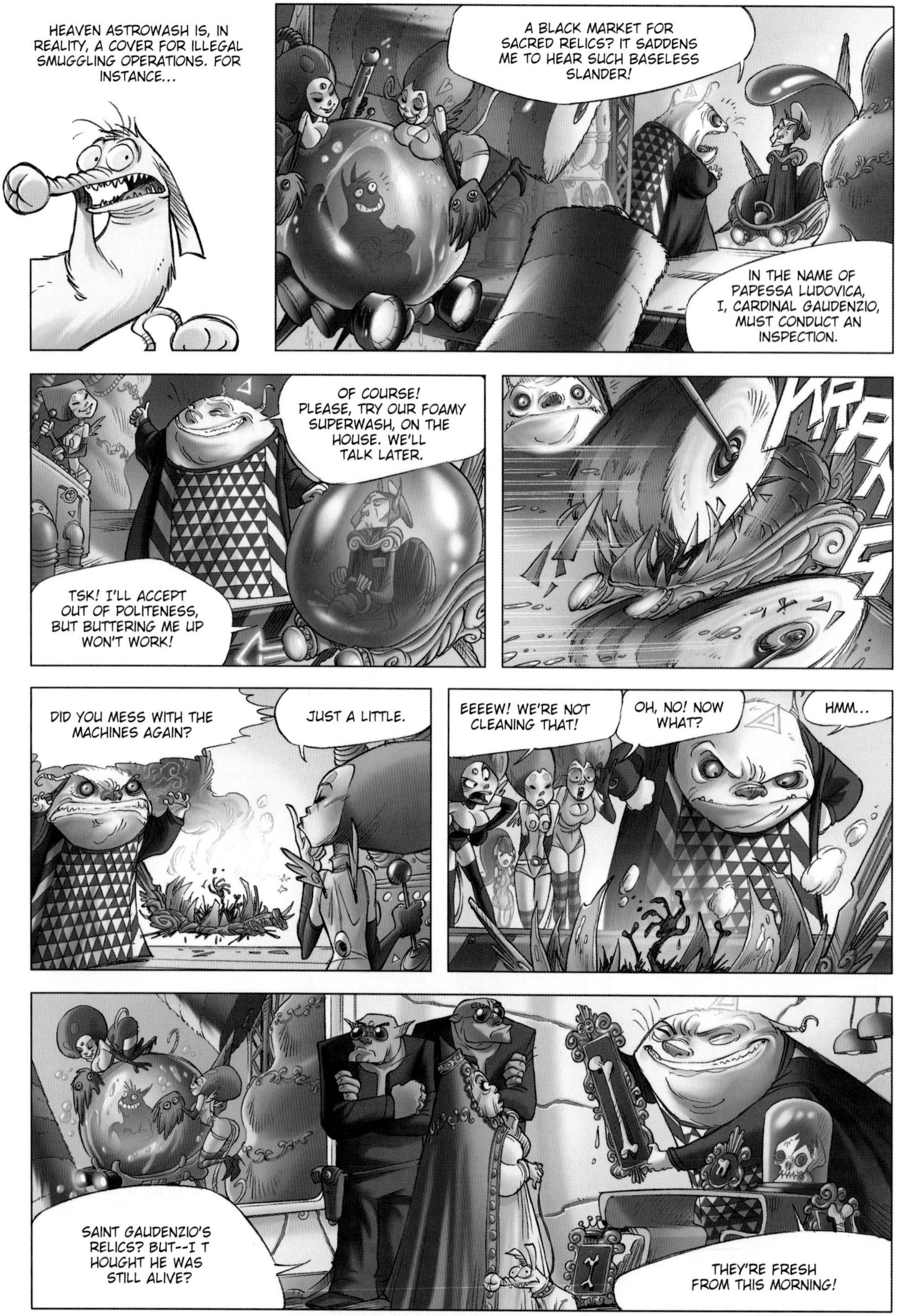
HEAVEN ASTROWASH IS, IN REALITY, A COVER FOR ILLEGAL SMUGGLING OPERATIONS. FOR INSTANCE...
A BLACK MARKET FOR SACRED RELICS? IT SADDENS ME TO HEAR SUCH BASELESS SLANDER!
IN THE NAME OF PAPESSA LUDOVICA, I, CARDINAL GAUDENZIO, MUST CONDUCT AN INSPECTION.
OF COURSE! PLEASE, TRY OUR FOAMY SUPERWASH, ON THE HOUSE. WE'LL TALK LATER.
TSK! I'LL ACCEPT OUT OF POLITENESS, BUT BUTTERING ME UP WON'T WORK!
DID YOU MESS WITH THE MACHINES AGAIN?
JUST A LITTLE.
EEEEW! WE'RE NOT CLEANING THAT!
OH, NO! NOW WHAT?
HMM...
SAINT GAUDENZIO'S RELICS? BUT--I T HOUGHT HE WAS STILL ALIVE?
THEY'RE FRESH FROM THIS MORNING!

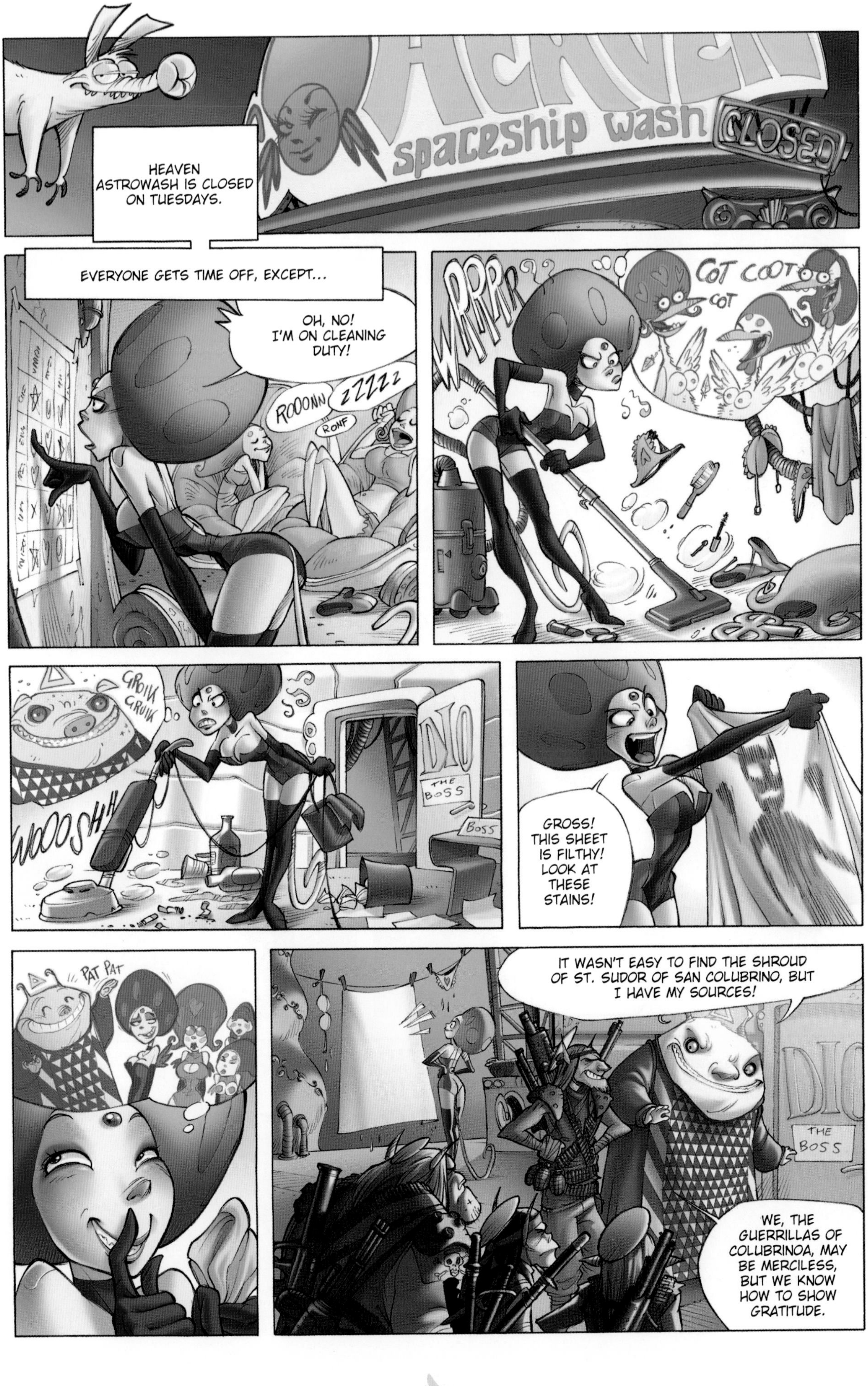
HEAVEN
spaceship wash
CLOSED
HEAVEN ASTROWASH IS CLOSED ON TUESDAYS.
EVERYONE GETS TIME OFF, EXCEPT...
OH, NO! I'M ON CLEANING DUTY!
ROOONN
ZZZZZ
RONF
WRRRRR
COT COOT
COT
GROINK GRUIK
WOOOSHH
DIO THE BOSS
BOSS
GROSS! THIS SHEET IS FILTHY! LOOK AT THESE STAINS!
PAT PAT
IT WASN'T EASY TO FIND THE SHROUD OF ST. SUDOR OF SAN COLUBRINO, BUT I HAVE MY SOURCES!
DIO THE BOSS
WE, THE GUERRILLAS OF COLUBRINOA, MAY BE MERCILESS, BUT WE KNOW HOW TO SHOW GRATITUDE.

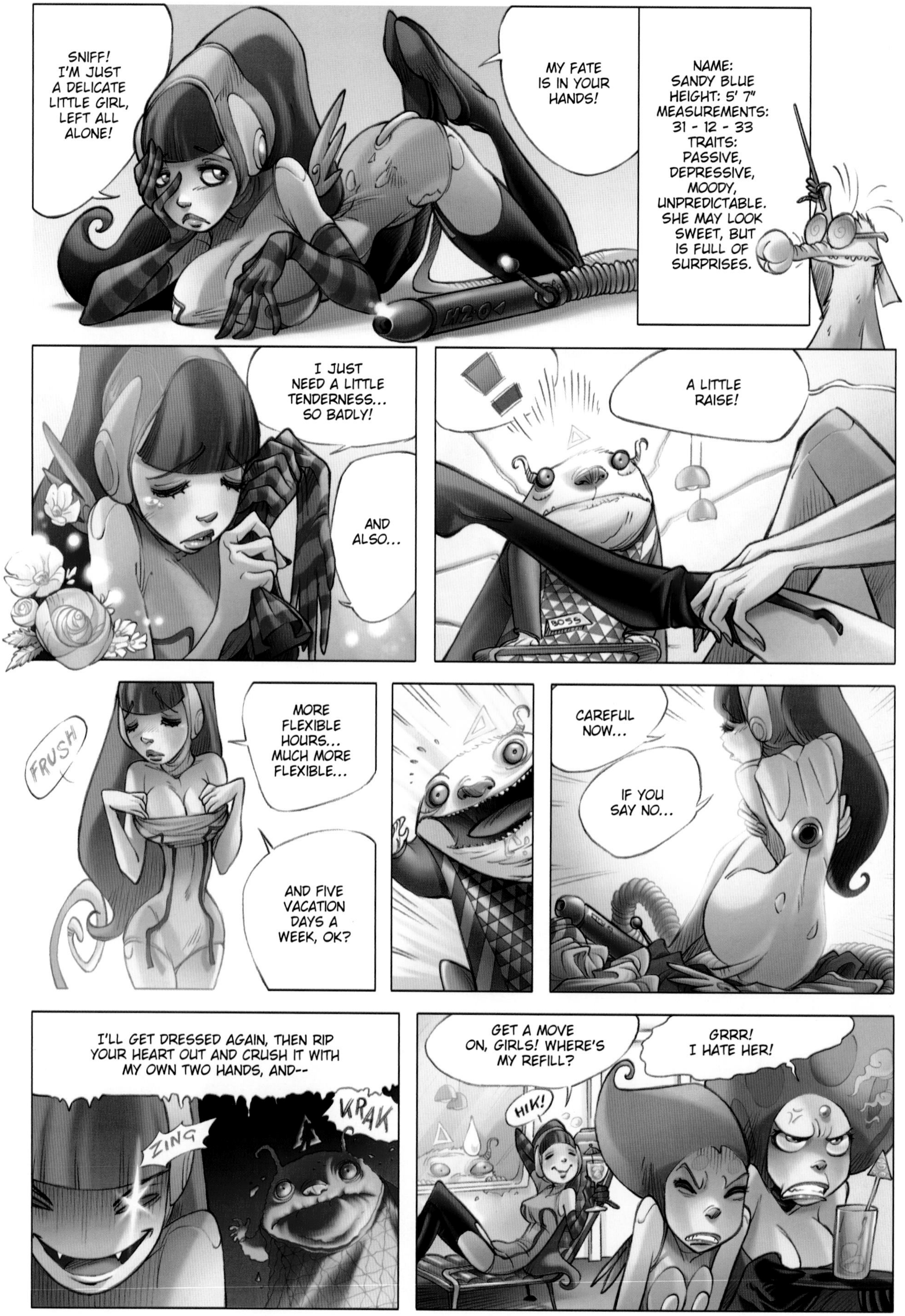
SNIFF! I'M JUST A DELICATE LITTLE GIRL, LEFT ALL ALONE!
MY FATE IS IN YOUR HANDS!
NAME: SANDY BLUE HEIGHT: 5' 7" MEASUREMENTS: 31 - 12 - 33 TRAITS: PASSIVE, DEPRESSIVE, MOODY, UNPREDICTABLE. SHE MAY LOOK SWEET, BUT IS FULL OF SURPRISES.
H2O
I JUST NEED A LITTLE TENDERNESS... SO BADLY!
AND ALSO...
A LITTLE RAISE!
BOSS
FRUSH
MORE FLEXIBLE HOURS... MUCH MORE FLEXIBLE...
AND FIVE VACATION DAYS A WEEK, OK?
CAREFUL NOW...
IF YOU SAY NO...
I'LL GET DRESSED AGAIN, THEN RIP YOUR HEART OUT AND CRUSH IT WITH MY OWN TWO HANDS, AND--
ZING
KRAK
GET A MOVE ON, GIRLS! WHERE'S MY REFILL?
GRRR! I HATE HER!
HIK!

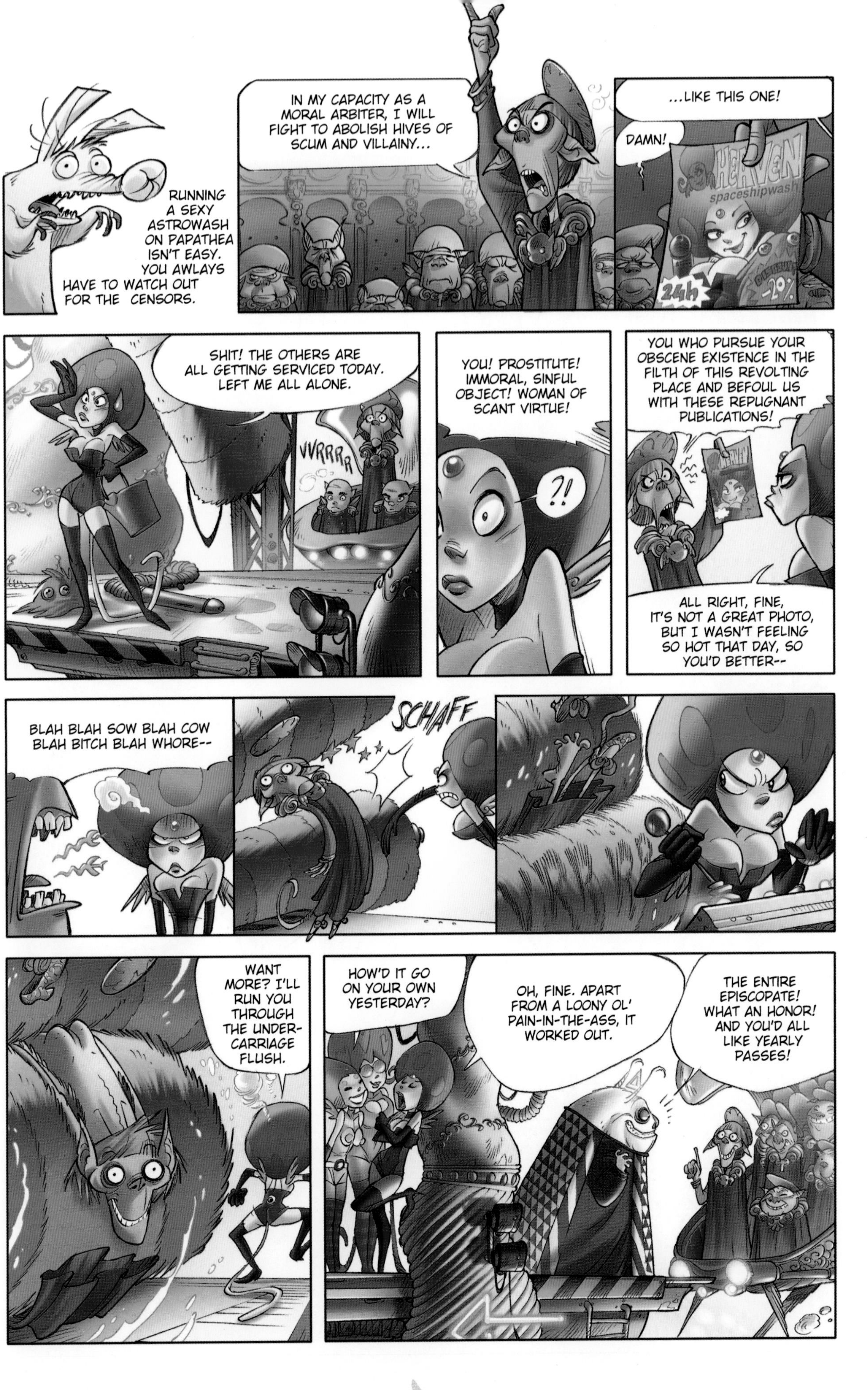
RUNNING A SEXY ASTROWASH ON PAPATHEA ISN'T EASY. YOU AWLAYS HAVE TO WATCH OUT FOR THE CENSORS.
IN MY CAPACITY AS A MORAL ARBITER, I WILL FIGHT TO ABOLISH HIVES OF SCUM AND VILLAINY...
...LIKE THIS ONE!
DAMN!
HEAVEN
spaceshipwash
24h
DISCOUNT
-20%
SHIT! THE OTHERS ARE ALL GETTING SERVICED TODAY. LEFT ME ALL ALONE.
VVRRRRR
YOU! PROSTITUTE! IMMORAL, SINFUL OBJECT! WOMAN OF SCANT VIRTUE!
?!
YOU WHO PURSUE YOUR OBSCENE EXISTENCE IN THE FILTH OF THIS REVOLTING PLACE AND BEFOUL US WITH THESE REPUGNANT PUBLICATIONS!
ALL RIGHT, FINE, IT'S NOT A GREAT PHOTO, BUT I WASN'T FEELING SO HOT THAT DAY, SO YOU'D BETTER--
BLAH BLAH SOW BLAH COW BLAH BITCH BLAH WHORE--
SCHAFF
WANT MORE? I'LL RUN YOU THROUGH THE UNDER-CARRIAGE FLUSH.
HOW'D IT GO ON YOUR OWN YESTERDAY?
OH, FINE. APART FROM A LOONY OL' PAIN-IN-THE-ASS, IT WORKED OUT.
THE ENTIRE EPISCOPATE! WHAT AN HONOR! AND YOU'D ALL LIKE YEARLY PASSES!

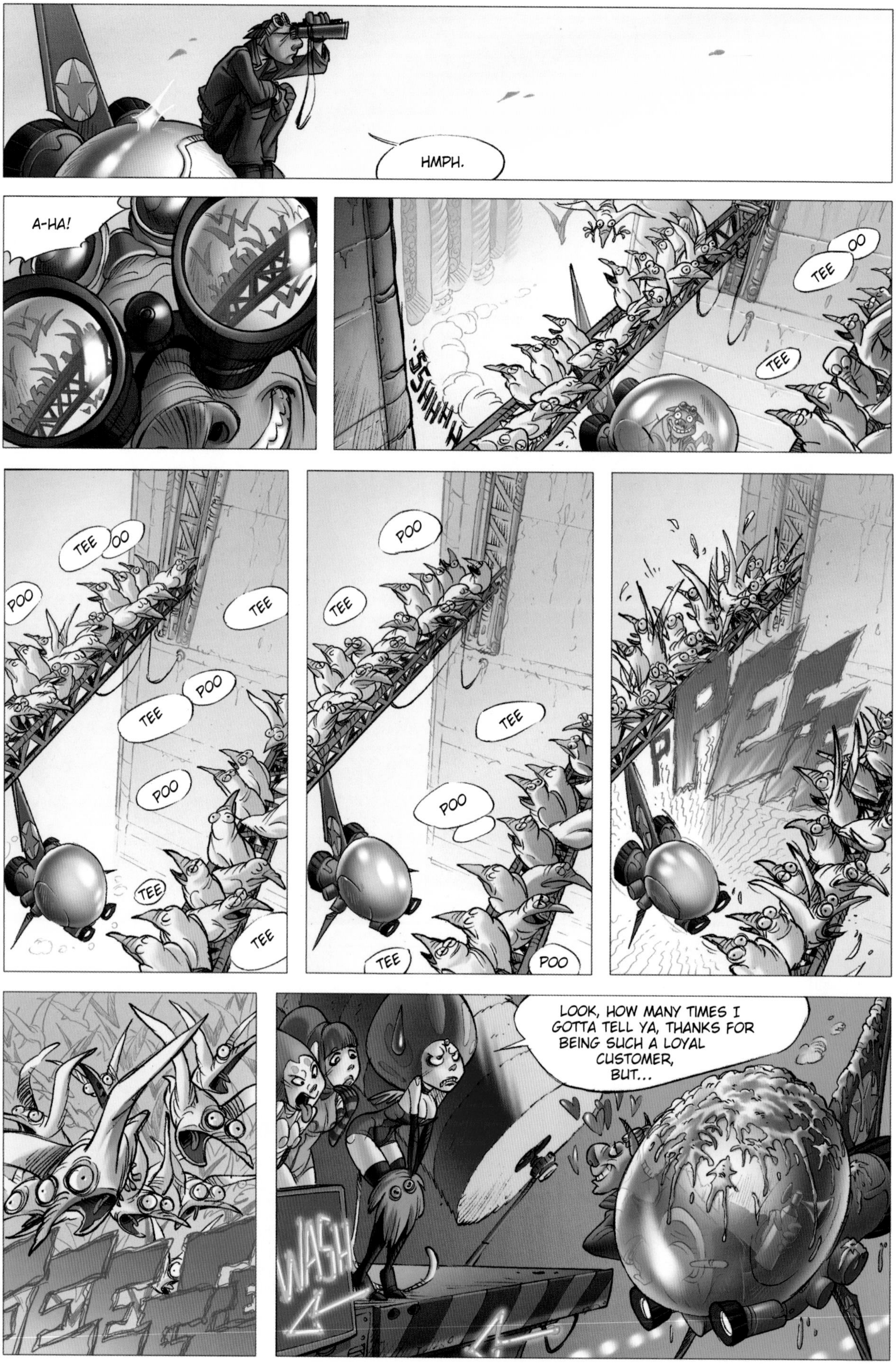
HMPH.
A-HA!
SSHHHHH
TEE
OO
TEE
TEE
OO
POO
TEE
TEE
POO
POO
TEE
TEE
POO
TEE
TEE
POO
TEE
POO
P
LOOK, HOW MANY TIMES I GOTTA TELL YA, THANKS FOR BEING SUCH A LOYAL CUSTOMER, BUT...
WASH

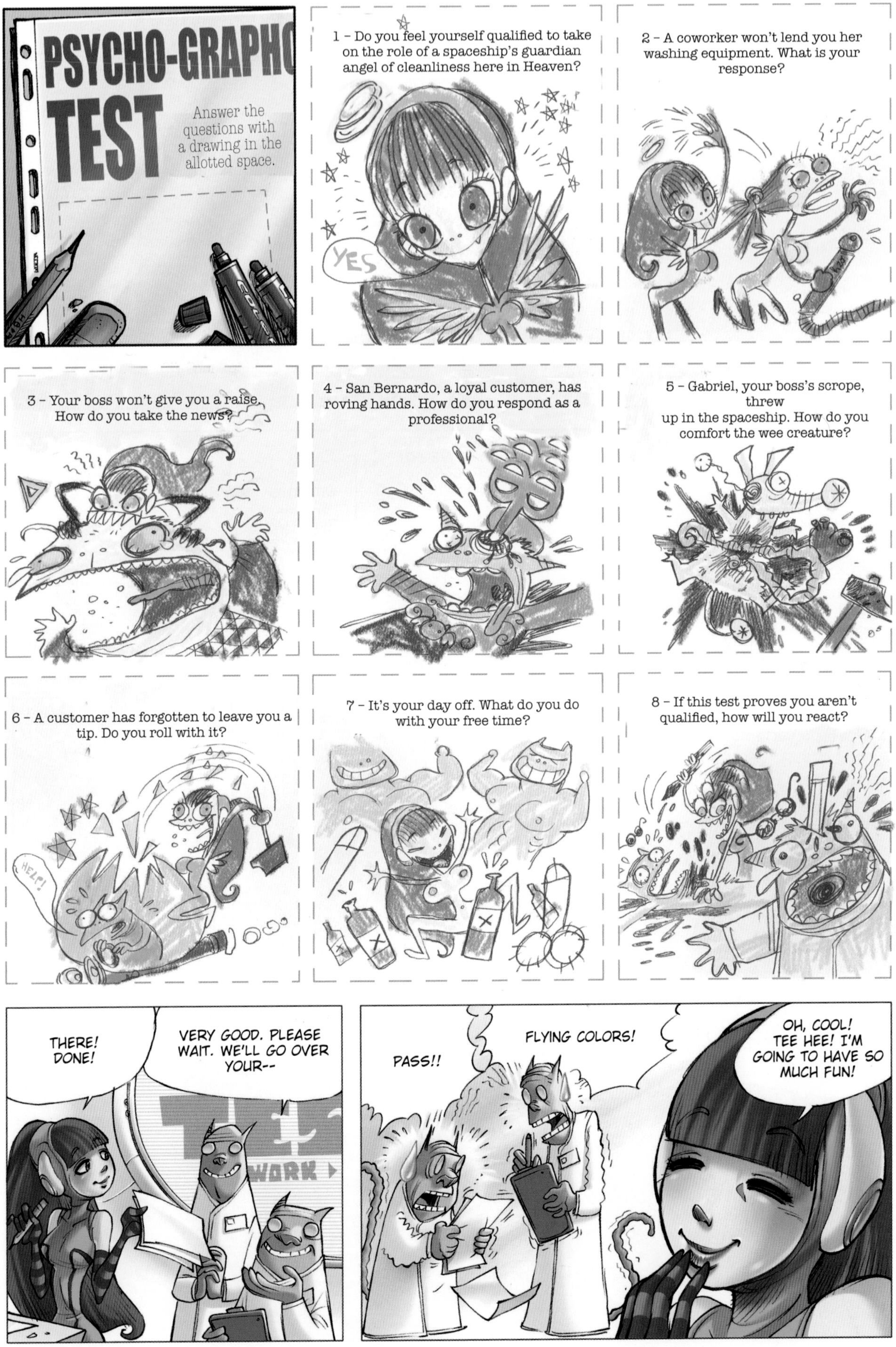
PSYCHO-GRAPHO
TEST
Answer the questions with a drawing in the allotted space.
1 - Do you feel yourself qualified to take on the role of a spaceship's guardian angel of cleanliness here in Heaven?
YES
2 - A coworker won't lend you her washing equipment. What is your response?
3 - Your boss won't give you a raise. How do you take the news?
4 - San Bernardo, a loyal customer, has roving hands. How do you respond as a professional?
5 - Gabriel, your boss's scrope, threw up in the spaceship. How do you comfort the wee creature?
6 - A customer has forgotten to leave you a tip. Do you roll with it?
HELP!
7 - It's your day off. What do you do with your free time?
8 - If this test proves you aren't qualified, how will you react?
THERE! DONE!
VERY GOOD. PLEASE WAIT. WE'LL GO OVER YOUR--
WORK
PASS!!
FLYING COLORS!
OH, COOL! TEE HEE! I'M GOING TO HAVE SO MUCH FUN!

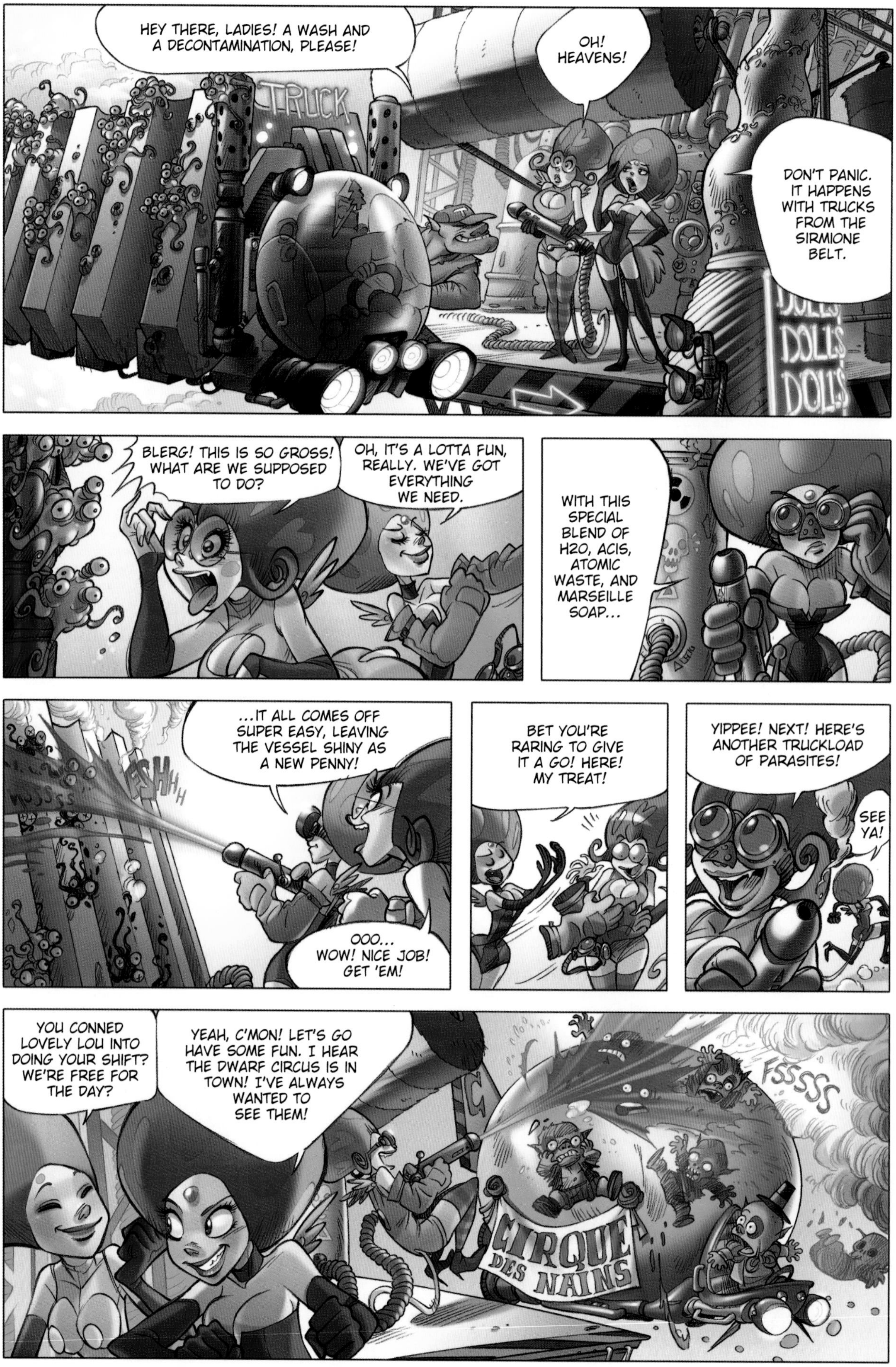
HEY THERE, LADIES! A WASH AND A DECONTAMINATION, PLEASE!
TRUCK
OH! HEAVENS!
DON'T PANIC. IT HAPPENS WITH TRUCKS FROM THE SIRMIONE BELT.
DOLLS DOLLS DOLLS
BLERG! THIS IS SO GROSS! WHAT ARE WE SUPPOSED TO DO?
OH, IT'S A LOTTA FUN, REALLY. WE'VE GOT EVERYTHING WE NEED.
WITH THIS SPECIAL BLEND OF H2O, ACIS, ATOMIC WASTE, AND MARSEILLE SOAP...
...IT ALL COMES OFF SUPER EASY, LEAVING THE VESSEL SHINY AS A NEW PENNY!
FSHHH
OOO... WOW! NICE JOB! GET 'EM!
BET YOU'RE RARING TO GIVE IT A GO! HERE! MY TREAT!
YIPPEE! NEXT! HERE'S ANOTHER TRUCKLOAD OF PARASITES!
SEE YA!
YOU CONNED LOVELY LOU INTO DOING YOUR SHIFT? WE'RE FREE FOR THE DAY?
YEAH, C'MON! LET'S GO HAVE SOME FUN. I HEAR THE DWARF CIRCUS IS IN TOWN! I'VE ALWAYS WANTED TO SEE THEM!
FSSSSS
CIRQUE DES NAINS

SKY·DOLL DECADE 00 > 10

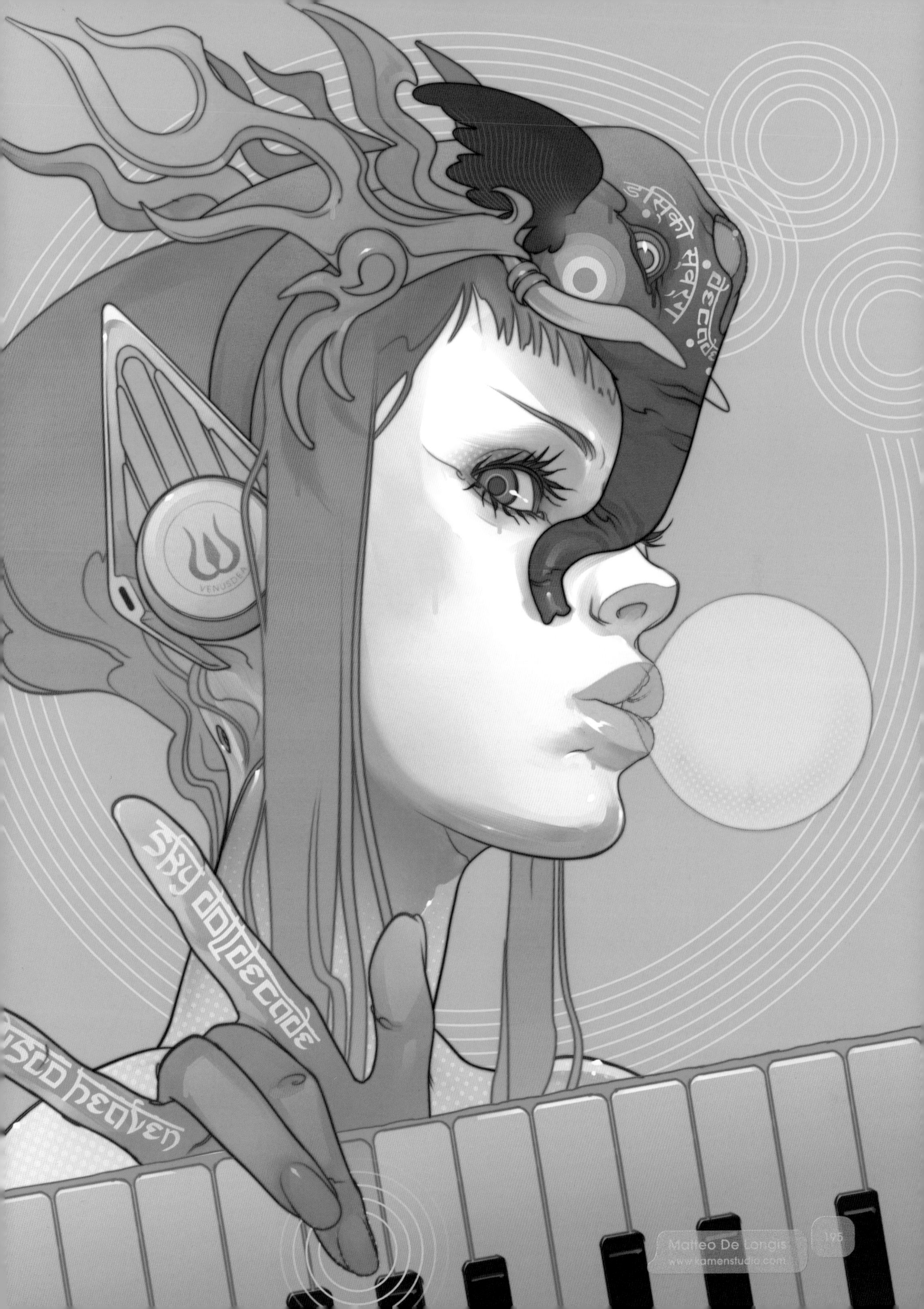
sky dolldecode
heaven

Matteo De Longis
www.kamenstudio.com

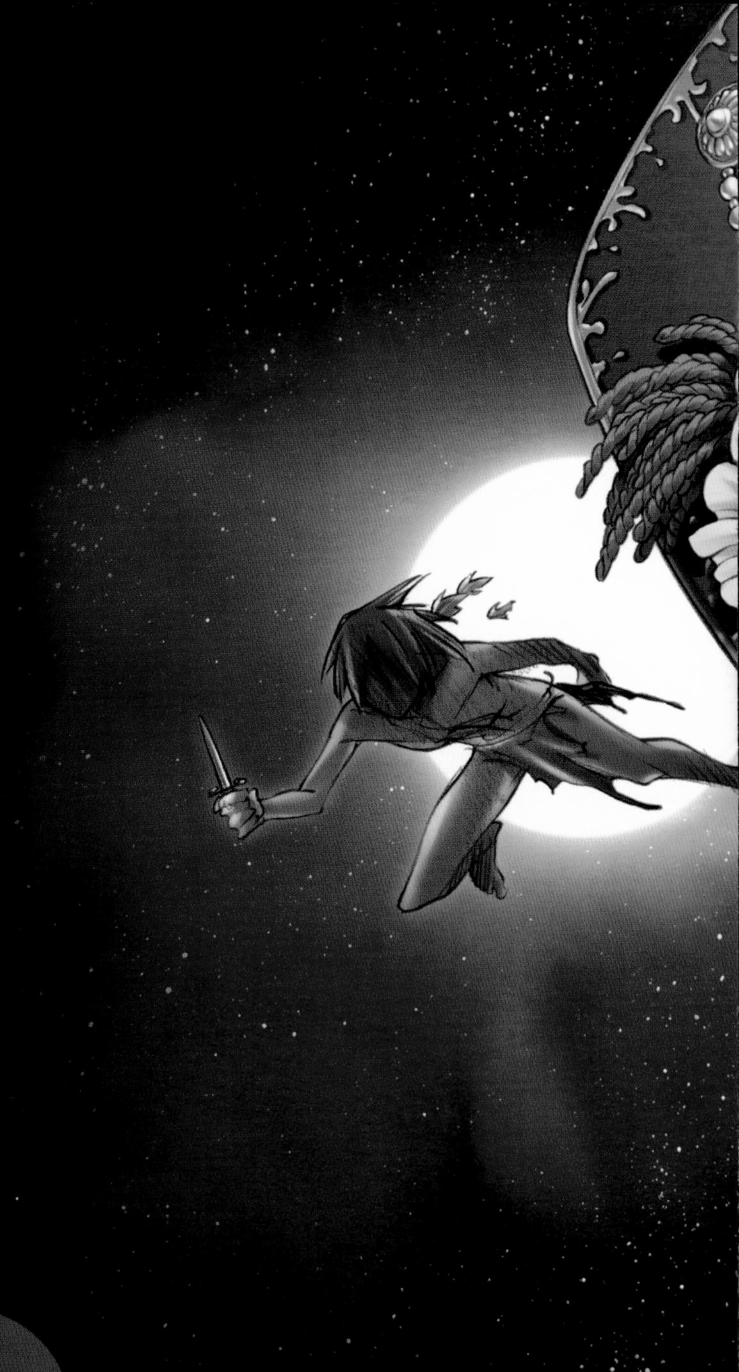

SKY·DOLL DECADE 00 > 10

HOMAGES

various artists

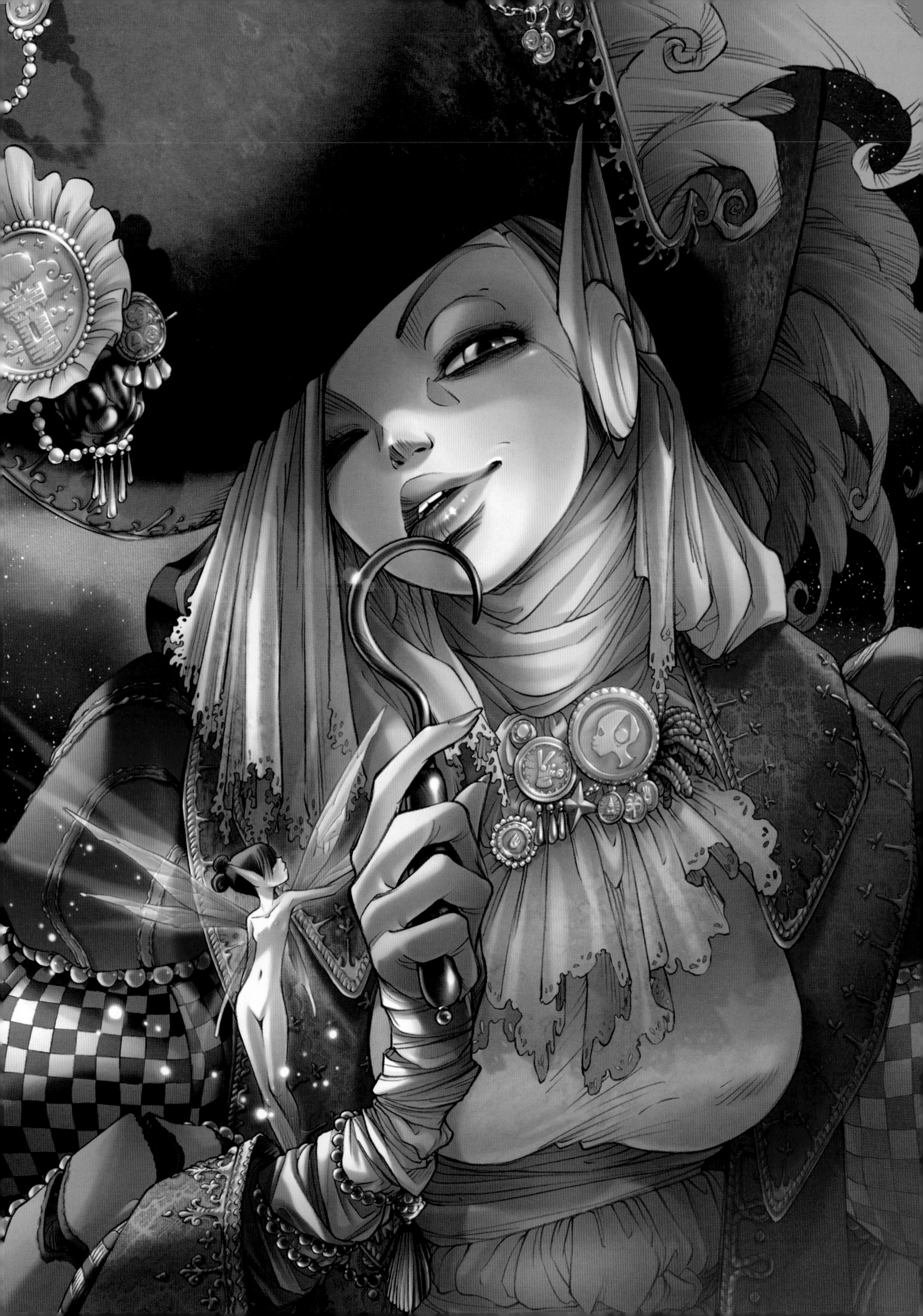

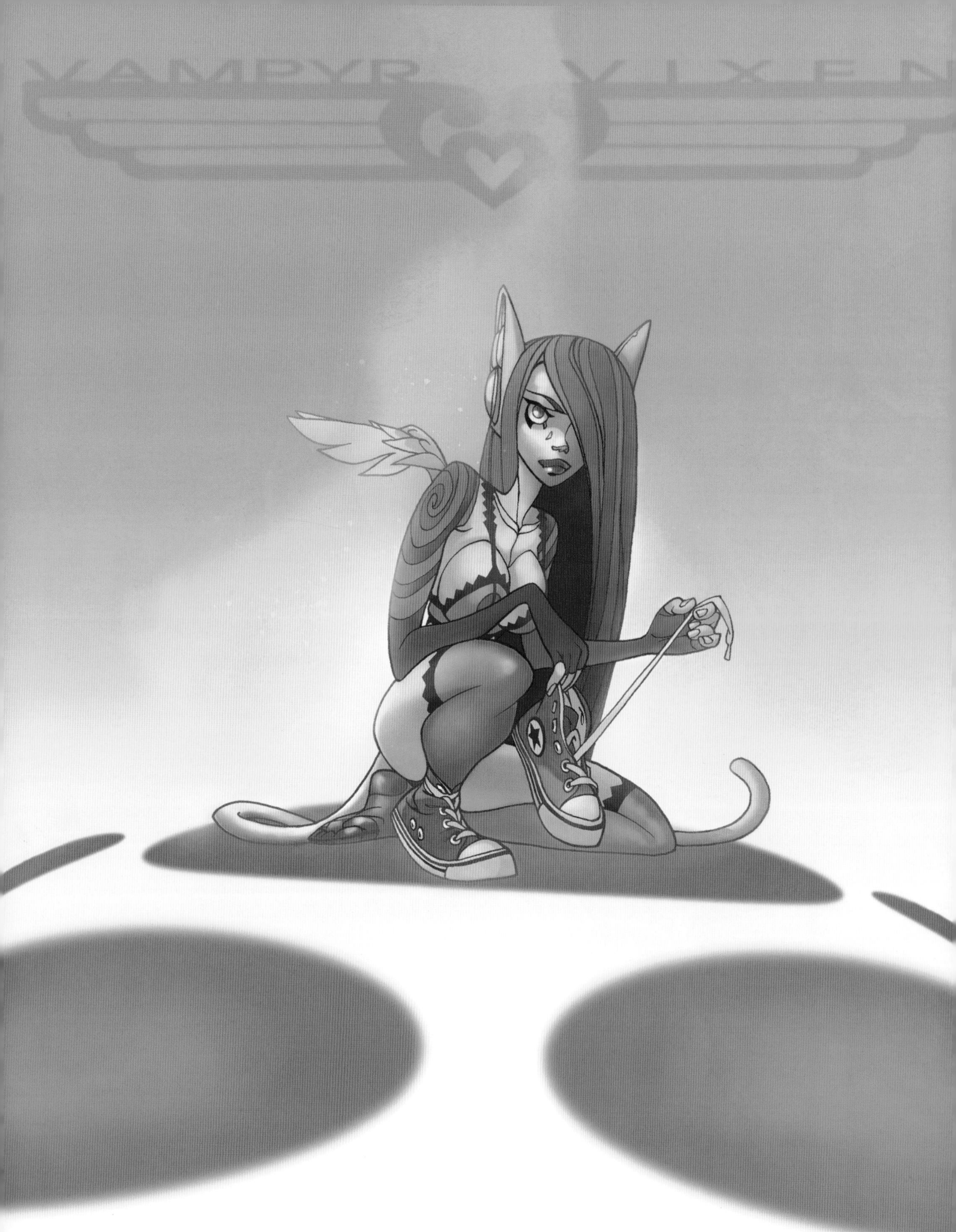
VAMPYR VIXEN

Claire Wendling
www.claire-wendling.net

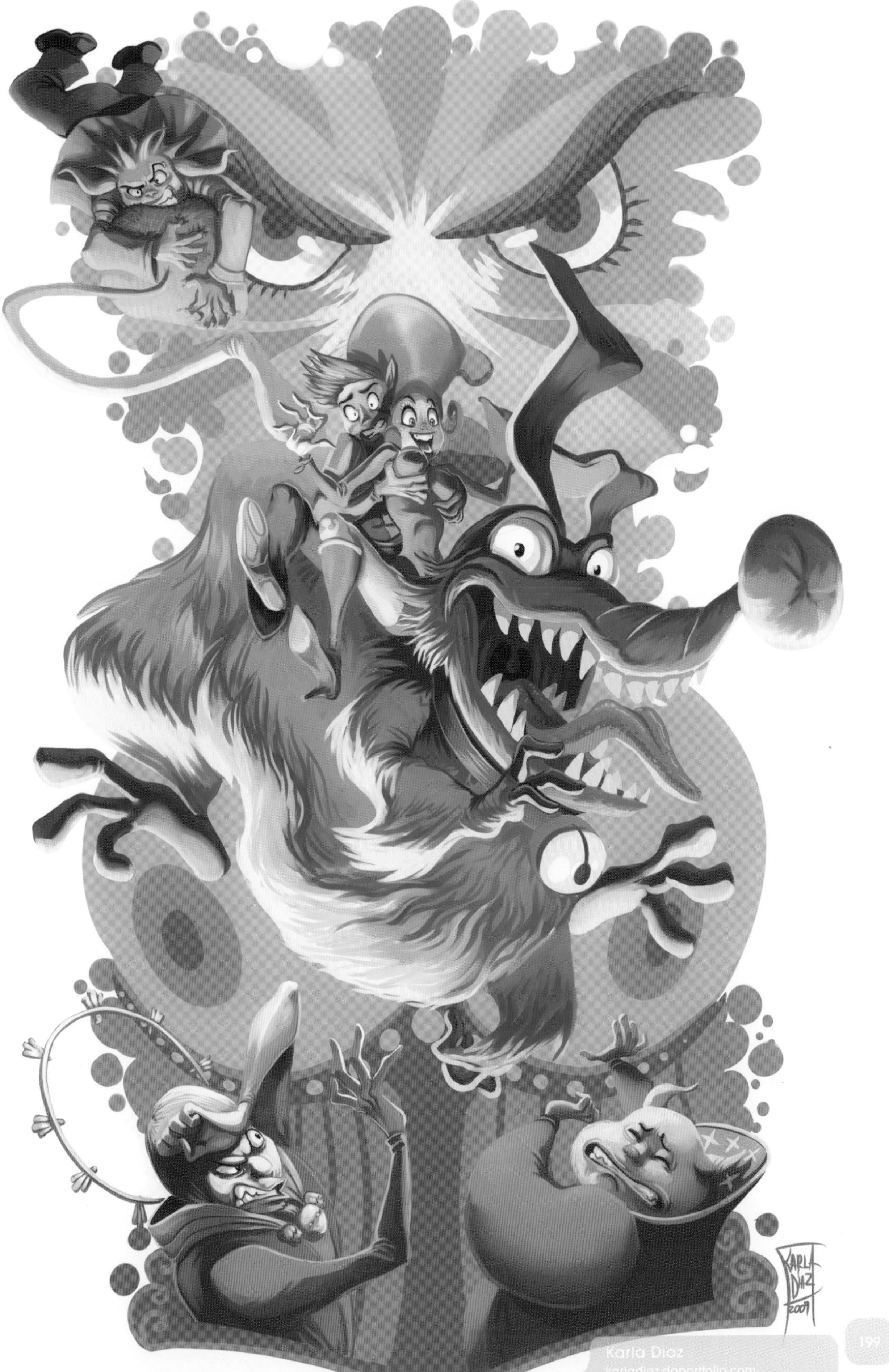
KARLA DIAZ
2009

Karla Diaz
karladiaz.daportfolio.com

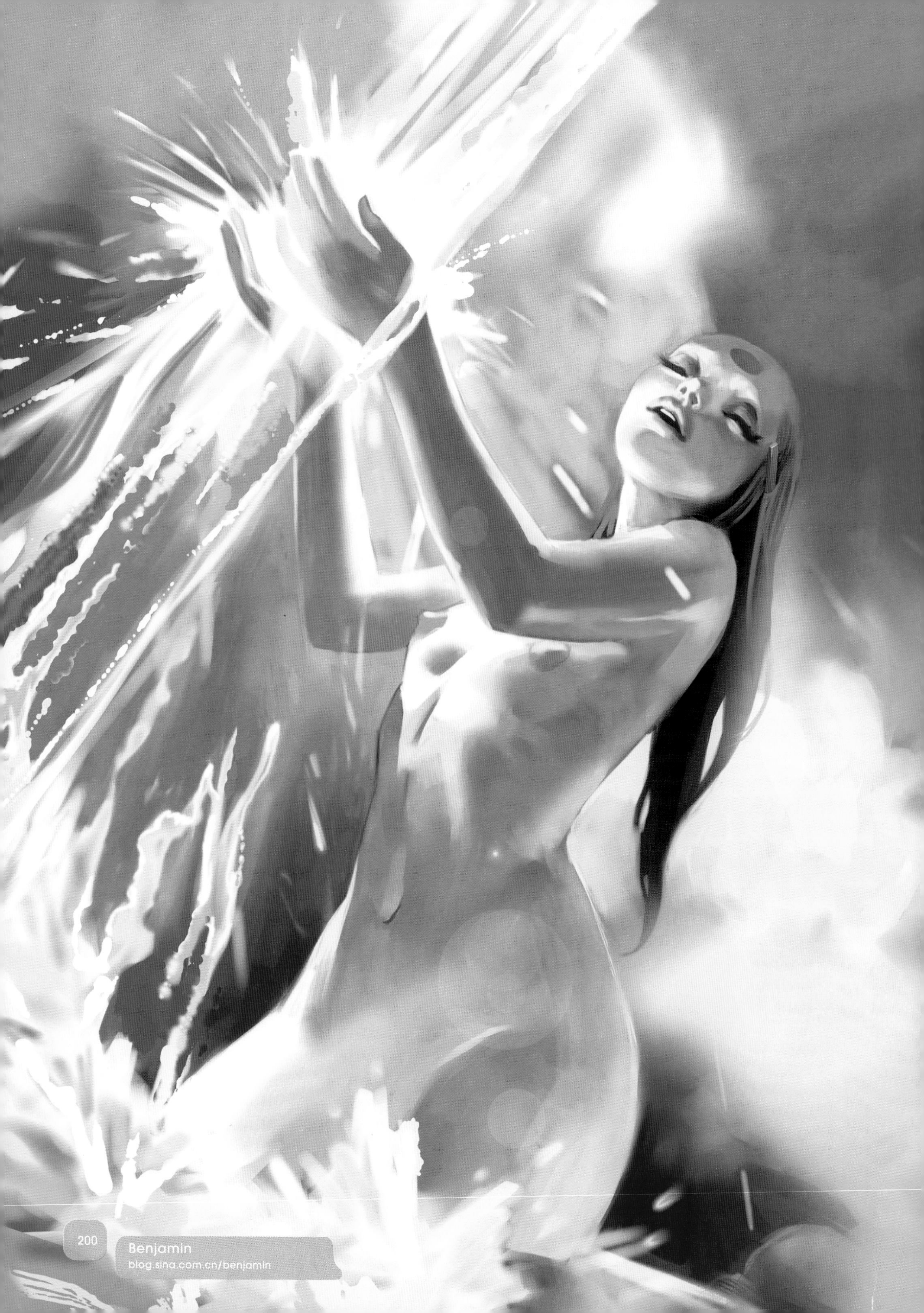

Benjamin
blog.sina.com.cn/benjamin

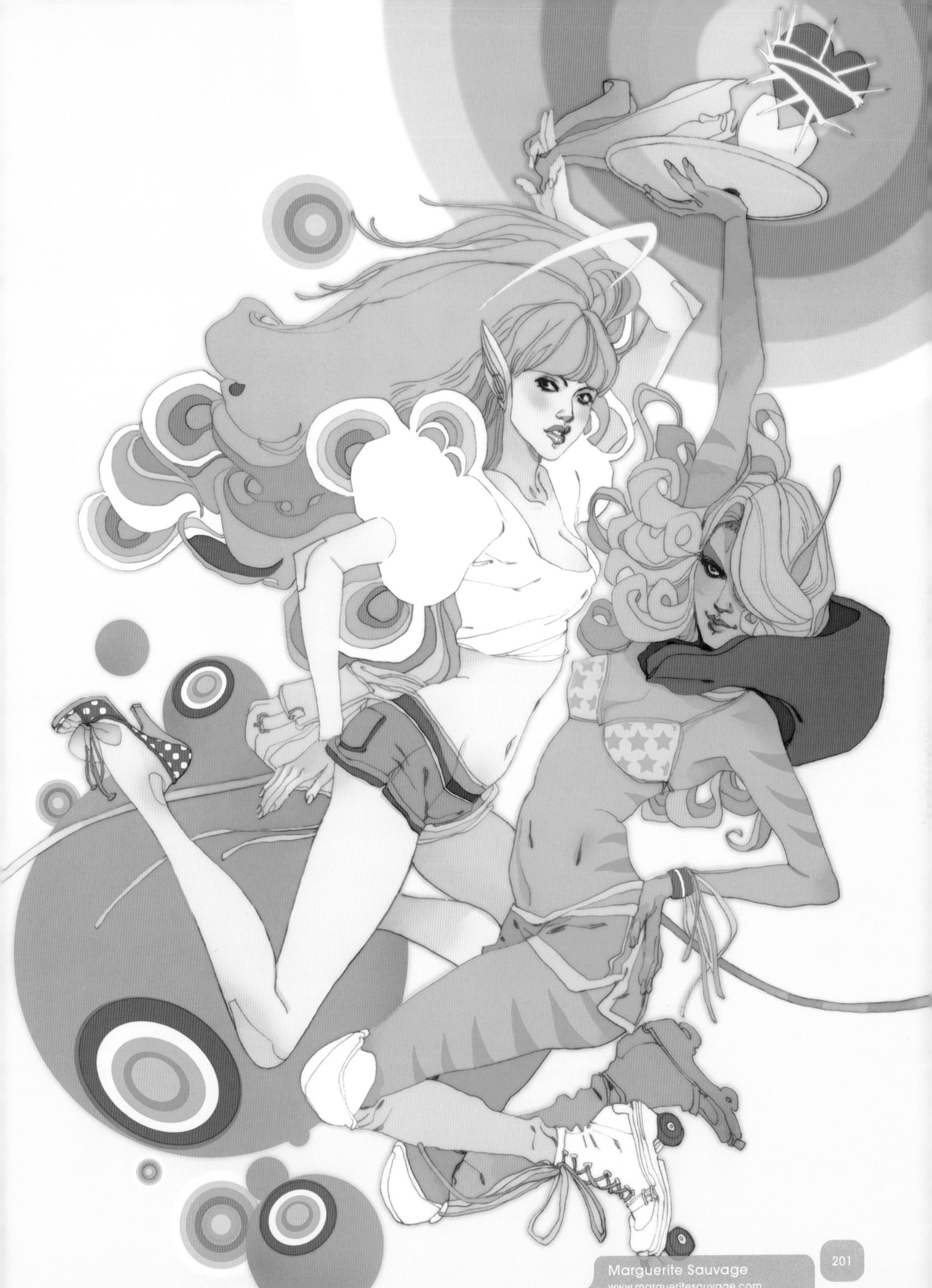

Marguerite Sauvage
www.margueritesauvage.com

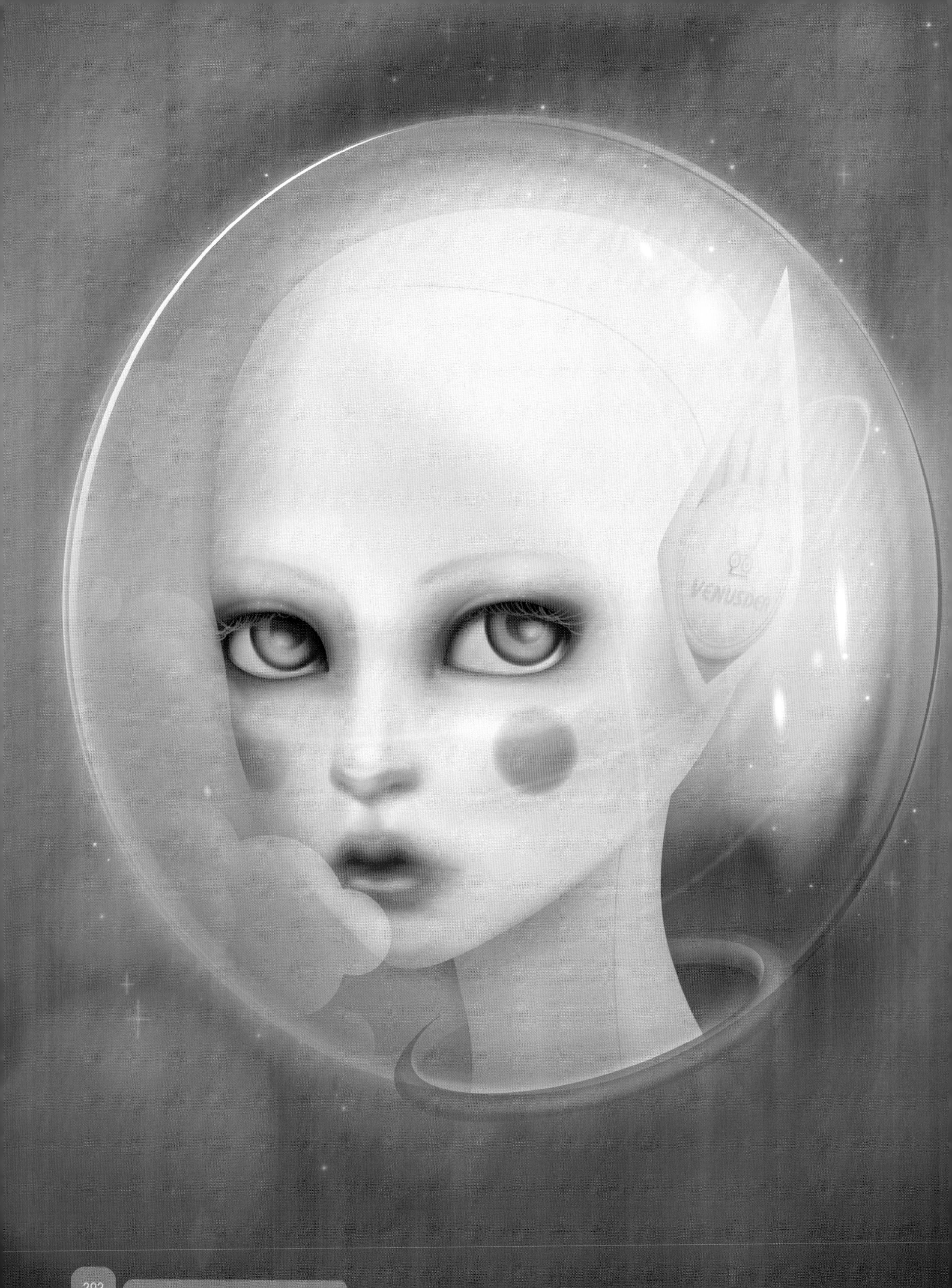

Mijin Shatje
www.mijnschatje.fr

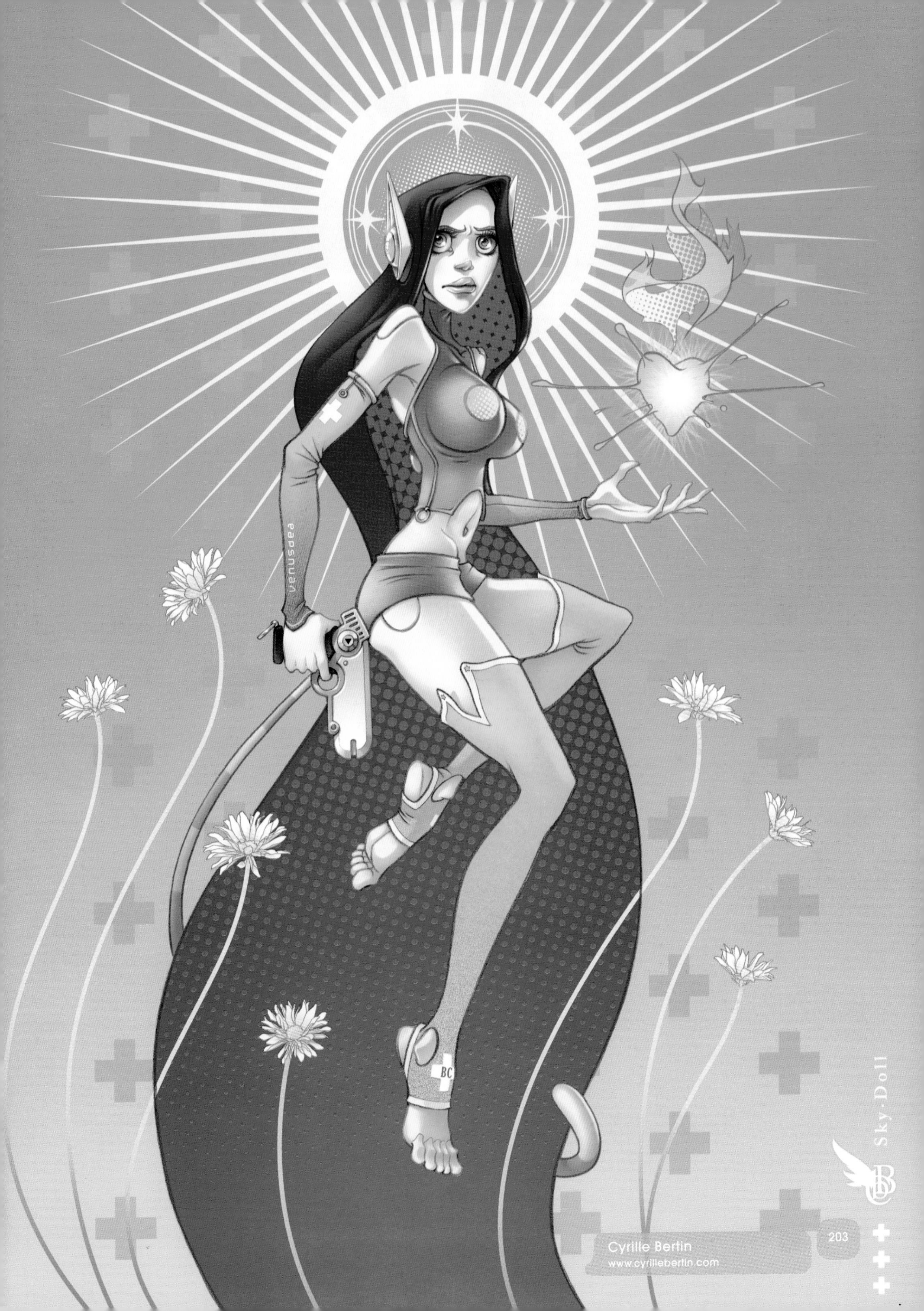
BC
Sky·Doll

Cyrille Bertin
www.cyrillebertin.com

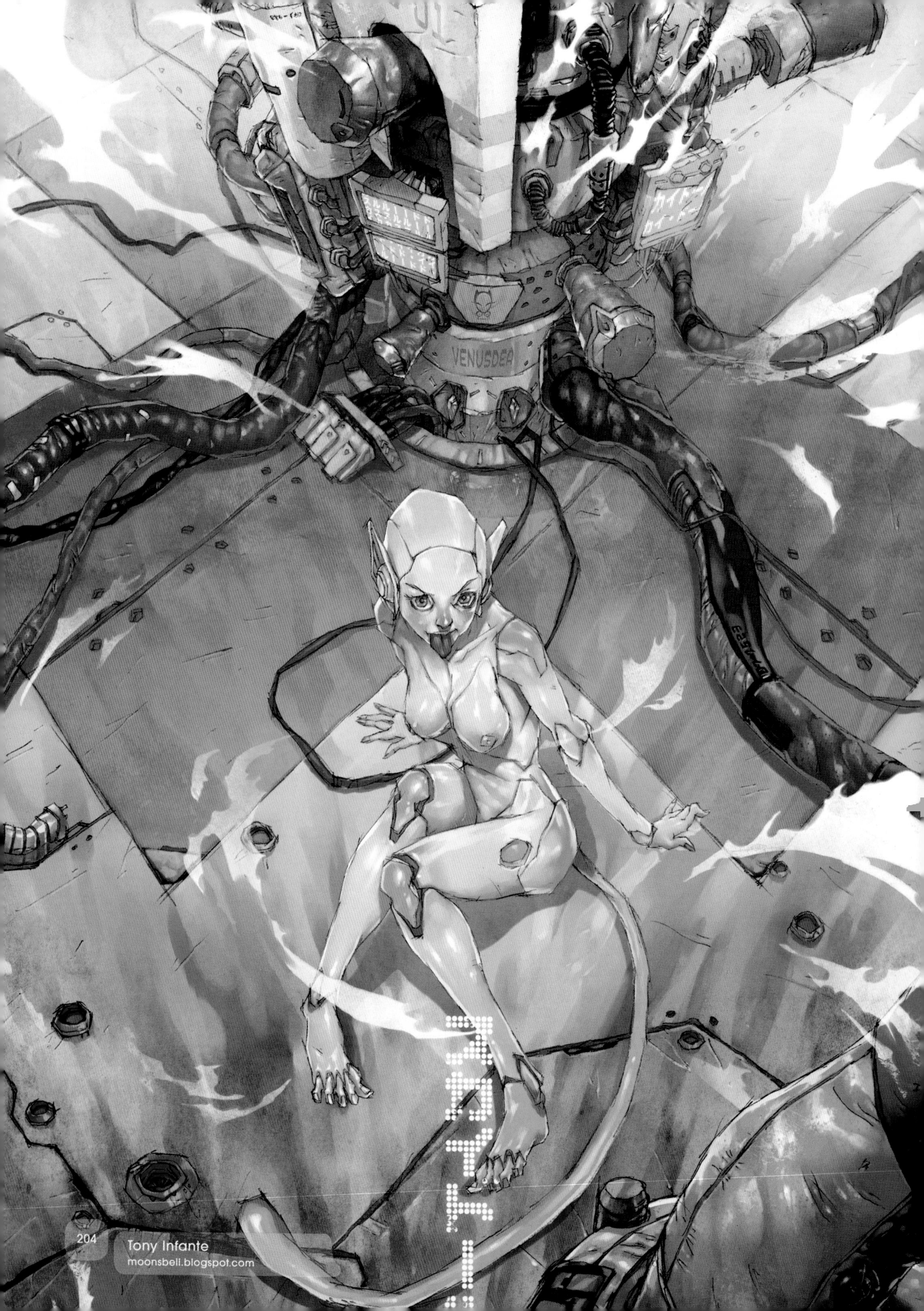
VENUSDEA

Tony Infante
moonsbell.blogspot.com

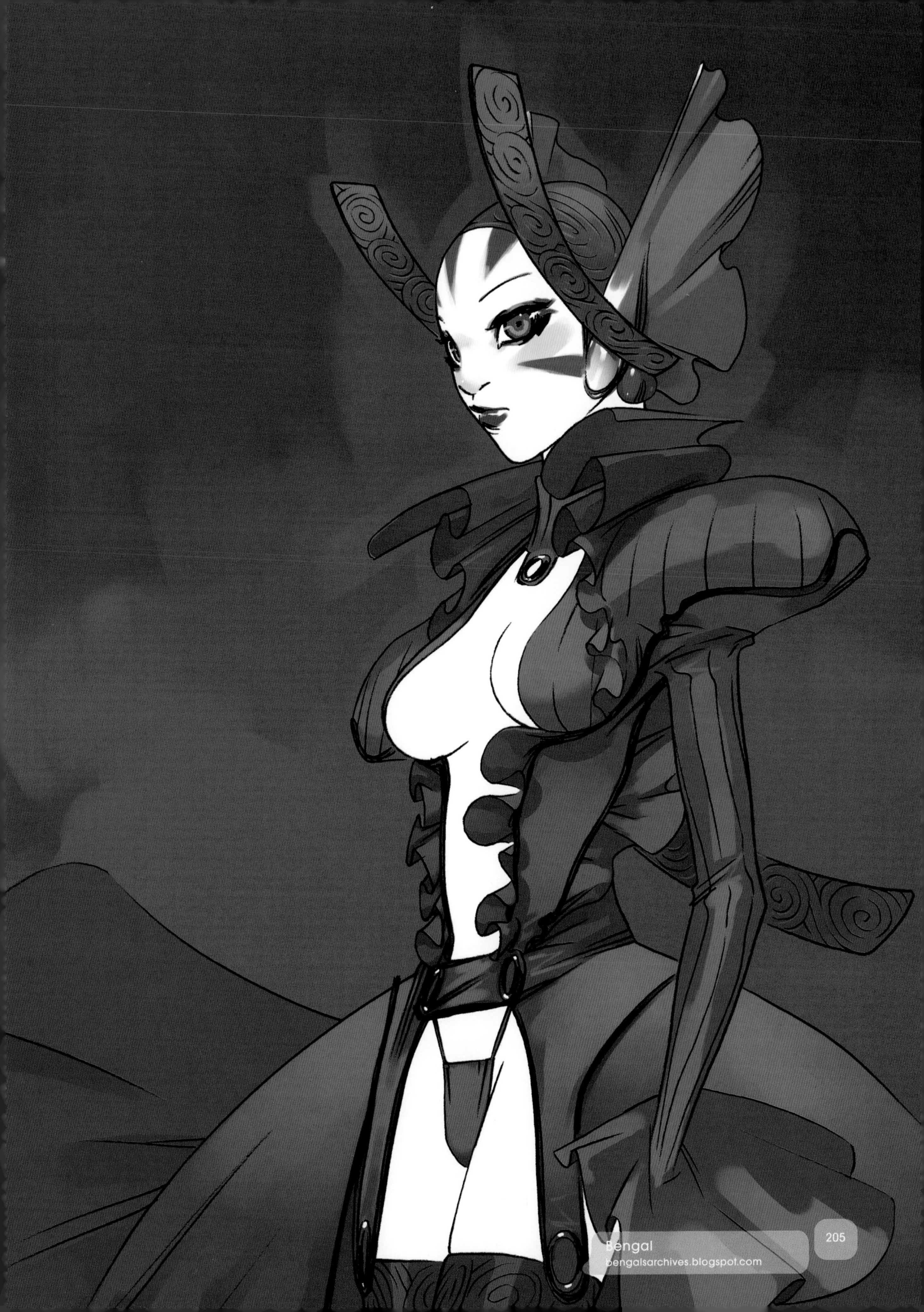

Bengal
bengalsarchives.blogspot.com

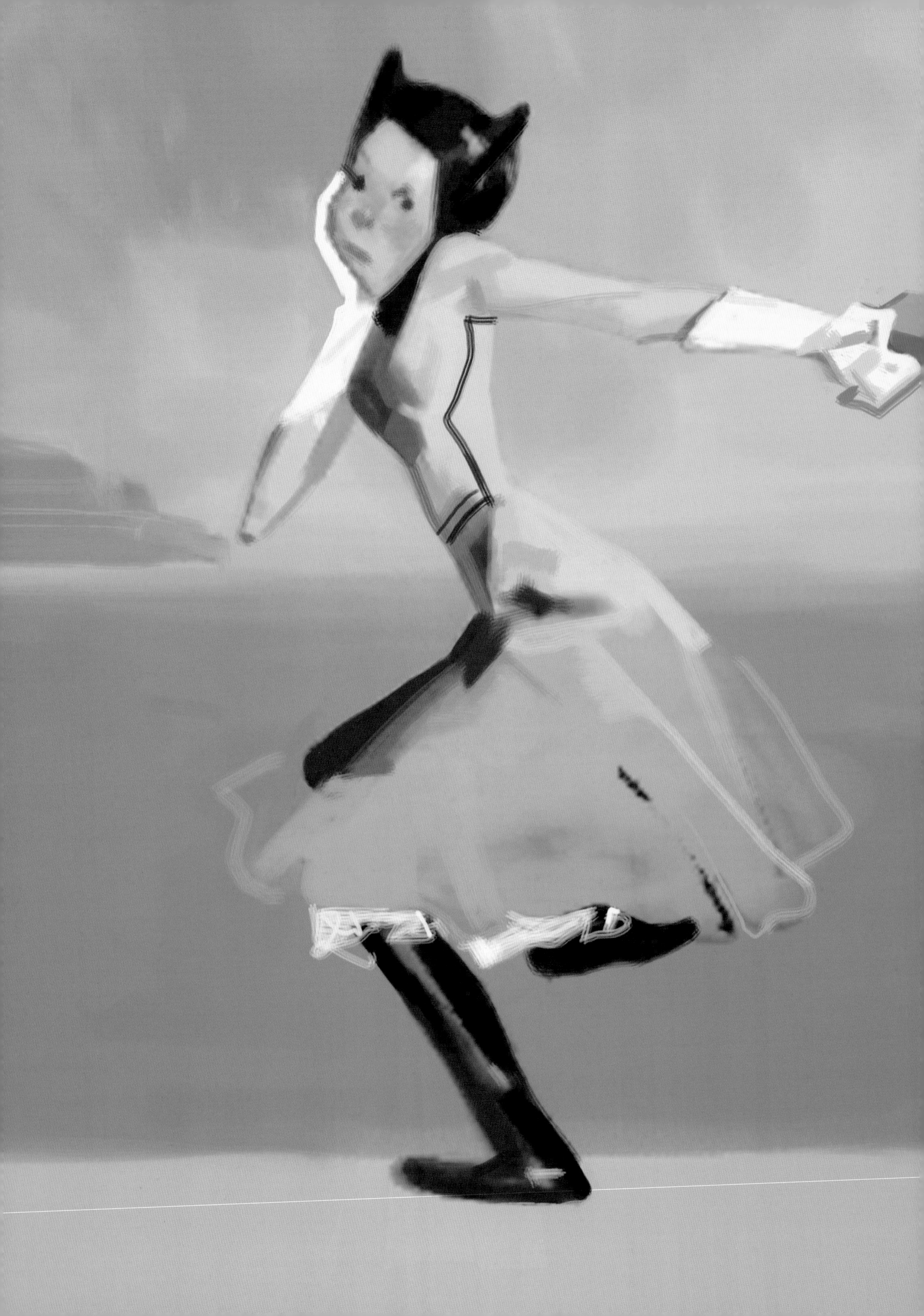

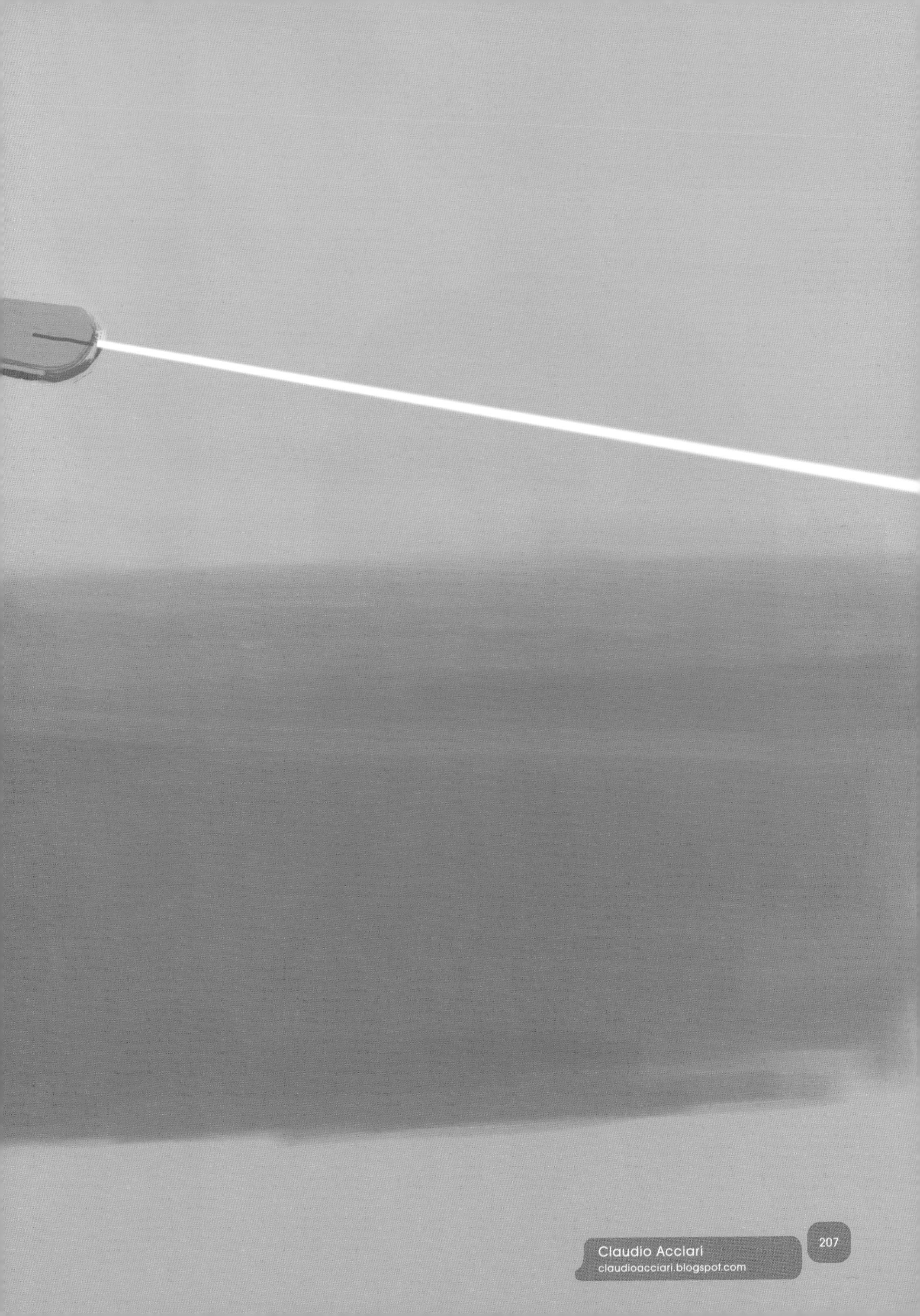

Claudio Acciari
claudioacciari.blogspot.com

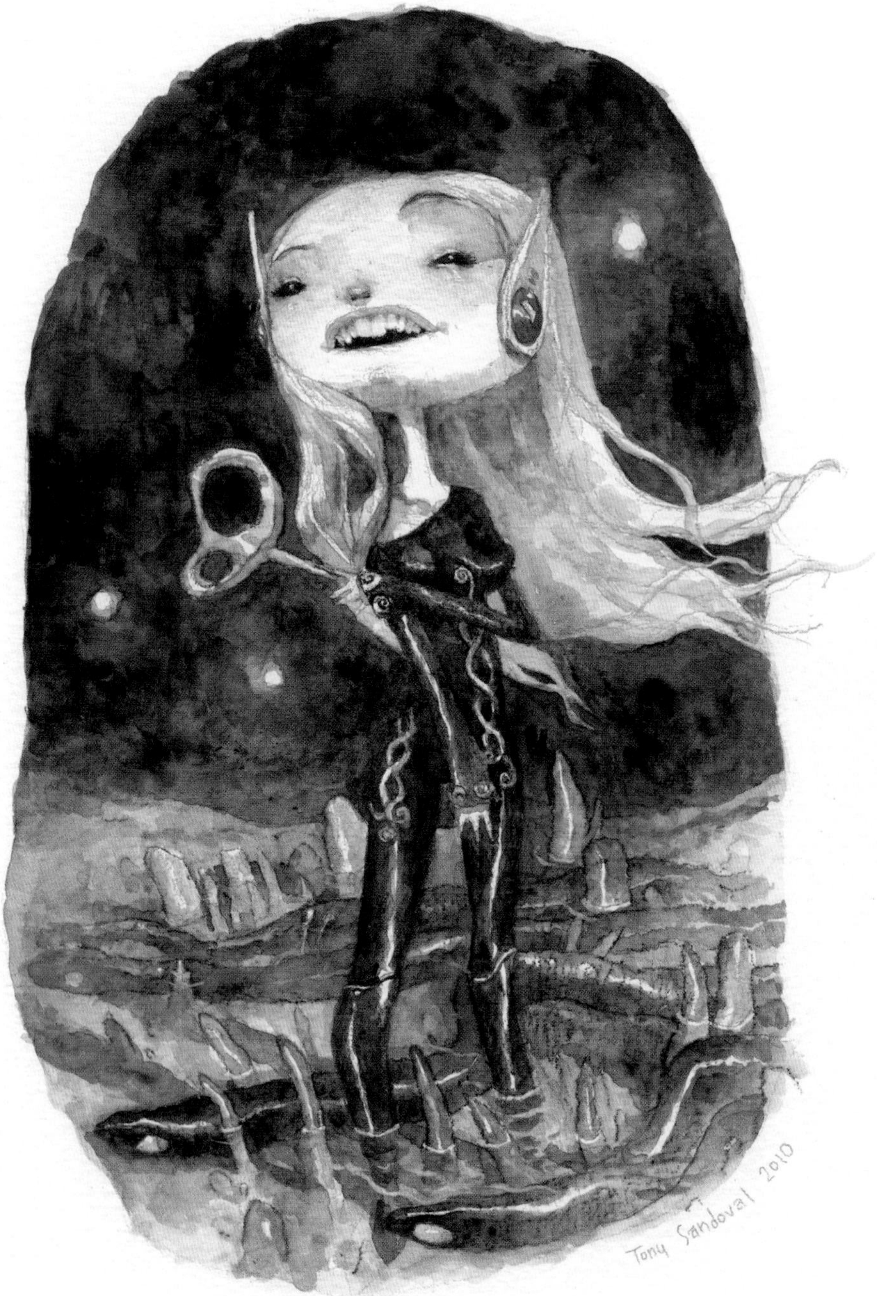
Tony Sandoval 2010

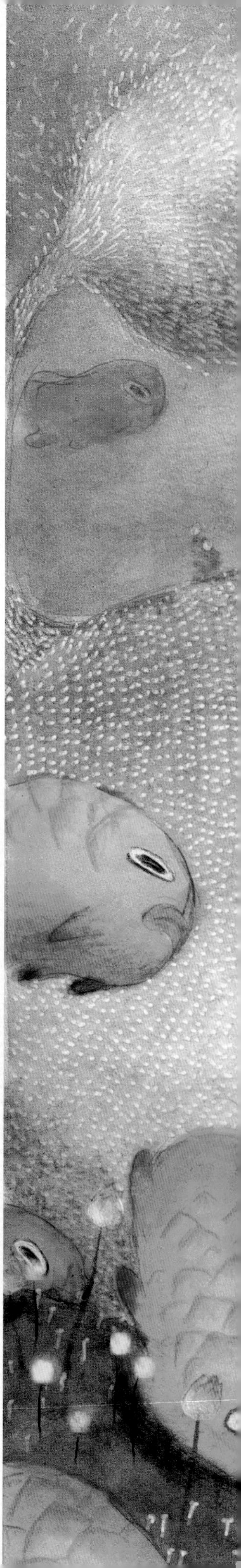

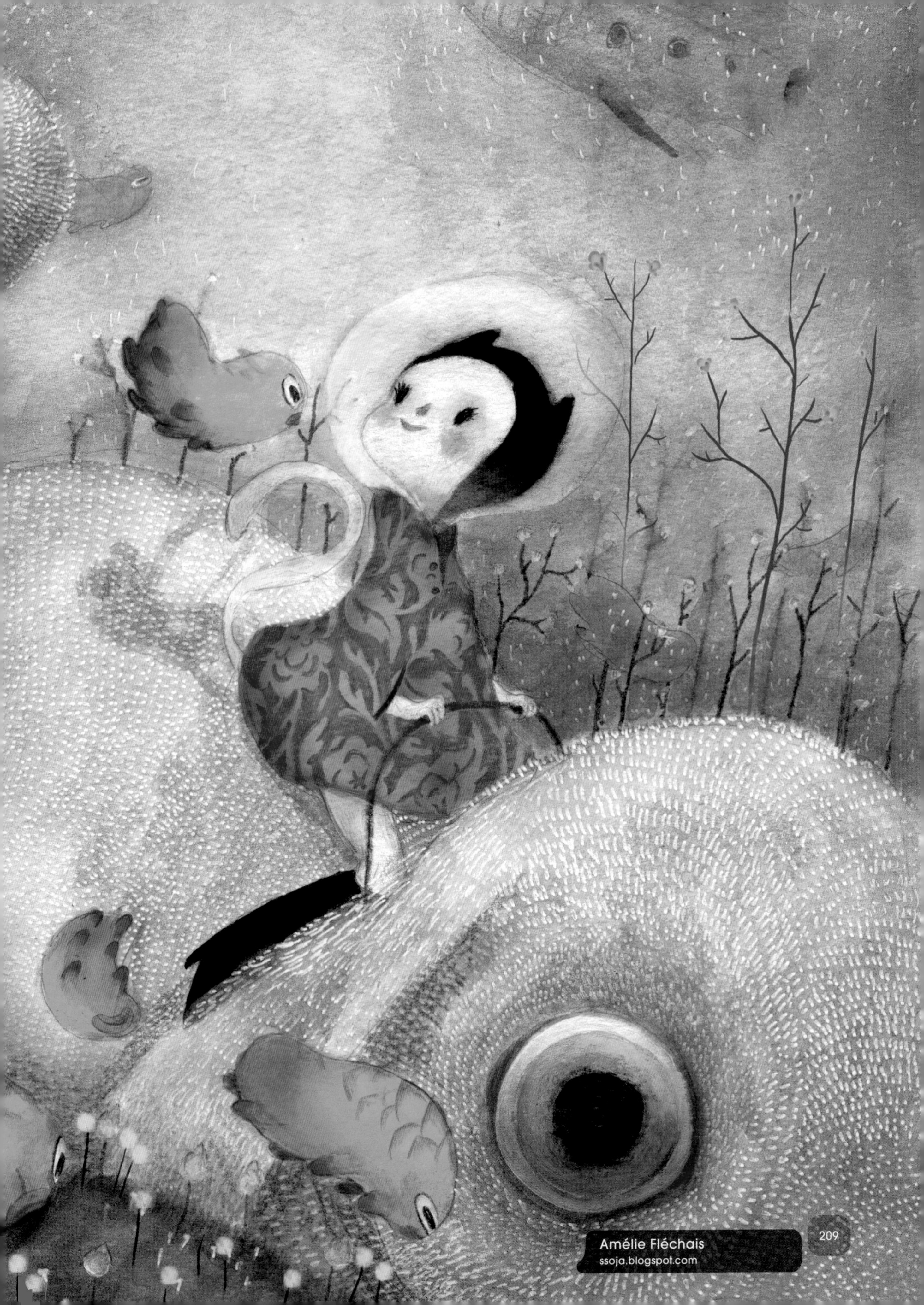

Amélie Fléchais
ssoja.blogspot.com

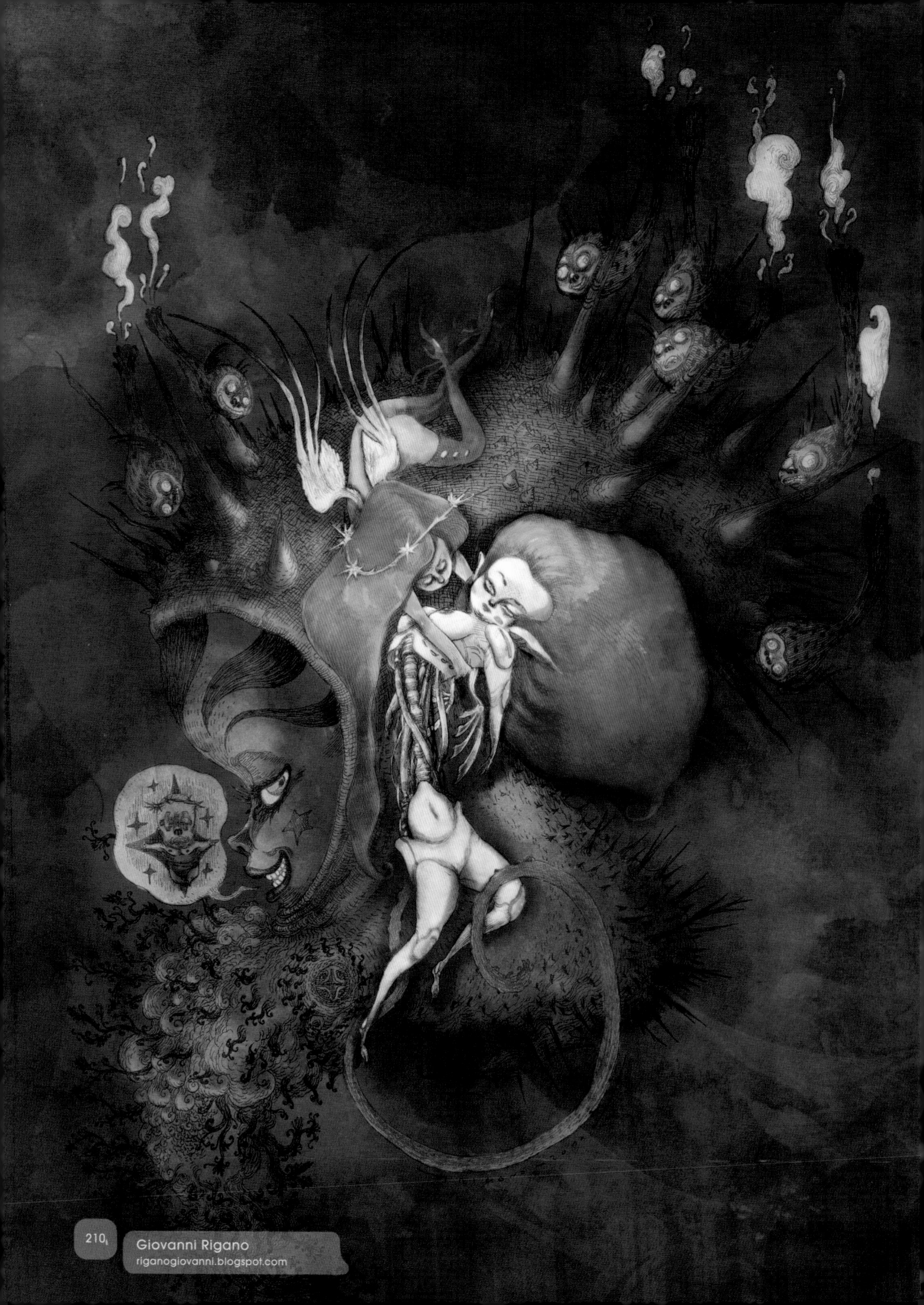

Giovanni Rigano
riganogiovanni.blogspot.com

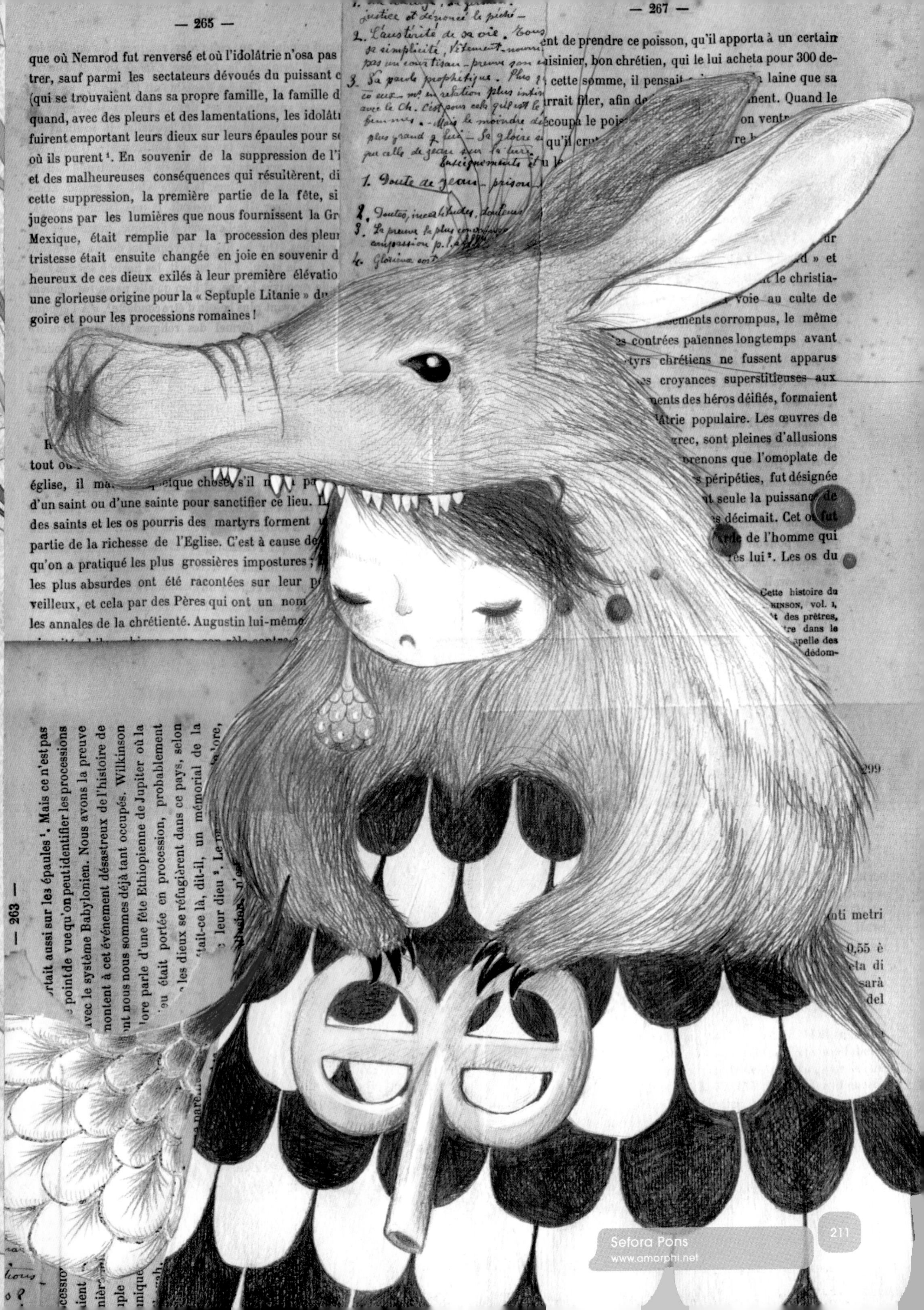
— 265 —
que où Nemrod fut renversé et où l'idolâtrie n'osa pas
trer, sauf parmi les sectateurs dévoués du puissant c
(qui se trouvaient dans sa propre famille, la famille d
quand, avec des pleurs et des lamentations, les idolâtı
fuirent emportant leurs dieux sur leurs épaules pour se
où ils purent. En souvenir de la suppression de l'i
et des malheureuses conséquences qui résultèrent, di
cette suppression, la première partie de la fête, si
jugeons par les lumières que nous fournissent la Gr
Mexique, était remplie par la procession des pleur
tristesse était ensuite changée en joie en souvenir d
heureux de ces dieux exilés à leur première élévatio
une glorieuse origine pour la « Septuple Litanie » du
goire et pour les processions romaines !
— 267 —
ent de prendre ce poisson, qu'il apporta à un certain
isinier, bon chrétien, qui le lui acheta pour 300 de-
d'un saint ou d'une sainte pour sanctifier ce lieu.
des saints et les os pourris des martyrs forment
partie de la richesse de l'Eglise. C'est à cause de
qu'on a pratiqué les plus grossières impostures ;
les plus absurdes ont été racontées sur leur
veilleux, et cela par des Pères qui ont un nom
les annales de la chrétienté. Augustin lui-même
s contrées païennes longtemps avant
rtyrs chrétiens ne fussent apparus
s croyances superstitieuses aux
nents des héros déifiés, formaient
lâtrie populaire. Les œuvres de
grec, sont pleines d'allusions
prenons que l'omoplate de
s péripéties, fut désignée
t seule la puissance de
s décimait. Cet os fut
rde de l'homme qui
rès lui. Les os du
— 263 —
rtait aussi sur les épaules. Mais ce n'est pas
point de vue qu'on peut identifier les processions
avec le système Babylonien. Nous avons la preuve
montent à cet événement désastreux de l'histoire de
nt nous nous sommes déjà tant occupés. Wilkinson
lore parle d'une fête Ethiopienne de Jupiter où la
eu était portée en procession, probablement
les dieux se réfugièrent dans ce pays, selon
était-ce là, dit-il, un mémorial de la
leur dieu.

Sefora Pons
www.amorphi.net

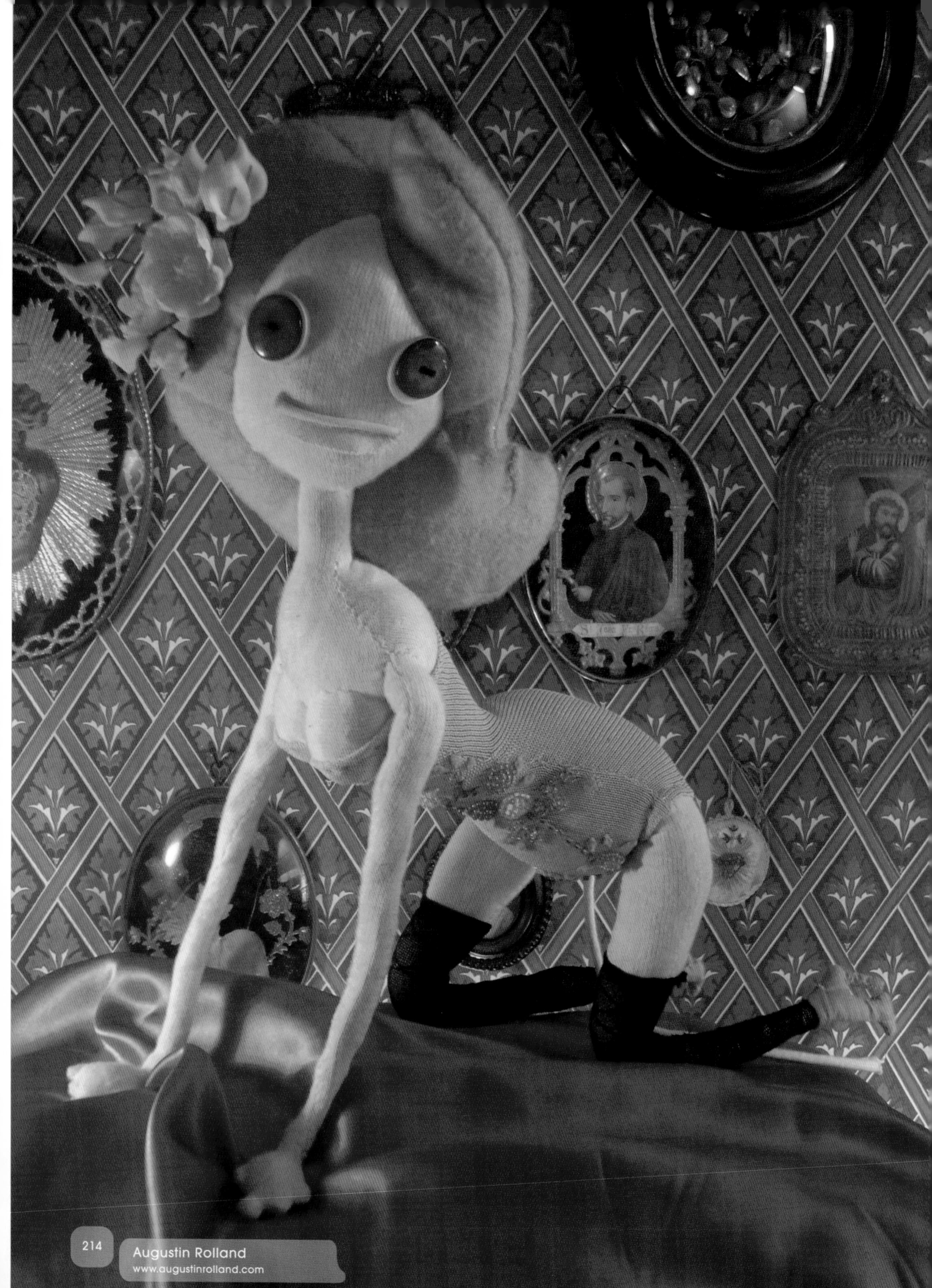

Augustin Rolland
www.augustinrolland.com

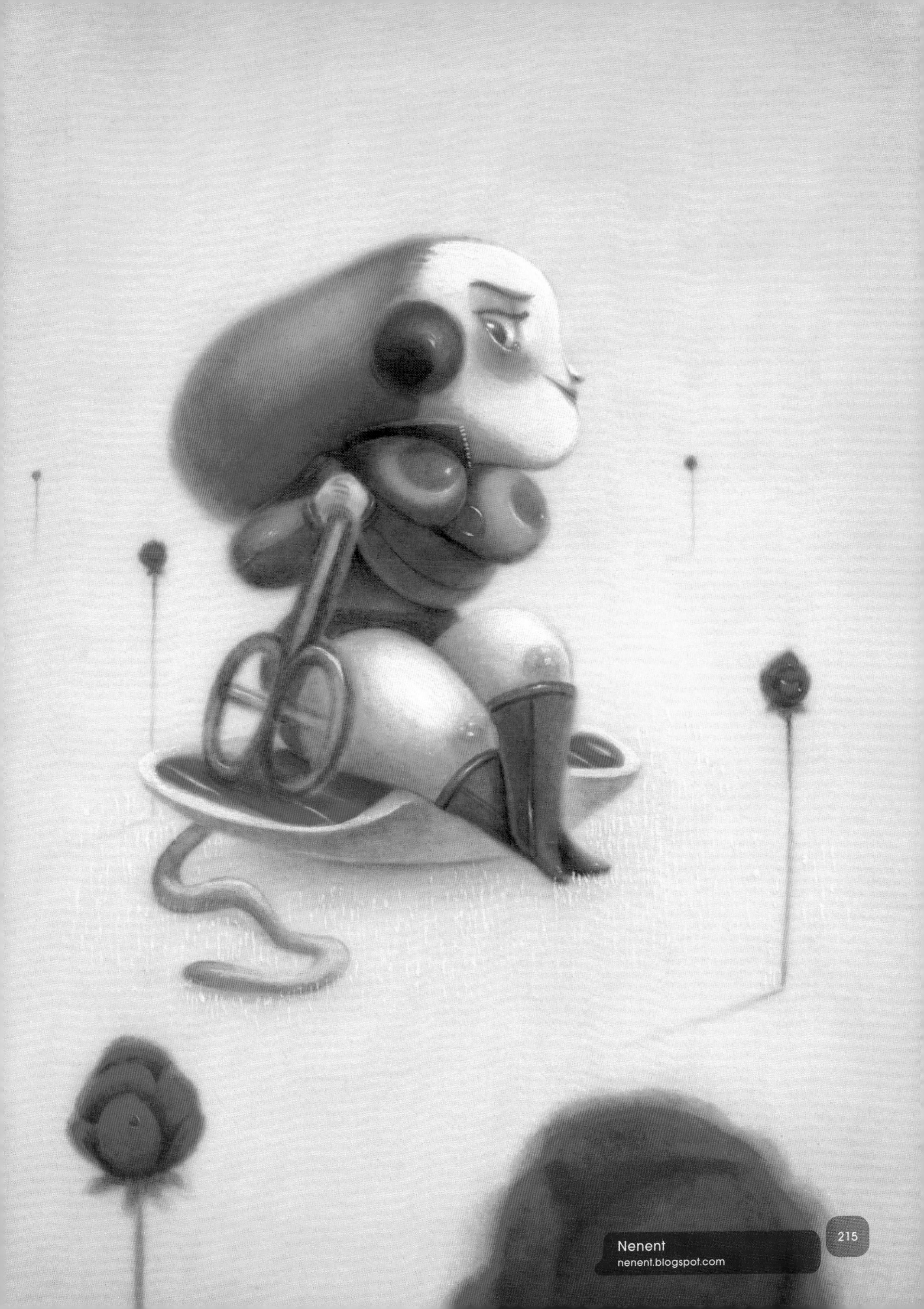

Nenent
nenent.blogspot.com

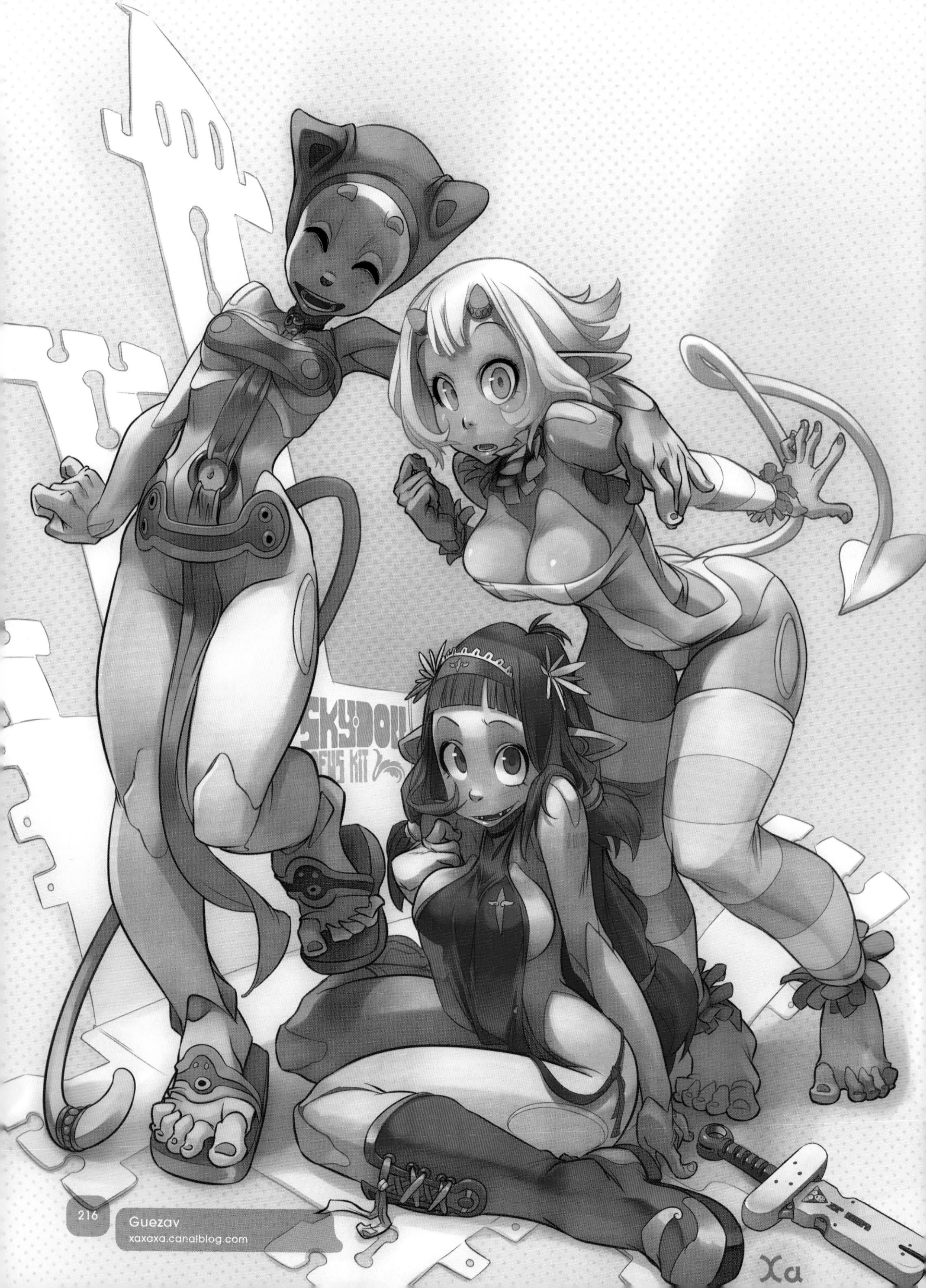

Guezav
xaxaxa.canalblog.com

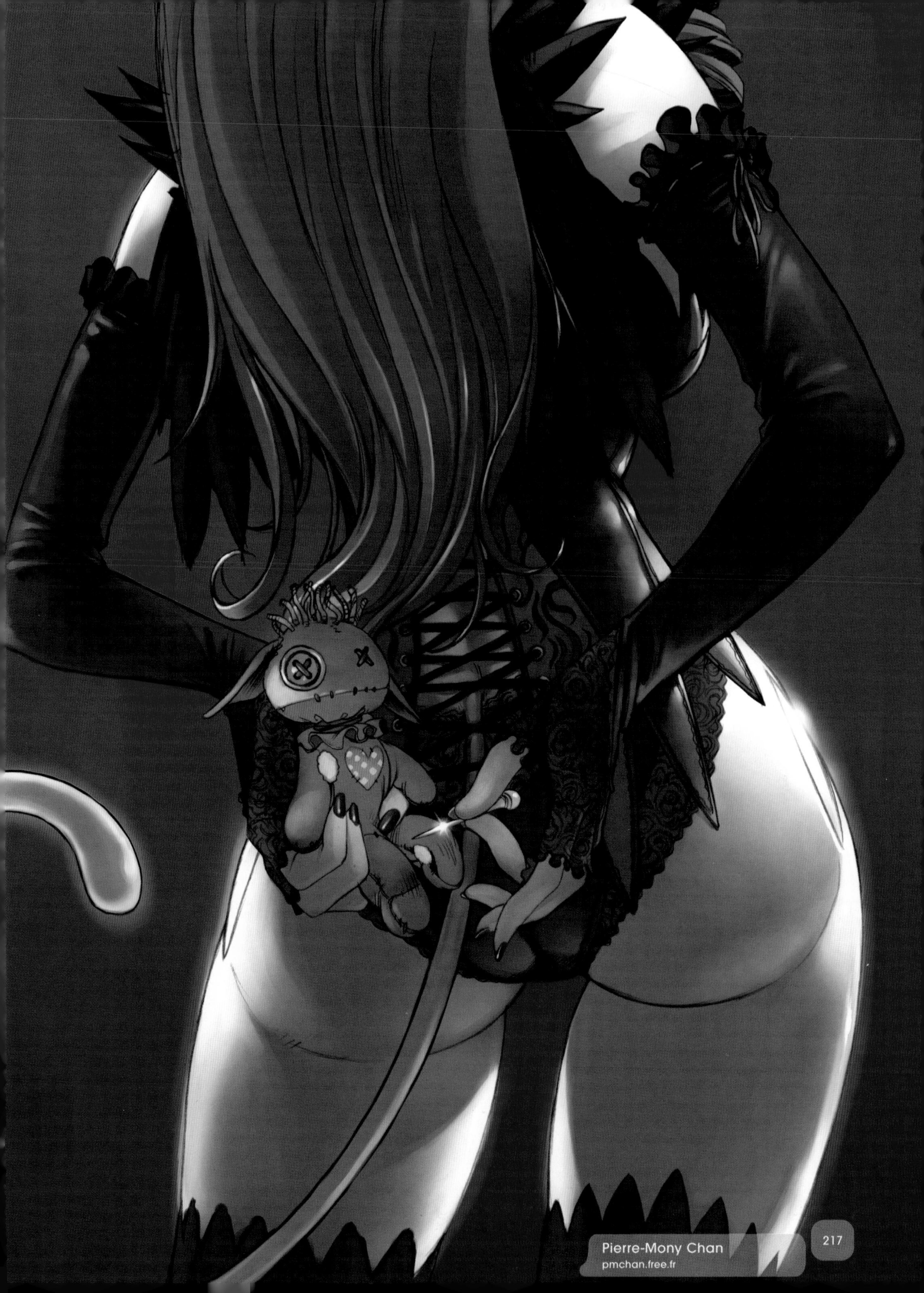

Pierre-Mony Chan
pmchan.free.fr

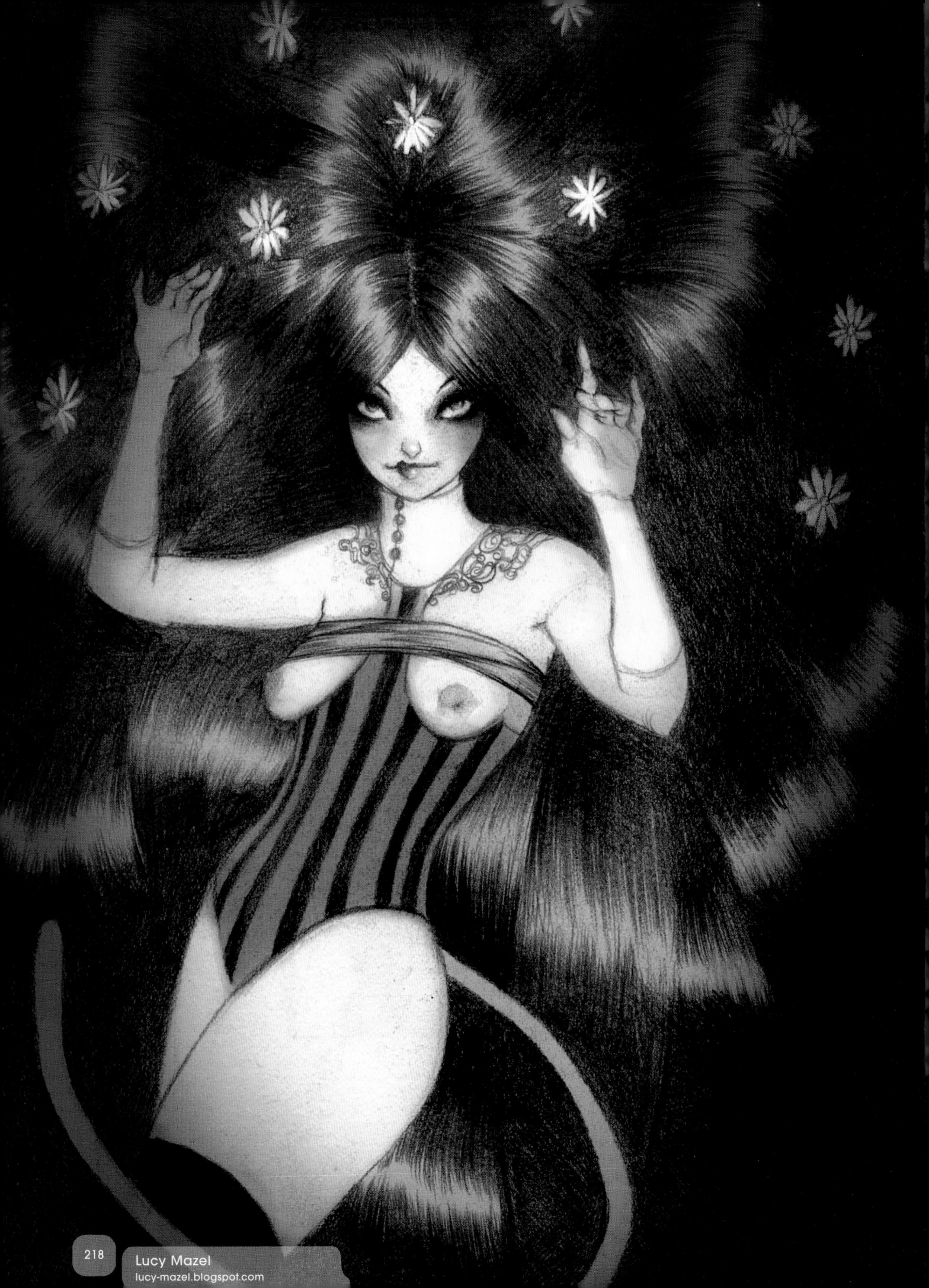

Lucy Mazel
lucy-mazel.blogspot.com

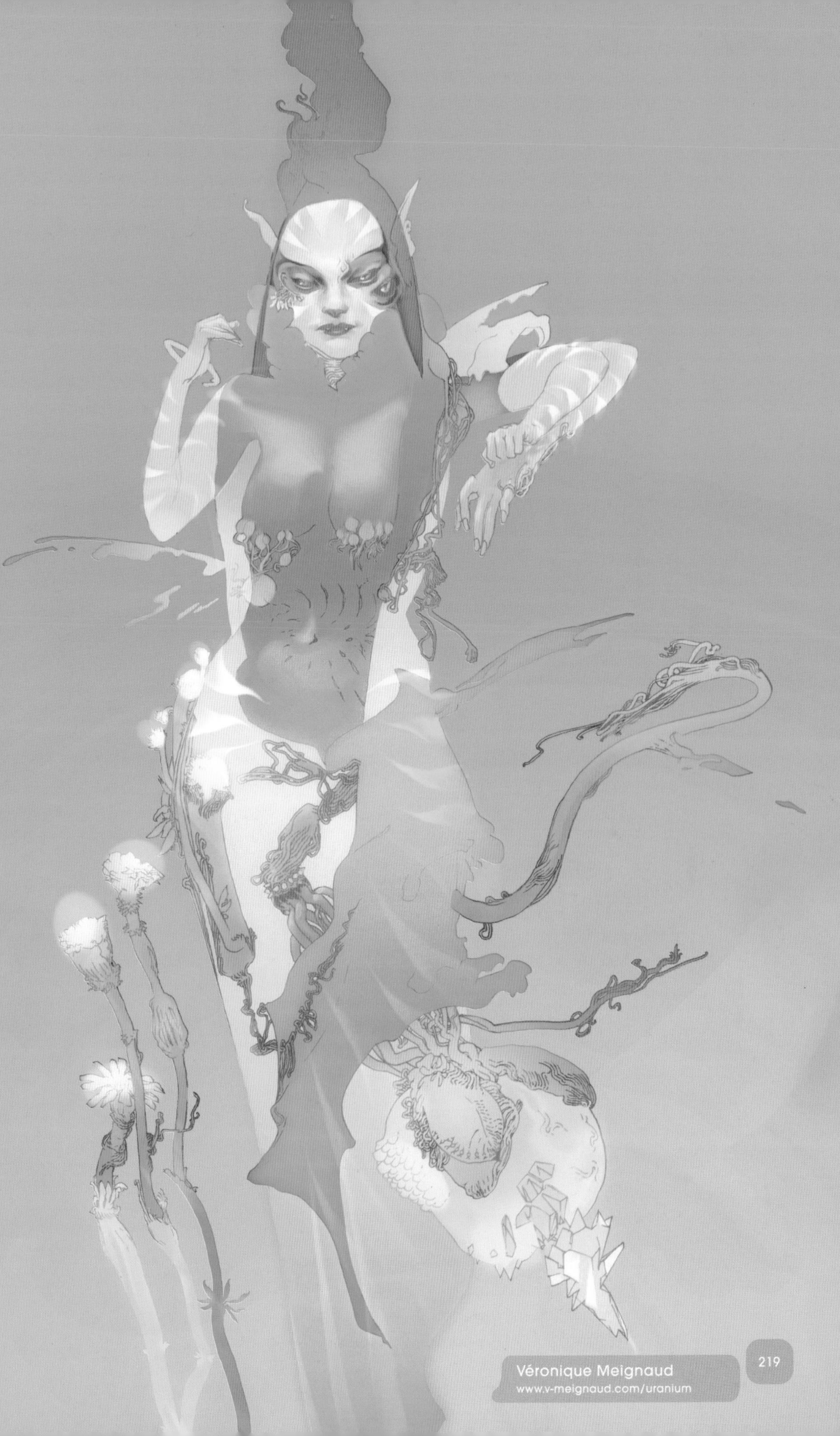

Véronique Meignaud
www.v-meignaud.com/uranium

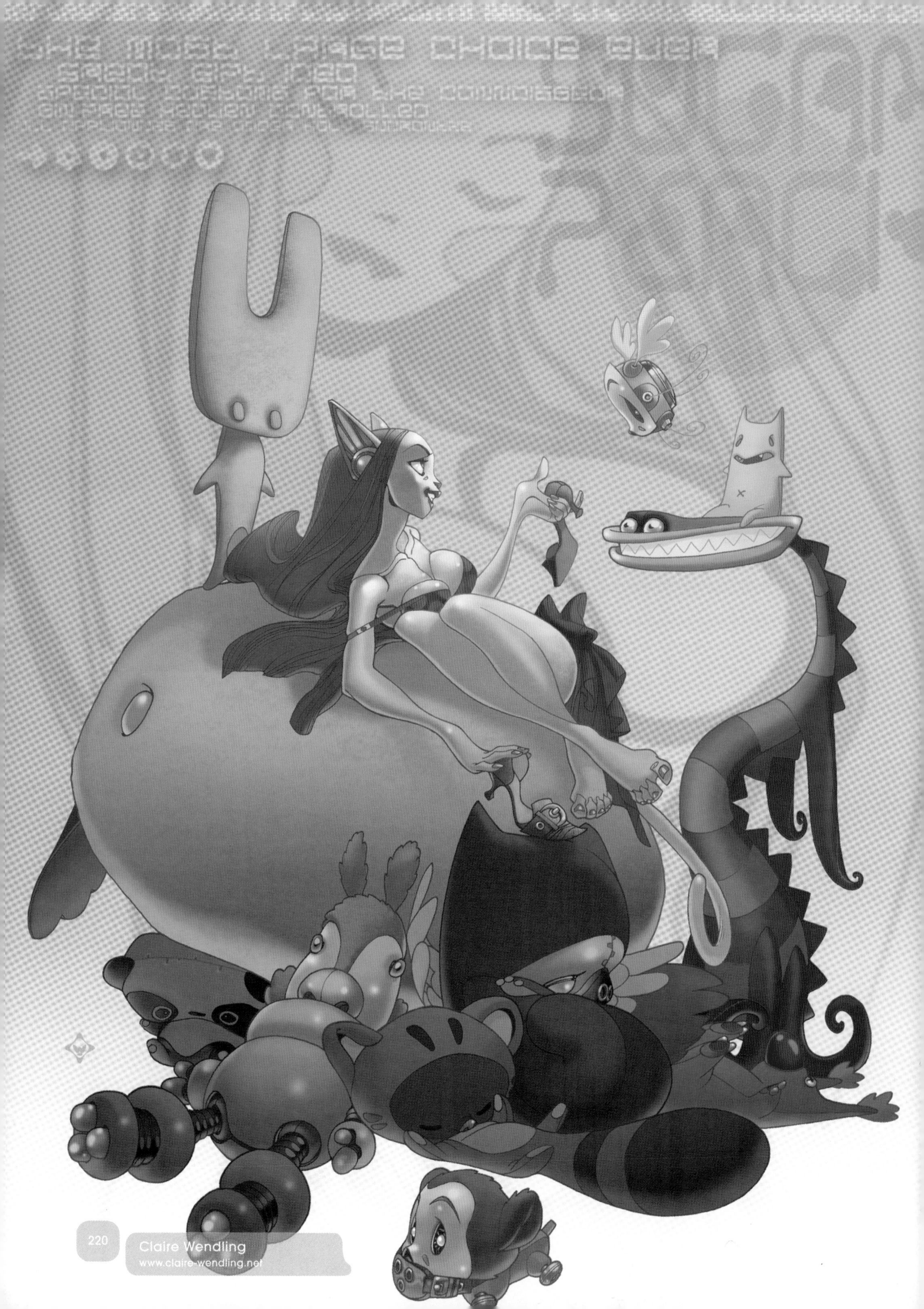

Claire Wendling
www.claire-wendling.net

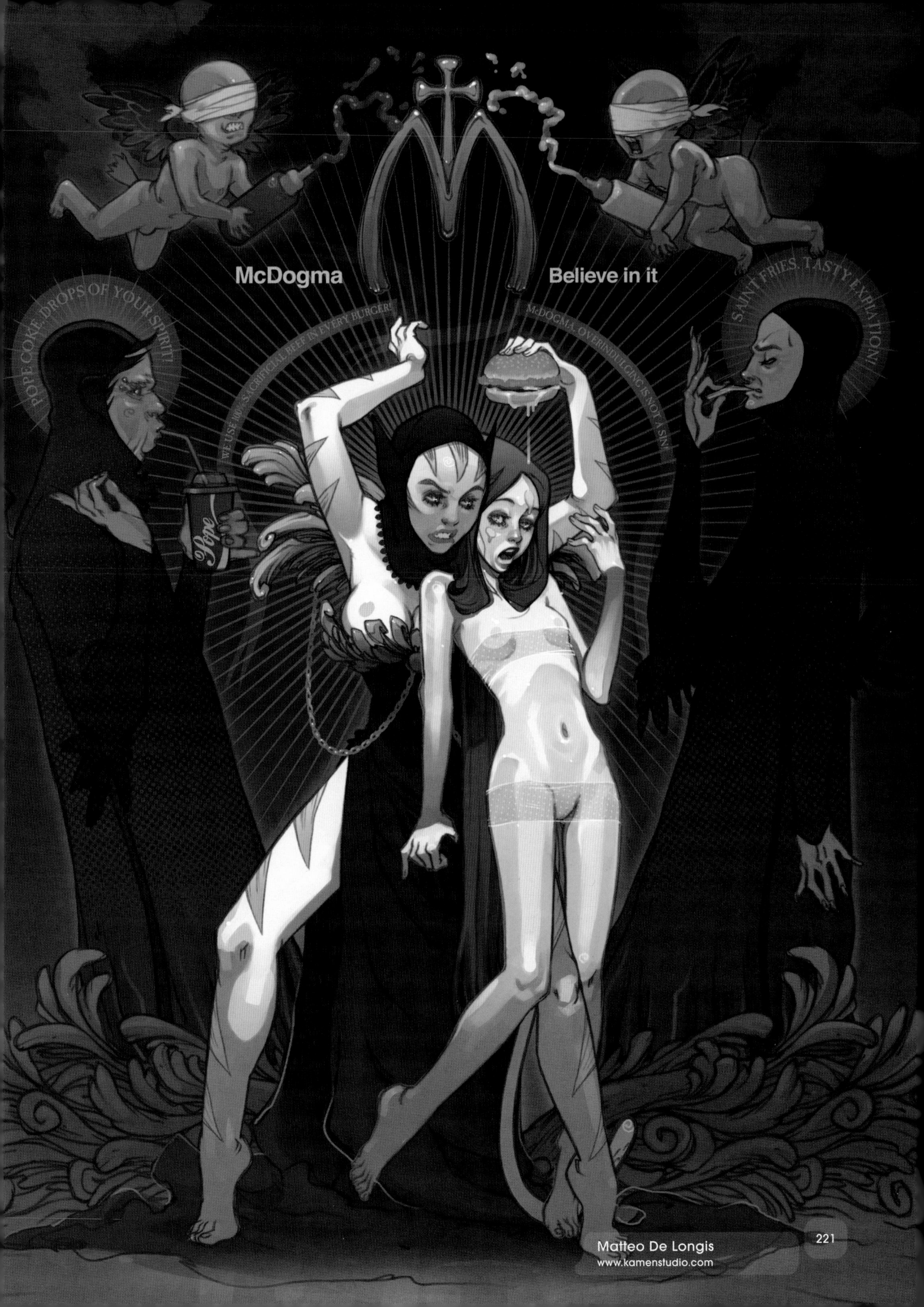
McDogma
Believe in it
POPE COKE. DROPS OF YOUR SPIRIT!
WE USE 100% SACRIFICIAL BEEF IN EVERY BURGER!
McDOGMA. OVERINDULGING IS NOT A SIN!
SAINT FRIES. TASTY EXPIATION!
Pope

Matteo De Longis
www.kamenstudio.com

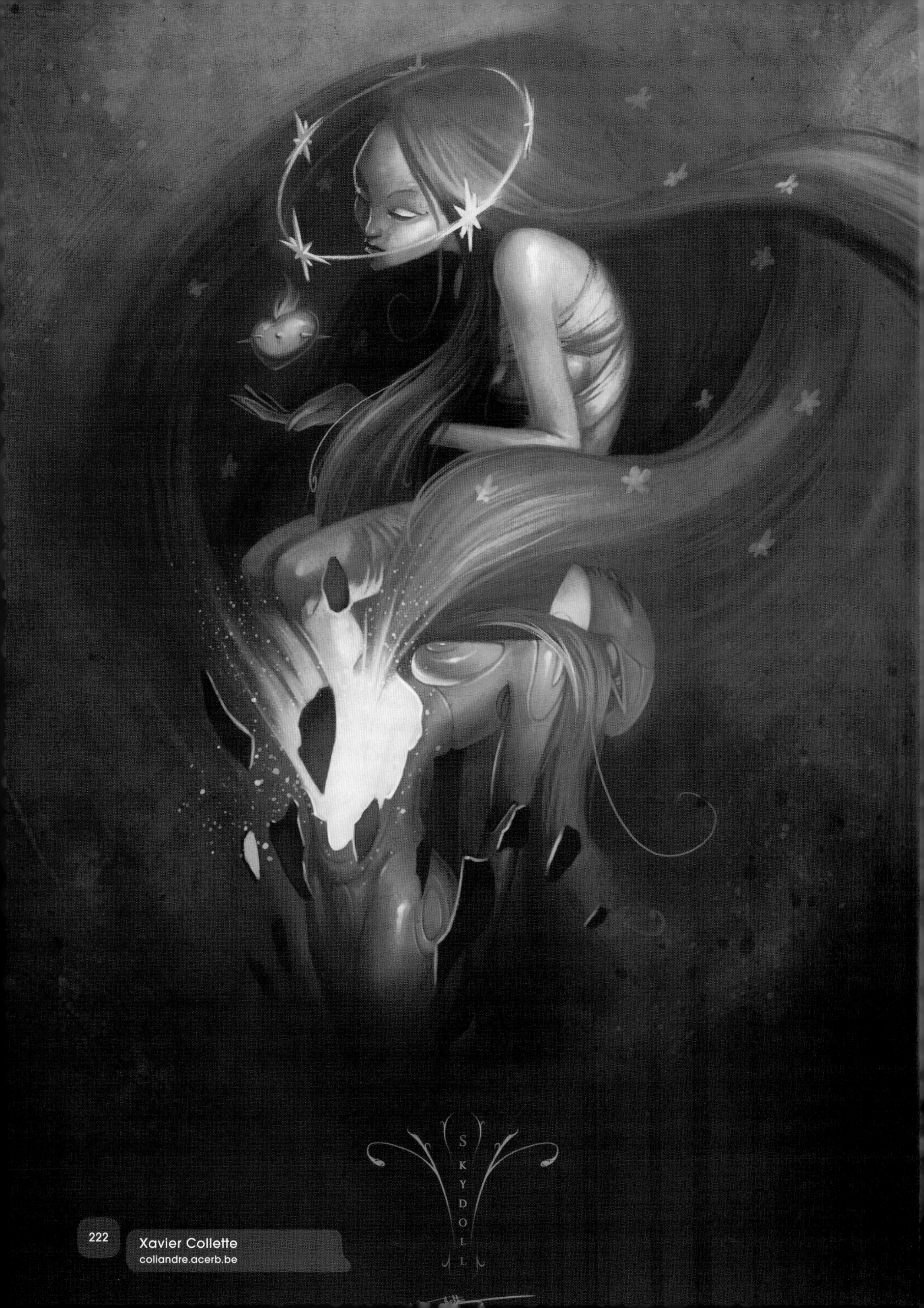
SKYDOLL

Xavier Collette
coliandre.acerb.be

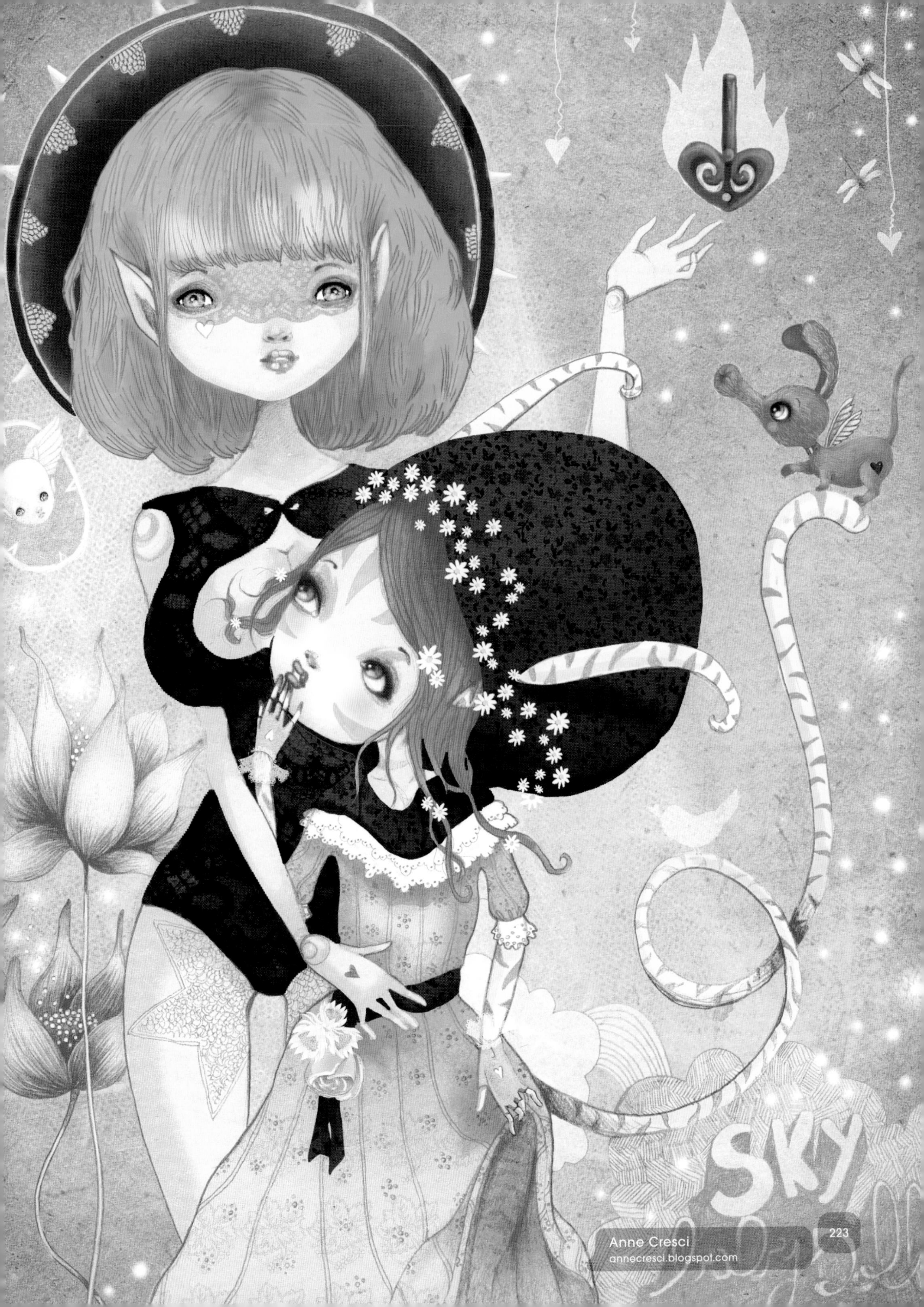
SKY
Anne Cresci
annecresci.blogspot.com

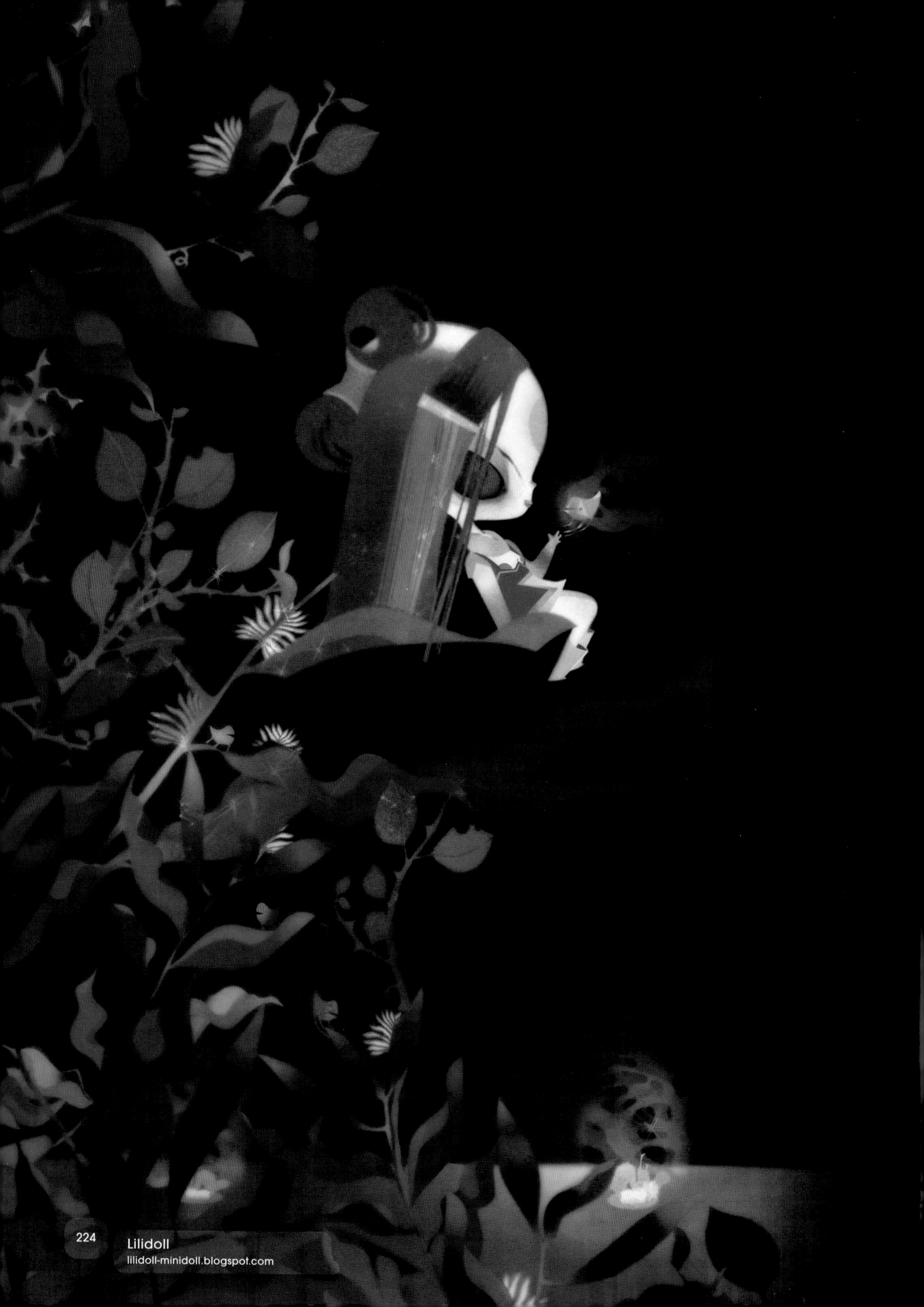

Lilidoll
lilidoll-minidoll.blogspot.com

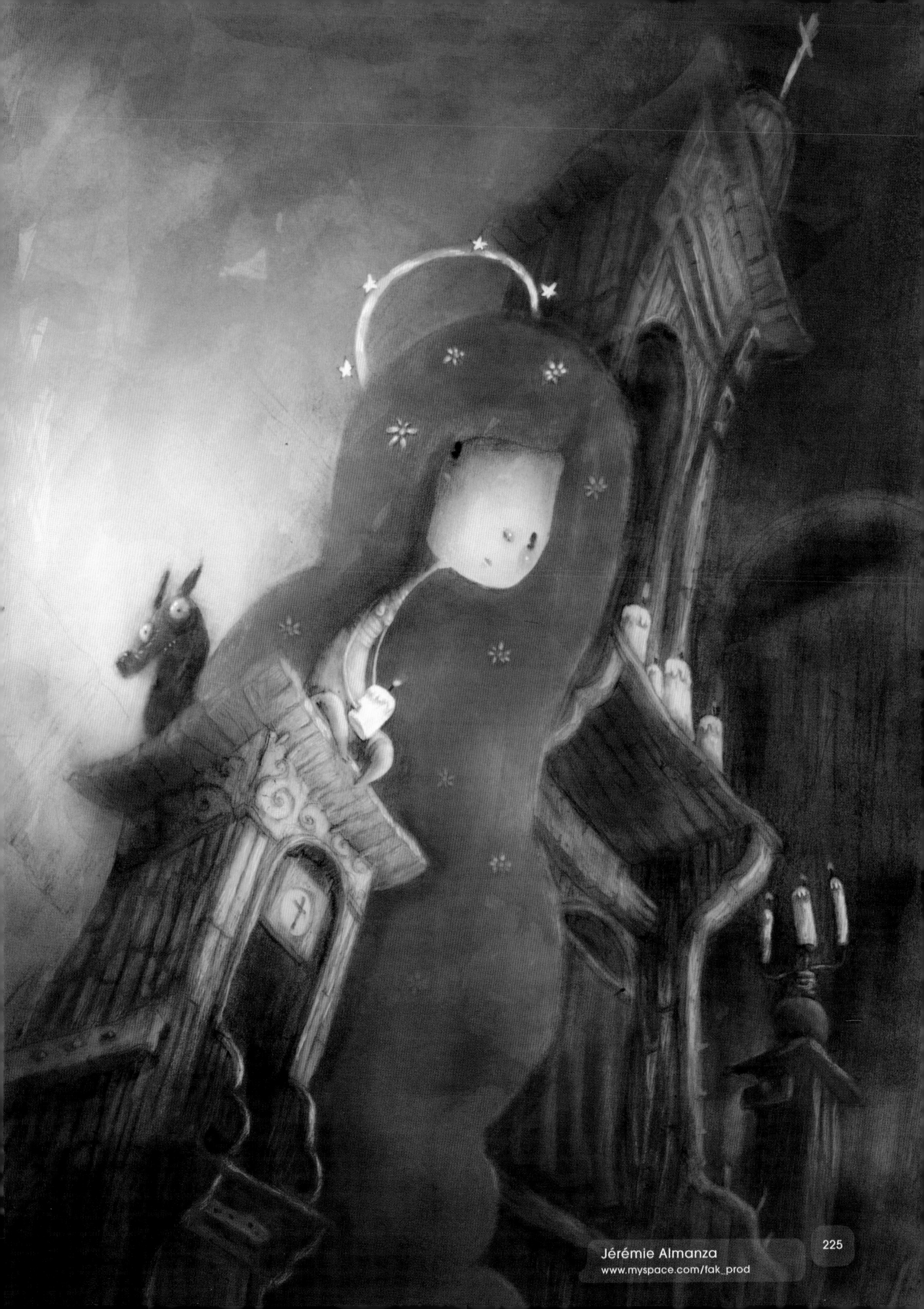

Jérémie Almanza
www.myspace.com/fak_prod

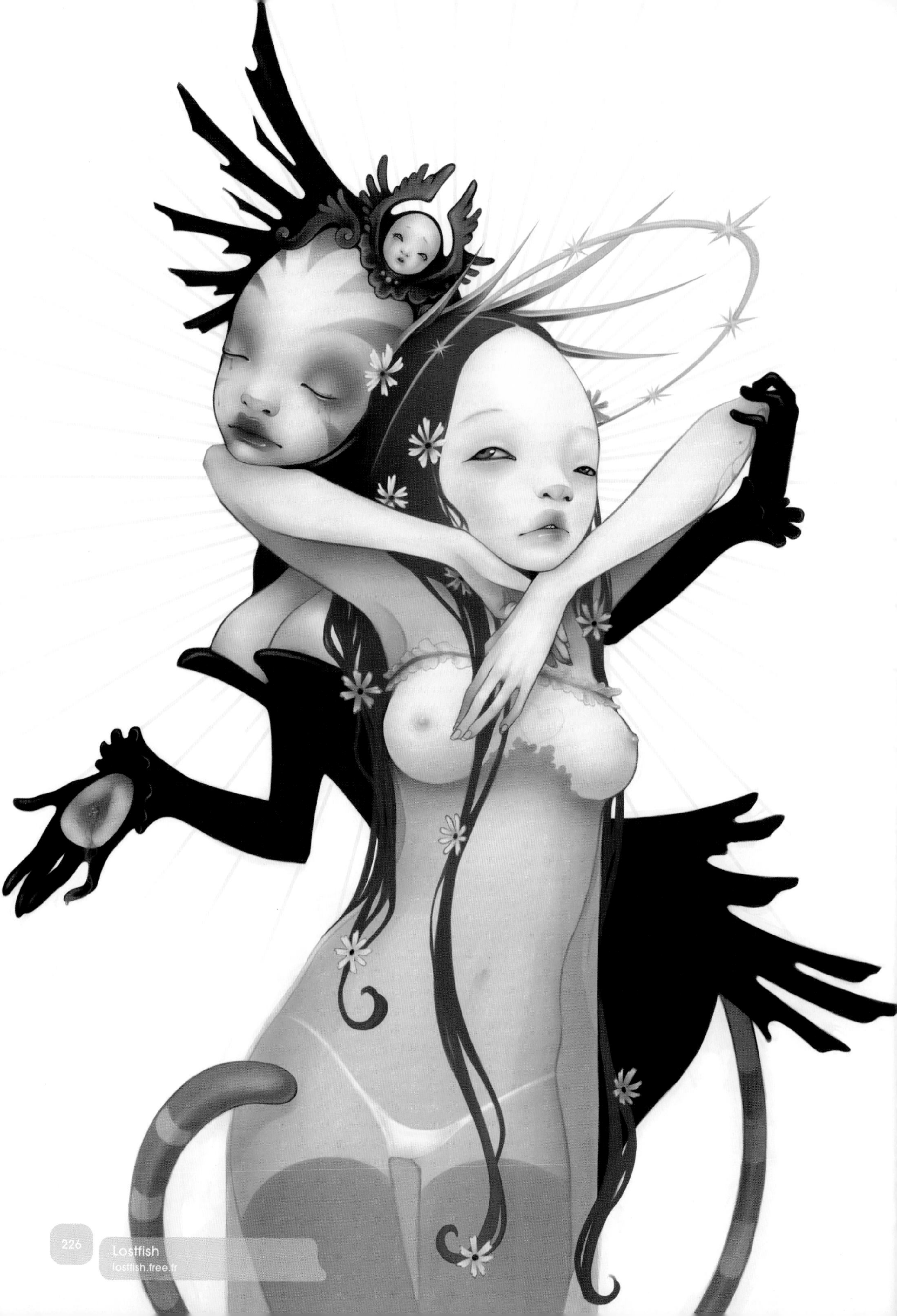

Lostfish
lostfish.free.fr

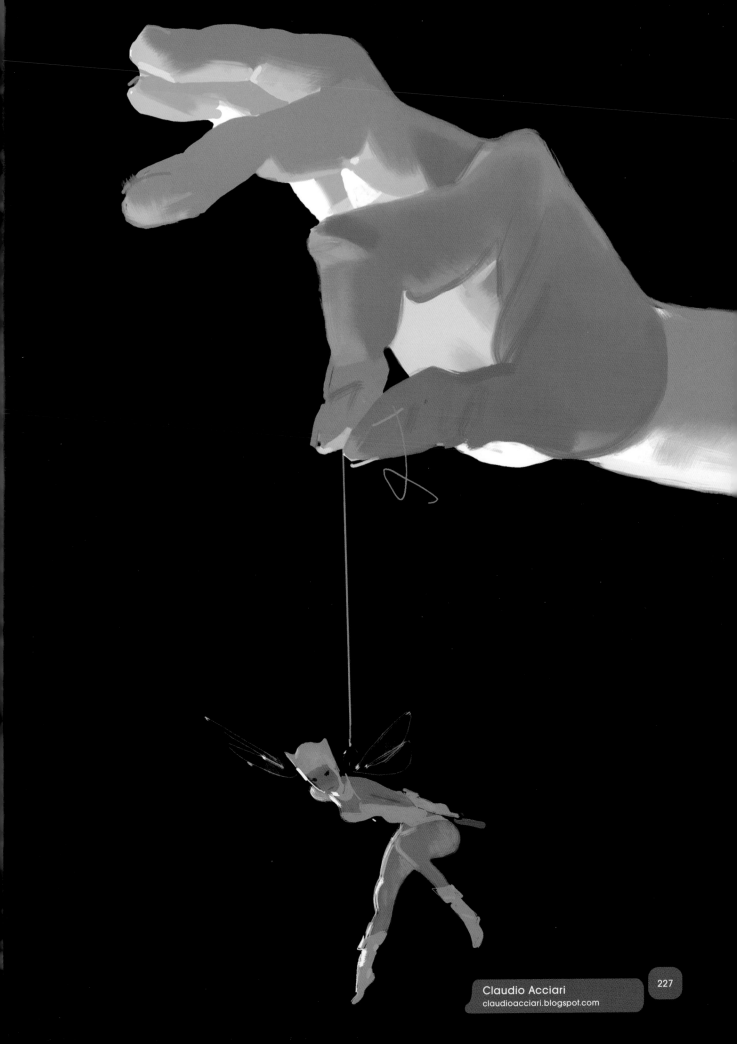

Claudio Acciari
claudioacciari.blogspot.com

227

SKYDOLL DECADE 00 > 10

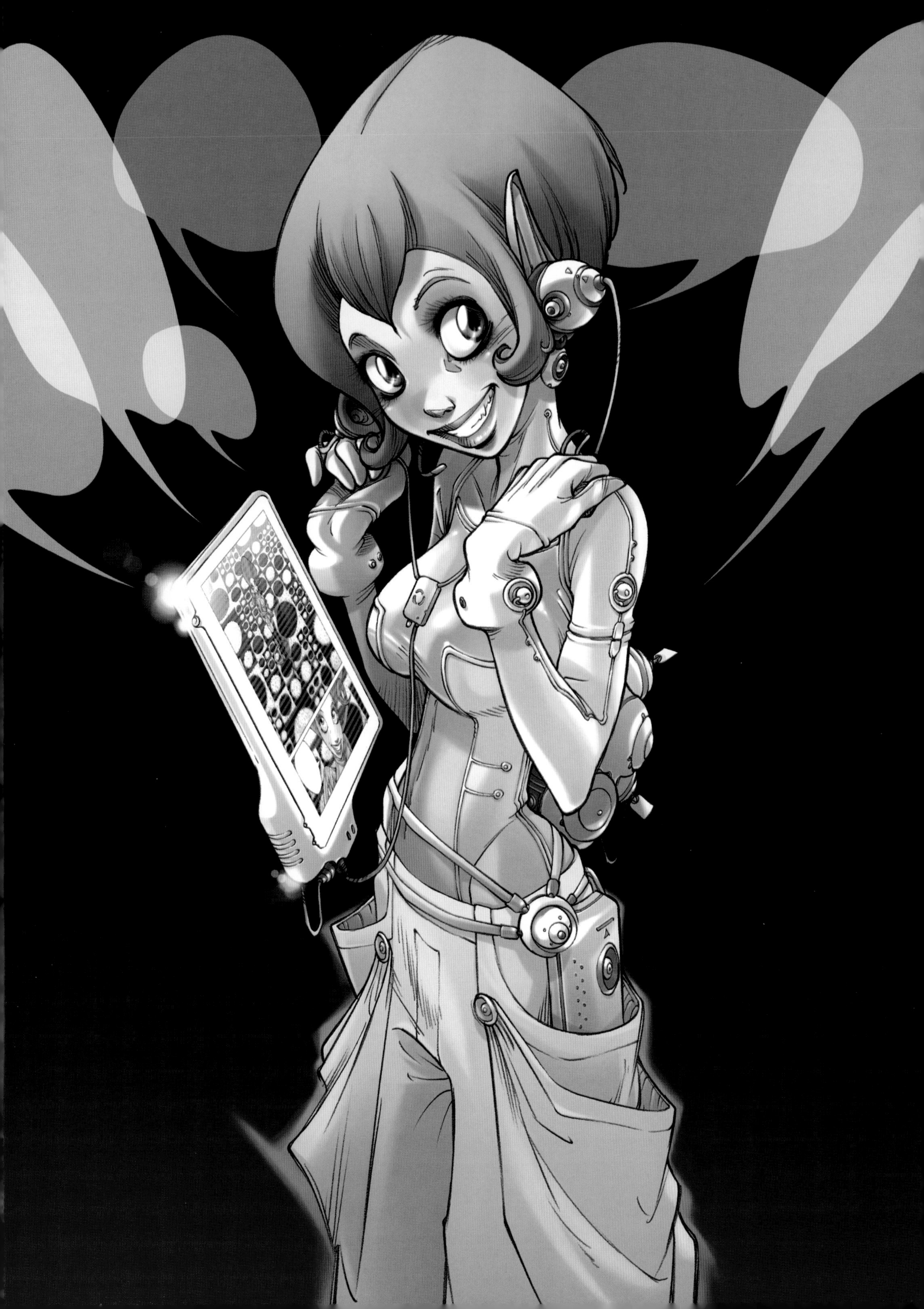

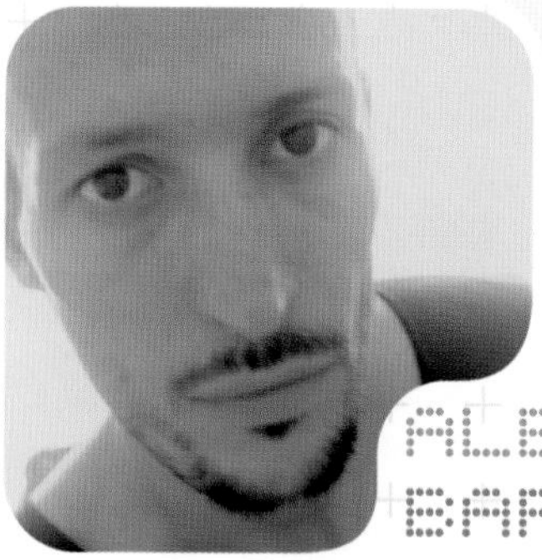

ALESSANDRO BARBUCCI

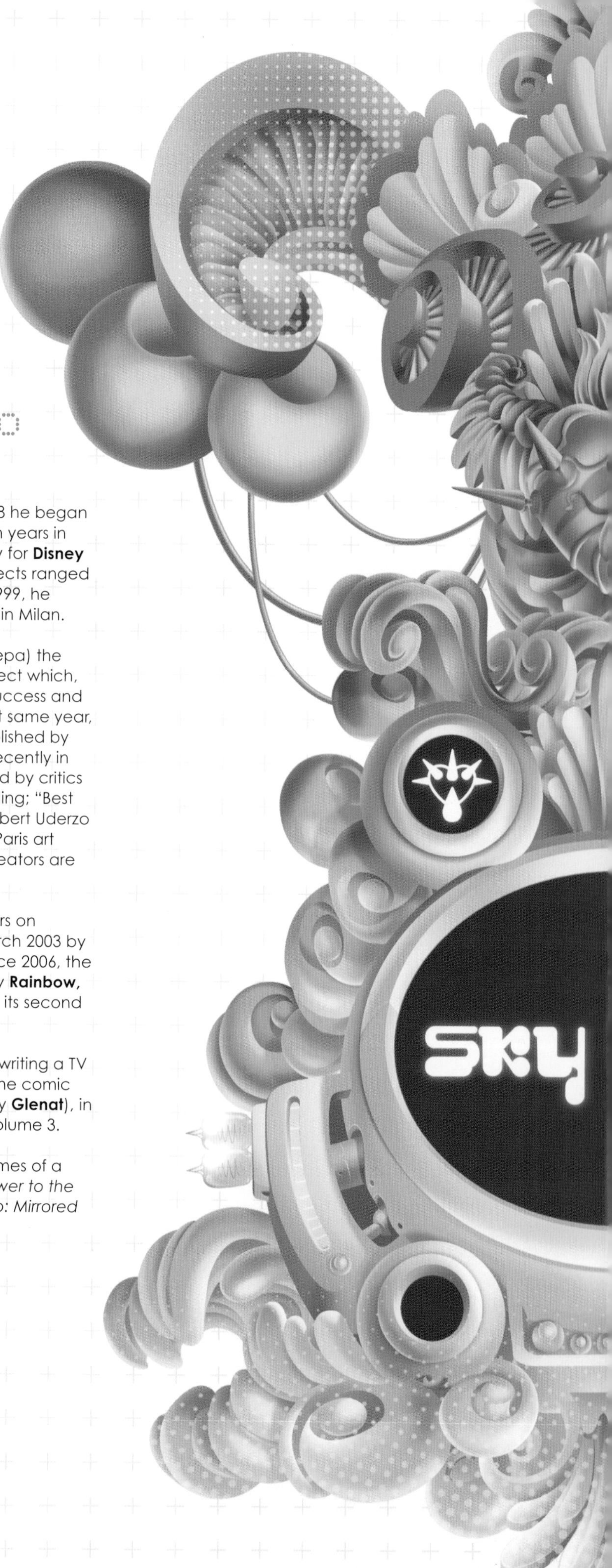
SKY

...was born in 1973 in Genoa, Italy. From the age of 18 he began to explore the world of comic books: within his first ten years in the industry he had drawn around 1200 pages, mostly for **Disney Editorial**. His contributions on numerous creative projects ranged from; storyboarding, animation, and directing. Until 1999, he taught comic art techniques at the Disney Academy in Milan.

In 1997 Alessandro created (along with Barbara Canepa) the universe and characters of the *W.I.T.C.H* series, a project which, since 2001, has experienced immense international success and has been published in over a hundred countries. That same year, the two created the science-fiction saga *Skydoll*, published by **Soleil** and distributed throughout Europe; and more recently in Korea, Japan and the USA by **Marvel Comics**. Lauded by critics and public alike, the series won several awards including; "Best Series of the Year," " Best Art and Colors," and "The Albert Uderzo Prize for Young Talent." Its success even extended to Paris art galleries, who regularly exhibit original artwork. The creators are currently working on the next volumes of the series.

Alessandro and Barbara are also the graphic designers on *Monster Allergy*, a comic for children published in March 2003 by **Soleil** in France, and distributed around the world. Since 2006, the series has been adapted into a cartoon, produced by **Rainbow, Futurikon** and **Disney Channel**. The show is currently in its second season.

In 2010, Alessandro re-joined the world of animation , writing a TV series for young audiences. He also collaborated on the comic *Lord Burger* (story by Arleston and Alwett, published by **Glenat**), in which he took over character designs and art after Volume 3.

Finally, in 2010, Alessandro published the first two volumes of a new series that he had written and drawn: *Chosp- Power to the Flies!* He is also now working on the fantasy series *Ekho: Mirrored World*.

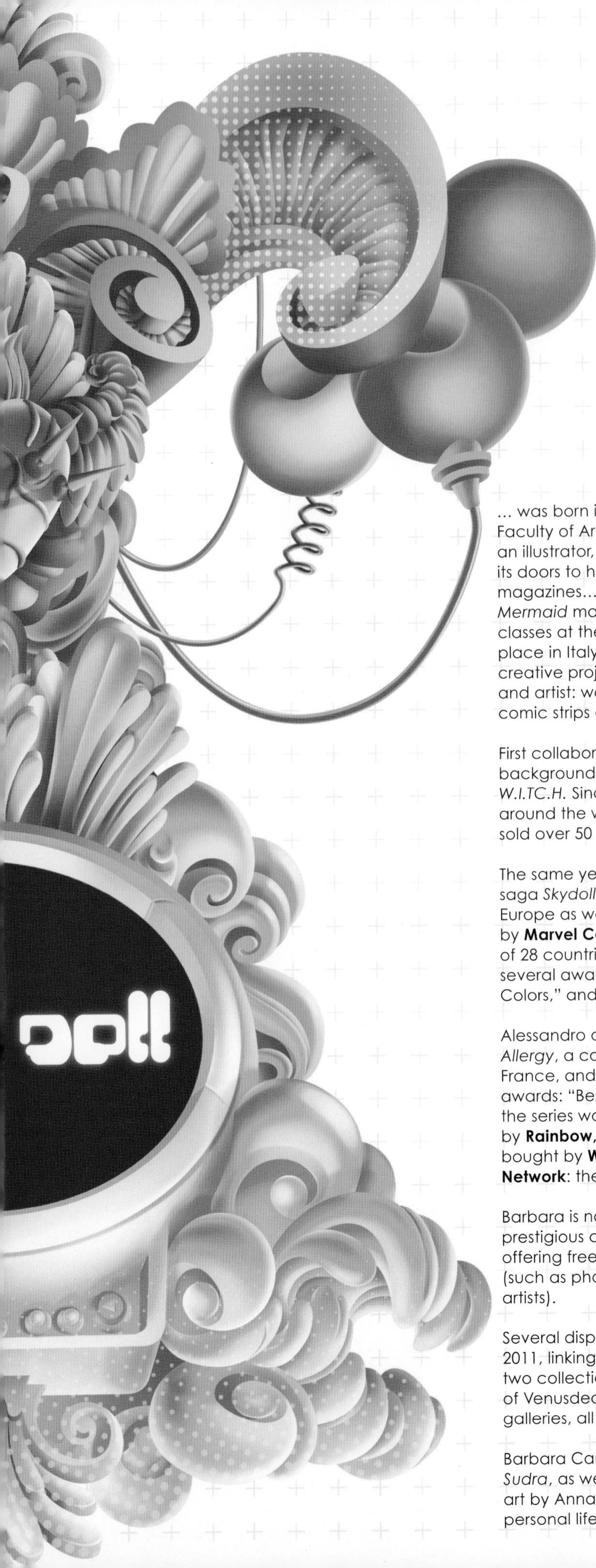
doll

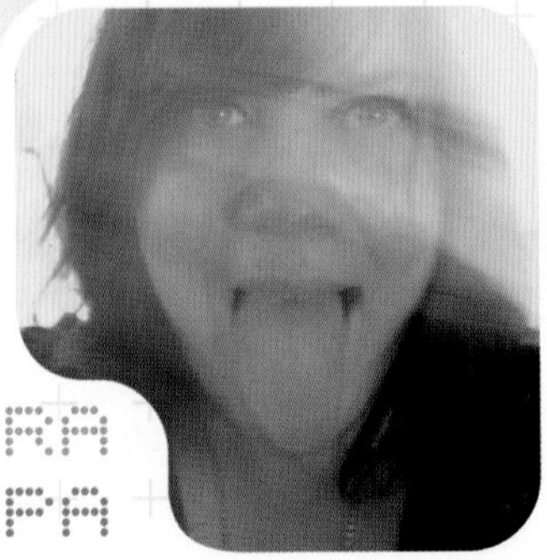

BARBARA CANEPA

... was born in 1969 in Genoa, Italy. After her studies at the Faculty of Architecture in the University of Genoa, she worked as an illustrator, and notably in advertising. In 1996, **Disney** opened its doors to her: offering her the job of illustrating books and magazines... Up until 2002, she drew stories and covers for *The Little Mermaid* magazine, all the while attending 'pictorial techniques' classes at the Disney Academy. Exhibits of her oil paintings took place in Italy and the United States. She collaborated on numerous creative projects, still all for Disney, as both a character designer and artist: working together with Alessandro Barbucci to create comic strips and illustrations for the magazines press.

First collaborating in 1997, they created the concept, characters, backgrounds, graphic style and color pallet of a new magazine, *W.I.TC.H.* Since 2001, its success has been considerable: published around the world, and winner of several awards, *W.I.T.C.H* has now sold over 50 million copies.

The same year in 1997, Barbara and Alessandro created the sci-fi saga *Skydoll*, published in France by **Soleil**, and diffused throughout Europe as well as in Korea, Japan, China and the USA (published by **Marvel Comics**)...meaning that it has been published in a total of 28 countries. Lauded by critics and public alike, the series won several awards including; "Best Series of the Year," " Best Art and Colors," and "The Albert Uderzo Prize for Young Talent."

Alessandro and Barbara are also the graphic designers on *Monster Allergy*, a comic for children published in March 2003 by Soleil in France, and distributed around the world. It too has won several awards: "Best Children's Comic" in Italy, France and Germany, and the series was made into a TV show in January 2006. Produced by **Rainbow, Futurikon** and **Disney Channel**, *Monster Allergy* was bought by **Warner Brothers** America and is now shown on **Cartoon Network**: the first European comic to be purchased by Warner.

Barbara is now an Editor at **Soleil**. She is in charge of several prestigious collections: Metamophosis and Venusdea, famous for offering freedom of expression to those with an Arts background (such as photographers, designers, illustrators, and pop Surrealist artists).

Several displays of her work were exhibited in late 2010/early 2011, linking both her personal projects (*Skydoll, End*) and these two collections she has helped put together for Soleil. The artists of Venusdea and Metamorphosis showed their work in European galleries, all curated by Barbara herself.

Barbara Canepa is currently working on the next volume *Skydoll: Sudra*, as well as the scripts for her new comic series, *End,* with art by Anna Merli. She is also working on a novel inspired by her personal life...

SKY DOLL DECADE

CREATORS : ALESSANDRO BARBUCCI – BARBARA CANEPA
WRITERS : ALESSANDRO BARBUCCI - BARBARA CANEPA
DRAWINGS : ALESSANDRO BARBUCCI
COLORS : BARBARA CANEPA

TRANSLATED BY EDWARD GAUVIN

ACKNOWLEDGMENTS

We'd like to thank everyone who contributed to making SKY DOLL a reality. These include:

Stefano Enna; Mara Domiani; Francesco Artibani; Barbara Bargiggia; Eloisa Scicolone; Mauro Gandini; Andrea Cagol; Stefano Attardi; Guillaume Bianco; Mourad Boudjellal; Jean Wacquet; Olivier Jalabert; Matteo De Longis; Adeline Richet; Sylvie Guillon and Clotilde Vu.

And finally, many thanks to all the wonderful artists who generoursly contributed their magnificent illustrations inspired by the SKY DOLL universe.

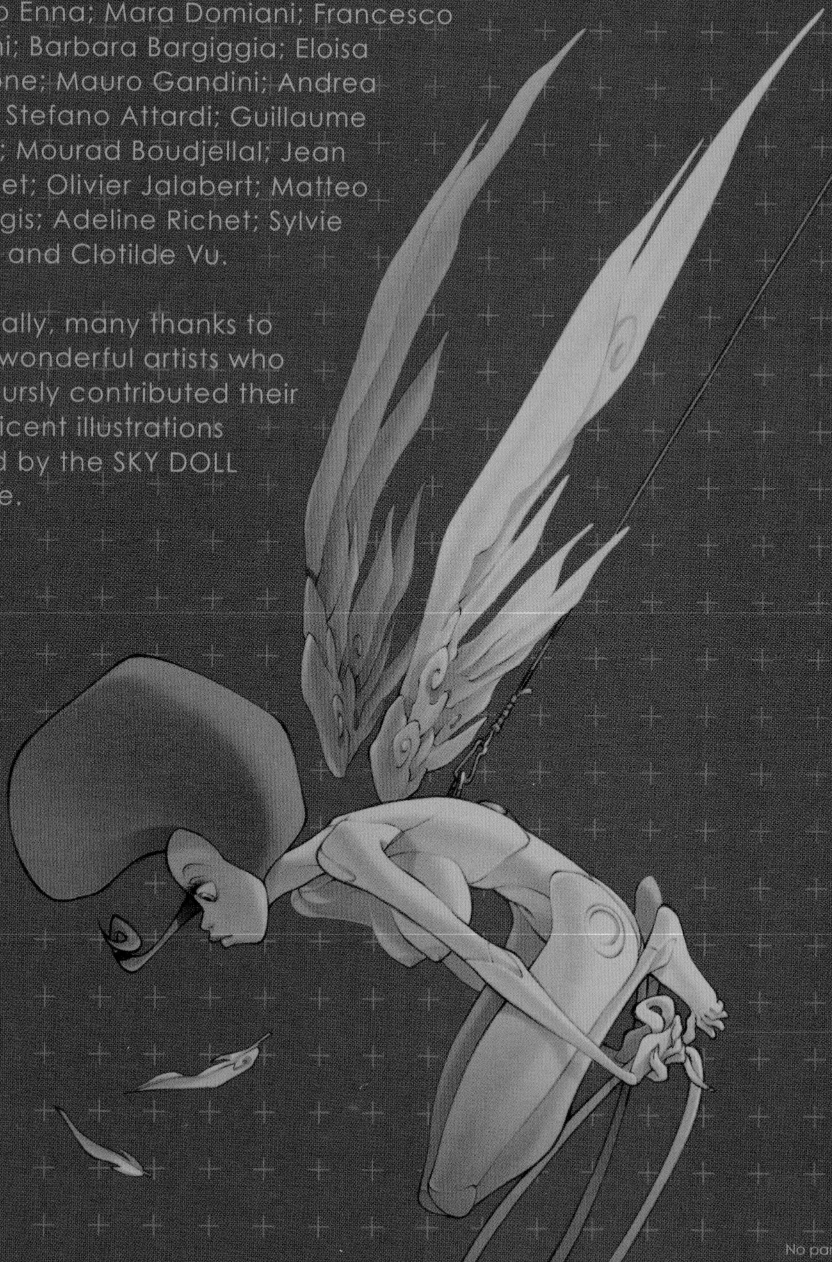

TITAN COMICS

Collection Editor
Lizzie Kaye

Collection Designer
Dan Bura

Senior Editor
Steve White

Titan Comics Editorial
Andrew James, Tom Williams, Kirsten Murray

Production Manager
Obi Onuora

Production Supervisors
Jackie Flook, Maria Pearson

Production Assistant
Peter James

Art Director
Oz Browne

Studio Manager
Selina Juneja

Circulation Manager
Steve Tothill

Sales and Marketing Manager
Ricky Claydon

Senior Marketing and Press Executive
Owen Johnson

Publishing Manager
Darryl Tothill

Publishing Director
Chris Teather

Operations Director
Leigh Baulch

Executive Director
Vivian Cheung

Publisher
Nick Landau

SKY DOLL: Decade
ISBN: 9781782767367

Published by Titan Comics. A division of Titan Publishing Group Ltd. 144 Southwark St. London, SE1 0UP

A CIP catalogue record for this title is available from the British Library.
First edition: February 2016

10 9 8 7 6 5 4 3 2 1
Printed in China. Titan Comics. TC0918